IN THE FOREGROUND:

BEOWULF

IN THE FOREGROUND:

BEOWULF

Eric Gerald Stanley

D. S. BREWER

First published 1994 by D. S. Brewer, Cambridge

D. S. Brewer is an imprint of Boydell & Brewer Ltd
PO Box 9, Woodbridge, Suffolk IP12 3DF, UK
and of Boydell & Brewer Inc.
PO Box 41026, Rochester, NY 14604, USA

ISBN 0 85991 394 5

British Library Cataloguing-in-Publication Data
Stanley, E. G.
    In the Foreground : "Beowulf"
    I. Title
    829.09
    ISBN 0–85991–394–5

Library of Congress Cataloging-in-Publication Data
Stanley, Eric Gerald.
    In the foreground : Beowulf / Eric Gerald Stanley.
        p.   cm.
    Includes bibliographical references (p.) and indexes.
    ISBN 0–85991–394–5 (alk. paper)
    1. Beowulf.   2. Epic poetry, English (Old) – History and
criticism – Theory, etc.   3. English literature – Old English,
ca. 450–1100 – History and criticism – Theory, etc.   I. Title.
PR1585.S7   1994
829′.3–dc20   93–5363

Printed in Great Britain by
St Edmundsbury Press Ltd, Bury St Edmunds, Suffolk

To
Antonette diPaolo Healey
Roberta Frank
Helmut Gneuss
and
Fred C. Robinson

CONTENTS

ABBREVIATIONS

AF	Anglistische Forschungen
Archiv	*Archiv für das Studium der neueren Sprachen und Literaturen*
ASE	*Anglo-Saxon England*
ASPR	G. P. Krapp and E. V. K. Dobbie (eds), The Anglo-Saxon Poetic Records
BB2A	Bonner, *Beiträge zur Anglistik*
Beiträge	*Beiträge zur Geschichte der deutschen Sprache und Literatur*
col(s)	column(s)
DOE	*The Dictionary of Old English* (Toronto)
EEMF	Early English Manuscripts in Facsimile (Copenhagen)
EETS	Early English Text Society, o.s. original series; s.s. supplementary series
EHR	*English Historical Review*
EStn	*Englische Studien*
ESts	*English Studies*
fo(s)	folio(s)
JEGP	*Journal of English and Germanic Philology*
LSE	*Leeds Studies in English*
MÆ	*Medium Ævum*
ME	Middle English
MLN	*Modern Language Notes*
MLR	*Modern Language Review*
MnE	Modern English
MP	*Modern Philology*
N&Q	*Notes and Queries*
NM	*Neuphilologische Mitteilungen*
n.s.	new series
OE	Old English
OF	Old French
OHG	Old High German
PBA	*Proceedings of the British Academy*
PMLA	Publications of the Modern Language Association of America
PQ	*Philological Quarterly*
QF	Quellen und Forschungen zur Sprach- und Culturgeschichte der germanischen Völker
RES	*Review of English Studies*
rev.	revised
s.	under (the heading)

SP	*Studies in Philology*
StNeophil	*Studia Neophilologica*
StePh	Studien zur englischen Philologie
s.v(v).	under the word(s)
YSE	Yale Studies in English
ZfdA	*Zeitschrift für deutsches Altertum*
ZfdPh	*Zeitschrift für deutsche Philologie*
*	hypothetical form (not recorded in manuscripts)
>	changed to
<	derived from

PREFACE

Prefaces are the last labour in writing a book, as Jacob Grimm says,[1] 'epiloge, welche wir unsern büchern voran zu setzen pflegen' [epilogues which we are wont to put first in our books], and that position is not paradoxical: some acknowledgements must be made at the outset because of debts incurred in the production of the book. To Peter Godman (Tübingen University) who first suggested that I write this book, to the late Ashley Crandell Amos (of *The Dictionary of Old English*, Toronto) who read an early draft of some parts of it, and made many suggestions for improvements of what she read, and to Roberta Frank (University of Toronto) who also read an early draft of parts of the book and not only made valuable suggestions, especially bibliographical, but also urged me, as the years went by, to finish it.

The book is heavy with notes and indexes; and some directions for its use may be helpful. I do not provide a bibliography, partly because it would have duplicated much of what is to be found well set out in the standard bibliography of the subject:

Stanley B. Greenfield and Fred C. Robinson. *A Bibliography of Publications on Old English Literature to the end of 1972* (Toronto and Buffalo, 1980).

I have used it often. But for publication of the last twenty years there is no such useful, single compilation.

Not an insignificant number of publications used by me lie outside the subject as conceived by Greenfield and Robinson. I hope to have covered the need to find the bibliographical details by giving access to the author's name through an 'Index of Scholars and Critics referred to in the notes'. That description must serve to include: Augustine of Hippo, Isidore, Jerome, Gregory the Great, pseudo-Quintilian, Richard Tottel, Sir Philip Sidney, Pope and Swift, J. J. Winckelmann, Goethe, Sir Walter Scott, and W. E. Gladstone, not all of whom would, I presume, have willingly condescended to be described in such narrow, academic terms, though others in the 'Index of Scholars and Critics' might well have been flattered to be so described. All bibliographical references in the notes are indexed, and under the first reference some details are to be found, sufficient, I hope, to identify the work used by me. Subsequent references take the form of author, short title (for convenient identification), and date, followed by the chapter number and the note number where the fuller reference is given. I have not used the system now sometimes adopted – even in our bibliographically

---

[1] 'Vorrede' to *Deutsche Grammatik*, IV (Göttingen, 1837), p. v.

rich subject, for which it is not very suitable – of name and date, for example, 'Sievers 1925', together with an extensive biliographical section, because even a reader familiar with the material is not likely to recall, without having to look it up in the bibliographical section, what work of Sievers is being referred to. It also necessitates fuller bibliographical treatment than does the system which I have adopted. At pp. viii-ix, above, there is a list of the abbreviations used in this book.

Some works were used often, but I have given an explicit reference to them only exceptionally when I thought it specifically helpful. They include the obvious dictionaries and concordances:

J. Bosworth and T. N. Toller, *An Anglo-Saxon Dictionary* (Oxford, 1882-1898), with a *Supplement* by Toller (Oxford, 1908-21), and *Enlarged Addenda and Corrigenda* by A. Campbell (Oxford, 1972).

A. Cameron, A. C. Amos, and A. diP. Healey, *The Dictionary of Old English* (Toronto, 1986-).

H. Kurath, S. M. Kuhn, J. Reidy, R. E. Lewis, and M. J. Williams, *Middle English Dictionary* (Ann Arbor, 1952-).

J. A. H. Murray, H. Bradley, W. A. Craigie, and C. T. Onions, *The Oxford English Dictionary* (originally *A New English Dictionary*) and first *Supplement* (Oxford 1882-1933); R. W. Burchfield, second *Supplement* (Oxford, 1972-1986); *OED* and Burchfield's *Supplement* were integrated by J. A. Simpson and E. S. C. Weiner in a 'Second Edition' (Oxford, 1989).[2]

J. B. Bessinger, Jr., and P. H. Smith, Jr., *A Concordance to Beowulf* (Ithaca, 1969).

J. B. Bessinger, Jr., and P. H. Smith, Jr., *A Concordance to The Anglo-Saxon Poetic Records* (Ithaca, 1978).

R. L. Venezky and A. diP. Healey, *A Microfiche Concordance to Old English* (Toronto, 1980)

R. L. Venezky and S. Butler, *A Microfiche Concordance to Old English. The High-Frequency Words* (Toronto, 1985).

Two familiar, standard editions have been used:

F. Klaeber, *Beowulf and the Fight at Finnsburg* (3rd edn with first and second supplements; Lexington, Massachusetts: 1950). Earlier editions (1st edn, Boston, New York, and Chicago: 1922; 2nd edn with supplement, Boston, New York, Chicago, etc.: 1928) are referred to explicitly when used for some reason.

---

[2] *OED* does not claim to be comprehensive for Old English; cf. E. G. Stanley, 'Old English in *The Oxford English Dictionary*', in R. W. Burchfield (ed.), *Studies in Lexicography* (Oxford, 1987), 19–35. For the 1989 edition of *OED*, cf. E. G. Stanley, 'The *Oxford English Dictionary* and *Supplement*: The Integrated Edition of 1989', *RES*, n.s. 41 (1990), 75–88, and I. S. Asquith and E. G. Stanley, 'Correspondence', *RES*, n.s. 42 (1991), 81–3.

G. P. Krapp and E. V. K. Dobbie, *The Anglo-Saxon Poetic Records* [ASPR].

G. P. Krapp, *The Junius Manuscript*, ASPR, I (New York and London, 1931).

G. P. Krapp, *The Vercelli Book*, ASPR, II (New York, 1932).

G. P. Krapp and E. V. K. Dobbie, *The Exeter Book*, ASPR, III (New York, 1936).

E. V. K. Dobbie, *Beowulf and Judith*, ASPR, IV (New York, 1953).

G. P. Krapp, *The Paris Psalter and the Meters of Boethius*, ASPR, V (New York, 1932; London, 1933).

E. V. K. Dobbie, *The Anglo-Saxon Minor Poems*, ASPR, VI (New York, 1942).

Usually these editions have been used without an explicit reference to them, except when some commentary or other detail is actually quoted or immediately derived from them, or for some other specific reason (such as the fact that for some poems ASPR may not be the obvious or only edition used). In this book the titles of poems, all of them modern inventions, are as in ASPR. In quoting the poems, the punctuation and capitalization of the editions have not been followed in all respects. Klaeber's diacritics have not been reproduced. ASPR has not been followed in silent departures from the manuscript readings; in this book all such departures are made apparent by italics.

Facsimiles have been consulted very often, and occasionally the manuscripts themselves, to confirm difficult readings; and I have usually not acknowledged that I have done so. The following facsimiles have been used often:

Bodleian MS Junius 11: I. Gollancz, *The Cædmon Manuscript of Anglo-Saxon Biblical Poetry Junius XI in the Bodleian Library* (London, 1927).

The Vercelli Book: M. Foerster, *Il Codice Vercellese con Omelie e Poesie in Lingua Anglosassone* (Rome, 1913); C. Sisam, *The Vercelli Book. A Late Tenth-Century Manuscript Containing Prose and Verse Vercelli Biblioteca Capitolare CXVII*, EEMF, XIX (1976).

The Exeter Book: R. W. Chambers, M. Förster, and R. Flower, *The Exeter Book of Old English Poetry* (London, 1933).

The *Beowulf* MS: K. Malone, *The Nowell Codex British Museum Cotton Vitellius A. XV second MS*, EEMF, XII (1963). For *Beowulf* alone, J. Zupitza, *Beowulf Reproduced in Facsimile from the Unique Manuscript in the British Museum MS. Cotton Vitellius A. xv* (2nd edn; N. Davis), EETS, 245 (1959); for *Judith*, see also Robinson and Stanley, below.

The Paris Psalter: B. Colgrave (ed.), with J. Bromwich, N. R. Ker, F. Wormald, K. and C. Sisam, *The Paris Psalter MS. Bibliothèque Nationale fonds latin 8824*, EEMF, VIII (1958).

All other verse, including *The Meters of Boethius*: F. C. Robinson and E. G. Stanley, *Old English Verse Texts from Many Sources A Comprehensive Collection*, EEMF, XXIII (1991).

The Bible used is the Vulgate (though that is not identical with the Latin Bible the Anglo-Saxons knew):

R. Weber (ed.): *Biblia Sacra iuxta Vulgatam Versionem* (Stuttgart, 1969, 2nd edn 1975).

The Modern English translation used is Doway-Rhemes, because of its closeness to the Vulgate:

The Holie Bible Faithfully Translated into English, out of the Authentical Latin. Diligently conferred with the Hebrew, Greeke, and other Editions in diuers languages. By the English College of Doway. I, Genesis to The Booke of Iob (Doway, 1609). *The Second Tome*, The Booke of Psalmes to the end of the Old Testament (Doway, 1610).
The New Testament of Iesus Christ Translated faithfully into English, out of the authentical Latin, according to the best corrected copies of the same, diligently conferred with the Greeke, and other Editions in diuers languages. In the English College of Rhemes (Rhemes, 1582).

This version has been preferred to the Authorized Version which has been referred to only occasionally for its more familiar wording.

There is a dedication, to celebrate my association with *The Dictionary of Old English*, in the persons of its Editor and my colleagues on its International Advisory Committee.

Thanks are due and gladly given to Derek Brewer for his willingness to let my book come out from D.S. Brewer, an imprint of Boydell & Brewer, to whose scholarly publishing house medievalists throughout the world owe so much; and to Pru Harrison of Boydell & Brewer who saw the book through proof and press with enviable accuracy and skill: what faults remain are mine.

Here I will end with a grateful mention of Mary who has had to bear with me for a third of a century, and of Ann who has borne with me for not quite so long.

Eric Stanley

January 1993
Pembroke College, Oxford

BEOWULF IN LITERARY HISTORY

I

The Period up to the Second World War

The History of Taste, the History of Scholarship and even Political History play their part in Literary History. The very concept of Literary History is based on, at least, two assumptions: first, that the composition of a work under discussion, whatever it may be and whenever it may have been written, has its antecedents and its own contemporariness; and secondly, that the reader comes to the work with a mind not a *tabula rasa* on which all writing entering it is freshly perceived, but rather with a mind stuffed full of preoccupations and predilections as a result of which every reading is at once a reading *of* and a reading *into* the work. It is thus when the reader is what used to be called a Modern Philologist, a scholar interested in textual and linguistic details, or when the reader is a Literary Critic; it was no different with more old-fashioned exegetical readings:[1]

> Im Auslegen seyd frisch und munter!
> Legt ihr's nicht aus, so legt was unter.

Freely translated, the meaning of this *xenion* of Goethe's is:

> As exegetes, you in each text display,
> Not what it says, but what you'd have it say.

This is especially significant for the reading of ancient texts in a language not immediately accessible to the reader.

That brings with it another problem. Old English, especially the complex language of *Beowulf* as also of other difficult poems, such as *Exodus*, is not easy enough for any modern reader ever to feel truly at home in, so as to respond directly to it, as one responds to literature in one's own modern language, or as really competent Classicists or modern linguists may in time come to respond to literature in an acquired dead or modern foreign language. The acquisition of *Beowulf* is, by the usual pedagogic method, through translation.

---

[1] *Goethe's Werke, Vollständige Ausgabe letzter Hand*, iii (Stuttgart and Tübingen, 1828), 270.

At a first reading a translation is made (perhaps with the help of one of many existing, published translations), in subsequent readings that translation is re-called through memory or by repeating the process. Such a translation is not merely an understanding of the text: it becomes the only text of the poem readily accessible to the reader's understanding.

The reading of a work of literature against a background of the history of scholarly and critical writings on it requires, if not a defence, at least some explanation. As a result of such a reading of a work of literature, each new piece of writing on it is assessed by the reader in the light – or relative darkness – of his or her preoccupations and predilections: the reader's own understanding of the work and his or her understanding, acceptance or rejection, of previous writings on it. Such previous writings form the prevailing scholarship of the subject, or a critical consensus.

This study of *Beowulf* in Literary History makes no pretence to be complete. That would require something even longer than the selective presentation here attempted. To a large extent the selection is based on my own preoccupations and predilections, which sometimes lead me to include items on *Beowulf* neglected by others; and since some such items are trivial, that is significant only in exemplifying a direction error may take, that general neglect may not seem undeserved. Some of the items now in general neglect do, however, seem to me significant enough to deserve an airing on merit, and not for merriment. In these first two chapters I include hardly anything on metre, on dating the composition of the poem relatively or absolutely, on language, on textual scholarship, on possible influences of other Old English poems on *Beowulf* or on the possible influence of *Beowulf* on other Old English poems. Yet these are subjects relevant to the historical study of the poem within Anglo-Saxon lit-erature, and some of them are discussed elsewhere in this book.

If I include nothing much in this book on paganism and Christianity at the cradle of English poetry, it is not because I am not interested. Far from it; it is because I have elsewhere written at such length on it that it may seem, to the less than benevolent reader, that I have already thrown out that baby with the bath-water.[2]

Entry of Beowulf *into Literary History*

Though *Beowulf* enters Literary History at the end of the eighteenth century, the poem was too little understood for sophisticated intellectual awareness. In 1805 Sharon Turner's *History of the Anglo-Saxons* has a very brief treatment of the

---

[2] See E. G. Stanley, *The Search for Anglo-Saxon Paganism*, originally published in a series of nine articles, *N&Q*, 209-10 (1964-1965); reprinted, with corrections, in book-form (Cambridge, and Totowa, New Jersey: 1975).

poem, with passages translated into Modern English.[3] The elegant but, in philological grasp, very insufficient *editio princeps* of 1815 by G. J. Thorkelin has an
inaccurate translation into Latin.[4] In 1820 N. F. S. Grundtvig, however, in his
translation of the poem into Danish[5] showed excellent understanding both of the
text and the language in which it is written, as is shown incidentally by his very
good prefatory verses in Old English, heavily dependent on *Beowulf*. Nevertheless, for non-Scandinavian scholars Danish is not an easy language in which to
read a difficult poetic rendering with often complicated notes, so that, in effect,
before J. M. Kemble published his translation into English in 1837, only extracts
were available to most readers of English, the most accomplished by J. J.
Conybeare, published in 1826, together with a literal Latin rendering of the
extracts translated more freely into English.[7] The first translation into German
was that by Ludwig Ettmüller in 1840, into alliterative verse.[8] Translation into
German was important in the nineteenth century, because German philological
scholarship was pre-eminent then in Anglo-Saxon studies, a period when, it may
now seem, literary good sense was wanting.

Terms used for literary kinds and concepts

Beowulf was at once given recognition as heroic poetry, *Helte-Digt*, *Heldengedicht*, but the terminology of literary kinds has shifted over the centuries, and
the major European languages are not agreed in the use of recognizably similar
terms: for example, *epic*, *Epos*, *épopée*; *romance*, *Romanze*, *roman*. One of the
very earliest allusions to the poem, John Pinkerton's in 1790,[9] describes it as 'a
noble specimen of Anglo-Saxon poetry of the tenth century, being a romance of

---

3 S. Turner, *The History of the Manners, Landed Property, Government, Laws, Poetry, Literature, Religion, and Language of the Anglo-Saxons*, in fact, *The History of the Anglo-
   Saxons*, IV (London, 1805), 398-408.
4 Grim. Johnson Thorkelin (ed.), *De Danorum Rebus Gestis Secul. III & IV. Poëma danicum
   dialecto anglo-saxonica* (Copenhagen, 1815).
5 Nik. Fred. Sev. Grundtvig, *Bjowulfs Drape. Et Gothisk Helte-Digt fra forrige Aar-Tusinde af
   Angel-Saxisk paa Danske Riim* (Copenhagen, 1820).
6 John M. Kemble, *A Translation of the Anglo-Saxon Poem of Beowulf* (London, 1837), vol. II
   of his edition, *The Anglo-Saxon Poems of Beowulf The Travellers Song and The Battle of
   Finnesburh* (London, 1835). Kemble's first edition of *Beowulf* had appeared in 1833, the
   second is greatly revised. According to B. Dickins, 'John Mitchell Kemble and Old English
   Scholarship', *PBA*, XXV (1939), 79 (= p. 31 of separate) [reprinted in E. G. Stanley (ed.),
   British Academy Papers on Anglo-Saxon England (Oxford, 1990), 85], vol. I of this second
   edition, though dated 1835, was not issued till 1837.
7 John Josias Conybeare, *Illustrations of Anglo-Saxon Poetry*, ed. by William Daniel
   Conybeare (London, 1826), 30-167.
8 Ludwig Ettmüller, *Beowulf. Heldengedicht des achten Jahrhunderts – Zum ersten Male aus
   dem Angelsächsischen in das Neuhochdeutsche stabreimend übersetzt* (Zürich, 1840).
9 J. Pinkerton (ed.), *The Bruce; or, The History of Robert I King of Scotland. Written in Scotish
   Verse By John Barbour* (London, 1790), I, p. xii. Cf. E. G. Stanley, 'A *Beowulf* Allusion,
   1790', *N&Q*, 234 (1989), 148.

the wars between Denmark and Sweden'. Since Pinkerton knew no Old English
it is likely that he derives the praise from Humfrey Wanley's account of the
manuscript and the mention that the poem is about war between Denmark and
Sweden from Thomas Warton's *History of English Poetry*, both standard auth-
orities in their day.[10] Pinkerton's allusion is of no significance, and I published it
a short time ago merely to draw the attention of the bibliographers of Old
English literature to it. One of them included my reference in a survey of
publications, and in doing so suggested that 'it would be an interesting study to
list the genres into which the poem has been placed since its discovery'.[11]

This is perhaps putting it the wrong way round. A study of the terms used for
poetic genres, from the eighteenth century onwards, would be of value for a
history of literary criticism; not merely terms for poetic genres but also descriptive terms, 'popular', 'pagan', 'oral', for example, adjectives which have been
used of *Beowulf*. Under each term the study would list the poems to which the
term has been applied at some time or at various times. It would be quite
interesting to see where *Beowulf* has been thought to belong. The use of the
word *romance* in 1790 does, of course, not mean that Pinkerton, if he had been
able to read the poem, would have thought of it as constituting what we now call
a romance or a metrical romance. A very good account of the history of that
literary term in the eighteenth century is available in Arthur Johnston's *Enchanted Ground*,[12] from which it emerges that 'scholars of taste and genius'
were in profound sympathy with medieval romances, and attached the term
particularly to the marvellous in medieval narrative. Monster- and dragon-
slaying deeds of heroism give *Beowulf* a secure place in this genre as perceived
in the eighteenth century and early nineteenth.

In translating from German into English (or *vice versa*) there are further
terminological difficulties. *Sage* is 'legend' as well as 'tale', perhaps 'folk-tale'
but less precisely defined than in modern Folk-Tale Studies; it has not the same
meaning as *saga*, as that term is used especially with reference to Icelandic
literature. *Gedicht* is close in sense to what Sir Philip Sidney understood by
'Poetry', that is, imaginative literary creation, not unlike Greek *poesis*:[13]

---

[10] H. Wanley, *Librorum Vett. Septentrionalium*, liber alter (1705) of G. Hickes, *Linguarum Vett.
Septentrionalium Thesaurus* (Oxford, 1703-1705), 218-19; T. Warton, *The History of English
Poetry*, I (London, 1774), 2 note d.

[11] R. M. Liuzza, in 'The Year's Work in Old English Studies 1989', *Old English Newsletter*,
24/2 (1991), 36. For more recent uses and definitions of 'epic', see pp. 45-6 and notes 22 and
24, below.

[12] A. Johnston, *Enchanted Ground The Study of Medieval Romance in the Eighteenth Century*
(London, 1964), Introduction.

[13] Sir Phillip Sidney, *An Apologie for Poetrie* (London: Henry Olney, 1595); or Sir Phillip
Sidney, *The Defence of Poesie* (London: William Ponsonby, 1595). For the quotation, see G.
Shepherd (ed.), *Sir Philip Sidney An Apology for Poetry or The Defence of Poesy* (London,
1965), 103. The basis of Sidney's Renaissance view of 'Poetry' (and related words), for
which cf. Shepherd, Introduction, *passim* (especially pp. 18-19), is, of course, radically
different from that of more recent German handling of *Dichtung* (and related words based on
dichten); the effects, however, are similar.

... verse being but an ornament and no cause of Poetry, since there have been many most excellent poets that never versified, and now swarm many versifiers that need never answer to the name of poets. ... But it is that feigning notable images of virtues, vices, or what else, with that delightful teaching, which must be the right describing note to know a poet by.

Märchen is 'story, tale', very close to *Sage*, and not usually to be rendered by 'fairy tale'. *Lied* is 'song', but also 'poem', both short and long, especially if it is thought unbookish. A translator's decision of what English words correspond to the German terms is difficult and largely arbitrary.

Jacob and Wilhelm Grimm and their immediate followers

Jacob Grimm's references to the genre of *Beowulf* are central early in the Literary History of the poem, because he occupied a central position in the history of philological scholarship, embracing the study of both language and literature. A section of the introduction to the first edition of the first volume of *Deutsche Grammatik*, 1819, is devoted to the Anglo-Saxon sources; he says this of *Beowulf*:[14]

> Die angelsächsische Literatur stehet an Reichthum und Gehalt weit über der althochdeutschen und weit unter der altnordischen. Die altsächsischen Heldenlieder sind, gleich den gothischen und althochdeutschen, verloren gegangen, wenige Spuren im Beowulf beweisen ihr ehemaliges Vorhandenseyn. Die Dichtung nahm seit der Einführung des Christenthums eine geistliche Richtung, der wir wohl manches merkwürdige Gedicht verdanken; aber um die Freiheit und Volksmäßigkeit der Poesie war es geschehn.

> [In wealth and content Anglo-Saxon literature is far superior to Old High German literature, and far inferior to that in Old Norse. Old Saxon heroic songs were lost, like those in Gothic and Old High German; a few traces in *Beowulf* prove their former existence. After the introduction of Christianity poetry took a religious direction to which indeed we owe many remarkable poems; but the freedom of the poetry and its rootedness in the folk perished.]

Grimm, in his edition of *Andreas und Elene*, 1840, defines the nature of 'epic', German *Epos*, in relation to *Beowulf*:[15]

> Die sage von Beóvulf müssen, sonst hätte ihr ganzer inhalt keinen verständlichen sinn, Angeln und Sachsen schon mit sich aus der alten in die neue heimat geführt haben, und es liegt in der natur solcher überlieferungen, dass sie längst in lieder gefasst waren. Diese epen wachsen und mindern sich ohne unterlass: es ist gleich unstatthaft die form des fünften oder sechsten jahrhun-

---

14 J. Grimm, *Deutsche Grammatik*, Erster Theil (Göttingen, 1819), p. lxvii.
15 J. Grimm (ed.), *Andreas und Elene* (Cassel: Fischer, 1840), pp. xlvi-xlvii.

derts in der umarbeitung des achten oder neunten zu erkennen und manche
ungetilgte spur höheres alterthums in der jüngeren gestaltung zu verkennen.
Weder das gewebe des inhalts der lieder noch die damit verwachsne form der
poesie kann entsprungen sein zu der zeit, wo sie das letztemal nieder-
geschrieben werden, wol aber war damals jene frühere ausdrucksweise immer
noch so verständlich und zusagend geblieben, dass sie sich mit dem fortschritt
der sprache und dichtkunst vereinigen und bis auf einen gewissen punct hin
durchdringen konnte. Hieran eben scheint alles gelegen: die poesie will nicht
ihrer vergangenheit entsagen, zugleich aber der gegenwart huldigen. Man
begreift, dass sich vom siebenten jahrhundert bis ins zehnte ein ziemlich fester
stil der dichtkunst bildete und erhielt, der ohne der christlichen ansicht zu
widerstreben noch manche gewohnheiten des heidenthums in sich trug.

[The Angles and Saxons must have brought with them from their old home
to their new home the tale of Beowulf, or its whole content would have no
comprehensible meaning; and it lies in the nature of such traditions that they
were composed long ago in songs. Such epics grow and decrease ceaselessly.
It is no more permissible to recognize in the eighth- or ninth-century rifa-
cimento their fifth- or sixth-century form, than not to recognize in the more
recent revision many an uneffaced trace of greater antiquity. Neither the textual content of the songs nor the poetic form closely connected with it can be
the product of the age when it was written down for the last time; the earlier
manner of expression remained, however, still so well understood and congenial in that more recent age that it was able up to a point to permeate and
combine readily with language and poetic art as it had progressed. Everything
seems to depend on that: Poetry has no wish to renounce its past, and at the
same time seeks to do homage to the present. It is to be understood that from
the seventh to the tenth century a fairly fixed style of poetry was formed and
maintained which, without resisting a Christian view still bore within it many
habits of paganism.]

In a paper as early as 1813, unconnected with *Beowulf*, Jacob Grimm wrote
on the relationship of epic to myth and history in terms as evanescent as
mountain air transcending distances:[16]

Das erste, was ein aufrichtiges Gemüth aus der Betrachtung alter Fabel und
Sage lernen kann, ist, daß hinter ihnen kein eitler Grund, keine Erdichtung,
sondern wahrhafte dichtung liegt; wenn ich mich . . . so ausdrücken darf:
objective Begeisterung. Bald aber wird die tiefer schreitende Untersuchung
auf den Punct dringen, wo man zu fragen hat: wie sich Sagenwahrheit verhalte
zu der historischen Wahrheit, gleichsam zu einer greiflichen eine fühlbare. . . .
    Es scheint mir, als sey hier eigentlich blos zweyerley zu antworten möglich:

16 'Gedanken über Mythos, Epos und Geschichte. Mit altdeutschen Beispielen', in F. Schlegel
(ed.), *Deutsches Museum*, 3 (1813), 53-75 [reprinted in J. Grimm, *Kleinere Schriften*, IV
(Berlin, 1869), 74-85]. I quote from the facsimile reprint of *Deutsches Museum* (Hildesheim
and New York, 1973), 3, 53-6; but I have corrected a mispunctuation and minor misprints, of
which the only significant one is that the second sentence quoted has *auf den punct bringen*
in the 1813 version.

entweder müßte die mythische wahrheit eine himmlische oder eine irdische genannt werden.

Lösen sich alle Sagen in einfache, immer einfachere Offenbarungen des Heiligsten auf? sind sie nur ein wechselndes, für das Unendliche, Unfaßliche, sich neuversuchendes Wort und fließen sie, im Schein wandelbar, im Grund unwandelbar, endlich in dem Urgedicht zusammen, von dem sie ausgegangen waren? Oder aber haben sie sich, wie Gebirgsduft über Fernen tritt, an die vergangene Menschenzeit gesetzt, gehören sie zu unserer Geschichte mit, und sind sie gleich dieser ewig hin etwas neues, verschiedenes, höchstens ähnliches?

Zu der letzten Meinung führt und gewöhnt die Geschichte selbst, die überall aus dem Schoos der Fabel aufgetaucht ist, und sich weder früher so rein von diesem mütterlichen Element losreißen will, noch späterhin es kann, wenn sie gleich wollte, ohne daß dort ein Stück des Mythus, hier ein Stück der Geschichte preisgegeben werden müßte. . . .

Nur dadurch wird der Widerspruch versöhnt und gehoben werden, daß man beyde Meinungen vereinbart, d. h. dem Volksepos weder eine reinmythische (göttliche) noch reinhistorische (factische) Wahrheit zuschreibt, sondern ganz eigentlich sein Wesen in die Durchdringung beyder setzt. . . . so ist auch zu dem Epos eine historische That nöthig, von der das Volk lebendig erfüllt sey, daß sich die göttliche Sage daran setzen könne, und beyde sind durch einander bedingt gewesen.

[The first lesson a sincere mind may learn through the contemplation of ancient fable and legend is that they are based on no vain foundation, no fabulosity, but on truthful *poesis*; if I may . . . so express it: they are based on objective inspiration. However, as the investigation advances more deeply, it will soon penetrate to a point where the question has to be asked: In what relationship does narrative truth stand to historical truth; as it were, how does what may be sensed stand in relation to what is palpable and to be grasped? . . .

It seems to me that essentially only two ways of answering are possible: mythical truth will have to be designated either a heavenly truth or an earthly truth.

Do all legends dissolve into simple, ever simpler, revelations of the most sacred? Are they only a variable utterance for the infinite, an utterance striving to find new expression for the intangible? And do they, seemingly variable yet in fact invariable, ultimately run together in the *Urgedicht* from which they took their origin? Or, on the other hand, did they, like mountain air transcending distances, associate themselves with a bygone age of humanity; do they pertain to our history, and are they like our history something ever new, ever different, at most with some similarities?

History itself leads and accustoms us to the latter view, for History everywhere emerges from the womb of fable, and neither strives to tear itself loose early from this matrical element, nor is History, however much it might desire it, able to do so later without having to relinquish sometimes a mythical item, sometimes an historical item. . . .

This contradiction is to be reconciled and eliminated only by combining both views, that is, neither a purely mythical (divine) truth nor a purely historical (factual) truth is to be ascribed to folk-epic, but by placing the very nature of folk-epic essentially in the permeation of both truths.... For epic, an historical action is required to give to the folk a sense of lively fulfilment, so that divine myth can attach itself to it, each conditioned by the other.]

Jacob Grimm's brother Wilhelm wrote similarly at exactly the same time, especially when he divides Germanic heroic legends into four periods:[17]

Das Ganze ist in vier Perioden, welche mir hier die natürlichsten schienen, abgetheilt. In die erste fällt auch die Z e i t s e l b s t, wo die Sage und Geschichte in ihrer ursprünglischen Vereinigung sich zeigen. Darum sollen hier alle Puncte, worin die Monumente beider sich begegnen, es sey nun ganz in Uebereinstimmung oder in eigenthümlicher Abweichung, bemerkt seyn; denn weil beide unabhängig von einander sind, so legt die letztere von der erstern in eben diesen Puncten gewiß das glaubwürdigste Zeugniß des Daseyns ab. Zugleich wird hierdurch das Verhältniß der Fabel zur urkundlichen Geschichte dargelegt, doch nur zum Theil; wo dieses einmal der eigentliche Gegenstand einer Untersuchung ist, muß wohl der Gesichtspunct erweitert, und es dürfen Uebereinstimmungen, die sich im Ganzen und Großen ähnlicher Sagen und Geschichte zeigen, wie etwa in der fränkischen und burgundischen, wo die alte Mythe noch einwirkend und thätig lebend erscheint, nicht übersehen werden; denn nicht blos in sich abgeschlossen hat sie bestanden, sondern auch auf anderes sich überbreitend. . . . Sobald aber Geschichte und Sage sich einmal geschieden und eine neuere Annäherung und Verflechtung durch große chronologische Widersprüche sich bezeichnet (weil das Epos nur in seinem Geist, nicht gleiches Schritts mit der Geschichte fortgeht), so sind Berührungen . . . hier übergangen, weil aus ihnen nicht a n s i c h das Daseyn des Epos folgt, so merkwürdig sie in anderer Hinsicht bleiben.

[The whole is divided into four periods which seemed to me the most natural. That age when myth and history show themselves in their original union belongs to the first period. For that reason all points in which the monuments of both myth and history concur are to be noted here, whether they meet in complete agreement or in peculiar deviation; for since both myth and history are independent of each other, history bears in precisely these points the most credible witness to existence in myth. By this means the relationship of fable to documentary History is revealed, but only in part: where this is the proper subject of a study the point of view must be enlarged, and the correspondences must not be overlooked which manifest themselves in general and as a whole in similar legends and history, as, for example, in the Frankish and Burgundian material where ancient myth appears as still influential and actively alive; for myth did not merely exist self-contained, but it also spread

---

[17] Wilhelm Grimm, 'Zeugnisse über die deutsche Heldensage', alternative title (in the table of contents), 'Zeugnisse für die altd[eutsche] Heldensage', in Jacob and Wilhelm Grimm (eds), *Altdeutsche Wälder*, I (Cassel, 1813), 195-323. His introduction (pp. 195-8) is theoretical, especially pp. 196-7 from which I quote. Wilhelm Grimm's *Die Deutsche Heldensage* (Göttingen, 1829) has no theoretical discussion; its brief 'Vorrede' opens with a reference to this preliminary study.

over on to other matter. . . . As soon as history and myth were separate and a more recent convergence and interconnection would be marked by great chronological contradictions (because epic marches forward with history only in spirit, without keeping step), therefore such contacts . . . are ignored here, because from them *in themselves* the existence of epic does not follow, however remarkable they may be in other respects.]

These visionary, oracular utterances of the Brothers Grimm – as imprecise in application as most visionary, oracular utterances – gave the lead to thinking about folk-epic, a concept in which *Beowulf* was comprehended, certainly for the rest of the century, at least among German-speaking scholars. The preface to Ettmüller's translation takes for granted general assumptions about epic poetry being of the folk and drawing on History and Myth:[18]

Aus jener frühern Zeit ist uns von deutscher Volksdichtung bekanntlich in Deutschland selbst nichts übrig geblieben als das Lied von Hiltibrand und Hadubrand, ein Gedicht welches den Untergang der ohne Zweifel grossen Menge ähnlicher Dichtungen um so mehr beklagen lässt, als es ungeachtet seiner Lückenhaftigkeit das Grossartige des ältesten deutschen Volksgesanges deutlich uns vor Augen stellt. Um so mehr also, wie mich dünkt, müssen wir uns Glück wünschen, dass England durch sein Beowulflied unsern Verlust einiger Massen zu ersetzen im Stande ist. . . . Wie belehrend endlich wird nicht das Beowulflied für die Geschichte unserer alten epischen Dichtung! Bekanntlich giebt es zwo Quellen derselben, Geschichte und Mythus. Unter den Epen, die ich geschichtlich nennen möchte, verstehe ich aber keineswegs solche, die aus der geschriebenen Geschichte geschöpft wurden, wie mehrere der neuern, sondern solche, die dadurch entstunden, dass das Volk selbst geschichtliche Ereignisse nach seiner Art und Weise auffasste, unbewusst mehr oder minder umgestaltete und in dichterischer Form von Geschlecht auf Geschlecht fortpflanzte. So allein ist es zu erklären, wie das Volk lange Zeiten hindurch, bis zur Verbreitung rein geschichtlicher Kenntnisse und somit des geschichtlichen Sinnes, an seine Gedichte als an wahrhafte Darstellung ehemaliger Ereignisse glauben konnte. Mythische Epen dagegen sind mir diejenigen, welche dadurch entstanden, dass das Volk in Folge des Christenthumes seine Götter entweder geradezu in menschliche Helden verwandelte, oder aber Thaten der Götter geschichtlichen Helden beilegte.

[As is well known, in Germany itself nothing of Germanic folk-poetry has survived other than *Hildebrandslied*, a poem which makes all the more regrettable the loss of what were, no doubt, a great multitude of similar poetic compositions, since it brings into view, in spite of its fragmentary character, the magnificence of the oldest Germanic folk-song. We therefore have reason, it seems to me, to congratulate ourselves that England is able by means of her *Beowulf* to make good our loss in some measure. . . . Lastly, how instructive *Beowulf* is for the history of our ancient epic poetry! As is well known, epic

---

[18] *Beowulf. Heldengedicht . . . stabreimend übersetzt* (1840; see I⁸), pp. 1-2.

poetry has two sources: history and myth. Among epics which I wish to
designate historical I by no means understand such as were created from
recorded history (as are several of the more modern epics), but such as take
their origin from this, that the folk itself understood historical events in its own
way, unconsciously recasting them more or less, and transmitting them in
poetic form from generation to generation. Only thus is it explicable how the
folk found it possible to believe in its poetry as a truthful representation of past
events, through long periods until the dissemination of strictly historical
knowledge and with it of historical understanding. I designate as mythical
epics such as arose either because, as a consequence of Christianity, the folk
transformed its gods directly into human heroes, on the other hand, attributed
the deeds of gods to historical heroes.]

It took another seventeen, formative years till the next translation into German was published, that by C. W. M. Grein, as part of his comprehensive
collection of Old English verse in Modern German alliterative verse translation.[19] Till 1857, therefore, Ettmüller provided German readers with the only
available text for them to read, and he provided it in a package gift-wrapped in
his preoccupations and predilections. The more important of these are worth
stressing, not least because his underlying assumptions were generally known,
as he himself recognized and stated in an 'as is generally known' (*bekanntlich*),
and were presumably very generally accepted.

First, the Germanic peoples had epics, and *Beowulf* is highly informative for
the history of ancient German epic, all the more so since, as is also well known,
the *Hildebrandslied* is all that remains of what must have been an abundance:
the ancient popular poetry of Germany herself. In these pleasing thoughts
Ettmüller follows the high praise given to the *Hildebrandslied* by the Brothers
Grimm in their edition, in terms that left no room for doubt:[20]

Wenn uns von der ohne Zweifel herrlichen, liederreichen Poesie der ältesten
Deutschen bis auf so weniges leider alles verloren gegangen ist, so konnte
nicht leicht ein angenehmeres Bruchstück als das von Hildebrand übrig ge-
lassen werden.

[If unfortunately, everything, except only so very little, of the, no doubt,
magnificent poetry, rich in song, of the oldest Germanic peoples was to be
lost, then a more acceptable fragment could not easily have remained to us
than that of Hildebrand.]

There is glaring lack of logic in this statement, that – with only the one specimen extant on the basis of which to generalize about the abundant class to

---

[19] C. W. M. Grein, *Dichtungen der Angelsachsen stabreimend übersetzt*, 2 vols (Göttingen,
1857-1859), I, 222-308.

[20] Die Brüder [Jacob and Wilhelm] Grimm (eds), *Die beiden ältesten deutschen Gedichte aus
dem achten Jahrhundert: Das Lied von Hildebrand und Hadubrand und das Weißenbrunner
Gebet* (Cassel, 1812), Vorrede [p. 1].

which it belonged – nothing more pleasing could have survived. They are not guilty, however, of another Romantic fallacy: that the very survival of an early Germanic poem may be the result of the high regard in which it was held, so that survival itself is evidence of poetic excellence. In Old English poetry one thinks of *The Battle of Maldon* burnt up in the Cottonian fire of 1731, the flames of which licked the *Beowulf* codex, damaged it, but then turned back leaving it somewhat charred. At least, the manuscript survives; while that of *The Battle of Maldon* is lost, and we know the poem only because it was transcribed before 1731.

Yet even the Brothers Grimm could not make it seem that *Hildebrandslied*, sixty-eight lines long in modern editions (sixty-one lines long in theirs), is an extensive work; and the absurdity of their statement becomes palpable when translated into terms of more recent poetic quantity and quality. In Shakespeare's 'The Phoenix and the Turtle' and Goethe's fragmentary 'Mahomets Gesang' we have two poems of about the same number of lines as the fragmentary *Hildebrandslied*. If we could imagine that one or other of them had alone survived of the works of Shakespeare or Goethe, would it make sense to claim that no more acceptable poem or poetic fragment could have survived to enable us to form some notion of the lost glories of which they were a small part?

No wonder that Ettmüller sought to supply from *Beowulf* the riches for which one looks in vain in Old High German poetry. By 1840 the poem had acquired what might now be described as a 'critical heritage'. J. J. Conybeare, as early as 1826, had referred to 'the literary history of this ancient poem', and had supported an earlier opinion concerning 'the probability that it may be a translation or rifaccimento of some earlier work', perhaps recalling Thorkelin's edition of 1815, at the same time drawing attention to some fact concerning the poet:[21]

> The writer speaks of his story as one of ancient days, and more than once appeals for his authority either to popular tradition or to some previously existing document. Whatever was his age, it is evident that he was a Christian, a circumstance which has perhaps rendered his work less frequent in allusions to the customs and superstitions of his pagan ancestors, and consequently somewhat less interesting to the poetical antiquary than if it had been the production of a mind acquainted only with that wild and picturesque mythology which forms so peculiar and attractive a feature of the earlier productions of the Scandinavian muse.

Continental scholars built on that. F. J. Mone, ten years later, basing himself on Conybeare's criticism, gives detailed examples to illustrate the underlying oral traditions expressed in formulas of 'I heard tell', 'I will recount', 'others say', 'as far as I could learn', and the like, and finally also, with a reference to

---

[21] J. J. Conybeare, *Illustrations* (1826; see I⁷) pp. 32-4; cf. G. J. Thorkelin (ed.), *De Danorum Rebus Gestis Poëma* (1815; see I⁴), pp. xii-xiii.

the page of Thorkelin's edition containing lines 861-74, to their knowing many ancient stories by heart.[22] For example, *Beowulf* lines 868-70a:

> guma gilphlæden,   gidda gemyndig,
> se ðe ealfela   ealdgesegena
> 870   worn gemunde
>
> [. . . a man rich in rhetoric and the memory of songs, one who recalled an ample multitude of ancient traditions . . .]

Among several adverse comments on the poem is a brief account of what Mone regards as flaws in the narrative, including 'lack of steady advance' and a very early use of the term 'episodes' in connection with the poem (p. 130):

> Daraus [that the poem depends on oral tradition and memory] ist begreiflich, warum die Darstellung epischer Ruhe und Stätigkeit ermangelt. Sie ist abgebrochen und macht Sprünge. . . . Daher denn häufige Wiederholung, Andeutung u. dgl. . . . Auch die Folge des Gedichtes ist hie und da gestört. Einzelne Theile, die keine Episoden sind, stehen an Orten, wo sie nicht hingehören.

> [The dependence of the poem on oral tradition and memory explains why the portrayal lacks epic calm and steadiness. The depiction breaks off and makes leaps. . . . Frequent repetition, allusion, and the like, arise from that cause. . . . Now and again the correct sequence of the poem is disturbed. Some parts, which are not episodes, come where they do not belong.]

Mone (1796-1871) was a major liturgist, but on *Beowulf* not as influential as Heinrich Leo who edited, from Kemble's edition, 'Hengest's Fride mit Finn (Episode aus dem Bëóvulf)' in 1838, and wrote a monograph on the historical elements, stressing the historicity of Hygelac.[23] Under the heading of 'Mythischer Inhalt', Leo discusses line 1553b-1555a, claiming that these lines refer

---

[22] F. J. Mone, *Untersuchungen zur teutschen Heldensage*, Bibliothek der gesammten deutschen National-Literatur, II/i (Quedlinburg and Leipzig, 1836), 130-1, § 116.

[23] H. Leo (ed.), *Altsächsische und Angelsächsische Sprachproben* (Halle, 1838), 88-92; cf. Kemble, *Beowulf* (1835-1837; see I[6]), 238-41. H. Leo, *Bëówulf, daß älteste deutsche, in angelsächsischer mundart erhaltene, heldengedicht nach seinem inhalte, und nach seinen historischen und mythologischen beziehungen betrachtet. Ein beitrag zur geschichte alter deutscher geisteszustände* (Halle, 1839).

On the historicity of Hygelac, see R. W. Chambers, *Beowulf An Introduction* (Cambridge, 1921), p. 4 note 1. N. F. S. Grundtvig, in his review of Thorkelin's *De Danorum Rebus Gestis Poëma* (1815; see I[4]) 'Et Par Ord om det nys udkomme angelsaxiske Digt', *Nyeste Skilderie af Kjøbenhavn*, 1815, col. 1030, and 'Om Bjovulfs Drape', *Danne-Virke*, 2 (1817), 285, and N. Outzen, in his review of Thorkelin's edition, 'Das angelsächsische Gedicht Beovulf, als die schätzbarste Urkunde des höchsten Alterthums von unserm Vaterlande', *Kieler Blätter*, 3 (1816), 312, had given details of Chochilaicus' raid as recorded by Gregory of Tours.

immediately to Woden, and that the poem has been little altered in the direction of Christianity (p. 19):

> Kurz! außer einigen zusätzen und außer der vertilgung der heidnischen götter-namen hat daß lied schwerlich eine veränderung nach dieser seite hin erfaren, und steht uns so da als treueß abbild der gesinnung und lebensauffaßung der d e u t s c h e n heidenwelt.
>
> [In short, except for a few additions and except for the deletion of the names of pagan gods, the poem has hardly undergone any alteration in the direction of Christianity; and therefore it represents to us a faithful picture of the beliefs and view of life of the world of *German* paganism.]

That there is much here that no one now would agree with is, after more than a century and a half, not surprising: but Leo's bold claim that his monograph was a contribution to the history of ancient German or Germanic intellectual condi-tions remains amazing since so much of it is based on his preoccupations and predilections. He found in the poem what he was looking for rather than what was there – 'Legt ihr's nicht aus, so legt was unter'.

A Scandinavian poem?

Thorkelin believed *Beowulf* to be a Scandinavian poem translated into Anglo-Saxon. It seems an absurd notion for a variety of reasons, of which the two most frequently advanced are that there is not a shred of evidence for it; and that the style and sentiments of Scandinavian verse are very far from those of *Beowulf*, as is emphasized by W. W. Lawrence as late as 1928,[24] about a hundred years after Conybeare's rejection of that view was published (in 1826), and it seems supererogatory to give reasons for not believing what no one believes. There is a third reason, which I have never heard given by scholars versed in Icelandic literature: that the extant Scandinavian material is so much later, its most ancient ingredients, if truly ancient, so fragmentary, that no valid view can be formed of the nature of Scandinavian, presumably East Norse, heroic poetry of the eighth, ninth or tenth centuries.

---

[24] W. W. Lawrence, *Beowulf and Epic Tradition* (Cambridge, Massachusetts, 1928; reprinted, New York, 1961), 157-8. For H. Leo's views, see I[31]. For B. Thorpe's view that the origin of *Beowulf* is to be sought in 'an heroic Saga composed in the south-west of Sweden', see his edition, *The Anglo-Saxon Poems of Beowulf, The Scôp or Gleeman's Tale, and The Fight at Finnsburg* (Oxford, 1855), and cf. I[44], below, referring to the fuller context quoted there.

The name of the hero

The etymology and meaning of the name Beowulf have been discussed ever since Grimm gave its sense in 1823, 'Beowulf (d.h. Bienenwolf)', and thirteen years later identified the 'bee-wolf' with the woodpecker.[25]

> . . . in ihm [Beovulf] wird sich etwas Göttliches erkennen lassen. Schon vor dreyzehn Jahren . . . habe ich den Namen richtig übersetzt Bienenwolf. B i e - n e n w o l f, I m m e n w o l f ist nichts anders als der S p e c h t, weil alle Spechte den Bienen nachstellen.

> [. . . in the name 'Beowulf' something divine is discernible. As long ago as thirteen years . . . I correctly translated the name as 'bee-wolf'. *Bee-wolf* is nothing other than the woodpecker because all woodpeckers persecute bees.]

There are several comprehensive accounts of the history of the etymology, and of the switch of interpretation from 'woodpecker' to 'bear'.[26] It was noted that the name was given to real people: Mone in 1836 had adduced a German called Bewolf, but the name of one of the monks listed in the *Liber Vitae* of Durham was not read as Biuᵘulf till 1885.[27] Soon after that the phonological difficulties of the first element of the name were much discussed;[28] and, indeed, Phonology could be said to belong to the realm of Old English Literary History when the *Junggrammatiker* were at their height, roughly during the last third of the nineteenth century and the first third of the twentieth.

The onomastic concern of literary historians lies mainly in the question: Was Beowulf his real name, or was it a nickname? If a real name, it is surprising that

---

[25] See Jacob Grimm's review of N. F. S. Grundtvig, *Bjowulfs Drape* (Copenhagen, 1820), in *Göttingische gelehrte Anzeigen*, 2 January 1823 (1. Stück), p. 2 [reprinted in Jacob Grimm, *Kleinere Schriften*, IV Recensionen und vermischte Aufsätze (Berlin, 1869), 179]; 'Bienen-wolf' not yet specifically identified by him with 'Specht' till his review of J. M. Kemble, *Über die Stammtafel der Westsachsen* (Munich, 1836), *Göttingische gelehrte Anzeigen*, 28 April 1836 (66. and 67. Stück), 653-4 [reprinted Jacob Grimm, *Kleinere Schriften*, V/2 Recensionen und vermischte Aufsätze (Berlin, 1871), 242-3; and cf. Jacob Grimm, *Deutsche Mythologie* (2nd edn; Göttingen, 1844), 342 (and 639).

[26] Cf. R. W. Chambers, *Beowulf An Introduction* (1921; see I²³), 365-9; Klaeber's *Beowulf* (1936; and reprinted, 1950), pp. xxv-xxvi, xxviii; E. Björkman, *Studien über die Eigennamen im Beowulf*, StePh, 58 (1920), 145-93; H. B. Woolf, *The Old Germanic Principles of Name-Giving* (Baltimore, 1939), 154-6; G. Schramm, *Namenschatz und Dichtersprache* (Göttingen, 1957), 82.

[27] Mone, *Untersuchungen* (see I²²), p. 129 note. A monk's name, early in the Durham *Liber Vitae* (British Library MS Cotton Domitian vii) fol. 34ᵇ col. 1, was read as Brinulf in J. Stevenson (ed.), *Liber vitæ ecclesiæ Dunelmensis*, Surtees Society, xiii (1841), p. 34 col. 1; it was read as biu[u]ulf in H. Sweet (ed.), *The Oldest English Texts*, EETS, o.s. 83 (1885), p. 163 line 342. See the facsimile, A. Hamilton Thompson (ed.), *Liber vitae ecclesiae Dunelmensis*, Surtees Society, cxxxvi (1923).

[28] See the convenient summary in R. W. Chambers, *Beowulf An Introduction* (1921; see I²³), p. 367 note 3. Cf. R. Müller, *Untersuchungen über die Namen des nordhumbrischen Liber Vitae*, Palaestra, ix (1901), p. 17 § 14. 3. a., p. 94 § 54.

it does not alliterate with the other names of the dynasties to which he belongs, alliterating on *h* if Geatish, on vowels if Swedish. If it was a real name, and if he was a genuine historical figure, then it hardly matters what the two elements of the name may mean; the elements of real names do not need to combine to make sense in Germanic. In fact, we know little of name-giving in Anglo-Saxon England; we know little of nicknames. The Anglo-Saxon royal houses did use remarkable animal names for their scions, such as cannot have seemed complimentary: the younger brother of Ceadwalla of Wessex (the West Saxon dynasty alliterated on *c*) bore the name Mul 'mule', presumably a nickname; we know little about him, only that he ravaged Kent with his brother in 686 and got killed by burning in 687.[29] The question of nickname – for a person whose real name Ælfhere may be given at *Beowulf* line 2604, according to H. B. Woolf writing in 1937[30] – was never discussed as such until the concepts of myth-making had been radically changed in relation to *Beowulf*.

Mythical content

'Mythischer Inhalt' forms the second chapter of Leo's monograph of 1839, immediately after the chapter on 'Historische Anlehnung' (historical backing). To some extent this chapter is based on the prefaces to Kemble's two volumes, the text of *Beowulf* and the translation. In the preface to the text he had barely introduced the notion of myth:[31]

> I do not say that the poem which is now published was not written in England; but I say that the older poem of which this is a modernized form, was shaped upon Angle legends, celebrates an Angle hero, and was in all probability both written in Anglen, and brought hither by some of the earliest Anglo-Saxon chieftains who settled upon our shores.

Kemble in that preface did not firmly distinguish historical and mythical matter. In 1836 he published in German a monograph on the West Saxon genealogy which elicited an important review from Jacob Grimm, the opening of which emphasized the development from a mythical to an historical age:[32]

---

[29] On the name, see H. B. Woolf, *Name-Giving* (1939; see I[26]), 80 and 84. Spurious biographical details are given by Henry of Huntingdon and William of Malmesbury; see T. Arnold (ed.), *Henrici Archidiaconi Huntendunensis Historia Anglorum*, Rolls Series, 74 (1879), 105-7, W. Stubbs (ed.), *Willelmi Malmesbiriensis . . . de Gestis Regum Anglorum*, Rolls Series, 90, I (1887), 16-17.

[30] H. B. Woolf, 'The Name of Beowulf', *EStn*, 72 (1937), 7-9.

[31] J. M. Kemble (ed.), *Beowulf* (1835-1837; see I[6]), p. xxii. H. Leo, *Bëówulf* (1839; see I[23]), 19, followed Kemble, arguing that the poem can hardly have originated in England since it lacks all reference to the Angels and Saxons in England; and since it lacks also the characteristics of Norse story it cannot easily be Scandinavian in origin. No other conclusion seems therefore possible to Leo than that the poem originated in continental Angeln.

[32] For Kemble's *Stammtafel* (1836) and Grimm's review (1836), see I[25].

Von den ältesten gothischen, langobardischen und angelsächsischen
Königen sind uns Geschlechtsreihen überliefert worden, sämmtlich auf einer
Verknüpfung der historischen Zeit an die mythische beruhend. Diese Namen
und ihre Verhältnisse scheinen für die deutsche Mythologie und die ersten
Anfänge unserer Geschichte wichtig. . . . Alles noch zu erklären scheint
unmöglich; manches wird sich unerwartet nach und nach wieder aufschließen,
so bald es der Forschung das mythische Element zu erfassen und zu ent-
wickeln gelingt. Die Deutung ist also durch die Fortschritte bedingt, welche
wir in Herstellung der deutschen Mythologie überhaupt machen werden.

[Genealogies of the earliest Gothic, Langobard and Anglo-Saxon kings have
come down to us, all of them dependent on a connection of the historical age
with the mythical age. These names and their background appear to be of
importance for Germanic mythology and the first beginnings of our history. . .
It seems to be impossible at this stage to explain everything; much of it will be
elucidated unexpectedly little by little as soon as our scholarship succeeds in
comprehending and unravelling the mythical element. The interpretation is
therefore dependent on the advances which we shall be making in producing a
Germanic mythology in general.]

Grimm's optimism looks heady in retrospect. Progress seemed sure, and with
every scholarly advance the Germanic mythical age of prehistory, on which the
first beginnings of historical Germanic antiquity depend, will yield up its secret:
the mythical element itself will be understood.

Generations of Germanic and Anglo-Saxon scholars, among them Müllenhoff, his disciple Möller, Panzer, Berendsohn, and, from the 1840s onwards, the
advocates of a Germanic oral-formulaic theory, all take their cue from Grimm
and are in varying degree infected by the optimism from which his work on the
literary prehistory and history of the Germanic peoples suffered.

For about half a century, Karl Müllenhoff (born 1818, died 1884) produced a
series of influential articles on *Beowulf* culminating in the 1880s in two books,
the first by the Danish scholar Hermann Möller (Martin Thomas Herman
Møller; born 1850, died 1923) published in 1883, and the second, by Müllenhoff himself, published posthumously in 1889.[33] Möller's endeavours were
based on Müllenhoff's distinguished model. As might be expected in that unex-
pectable world of Germanic myth, we encounter gods, giants and heroes at
every turn in an early article by Müllenhoff, 'Der mythus von Beówulf'.[34] But
there is more than that to it, for names of denizens in the poem are etymologized
or discussed linguistically till they cease to be what they appear to be to a reader

[33] H. Möller, *Das altenglische Volksepos in der ursprünglichen strophischen Form*, I Abhandlungen, II Texte (Kiel, 1883). K. Müllenhoff, *Beovulf Untersuchungen über das angelsächi-
sche Epos und die älteste Geschichte der germanischen Seevölker*, with a preface by H.
Lübke (Berlin, 1889); the first part of the book was the introduction to his Berlin course of
Beowulf lectures, the second part had appeared as an article twenty years earlier, 'Die innere
geschichte des Beovulfs', *ZfdA*, 14 (1869), 193-244.
[34] *ZfdA*, 7 (1849), 419-41.

unaware of the mythical cargo carried. For example (pp. 420-1, footnote), Breca and his Brondings yield, by way of Old Icelandic poetic *breki* 'breaker, heavy ocean-wave' as well as 'Brandingi ein nordischer Riesenname' [the Norse name of a giant] (not to be directly related to Modern High German *Brandung* 'the place where the sea dashes on the rocks', for that is not attested early), and the word may be of fire rather than water. In such an exegesis the Breca story becomes the elemental struggle of our hero with the wild unfathomable sea. That view lived on, with the Brondings compared with Dutch *branding* and Danish *brænding* (identical in sense with Modern German *Brandung*); it is to be found as late as 1912 in R. W. Chambers's explanation of *Breoca* [*weold*] *Brondingum* (*Widsith* line 25), and similarly in R. Much on *Widsith* in 1925:[35]

> [Breca's] name deckt sich buchstäblich mit an. *breki* 'woge', eigentlich 'brecher'; vgl. engl. *breaker* 'sturzsee'. da nun von einem schwimmwettkampf Beowulfs mit ihm berichtet wird, macht sein name und seine gestalt einen mythologischen beziehungsweise märchenhaften eindruck.

> [Breca's name agrees literally with Old Norse *breki* 'wave', more exactly 'breaker', cf. English *breaker* 'heavy sea breaking over the ship'. Now, since a swimming contest is reported between Beowulf and him, his name and his stature give a mythological impression, or, as the case may be, the impression of a folk-tale.]

For onomastic reasons that seem far from clear, Müllenhoff (p. 421) asserts that Beowulf

> ist seinem namen nach eigentlich nur ein agrarischer heros und deswegen muß er schon sonst für einen diener oder kämpen des land und meer beherschenden gottes gegolten haben.

> [Beowulf is on the evidence of his name ultimately an agrarian hero, and for that reason alone he must have been considered a retainer or warrior of the god who ruled land and sea.]

Müllenhoff (p. 423) merges Grendel with Loki, both elemental beings of fire and water, and of gigantic stature; smaller, however, than Grendel's mother in whom, one would have thought without much help from the text, Jacob Grimm had seen the devil's grandmother; Müllenhoff too refers to that argument, and echoes were still to be heard early this century.[36] Yet in Müllenhoff's opinion (p. 624) Grendel's mother is 'gleichsam nur eine personifikation der meerestiefe' [as it were, only a personification of the depth of the sea].

---

[35] See R. W. Chambers (ed.), *Widsith A Study in Old English Heroic Legend* (Cambridge, 1912), 110-11. R. Much, 'Widsith', *ZfdA*, 62 (1925), 133.

[36] *Deutsche Mythologie* (1844; see I[25]), p. 959. Cf. E. Lehmann, 'Fandens oldemor', *Dania Tidsskrift for dansk sprog og litteratur samt folkeminder*, 8 (1901), 179-94, *Beowulf* at 185-90; translated into German, 'Teufels Großmutter', *Archiv für Religionswissenschaft*, 8/3-4 (1906), 411-30, *Beowulf* at 419-24.

In all this stuff Müllenhoff felt able to distinguish what is Germanic, *deutsch*, from the un-Germanic, *undeutsch*; thus (p. 428) of the dragon, 'feuerspeien' and likewise 'umherfliegen in der luft muß ich für undeutsch halten' [fire-breathing (and likewise) flying about in the air I must regard as un-Germanic], an imported concept like the word *draca* itself. The dragon is quite a different beast really:

> die wahrheit also ist daß der drache den Beóvulf tödtet nichts anderes ist als was in andern guten deutschen sagen, ein wurm der neidisch über seinem horte liegt.

> [The reality therefore is that the dragon killed by Beowulf is nothing other than what is in other good German tales a worm lying jealously on top of its hoard.]

The fights in *Beowulf* symbolize the changing seasons of the year; Beowulf's presence is aestival, his death and burial hiemal (pp. 433-7). Since Müllenhoff elsewhere made a very considerable contribution to Germanic prehistory and early history, all his myth-mongering is perhaps surprising. Yet even in 'Der mythus von Beóvulf' occur interesting statements relating this figure or that to history not myth; for example (p. 430), Wiglaf son of Weohstan. That gains significance from the recent renewal of interest in the genealogy of the kings of East Anglia in Cotton MS Vespasian B.vi fol. 109[b] with the earliest king Wehha, his name so close in appearance to the first element of Weohstan, and his son Wuffa from whom the royal house of the Wuffings takes its name.[37] As we have seen, Jacob Grimm and Kemble took great interest in the Anglo-Saxon royal genealogies.[38]

It is difficult to distinguish between myth and history, and uncertain if the Anglo-Saxons themselves, who are unlikely to have made that distinction, had more than the vaguest notion of how the names in those listings might provide a factual core to story as they knew it. I do not believe that any scholar, before Kenneth Sisam in 1953, posed the following questions central to *Beowulf* in Literary History, based on the recognition that Anglo-Saxons, though intelligent, might have thought about or used the royal genealogies of their nation differently from the way we now think about them and use them:[39]

> How much did the Anglo-Saxons know about their early history in England, and about persons associated in legend with still earlier Germanic times? When a name appears incidentally in a sixth-century annal of the *Anglo-Saxon*

---

[37] See R. Bruce-Mitford, *The Sutton-Hoo Ship-Burial*, I (London, 1975), 690-5.

[38] Kemble's *Stammtafel* and Grimm's review of it, both 1836; see I[25]. See also, even earlier, Jacob Grimm, *Deutsche Mythologie* (1st edn; Göttingen, 1835), Anhang, 'Angelsächsische Stammtafeln', pp. i-xxix.

[39] Kenneth Sisam, 'Anglo-Saxon Royal Genealogies', *PBA*, 39 (1953), 353; reprinted in *British Academy Papers*, (1990; see I[6]), 203.

Chronicle or in *Beowulf*, did it unlock a store of well-ordered information in the mind of an intelligent Anglo-Saxon? Or did it often convey no more than the vague impression of remote times that adds to the enjoyment of old stories? Evidence bearing on such questions is hard to find. Modern scholars, whether expressly or by implication, seem to prefer the first and more congenial opinion. Yet scattered through this examination of the Anglo-Saxon genealogies [i.e. throughout Sisam's paper] there is a considerable amount of evidence in the other direction.

Modern literary scholarship as exemplified by Sisam has given greater precision to the study of Old English literature by dwelling on doubt where certainty is hard or impossible to come by. That scholarly attitude has had the result that one soon tires of the 'without doubt', or 'originally', or 'essentially', or 'in reality', the 'ohne Zweifel', or 'ursprünglich', or 'eigentlich', of earlier scholarship. Wherever in earlier scholars we meet with one or more of these words and phrases we must substitute doubt for their certainty. Thus in a paper which comes relatively late in Müllenhoff's critical involvement with *Beowulf*:[40]

Die mythen gehörten ursprünglich eben dem gotte an, dessen beiname in dem angegebenen sinne [*scil.* 'ein bienengott'] Beóva war, und bildeten ohne zweifel mit dem mythus von Sceáf eine zusammenhängende reihe von sagen, von seiner ankunft, jugend, heldenthat und seinem hingang.

[Originally these myths belonged to the god whose byname was Beowa in the sense indicated (namely, of a bee-deity), and together with the myth of Sceaf they formed doubtlessly a coherent sequence of tales about his arrival, youth, act of heroism, and his departure.]

Müllenhoff believed in the poets' own assurance when they created myths: they got everything right by instinct, and he marvelled at such 'instinctmässige Sicherheit'.[41] As confidently as he judged the writings of the ancient poets so he himself judged with absolute assurance right and wrong in the work of contemporary mythologists of Germanic antiquity: he knew what was right.

H. Möller took his master's principles even further and applied them to his chosen texts with similar, and similarly questionable, assurance. He proclaims that there is a genre of Old English popular epic, *Volksepos*, and the textual part of his book provides editorially altered versions of them: *Widsith*, the 'episodes' in *Beowulf*, namely, Scyld's burial, Finn (as well as *The Battle of Finnsburh*), two Heremod episodes, Sigemund, Offa's queen, Ingeld, Ongentheow (in several bits), Hygelac (four episodes), and Hrethel or 'The Father's Lament', the two 'Beowulf' epics or epic songs ('epen oder epische lieder', consisting of lines of lines 1-2199 and 2200-end, with the 'episodes' omitted), and *Waldere*.

---

40 'Zeugnisse und excurse zur deutschen heldensage', *ZfdA*, 12 (1865), 283-4.
41 See K. Müllenhoff, 'Ueber Tuisco und seine Nachkommen. Ein Beitrag zur Geschichte der altdeutschen Religion', *Allgemeine Zeitschrift für Geschichte*, 8 (1847), 223.

With the vehement certainty of a nineteenth-century *Neuphilologe* who has mastered the principles of Higher Criticism as well as Müllenhoff's 'innere Geschichte' of the relevant texts, Möller's book avers also, that the maritime Germanic peoples, those especially that sail the North Sea, employed strophic form for their *Volksepos*. The disintegration of the extant poems was undertaken, and based on an infallible ability to distinguish, for example, the original verses in the extant agglomerate called *das Beowulfepos* from the work of more than one interpolator. Among strophic forms the varieties found in Norse are to be recognized. Müllenhoff himself had asserted the strophic nature of Germanic verse,[42] and soon it becomes clear that, within the Finn episode, *fornyrðislag* was the form of the *Hengestlied*, whereas *lioðahattr* was the form of the *Hnæflied* and the *Hildeburhlied*. There is no need to spend longer on this kind of textual criticism, full of preoccupations and predilections, because R. W. Chambers has dealt with it sufficiently in *Beowulf An Introduction*, with the crucial and matter-of-fact dismissal (p. 254) of such textual scholarship as 'unsupported by any evidence'.

C. W. M. Grein

A year before Jacob Grimm's death in 1863, C. W. M. Grein (born 1825, died 1877) delivered his 'Habilitationsvorlesung'.[43] Of the three possible aspects under which *Beowulf* may be considered, history, mythology and literary criticism, he undertakes to confine himself to the first, but, in fact, has not a little on myth, and is critical of mythologists (p. 260):

> Wenn auch grade die Hauptthaten Beowulf's, deren Verherlichung die Aufgabe dieses Liedes bildet, unbestreitbar rein mythischer Natur sind, so sind dies eben Züge aus der alten Göttersage, welche die sagenbildende Tradition an einen historischen Helden angeknüpft hat: denn daß wir den Beowulf als einen solchen müssen gelten lassen, das geht unverkennbar hervor aus allen Beziehungen, in denen wir ihn außerdem werden auftreten sehen. Nach Abzug dieser und sonst noch einer wenigen offenbar mythischen Anlehnungen bleibt uns in unserem Liede noch eine reiche Fülle von Ueberlieferungen aus der wirklichen Geschichte übrig und zwar . . . aus der Geschichte einer Zeit, die kaum mehr als 200 Jahre hinter der Abfassungszeit des Gedichtes selber liegt. Einigen dieser Punkte haben selbst die eifrigsten Mythenforscher, bei denen sich sonst mitunter nur zu leicht Alles in mythischen Nebel zu verflüchtigen droht, die rein historische Natur nicht abzusprechen gewagt. Aber der kreis der geschichtlichen Ueberlieferungen ist in unserem Liede noch viel größer, als man gewöhnlich anzunehmen geneigt ist.

---

[42] K. Müllenhoff (ed.), *De carmine Wessofontano et de versu ac stropharum usu apud Germanos antiquissimo* (Berlin, 1861).

[43] 'Die historischen Verhältnisse des Beowulfliedes', published in *Jahrbuch für romanische und englische Literatur*, 4 (1862), 260-85.

[Even though the principal deeds of Beowulf, the glorification of which forms the task which the poem sets itself, are indisputably purely mythical, these are in fact the characteristic features of the ancient deity-tale which the tradition forming these legends attached to an historical hero; for it emerges unmistakably from all other matters in which he is active, that we must grant that he is historical. Once we have removed this and a very few other features which are obviously mythical in origin, we are left with a great abundance of factual historical traditions, and that moreover from a period of history which is not likely to go back further than two hundred years before the date of composition of the poem itself. Even the most energetic mythological scholars – with whom otherwise everything evaporates now and then all too easily in mythical haze – have not dared to deny the purely historical nature of some of these points. The compass of historical traditions is, however, much greater than one is usually inclined to suppose.]

Grein is not among the disintegrators of *Beowulf*, and regards the poem up to the arrival of Beowulf and his men as a suitable induction (p. 263):

Und was ist da wol natürlicher, als daß dieser Dänenkönig eingeführt werde durch einen kurzen Ueberblick über die Geschichte seiner Ahnen! Jener Eingang bildet somit grade einen wesentlichen Bestandtheil des Liedes, das ich überhaupt, sowie es uns vorliegt, nur für das zusammenhängende Werk eines einzigen Dichters halten kann.

[And nothing could be more natural than that the Danish king should be introduced by a short survey of the history of his ancestors! That induction therefore forms directly an essential element of the poem which, as we have it, I can only regard as the coherent work of a single poet.]

He accepts that myth is attached to Scyld Scefing (p. 263), to Grendel and his mother (p. 267), believes that the swimming exploits of Beowulf are the result of confusion of names and that Woden's son Beaw performed these deeds and perhaps also the fight with the dragon (pp. 277-8), and attributes the story of Offa's queen to monastic confusion of the historical queen with the legendary (p. 283):

Denn daß unsere Erzählung von der Jugend der Môdthryðo ein rein mythisch sagenhafter Zug, ein Stück unheimlicher Walkürennatur sei, übertragen auf die Gemahlin des Königs Offa, das braucht wol kaum ausdrücklich hervorgehoben werden.

[For it need hardly be emphasized explicitly that the narrative of Modthrytho's youth is purely mythical and legendary in character, a piece typical of the supernatural sphere to which the Valkyries belong and transferred to the consort of King Offa.]

Except for these myths, *Beowulf* is history.

More pragmatic views

Pragmatic English scholars hardly entered the arena of myth-mongering. Whatever misconceptions there may be in Benjamin Thorpe's speculations on *Beowulf* (including south-west Sweden as the original home of the subject-matter of the poem), they are not evaporations into mythical haze:[44]

> With respect to this the oldest heroic poem in any Germanic tongue, my opinion is, that it is not an original production of the Anglo-Saxon muse, but a metrical paraphrase of an heroic Saga composed in the south-west of Sweden [a footnote expresses 'the hope that the original Saga may one day be discovered in some Swedish library'], in the old common language of the North, and probably brought to this country during the sway of the Danish dynasty.
> . . .
> From the allusions to Christianity contained in the poem, I do not hesitate to regard it as a Christian paraphrase of a heathen Saga, and those allusions as interpolations of the paraphrast, whom I conceive to have been a native of England of Scandinavian parentage.

And more bluntly (pp. xvii-xviii):

> Preceding editors have regarded the poem of Beowulf as a myth, and its heroes as beings of a divine order. To my dull perception these appear as real kings and chieftains of the North, some of them, as Hygelac and Offa, entering within the pale of authentic history, while the names of others may have perished.

John Earle was less self-effacing than Thorpe in his rejection of the then 'prevalent view of German Higher Criticism' of *Beowulf* – an epidemic, infection with which he strove to avoid:[45]

---

[44] B. Thorpe, *Beowulf* (1855; see I²⁴), pp. viii-ix.

[45] J. Earle, *The Deeds of Beowulf* (Oxford, 1892), pp. xxviii-xxix. Earle had contributed three articles on *Beowulf* to *The Times*. The first, 'The Beowulf', 25 August 1884, p. 6, cols 4-5, is unsigned; it includes a good 'sketch of the modern literary history of the poem', and assigns its composition to the last decade of the ninth century, a date that seems wholly acceptable to me as appears from 'The Date of *Beowulf*: Some Doubts and No Conclusions', in C. Chase, *The dating of Beowulf*, Toronto Old English Series, 6 (1981), 197-211 [reprinted in E. G. Stanley, *A Collection of Papers with Emphasis on Old English Literature*, Publications of the Dictionary of Old English, 3 (Toronto, 1987), 209-31]. The second, '*Beowulf* I', 30 September 1885, p. 3 cols 3-4, revises his dating of the composition to the reign of Offa of Mercia, on the grounds that the quality of the coinage of Offa's reign shows that the age was capable of producing artistic excellence; and that argument is carried further in '*Beowulf* II', 29 October 1885, p. 3, cols 1-3, on the grounds that the high praise given to Offa of Angel in the poem can be related to the likely welcome of such prominent praise by a king of that name contemporary with the poet. Later writers on Old English verse have used similar arguments. First, on *Widsith*, for example by: A. Brandl, 'Die angelsächsische Literatur' [title of separate, *Geschichte der altenglischen Literatur*. I. Teil: Angelsächsische Periode bis zur Mitte des

It [*scil.* the prevalent view] is arbitrary, it did not spring from the data of the poem, though it may seem to find a justification there. If the data of the poem had really afforded a ground for this course of speculation, there might have been matter for combating it by argument; but as it is, we can only wait till the epidemic has passed over.

The real source of this criticism has been from without. Long ingrained notions about the fortuitous growth of Epics, grounded upon the authority of Wolff and Lachmann, had prepared in the German learned mind a welcome for the Beowulf, and at the same time a foregone sentence upon the nature of its composition. That great works in early literature forsooth were not made by art and device, but that they grew spontaneously and blindly, this was that imagination in the air which attended the first entertainment of Beowulf in the Fatherland.

Earle (p. xxxii) recognized the merits of Grein, similarly uninfected:

> Between 1857 and 1867 appeared the work of C. W. M. Grein. . . . On the whole it may be said, without hesitation, that Grein's output was of such eminence as to dwarf all other labours, before or since, upon Anglo-Saxon poetry in general, and upon the Beowulf in particular.

Earle lists Grein's major publications: the edition of virtually all extant poetry, *Bibliothek der angelsächsischen Poesie* (Göttingen, 1857-8); the translation of most of it, *Dichtungen der Angelsachsen* (Göttingen, 1857-9); the glossary to the verse, *Sprachschatz der angelsächischen Dichter* (Cassel and Göttingen, 1861-4); 'Die historischen Verhältnisse des Beowulfliedes' (1862; see I[43]); and finally the separate edition, *Beowulf nebst den Fragmenten Finnsburg und Waldere* (Cassel and Göttingen, 1867). Earle enjoyed these major publications because he agreed with Grein's views when they differed from those of other scholars.

Textual scholarship

Some of the disagreement concerned textual scholarship, not literary criticism and, therefore, not central to this book. Grein himself was a conservative editor of Old English verse, and he greatly admired the textual conservatism of F. E. C. Dietrich as advocated in his article 'Rettungen', a title embracing both 're-coveries' and 'rescue operations', in which he set out to save manuscript read-

---

zwölften Jahrhunderts], in H. Paul (ed.), Grundriss der germanischen Philologie (2nd edn; Strasburg, 1908), 968-9 [= 28-9]; R. W. Chambers (ed.) *Widsith* (1912; see I[35]), 166; K. Malone (ed.), *Widsith* (London, 1936), 53-4 [and so also 2nd edn, Anglistica, XIII (Copenhagen, 1962), 115]; and E. V. K. Dobbie in ASPR III (1936), p. xlv. Secondly, on *Beowulf* (as well as *Widsith*): D. Whitelock, *The Audience of* Beowulf (Oxford, 1951), 64 (with a reference to Earle's *Deeds of Beowulf*.

ings from editorial interference.[46] Dietrich opens the article with a bold defence of manuscript readings against conjectural emendation:

> Für die älteren schriftwerke unserer vorzeit hat sich die erwachte kritik gegen die angriffe und schäden die ihnen durch die überlieferung angethan sind mehr als anderwärts mit der conjectur bewaffnen müßen, was besonders in solchen denkmälern berechtigt und wohlthätig war die nur in éiner handschrift auf uns gekommen sind. da begegnet denn aber auch nichts leichter als daß sie sich verhauet und daß es nötig wird ungerechte beute, die bald der scharfsinn bald die bloße ungeduld wegführt, zu retten und zurückzustellen.

> [For the older written works of our antiquity, more than elsewhere, textual criticism has had to be alive to the attacks and damages inflicted by transmission, and has had to arm itself with conjecture against them. That is especially justified and salutary in the case of such monuments as have come down to us in only a single manuscript. Nothing occurs more easily in such cases than that textual criticism blunders; and then it becomes necessary to rescue and restore unjustified spoils carried off sometimes by acumen at other times by sheer impatience.]

Earlier in the same volume of the journal in which Dietrich published 'Rettungen', K. W. Bouterwek, an active conjectural textual critic, had published his many notes on the text of *Beowulf*,[47] charitably characterized by Klaeber as 'Some useful comments by the side of unprofitable guesses'.[48] Grein himself expressed his feelings less charitably. The example quoted by Grein, to illustrate Bouterwek's arbitrariness in dealing with textual problems and etymologizing wildly, refers to *walu* 'the slain' plural of *wæl* at *Beowulf* 1042b *ðonne walu feollon*. Grein says:[49]

> Im Jahr 1856 endlich veröffentlichte B o u t e r w e k in Haupt's Zeitschrift XI, 59-113 einen langen Aufsatz zur Kritik des Beovulfliedes, worin jedoch nur wenig Erspriessliches geschehen ist da B. auch hier wieder mit seiner gewohnten Willkür verfuhr; auch an wahren Curiosen fehlt es darin nicht: so soll z. B. p. 88 valu (Plur. von v ä l) ein Compositum von w e a l h und e o h sein! Ich dächte, die Zeit solcher Etymologien läge längst hinter uns.

> [Finally, in the year 1856 Bouterwek published in *ZfdA*, 11, 59-113, a long essay as a contribution to the textual criticism of *Beowulf*, in which, however, only little that is profitable is transacted, because Bouterwek here too operates again with his customary arbitrariness. Nor are genuine curiosities lacking; for example, *walu* (pl. of *wæl*) is said to be a compound of *wealh* ('stranger, foreigner') and *eoh* ('horse'). I should have thought that we have long left behind the age of such etymologies.]

---

46 *ZfdA*, 11 (1859), 409-48; cf. E. G. Stanley, 'Unideal Principles of Editing Old English Verse', *PBA*, LXX (1984), 241-2.

47 'Zur kritik des Beóvulfliedes', *ZfdA*, 11 (1859), 59-113.

48 Klaeber's *Beowulf* (all editions: 1922, 1928, 1936), Bibliography, V. 2.

49 C. W. M. Grein (ed.), *Bibliothek der angelsächischen Poesie*, I, 1 (Göttingen, 1857), 367.

Andreas Heusler

The Swiss scholar A. Heusler, at the beginning of this century, puts the matter well, acknowledging his debt to Svend Grundtvig, N. F. S. Grundtvig's son:[50]

> Zwei Klippen, so lehrte vor vierzig Jahren Svend Grundtvig, bedrohen die germanische Sagenforschung. Die deutschen Gelehrten leiden Schiffbruch an der Szylla der mythischen Auslegung; die Charybdis aber, die der nordischen Wissenschaft gefährlich wird, ist die geschichtliche Deutung. Grundtvig betonte, wie vor ihm Wilhelm Grimm,[51] das dritte, mitteninne liegende: die freie Dichtung; er wandte sich scharf gegen die Formel: Heldensage ist eine Mischung von Mythus und Geschichte.

> [Two perils threaten the study of Germanic legends, as Svend Grundtvig taught forty years ago. German scholars suffer shipwreck on the Scylla of mythical exegesis; historical interpretation, however, is the Charybdis endangering Scandinavian scholarship. Grundtvig stressed, as Wilhelm Grimm had done before him,[51] a third way, a *via media*: free *poesis*. He sharply opposed the formulation, 'Heroic legend is a mixture of myth and history.']

And a little later in the article (pp. 498-9):

> Dárin behalten W. Grimm und Grundtvig Recht: die Handlung einer germanischen Heldensage »erklärt« sich nicht aus der Geschichte. Und zwar nicht deshalb, weil wir die Geschichte jener Zeit zu wenig kennen; auch nicht weil uns die Sagen zu mangelhaft überliefert sind, sondern weil die germanische Heldensage i h r e m M o t i v s c h a t z e u n d G e d a n k e n k r e i s e n a c h unhistorisch ist, untauglich, Geschichte abzubilden.

> Denn sie kennt gar nichts von Zeitrechnung und wenig von Geographie, sie ist unpolitisch und unstrategisch, fragt nicht nach Herrschaftsbegründungen, nach Eroberung und Verlust von Ländern, nach Wanderung von Völkern, überhaupt nicht nach dem Volke. . . . Das Personal der Heldensage ist die *druht* mit ihrem *druhtin*, die Kriegerauslese um den Fürsten herum. Der Fürst ist keine politische Gestalt, kein Herrscher, der Länder verwaltet, zu Gericht sitzt, Volkskriege denkt: er ist der ideale, daher hochgeborene, über einen Hort und ein Gefolge gebietende Krieger.

> Es herrschen in unserer Sage die persönlichen Ideen: die Pflichten und Neigungen zu der Sippe, unter Schwurbrüdern und zwischen Herrn und Gefolge; die Kriegerehre des einzelnen, die sein Handeln bestimmt und deren

---

[50] A. Heusler, 'Geschichtliches und Mythisches in der germanischen Heldensage', *Sitzungsberichte der Preußischen Akademie der Wissenschaften*, 1909, 920-45 [reprinted in A. Heusler, *Kleine Schriften* (Berlin, 1969), II, 495-517]; I quote the opening. Svend Grundtvig expressed himself in such terms in a pamphlet containing three lectures by him, *Udsigt over den nordiske oldtids heroiske digtning* (Copenhagen, 1867), 10; much of the first lecture (pp. 1-30) on Germanic heroic story is concerned with mythical and historical elements.

[51] Heusler gives no reference where in Wilhelm Grimm's writings he advocates this view, but cf. I[17] (and the quotation from *Altdeutsche Wälder* to which the note refers).

Verletzung zum Neiding stempelt. Die p e r s ö n l i c h e F a b e l , dies müssen wir in die Definition des germanischen Heldenliedes aufnehmen. . . .

Durch die Heldendichtung andrer Länder zieht sich der große Gegensatz des eignen Volkes zum Nationalfeinde: Franzosen gegen Sarazenen, Serben gegen Türken, Iran gegen Turan. Die germanische Sage kennt keinen Nationalfeind. Im Beowulf besteht dauernder Zwist zwischen den Nachbarn Gauten und Schweden; aber schwedische Prätendenten kämpfen gelegentlich auf seiten der Gauten,[52] es ist ein Hader Fürstenhäuser, nicht der Völker. Die Feindschaft zwischen Dänen und Hadebarden, zwischen Hocingen und Friesen, zwischen Burgunden und Hunnen, zwischen Thüringern und Franken bekommt ihre Weihe dadurch, daß die streitenden Könige verschwägert sind.[53]

[In this respect Wilhelm Grimm and Svend Grundtvig are right: the action of a Germanic heroic legend is not to be 'explained' by History. And that *not* for such reasons as, because too little of the history of that age is known to us, or because the legendary material is transmitted to us too fragmentarily; but for this reason, that Germanic heroic legend is unhistorical *on account of its repertoire of motifs and its range of ideas*, that it is not fit to depict History.

For there is no notion of chronology in Germanic heroic legend and very little idea of geography. It is unpolitical and shows no interest in strategy, does not concern itself with the foundation of dynasties, with the conquest or loss of countries, or with the migrations of peoples; in fact, it has no sense of nationhood. . . . The figures of heroic legend are the *dryht* together with their *dryhten*, the select band of warriors around their lord. That lord is not a political personage, not a ruler governing provinces or sitting in judgement or planning national wars. He is the ideal and, therefore, wellborn warrior, having power over a treasure and a band of retainers.

In Germanic legend personal concerns predominate: the duties and affections relating to the sib, the duties and affections among men bound by oaths of fraternal loyalty, and those between lord and retainers; the martial honour of each individual warrior which governs his actions and the breach of which brands him as a nithing. In any definition of 'Germanic heroic song' we must include the concept *the narrative of the hero's person*. . . .

The great contrast between 'our nation' and 'the national enemy' manifests itself in the heroic poetry of other nations: the French against the Saracens, the Serbs against the Turks, the Iranians against the Turanians. Germanic legend has no national enemy. In *Beowulf* there is unending strife between the Geats and their neighbours the Swedes; yet occasionally pretenders to the Swedish throne fight on the side of the Geats,[52] and we are dealing with the dynastic quarrel of princes, not with a national enmity. The hostility between Danes and Heathobards, between Hocings and Frisians, between Burgundians and Huns, and between Thuringians and Franks are consecrated through the marital relationship of the warring kings.[53]]

---

[52] The reference is to Eanmund and Eadgils, *Beowulf* lines 2379-96 and 2611-16.

[53] The first two warring pairs have a place in *Beowulf,* namely in the Heathobard and Finn Episodes; for details about the last two pairs, see, for example, R. W. Chambers, *Widsith* (1912; see I[35]), 58-65, 112-15.

The importance of this definition for an understanding of Germanic heroic poetry, including *Beowulf*, is easy to see. Expressed in other terms, the lack of historicity as manifested by the lack of chronological and geographical realism leads to a lack of verisimilitude, as we see it. Not only the pair of amphibious monsters nor the fire-breathing dragon, contribute to that sense; but the hand-strength of Beowulf and his natatorial skill in competition with Breca and in carrying, as he swam from Friesland home to distant Geatland, thirty suits of armour. It is unhelpful to an understanding in tune with this view to provide, however tentatively, dates for those who figure in the Danish, Geatish and Swedish genealogies, as Klaeber does in the section 'The Historical Elements' in all three of his editions. Klaeber always has a note, which itself indicates a desire for 'probabilities' as if of an historical narrative while warning that definite dates 'at best could represent approximate dates only' and 'they are only designed to show the sequence of events'. His map, 'The Geography of Beowulf', gives the kind of information a modern reader may find helpful, but 'is not entirely consistent chronologically'.[54]

The poet

It is not unreasonable to take an interest in the anonymous poet who first gave *Beowulf* (as the poem has been called for nearly two centuries now).[55] Was he singing it to a listening audience, or was he a writer of verse catering for a reading public? I have traced elsewhere some of the early scholarship linking the composition of Germanic heroic verse with that of Serbian singers composing as they plucked the gusle. The first scholar to have made that connection,

---

[54] In the third edition the dates in the genealogies are changed slightly. The footnote about the map is at p. xxix in all editions. Klaeber in providing dates acknowledges his debt to an article by A. Heusler, 'Zeitrechnung im Beowulfepos', *Archiv*, 124 (1910), 9-14 [reprinted in his *Kleine Schriften* (1969), II, 555-60]. It carries a similar warning to Klaeber's; Heusler's actual 'Zeittafel' at the end of the article gives far less the appearance of precision than Klaeber's original datings. Heusler's dates (in five- or ten-year approximations) form the left-hand column of a table, the other columns of which give the names of, 1. Geats and Swedes, 2. Heathobards, and 3. Danes. On the other hand, H. Gering's 'Zeittafel' in the introduction to his translation, *Beowulf nebst dem Finnsburg Bruchstück* (2nd edn; Heidelberg, 1913), p. xi, gives precise dates: for example, 474 Beowulf's mother marries Ecgtheow, 489 the Breca contest, 515 Beowulf fights Grendel, 571 death of Beowulf; Klaeber refers to this set of dates (p. xxxi note 1), but seems not to have used it.

[55] Sharon Turner, in the index to the second edition of his *The History of the Anglo-Saxons* (London, 1807), had '*Beowulf*, a narrative poem'; cf. E. G. Stanley, 'Sharon Turner's First Published Reference to *Beowulf*', *N&Q*, 220 (1975), 3 [reprinted in *A Collection of Papers* (1987; see I[45]), 75].

the true founder of an oral-formulaic theory for Germanic verse, was, as far as I know, J. A. Schmeller in 1839.[56]

The anonymous poet, it was assumed, must be a *scop*, and that concept was soon equated with the notion of a *Volksdichter* 'a folk-poet', but equated also with a *Spielmann* 'a minstrel' by some scholars preoccupied with minstrelsy. Thus A. Brandl, in what was for a long time the standard history of Old English literature, who classified *The Battle of Finnsburh* as 'epic minstrel song':[57]

> Unter den erhaltenen Denkmälern kommt der Gattung des epischen Spiel-mannsliedes am nächsten das Gedicht K a m p f u m F i n n s B u r g .

> [Among the extant monuments *The Battle of Finnsburh* comes closest to the genre of epic minstrel song.]

Brandl (p. 988 [= 48]) saw the foundations of *Beowulf* in minstrelsy:

> Ihr Umfang ist so beträchtlich (3183 V.), die dargestellten Begebenheiten so mannigfach, die Anlage so weit biographisch, auch christliche Bildung so durchfühlbar, dass der vorliegende Text von vornherein den Eindruck eines Schreibepos macht, das allerdings, wie die Quellenuntersuchung zeigen wird, noch wesentlich auf spielmännischer, nicht buchmässiger Grundlage ruht.

> [The scope [of *Beowulf*] is so considerable (3182 lines long), the events depicted so manifold, the conception so extensively biographical, the Christian learning moreover so perceptible, that the extant text at once gives the impression of a book-epic, though that indeed, as the study of its sources will show, still rests on foundations of minstrelsy rather than of bookishness.]

Folk-tale or allegory

The closeness to folk-tales of those parts of *Beowulf* which seem least realistic, least historical therefore, has been the subject of scholarly interest from the very beginning. Offa's queen (*Beowulf* lines 1931b-57a) is unlikely history, but her story is close to that of other maidens, wellborn and beautiful, but wicked or arrogant or, at least, insufficiently compliant with the will of a father or of some other man with power over her.[58] A story so unrealistic, if not a folk-tale, may be an allegory, and since her name is an abstract, Þryðo 'strength' perhaps Modþryðo 'strength of mind, wilfulness', it is easy to find in her, as John Earle

---

[56] See p. 41 and n. 6, below; and cf. E. G. Stanley, 'The Scholarly Recovery of the Significance of Anglo-Saxon Records in Prose and Verse: A New Bibliography', *ASE*, 9 (1981), 258-9 [reprinted in *A Collection of Papers*, 1987 (see I[45]), 44-5].

[57] A. Brandl, 'Die angelsächsische Literatur' (1908; see I[45]), 983 [= 43].

[58] Cf. M. Schlauch, *Chaucer's Constance and Accused Queens* (New York, 1927); J. Schick, 'Die Urquelle der Offa-Konstanze-Sage', in *Britannica – Max Förster zum sechzigsten Geburtstage* (Leipzig, 1929), 31-56.

did in 1892, an onomastic and allegorical contrast with Hygelac's queen who also bears an abstract, allegorical name, Hygd 'thought, thoughtfulness';[59] and Hygelac too bears an abstract name, the first element of which means 'mind' and the second, more polysemous, 'offering, play, sacrifice, booty', perhaps 'play of mind'. And yet Hygelac is the only figure in the central narrative of *Beowulf* whose existence is confirmed by established historical sources; and Cynethryth, 'royal strength' if one were to translate the name, is the name borne by the queen of Offa of Mercia.

Dragons, they surely are the fauna of folk-tale, at least to Germanic scholars whether writing of the one slain by Beowulf and Wiglaf at the end of the poem or of the dragon of the Sigemund episode (lines 874b-97), however that may be related to Middle High German and Scandinavian dragon-slaying by Sigfrit (Sigurthr). Wilhelm Grimm drew attention to the problem:[60]

> Als eine Abweichung von der Annahme aller Sagen fällt sogleich auf, daß in der Besiegung des Drachen und dem Erwerbe des Horts Sigmund die Stelle Siegfried's vertritt, und dieser gar nicht genannt wird. Falsche Auffassung oder Entstellung des Originals hat nicht statt gefunden, denn es wird ausdrücklich gesagt, Sigmund habe die That allein verbracht und sein Gefährte Fitela sey nicht bei ihm gewesen. . . . Ich lasse mich auf keine Vermuthung über den Grund dieser Abweichung ein, die vorerst noch keinen Nutzen hat.

> [It is to be noted at once as a variation of the assumption in all other legends that Sigemund takes the place of Sigfrit in the victory over the dragon and the winning of the hoard, and that Sigfrit is not so much as mentioned. A misconception or distortion of the original has not taken place, for it is stated explicitly that Sigemund has done this deed alone and that his companion Fitela was not with him. . . . I refuse to speculate on how this deviation arose which in the present state of scholarship would be unprofitable.]

Not all scholars were as abstemious; indulging in speculation, some scholars displayed in *Beowulf* lines 885-6 what one might wish it to say rather than what it appears to be saying: that *æfter deaðdæge dom unlytel* refers, not to the glory that came to Sigemund after his death through the deeds, especially the dragon-slaying, he had performed in life, but to the glory that came to Sigemund after his death through the deed of *wiges hearde* 'one valiant in war', namely Sigfrit, his life and this deed so famous that he need not even be named to be recognized in the allusion; and Heusler himself favoured this interpretation.[61]

---

[59] See *Deeds of Beowulf* (see I[45]), pp. lxxxiv-lxxxv. For references to the many discussions of these names, see H. B. Woolf, *Name-Giving* (see I[26]): on Thryth 160 and note 39; on Hygd 152 and note 20. See also pp. 40-1, below.

[60] *Deutsche Heldensage* (1829; see I[17]), 16.

[61] See E. Jessen, 'Über die Eddalieder. Heimat, alter und charakter', *ZfdPh*, 3 (1871), 18-19, suggested that to take *wiges heard* as referring to Sigurthr may be possible, but is not the obvious interpretation; A. Heusler, 'Sigfrid', in J. Hoops (ed.), *Reallexikon der Germanischen Altertumskunde* (Strasburg, 1911-1919), III/2 (1918), 173 § 3; at 177 § 13 Heusler

That folklore is close to some aspects of *Beowulf* had been suggested by several writers, among them, as R. W. Chambers had pointed out, John Earle in letters to *The Times* in 1884-1885, 'The Beowulf itself is a tale of old folklore'.[62] In 1910, F. Panzer gave all such folkloristic connections far more systematic treatment, especially the fights of Beowulf with Grendel and his mother.[63] The work is impressive, not least because of its size, over four hundred pages long. The first part tries to establish a fundamental, widely distributed, ancient story-pattern of the hero with superhuman strength fighting superhuman adversaries with success. Such a hero is the son of a bear, the subject of the first half of the book. Whether the unprepossessed reader recognizes this type in every one of over two hundred stories may be doubtful, and whether Beowulf in his supernatural fights is one of them may not be as certain as Panzer suggests near the beginning of the second half of the book, the *Beowulf* half (p. 253):

> Eine brauchbare neue Erklärung der Beowulfsage aber ist gefunden: es kann wohl keinem, der den ersten Teil dieses Buches gelesen, zweifelhaft sein, daß in dieser Sage nichts anderes als das Bärensohnmärchen uns vorliegt.
>
> [A serviceable, new explanation of the tale of Beowulf has been found, however. It is unlikely that anyone who has read the first part of this book can be in doubt that in this legend we have anything other than the tale of the bear's son.]

At almost the same time as Panzer's book appeared, W. W. Lawrence had written an article in which he opposed allegorical interpretations.[64] Lawrence even then would seem to have been receptive to the kind of study Panzer undertook. That he was indeed in agreement with much of Panzer emerged when his own book on *Beowulf* appeared almost twenty years later:[65]

> Resemblances between the supernatural plot-material in *Beowulf* and popular tales had been observed by various scholars, but detailed investigation really began with the work of Friedrich Panzer, who, in 1910, published carefully tabulated plots of a large number of *märchen* illustrating the Grendel adventures, and similar material illustrating the dragon adventure. The former are far the more important and convincing. Despite all differences, the *märchen* resembling the story of Grendel and his dam preserve a common framework, which is of the utmost importance as showing what the earlier form of that story must have been. Panzer's work, while exhibiting errors of

gives a reference to Svend Grundtvig's *Udsigt* (1867; see note I[50]), 36, where Grundtvig argues that in *Beowulf* it is stressed that Sigemund always performed deeds together with Fitela, in contrast with Sigurthr (Sigfrit) who in all accounts of him always appears alone. In *Beowulf* the dragon-slayer killed the dragon alone, *ne wæs him Fitela mid* (line 889b); Grundtvig does not mention that Sigurthr (Sigfrit) nowhere performs deeds with Fitela (Sinfjǫtli), so that the explicit *ne wæs him Fitela mid* is not likely to refer to Sigurthr.

[62] *Beowulf An Introduction* (1921; see I[23]), 400; for Earle, see I[45]).

[63] F. Panzer, *Studien zur germanischen Sagengeschichte*, I *Beowulf* (Munich, 1910).

[64] 'Some Disputed Questions in *Beowulf*-Criticism', *PMLA*, 24 (1909), 220-73.

[65] *Beowulf and Epic Tradition* (1928; see I[24]), 171.

judgment and critical shortcomings, must be regarded as a landmark in the investigation of *Beowulf.* It struck boldly out into an almost unexplored field, and demonstrated the significance of the results thus gained. . . . Panzer presented material enough to show beyond question that the tale is of wide geographical distribution and of great antiquity.

Lawrence added the waterfall-troll of the thirteenth- or fourteenth-century *Samsons saga fagra* to the stock of analogues, a discovery hailed as important by Chambers.[66] Chambers himself, though he considered Panzer's study significant, received it more coolly than Lawrence, and not without a touch of irony about the absence in *Beowulf* of the princess who in most of the analogues was won by the hero (p. 381):

> The rather tragic and sombre atmosphere of the stories of Beowulf and Grettir fits in better with a version from which the princesses, and the living happily ever afterwards, have been dropped. On the other hand, it might be argued that the folk-tale is composite, and that the source from which the *Beowulf-Grettir*-story drew was a simpler tale to which the princesses had not yet been added.
> . . .
> But Panzer has, I think, proved that the struggle of Beowulf in the hall, and his plunging down into the deep, is simply an epic glorification of a folk-tale motive.

More prehistory of the poem

W. A. Berendsohn in 1935 showed a similar interest in the prehistory and the analogues of *Beowulf*, but within a discussion which ranges widely, most valuably perhaps in his listing of features of style and poetic language in the poem itself, features which he used to identify parts drawn from earlier versions.[67] He had a low opinion of the Anglian redactor to whom we are indebted for the extant version; for example, in discussing what Berendsohn runs down as *Reimspielereien* [playing around with rhymes], he quotes some two dozen of them (p. 187):

> Die vorkommenden Reimspielereien sind im allgemeinen . . . dem anglischen Bearbeiter zuzuschreiben, da sie zu seinem Sprachüberfluss passen.
>
> [Such playing around with rhymes as occurs is in general . . . to be ascribed to the Anglian redactor because it goes with his verbal superfluity.]

This attitude manifest itself similarly elsewhere, always with the same manner

---

[66] *Beowulf and the Epic Tradition*, pp. 188-91. Cf. R. W. Chambers, *Beowulf An Introduction* (2nd edn; Cambridge, 1932), 454-8; G. N. Garmonsway, J. Simpson and H. Ellis Davidson, *Beowulf and its Analogues* (London, 1968), 322-4.
[67] W. A. Berendsohn, *Zur Vorgeschichte des "Beowulf"* (Copenhagen, 1935).

of circular argument; what Berendsohn approves of is ancient, what he dislikes is the work of the aged Anglian (pp. 198-9):

> Es kommen auch in den älteren Teilen zusammengesetzte Satzgebilde vor; überall aber, wo Unübersichtlichkeit des Satzgefüges auffällt, wo die logische Verknüpfung Schwierigkeiten bereitet, dürfen wir annehmen, dass wir die sprunghafte Reflexion des Angeln vor uns haben. . . . Es muss . . . genügen, dass sich die Bruchstücke altüberlieferter dichterischer Kunst deutlich abheben von der reflexionsgetränkten Bearbeitung des bejahrten, christlichen Angeln.

> [Compound sentence conformations occur also in the older parts; but wherever a sentence structure is noticeable because it lacks clarity, wherever difficulties arise in logical connection, we may suppose that we have in front of us the disjointed reflexion of the Anglian. . . . It is . . . sufficient [to recognize] that the transmitted, ancient fragments of poetic art stand in clear contrast with the redaction, soaked in reflexion, of the aged, Christian Anglian.]

On the whole, Berendsohn's views and methods were out of date even when his book was published; he was out of step with the scholarship and criticism of *Beowulf* in the mid-thirties. The detection of original passages, the attribution of reflexions to the Christian redactor (who deserves to be abused for them), the wish to reconcile the various story elements as told in *Beowulf* with the same or analogous stories told elsewhere, these were lines of investigation no longer so actively pursued in the second quarter of the twentieth century.

In 1925 A. S. Cook still thought it profitable to consider if Cynewulf was the author of parts of 'our *Beowulf*'.[68] Attempts to reconcile the Finn Episode with *The Battle at Finnsburh* went on unabated, so much so that they might well form a separate study: Finn and Hengest, Hnæf and Hildeburh in the History of Literature from 1814 to our day.[69]

The poem to be read as a work of literature; L. L. Schücking

A new spirit was abroad just before the Second World War. *Beowulf* was being assessed for quality of expression; and questions were asked about the poet and the intended audience. J. Hoops's very factual commentary on the poem, published in 1932, rarely lets literary subjectivism show itself, but once or twice he utters a rapturous literary comment; thus at the end of the note on lines 2263-4 giving a brief history of falconry in Anglo-Saxon England, and intended, no

---

[68] A. S. Cook, 'Cynewulf's Part in Our *Beowulf*', *Transactions of the Connecticut Academy of Arts and Sciences*, XXVII (1925), 385-406.

[69] See D. K. Fry (ed.), *Finnsburh Fragment and Episode* (London, 1974), with a good bibliography referring to earlier work; J. R. R. Tolkien (ed.), *Finn and Hengest The Fragment and the Episode* (ed. by A. Bliss, London, 1982), in fact going back to lectures first given in the 1920s, and constantly revised till the 1960s.

doubt, as a comment on the whole of the 'Elegy of the Last Survivor' (lines 2247-66):[70] 'Die ganze Stelle ist übrigens poetisch ungemein schön' [Incidentally, the whole passage is poetically exceptionally beautiful]. The statement is merely assertive, and Hoops makes no attempt to analyse or justify his praise.

Levin Ludwig Schücking is, I think, the most distinguished critic of the art of the poem. One of his earliest works (of 1908), on Old English laments for the dead, commands all the relevant material as he deals with the various uses of laments, including, briefly, the father's lament at *Beowulf* lines 2444-69.[71] In line with an interpretation then widely held, he attributes this lament to Hrethel.[72] Schücking's article is interesting in general, but perhaps the most astonishing and unusual feature is a bold footnote (p. 9 note 2) in which he ironically criticizes Eduard Sievers, the *Altmeister* then at the height of his fame. A point of great significance is raised: can we genuinely differentiate between fine shades of the meaning of Anglo-Saxon words, and can we tell reliably what is literal and what is metaphorical or transferred? Sievers had expressed his certainty; he understood what was 'typically poetic', he knew when in *Beowulf* the word *leoð* was 'a song' expressed in words, or (especially as the second element of a poetic compound) wordless 'howling' such as animals and Grendel utter.[73] Schücking was unconvinced, and mocks the notion that the concept 'typically poetic' is helpful in solving the problem:

> Die frage, wo wir den ausdruck in seiner eigentlichen bedeutung, wo bildlich aufzufassen haben, scheint mir nicht so einfach zu beantworten, wie Sievers neuerdings . . . der schwierigkeit herr wird! . . . Sievers . . . hält in allen fällen den ausdruck [compounds with second element *-leoð*], wie es scheint, nicht einmal für bildlich, sondern nur für »typisch poetisch«. In wirklichkeit indes fehlte es uns wohl nur an den eigentlichen liedern selbst, denen jene ausdrücke entsprechen, sonst würde uns ihre gelegentliche bildlichkeit ausser frage stehen.

> [The problem in which use the expression is to be interpreted literally and in which use it is to be interpreted metaphorically seems to me to be not so easily soluble as in the recent mastery . . . Sievers has gained over it. . . . Sievers . . . regards, as it seems, expressions (using compounds the second element of which is *leoð*) not even as figurative, merely as 'typically poetic'. In reality, however, we are perhaps only lacking the actual songs themselves correspond-

---

70 J. Hoops, *Kommentar zum Beowulf* (Heidelberg, 1932), 246.

71 L. L. Schücking, 'Das angelsächsische totenklagelied', *EStn*, 39 (1908), 1-12. I did not know this article, aspects of it highly relevant to my argument, when I wrote 'Two Old English Poetic Phrases Insufficiently Understood for Literary Criticism: *þing gehegan* and *seonoþ gehegan*, in D. G. Calder (ed.), *Old English Poetry: Essays on Style* (Berkeley, Los Angeles, and London: 1979), 67-90 [reprinted in *Collection of Papers* (1987; see I[45]], 298-317.

72 See D. Whitelock, '*Beowulf* 2444-2471', *MÆ*, 8 (1939), 198-204, for the interpretation now generally accepted, that the lament is spoken by 'an old man' unnamed, and typifies bootless death through hanging, here compared with bootless death through (accidental) fratricide.

73 'Zum Beowulf', *Beiträge*, 29 (1904), 314-15.

ing to these expressions; otherwise their occasional figurativeness would not be questioned by us.]

Schücking's magisterial understanding of semantics (together with other, differently directed learning, especially syntactic) led a few years later to Schücking's excellent book on Old English poetic diction.[74] Some of these works are too linguistic for discussion here: Schücking's philological grasp encompassed both language and literature.

In one of Schücking's more minor writings (of 1919), his is the new voice, better on the so-called digressions than anyone before him; in the preliminary remarks to an extract (consisting of *Beowulf* lines 1888-2199) he writes:[75]

Die Ingeldsage (2026 ff.) scheint schon im 8. Jahrhundert in England ganz besonders beliebt gewesen zu sein. Sie erzählt vom Kampfe der auf Seeland wohnenden Hadubarden gegen die Dänen, der ein vorläufiges Ende durch die Vermählung des Hadubardenkönigs Ingeld mit der Dänenprinzessin Freawaru, Tochter Hroðgars, findet. Wie ihre Verwandte Hildeburg[76] vermag auch sie nicht den Rachedurst ihres Gatten auf immer in Fesseln zu schlagen. Der Streit entbrennt, namentlich infolge der Aufhetzung eines alten Hadubardenkriegers, aufs neue und findet seine für Ingeld unglückliche Entscheidung im Kampfe um die Halle Heorot, die dabei in Flammen aufgeht.[77] – Die Abschweifung auf

---

[74] L. L. Schücking, *Untersuchungen zur Bedeutungslehre der angelsächsischen Dichtersprache* (Heidelberg, 1915). Earlier he had made a major contribution to our understanding of the sentence structure of *Beowulf, Die Grundzüge der Satzverknüpfung im Beowulf*, StePh, 15 (1904). For another interesting article by Schücking on *Beowulf*, see p. 49 n. 34, below.

[75] L. L. Schücking (ed.), *Kleines angelsächsisches Dichterbuch. Lyrik und Heldenepos* (Cöthen, 1919), 42-3.

[76] The relationship of Hildeburh to Freawaru is distant; in L. L. Schücking's 11th and 12th edition of M. Heyne's *Beowulf* (Paderborn, 1918), nearest in date to Schücking's verse anthology, he has in the 'Namenverzeichnis' under Hnæf 'Heerführer eines den Dänen verwandten Stammes' [army chief of a tribe related to the Danes], taken over from earlier editions of Heyne, first in A. Socin's 5th edition (1888); Heyne himself, more cautiously, said merely that Hnæf is a Hocing, and the army chief of the Danish king Healfdene; thus 4th edn (1879).

[77] This was the widely accepted interpretation of events; the destruction of Heorot by flames, predicted in lines 81-5, was thought to have occurred at Ingeld's marriage feast which, according to this view, took place in the Danish hall, and was identified with the contest *æt Heorote* of *Widsith* line 49; cf. E. A. Kock, 'Interpretations and Emendations of Early English Texts, X', *Anglia*, 46 (1922), 174, 'Ingeld, staying at the time at the Danish court'. Others thought that the destruction by fire of Heorot took place on a different occasion, at some later stage of the Heathobeard wars; cf. F. Klaeber (ed.), *Beowulf* (3rd edn, 1936), p. 129 note on 82-85, 'Heorot was to be burned . . . in the Heaðo-Bard feud'. Hoops, *Kommentar* (1932; see I[70]), p. 227 (note on lines 2032-6) regards it as certain 'wie sich aus 2062 *con him land geare* deutlich ergibt' [as is the clear inference of line 2062b *con him land geare*] that the events described in lines 2024b-69a took place in the land of the Heathobeards, for only a Heathobeard would know the lie of the land well. That seems to force a lot of meaning on to the half-line, but has been generally accepted nevertheless; not quite, however, by E. von Schaubert (ed.), *Beowulf*, part 2 'Kommentar' (17th edn of the Heyne-Schücking *Beowulf*, Paderborn, 1961), p. 124 (note on line 2062), who points out that the special mention might indicate the opposite, namely, that these events took place in Denmark.

anderweitige Sagenstoffe geht im Beowulf noch weiter. Wir hören vom Brosinga mene (1199), dem berühmten Götterhalsband, von Ermanarich und Heime (1201), von Fitela und Sigemund (875 ff.), von König Hreðel (2439) u[nd] a[nderem] m[ehr]. Aber kaum eine andere Episode trägt in das sonst schönfärberisch bis zur Flachheit gezeichnete Bild germanischen Heldenlebens, wie es der Beowulf gibt, einen so lebensvollen Zug hinein, wie die Beschreibung des verbissenen alten Hadubardenkriegers, der das Blut seines jungen Landsmannes mit dem fortwährenden Hinweis darauf zum Überwallen bringt, daß der dänische Hofherr der Königin ohne Scheu mit dem Schwert von des Hadubarden gefallenem Vater an der Seite herumstolziert. Insofern zeigt gerade dieser Abschnitt also ein größeres Interesse an seelischen Vorgängen, als man es sonst dem Beowulf nachrühmen kann, dessen Dichter seiner Aufgabe als Epiker am besten in der Beschreibung gerecht wird, die uns anschauliche und liebevolle Bilder des äußeren altgermanischen Lebenshintergrundes entwirft.

[The story of Ingeld (lines 2026-69) appears to have been especially well liked in England as early as the eighth century. It tells of the hostility of the Heathobeards dwelling on Zealand against the Danes, strife which ends temporarily through the marriage of Ingeld, king of the Heathobeards, to the Danish princess Freawaru, Hrothgar's daughter. Like her relative Hildeburh[76] she too cannot always hold in check her husband's thirst for vengeance. A quarrel breaks out anew, especially as a result of the incitement of an old Heathobeard warrior, and comes to a head, unfortunate for Ingeld, in a battle for the hall Heorot which in that conflict goes up in flames.[77] – Digressions in *Beowulf* go into story-matter far beyond this: we hear of the *Brosinga mene* (line 1199), the famous necklace of the gods, of Eormenric and Hama (line 1201), of Fitela and Sigemund (lines 875-97), of King Hrethel, and of many more. But hardly any other episode introduces into the depiction of Germanic heroic life (drawn elsewhere in the poem with some embellishments or quite unadorned) a feature so vivid as the description of the grim old Heathobeard warrior who brings the blood of his young compatriot to the boil by incessant reference to the fact that the Danish courtier, without inhibition, parades up and down by the side of the queen, carrying the sword of the [young] Heathobeard's dead father. This passage shows a greater interest in psychological processes than *Beowulf* is usually given credit for, the poet best fulfilling the task of an epicist in descriptions which depict clear and affectionate scenes of the external circumstances of ancient Germanic heroic life.]

Several of Schücking's studies evaluate the ideals of *Beowulf*. A lecture on the ideal of kingship in *Beowulf* was first delivered in England as a presidential address given to the Modern Humanities Research Association.[78] Beowulf's

---

[78] 'Das Königsideal im Beowulf', originally published in the *Bulletin of the Modern Humanities Research Association*, 3 (1929), 143-54; it was reprinted in *EStn*, 67 (1932), 1-14, from which I quote. An English translation, 'The Ideal of Kingship in *Beowulf*' was published in L. E. Nicholson (ed.), *An Anthology of Beowulf Criticism* (Notre Dame, Indiana: 1963), 35-49.

kingship is analysed within the setting of the historical study of medieval
European literature (pp. 11-12):

> Der Beowulf aber zeigt nun – und das gibt ihm so außerordentliches Inter-
> esse – das erste Beispiel einer nach dem "sobrietas"- oder "mensura"-ideal
> ausgerichteten Persönlichkeitszeichnung. Hier wird ein Held beschrieben, der
> auf vorbildliche weise Stolz mit Bescheidenheit paart, Gottergebenheit mit
> Selbstvertrauen, Kühnheit mit Vorsicht, Lebensfreude mit Frömmigkeit, der
> besitzfroh, aber nicht habgierig, dankbar, pietätvoll und ehrerbietig gegen das
> Alter ist. Unter den Zügen die besonders in die Augen fallen, ist vielleicht an
> erster Stelle jene Klugheit zu nennen, von deren hoher Bewertung schon bei
> dem Königsideal die Rede gewesen ist.

> [Beowulf, however, and this makes him so extraordinarily interesting –
> provides the first example of a characterization the orientation of which is
> governed by the ideal of *sobrietas* or *mensura*. Here we have the description of
> a hero who combines in exemplary fashion pride with modesty, devotion to the
> will of God with self-confidence, boldness with caution, enjoyment of life
> with piety, a hero who rejoices in possessions yet is not avaricious, and is
> thankful, and full of piety and respect towards old age. Among his most
> striking traits, that wisdom is perhaps to be named in the first place, the high
> esteem of which we have spoken in connection with the ideal of kingship.]

A quarter of a century later R. E. Kaske,[79] in his consideration of a different
aspect of Beowulf as a heroic ideal, based it more on patristic learning without
ignoring the views of earlier scholars, Schücking's among them, both 'Das
Königsideal' and 'Heldenstolz und Würde'.[80] The latter is a central study of
heroic pride and dignity in Anglo-Saxon literature, and especially in *Beowulf*.
The opening words of the appendix on the technique of characterization in
Beowulf refer to Pope's well-known couplet (lines 233-4) from *An Essay on
Criticism*:

> A perfect Judge will *read* each Work of Wit
> With the same Spirit that its Author *writ*.

Schücking warned explicitly of the dangers of begging the question when little
is known of the author's spirit; nevertheless he tried to read *Beowulf* with that
spirit; he tried to understand the art of the poem from within, and tried, as far as
possible, to free himself from the preoccupations and predilections of a twentieth-century reader.
    In the course of this appendix (pp. 27-44) Schücking showed clearly that

---

[79] '*Sapientia et Fortitudo* as the controlling Theme of *Beowulf*', *SP*, 55 (1958), 423-57; reprinted in L. E. Nicholson's *Anthology* (1963; see I[78]), 269-310.
[80] L. L. Schücking, *Heldenstolz und Würde im Angelsächsischen mit einem Anhang: zur Cha-
rakterisierungstechnik im Beowulfepos*, Abhandlungen der Philologisch-Historischen Klasse
der Sächsischen Akademie der Wissenschaften, XLII/5 (1933).

'characterization' need not be the same in every age or in every literature. In his vision of the characters of the poem we have moved away from the warriors of the Germanic Heroic Age to a world of courtliness, Christian courtliness. As often, John Earle was early in detecting an association of *Beowulf* with post-heroic values; in a popular work he says of the poem:[81] 'It has much in it that seems like anticipation of the age of chivalry.' Schücking suggested new, Christian attitudes, as for example (p. 31), that, since Old Norse literature seems not to hold youth in low regard, Beowulf's excuse for the rather foolish contest with Breca (*cnihtwesende . . . wæron begen þa git on geogoðfeore*, lines 535-7) may derive from Christian values.

J. R. R. Tolkien

J. R. R. Tolkien's lecture on *Beowulf* was given in 1936, and at once was regarded highly.[82] No reader would wish to detract from the praise given to it, of which that by his colleague at Oxford, C. L. Wrenn, is a fair specimen:[83] 'Exceptionally important: probably the most widely influential critical appreci-ation of the poem.' Tolkien was widely read, especially in the medieval lit-eratures of England, Scandinavia (first and foremost, Iceland), continental Germanic, and Wales; he refers in a final note to Hoops's *Kommentar*; other-wise there are no references in 'The Monsters and the Critics' to secondary writings in German on the poem, but then the display of foreign references belongs to later generations of scholarship, and silence need not mean ignor-ance. On the whole, however, Tolkien formed his literary views by reading the texts themselves, and by understanding the words, the grammar, and the sounds heightened by the metre, and by reacting to the adverse criticism by critics whom he otherwise respects, in their comments on texts he likes. I do not know how well he knew Schücking's criticism of the poem. Even if he did not, Tolkien follows on well from Schücking. He quotes at length and with respect both W. P. Ker and R. W. Chambers.[84] Tolkien is at his best when he allows us at the end of

---

[81] *(The Dawn of European Literature.) Anglo-Saxon Literature*, Publication of the Society for Promoting Christian Knowledge (London, 1884), 120-1.

[82] J. R. R. Tolkien, 'Beowulf: The Monsters and the Critics', *PBA*, XXII (1936), 245-95 [reprinted in Nicholson's *Anthology* (1963; see I[78]), 51-103; and in D. K. Fry (ed.), *The Beowulf Poet. A Collection of Critical Essays* (Englewood Cliffs, New Jersey: 1968), 8-56]. A good example of scholarly acceptance of many of Tolkien's views, as well as an inde-pendent contribution of interest, is J. Blomfield, 'The Style and Structure of *Beowulf*', *RES*, 14 (1938), 396-403 [reprinted in Fry's *Collection*, pp. 57-65].

[83] In Wrenn's 'Supplementary Bibliography to 1958', in the 3rd edn of R. W. Chambers, *Beowulf An Introduction* (Cambridge, 1959), 606.

[84] W. P. Ker, *The Dark Ages*, Periods of European Literature, I (Edinburgh and London, 1904), is quoted by Tolkien at p. 251; see II[35], below, and the quotation to which it refers. R. W. Chambers's '*Beowulf* and the Heroic Age in England', Foreword to A. Strong's translation of the poem (London, 1925), is quoted by Tolkien at pp. 261-2.

his lecture to see the whole poem in a grander view than anyone else's before him or after (pp. 277-8):

> It is just because the main foes in *Beowulf* are inhuman that the story is larger and more significant . . . It glimpses the cosmic and moves with the thought of all men concerning the fate of human life and efforts; it stands amid but above the petty wars of princes, and surpasses the dates and limits of historical periods, however important. At the beginning, and during the process, and most of all at the end, we look down as if from a visionary height upon the house of man in the valley of the world. A light starts – *lixte se leoma ofer landa fela* – and there is a sound of music; but the outer darkness and its hostile offspring lie in wait for the torches to fail and the voices to cease. Grendel is maddened by the sound of harps.
>
> And one last point, which those will feel who to-day preserve the ancient *pietas* towards the past: *Beowulf* is not a 'primitive' poem; it is a late one, using the materials (then still plentiful) preserved from a day already changing and passing, a time that has now for ever vanished, swallowed in oblivion; using them for a new purpose, with wider sweep of imagination, if with a less bitter and concentrated force. When new *Beowulf* was already antiquarian, in a good sense, and it now produces a singular effect. For it is now to us itself ancient; and yet its maker was telling of things already old and weighted with regret, and he expended his art in making keen the touch upon the heart which sorrows have that are both poignant and remote.

It is not mere piety that one taught by Tolkien should see him, not as the end of the first age of *Beowulf* scholarship, but the beginning of a new age. The end of the first age is perhaps exemplified by G. Baesecke, and exemplified well by him in his account of the nature of the singers within the poem: but he saw *Beowulf* as preliterate, and so found 'herzbewegend' [heart-moving] the poet's account of the aged Scylding king reciting story true and sad (lines 2105b-14).[85] Tolkien did better: he too was moved by *Beowulf*, but he saw it as literate.

---

[85] G. Baesecke, *Vorgeschichte des deutschen Schrifttums*, in G. Baesecke, Vor- und Früh-geschichte des deutschen Schrifttums, I, Vorgeschichte (Halle, 1940), especially pp. 484-5. For the concept of the literate Anglo-Saxon, cf. J. E. Cross, 'The Literate Anglo-Saxon on Sources and Disseminations, *PBA*, LVIII (1972), 67-100, but that is concerned with source-based religious literature, not with the sourceless secular literature of the Anglo-Saxons of which *Beowulf* is the supreme example.

II

The Last Fifty Years

The literary history of *Beowulf* extends over nearly two hundred years now. As we look at past ages we notice, of course, some oddities of critical aim, but the sympathetic reader of earlier work in the field will recognize in it the foundations of our current thinking, and that too has its oddities. Our understanding of the poem is inevitably limited by our own preoccupations and predilections; and that goes also for our reading of past *Beowulf* criticism in whatever spirit of inquiry it is undertaken. The following account of the period after the Second World War is even more sketchy than the preceding chapter, the account of *Beowulf* criticism from the beginnings to J. R. R. Tolkien. Some attempt was made for the earlier period to proceed chronologically. In what follows, the organization will be more generally by themes.

Etymology and wordplay

It may be thought that today, nearly 150 years after Bouterwek wrote and Grein criticized him for it in the notes to his monumental *Bibliothek der angelsächsischen Poesie*,[1] it is hardly worth dragging such nonsense into the light of day out of the well deserved darkness of oblivion, however characteristic of Bouterwek's textual scholarship it may be. My justification for quoting it is that arbitrariness remained for a long time the besetting sin of Germanic textual scholars, a sin in which some modern and especially deconstructionist critics at the end of this century revel likewise; though, as far as I know, *Beowulf* lies only rarely at the centre of the intellectual penumbra they inhabit.

Raymond P. Tripp, Jr, who proudly proclaims in his preface to an edition of part of the poem:[2] 'The commentary combines many "methods," blending paleography, linguistics, semiotics, narrative theory, and a lot of hard-headed logic, into a fully eclectic approach, while it depends most upon sincere

---

[1] See p. 24 and I[47] and I[49], above.
[2] R. P. Tripp, Jr (ed.), *More about the Fight with the Dragon – Beowulf 2208b-3182, Commentary, Edition, and Translation* (Lanham, New York, and London, 1983), p. ix.

questioning of previous certainties.' It would be easy to quote from Tripp's work examples of wordplay detected by him in *Beowulf* by the side of which Bouterwek's etymologies take their natural place.

Whether we in the last quarter of the present century have quite left behind such etymologizing is uncertain. Anyone aware of Isidore of Seville's direction of etymological scholarship and aware also of the high esteem in which he was held by scholars in the centuries that followed may wonder if, what he called *etymologia* should not by us be called wordplay whenever the derivation is false (as far as we can tell from our more scientific kind of diachronic linguistics). True etymology of Old English, unless the relation and origination of a word is transparently obvious, is not likely to have been understood better by the Anglo-Saxons than by Bouterwek writing about their language. Associating words by superficial likeness, that is, in wordplay, does not require etymology. Is it likely that the Anglo-Saxons would have recognized that *æþele* 'noble' and its immediate derivative *æþeling* 'prince, nobleman', both with short stem-vowel, are somehow related to *ēþel* 'homeland' with stem-vowel phonemically different in both quality and quantity? I remain sceptical if that modern recognition of an etymological relationship, quite fun in itself, helps elementary or advanced readers of Old English literature towards an understanding in line with such understanding as the Anglo-Saxons themselves may have had. Yet that is suggested by S. A. Barney in an etymological attempt, only about fifteen years old, designed for elementary students:[3]

> In this list I have gone farther than the obvious, and have grouped together all of the words which are etymologically related – even a number which are not very obvious – in order to assist the memory [of the elementary learner of the language]. Once it is known that *æðele* means "noble," it is not very hard to learn that *æðeling* means "nobleman," and it is still not *very* hard to see that *ēðel* "native land" is related, and shares in a sense of concern with ancestors, of genealogical pride. These connections . . . can refine the student's sense of the connotations of words.

There is a danger. Such connections, based on modern scientific etymology, are likely to lead anyone who imposes the semantic implications of etymological relationships on a reading of the words in their literary context to pretend to an atavistic understanding of connotations of Old English words. It is highly unlikely to be an understanding shared with the Anglo-Saxon poet and the original audience who heard or read the poem.

As we have seen,[4] some of the names in the poem have long been regarded as in some measure figuring, by transparent etymology, the persons that bear them.

---

[3] S. A. Barney, *Word-Hoard An Introduction to Old English Vocabulary* (New Haven and London, 1977), p. vii. The etymological dictionaries set out the relationship of the words in the Germanic languages; see, for example, J. Pokorny (ed.), *Indogermanisches etymologisches Wörterbuch* (Berne and Munich, 1959-1969), I, 71.

[4] See pp. 28-9, above.

That, however, is quite another form of etymological understanding, a form familiar to Christian Anglo-Saxons in the exegesis of biblical names especially. Some Old English poets of saints' lives and biblical paraphrase seem to have exploited such etymologies. For probable examples, see: the name Andreas 'the manly one', therefore *gumcystum* (dative plural) 'manly virtues' in probable wordplay in *Andreas* (line 1606a); Guthlac 'battle-play, warfare' used in word-play in *Guthlac A* (line 182); in *Genesis A* there is play on the etymologies of the names Seth 'resurrection' (lines 1104-10) and Noah 'rest' (line 1304a); in *Exodus* Egypt 'ravaging, afflicting' (lines 37a and 501a); *Daniel* Daniel 'to/at judgement' (lines 150a, 531 and 547a).[5] Of these, the well-attested wordplay on the name Guthlac is particularly relevant to the names in *Beowulf*, especially in considering the possibility of wordplay on the name of Hygelac.

Oral poetry, the lyre and the formula, in the composition and delivery of epic, that is 'Epos' in German

It is not unreasonable to take an interest in the anonymous poet, in one view the singer who first gave *Beowulf* to a listening audience; in another view, the writer who was catering for a reading public. I have traced elsewhere some of the early scholarship linking the composition of Germanic heroic verse with that of Serbian singers composing as they plucked the gusle, beginning with J. A. Schmeller who, as early as 1839, brought Serbian song together with Old Saxon verse (with special reference to *Heliand*).[6] The Chadwicks had drawn attention to 'The abundance of static epithets' and other features which *Beowulf* shares with the Homeric epics.[7]

Attempts to establish Old English verse as composed within the frame of reference of a twentieth-century oral-formulaic theory are based on the connection seen by the Harvard Greek scholar Milman Parry between Homeric composition in ancient Greece and Serbian composition in modern times.[8] The leap to

[5] See F. C. Robinson, 'The Significance of Names in Old English Literature', *Anglia*, 86 (1968), 14-58, 'Some Uses of Name-Meanings in Old English Poetry', *NM*, 69 (1968), 161-71; R. Frank, 'Some Uses of Paronomasia in Old English Scriptural Verse', *Speculum*, 47 (1972), 207-26. (Cf. I[59].) Play on the meaning of the name of Guthlac goes back to his *Vita*; see B. Colgrave (ed.), *Felix's Life of Saint Guthlac* (Cambridge, 1956; reprinted 1985), text and translation 78-9 and note 174, reference to the Martyrology 25, for which see G. Kotzor (ed.), *Das altenglische Martyrologium*, Bayerische Akademie der Wissenschaften, Philosophisch-Historische Klasse, Abhandlungen, Neue Folge 88 (1981), II, 53, 301.

[6] See J. A. Schmeller, *Ueber den Versbau in der alliterirenden Poesie besonders der Altsachsen*, Königlich Bayerische Akademie der Wissenschaften, Abhandlungen der Philosophisch-Philologischen Classe, IV (1847), No. 5, 211 and note. Cf. E. G. Stanley, 'The Scholarly Recovery' (1981; see I[56]), 199 [reprinted in *A Collection of Papers* (1987; see I[45]), 45].

[7] H. M. and N. K. Chadwick, *The Growth of Literature*, I The Ancient Literatures of Europe (Cambridge, 1932), 22-3.

[8] A good, recent account of Parry's work, and of some doubts felt about it, is given by J. B. Hainsworth, 'Ancient Greek', in A. T. Hatto (ed.), *Traditions of Heroic and Epic Poetry*, I (London, 1980), 20-47, especially pp. 31-3 and p. 46 note 12.

Old English poetry was made by the Harvard Anglo-Saxonist F. P. Magoun, Jr,
by Parry's pupil A. B. Lord, and by a number of scholars, some of them pupils
of Magoun's, some of them still reaping grain from the seeds sown by Magoun
and Parry.[9]

Of course, nothing is known about how, if at all, the harp was used when the
Anglo-Saxons themselves recited or sang their verse; perhaps as accompaniment, perhaps between recited fits or *laisses*. What is known of the
harp is related to manuscript depictions of King David and archaeological
evidence of the Germanic round lyre, chiefly now in relation to the more recent
replica reconstructed to make sense of the fragments excavated at Sutton Hoo.[10]
Scholars in the humanities are sometimes eager to show that in their subjects
too, even in Anglo-Saxon Studies, advances in factual knowledge are made on
the basis of newly discovered realia, such as the harp at Sutton Hoo. But, alas,
the harp is a modern reconstruction, and how it was played, who knows?

That provides hardly a sufficiently firm basis for anything on how, if at all,
the harp went with *Beowulf* as we have it, or with the 'premonumental' *Ur-
Beowulf* some scholars still wish they had and the existence of which other
scholars doubt. We do not even know how Cædmon's fellow-servants sang to
the harp that circulated from singer to singer.[11] Sometimes Anglo-Saxon harp
accompaniment is related to the even less well attested early Irish recitation of
poetry to the harp, as in a paper, the first version of which was heard in 1962, by
J. B. Bessinger, Jr – it ranks high in unspecificity:[12]

> I would venture to argue only that amateurs of the Old English harp should be
> able to hypothesize inoffensively about the possibilities of such an appication
> [namely, to the extant Old English verse], and to do this one must perforce cite
> and on occasion indulge in the recitation of an existing written text. We need
> not take up arms here, therefore, about the orality or bookishness of *Beowulf*,
> for example, which must have been musical in some early stages of its pre-
> monumental formation and is undeniably bookish in the unique surviving
> manuscript. In what follows I use the verb *sing* not in its strict oral-formular
> sense but simply to mean an oral presentation to musical accompaniment,
> whether singing in the ordinary sense, or some style of formal chanting, or the

9 F. P. Magoun, Jr, 'Oral-Formulaic Character of Anglo-Saxon Narrative Poetry', *Speculum*, 28
   (1953), 446-67; Magoun, p. 446 note 3, acknowledges his debt to Parry and also to Lord's
   unpublished Harvard Ph.D. thesis (1949), *The Singer of Tales: A Study in the Process of
   Yugoslav, Greek, and Germanic Oral Poetry*, which, revised and expanded, gave A. B. Lord's
   The Singer of Tales, Harvard Studies in Comparative Literature, XXIV (1960), especially ch.
   10 'Some Notes on Medieval Epic'.
10 See M. and R. Bruce-Mitford, in R. Bruce-Mitford (ed., in vol. III with A. Care Evans), *The
   Sutton Hoo Ship-Burial*, (London, 1975-1983), III/2 (1983), ch. ix, 'The Musical Instrument'.
11 Cf. F. P. Magoun, 'Bede's Story of Cædman: The Case History of an Anglo-Saxon Oral
   Singer', *Speculum*, 30 (1955), 49-63.
12 'The Sutton Hoo Harp', in R. P. Creed (ed.), *Old English Poetry Fifteen Essays* (Providence,
   Rhode Island: 1967), 13-14.

use of some sort of mannered recitative style, a kind of *Sprechstimme*, which in public recital of Old English verse today is as far as most of us will dare to go.

First, then, Old English poetry could have been sung to an undifferentiated background of harp music with no regular relation between verse and instrumental melody or metrical ictus – a heterophonic style, if I understand that term correctly. Early Irish poetry was apparently sometimes recited in this fashion from the sixth century onwards.[13] Supposing that this free rhapsodic style were known in England, perhaps spreading to or from Anglo-Celtic areas along with the small harp,[14] it would have been as adaptable to later run-on verse as to early end-stopped verse, which fact would theoretically make available to would-be singers a musical accompaniment to the oral production of poems like *Beowulf*, now sometimes considered purely literary.

Or a harp could provide a rhythmic base without systematic melody, which would be likely enough if the strings on a small harp, already nearly equal in length because of the slight curvature of the peg-arm, were nearly equal in tension and thus in tone. Volume would be irrelevant; the rhythmic beat would be nonlinear and percussive, conceivably with occasional rapped tambour effects on the resonator or perhaps with a mixture of thrashing and chording.

The next study in the volume, J. Nist is generous in his praise of the poet, but does not reveal how Nist knows or how a future editor is to know the exact effects of the harp, and the poem is likely to cry in vain for an edition such as he demands. He ends thus:[15]

The artistry of the *Beowulf* poet is indeed superb.

Thus the percussional harp, even while executing its basic metrical function of strengthening weak measures, may serve to heighten the emotional tone of intensely dramatic lines by means of heavily emphasizing the syncopation. So important is the harp for the rhythm of *Beowulf* in all its metrical and aesthetic features that the poem itself cries for a future edition that will indicate the exact placing of every musical chord of the scop. Such an edition would be of incalculable value for bardic performance and critical commentary, for it would be a modern equivalent of Vitellius A.xv – a manuscript that perpetuates rather than replaces the oral tradition of *Beowulf*.[16] And that tradition

---

13 Bessinger, p. 25 note 39, gives references to early Irish poetic form, but does not reveal how, if at all, the harp may have been used with Irish song, whether in accompaniment or otherwise; nor does he say how secure the evidence is for the use of the harp in Ireland contemporary with the original *Beowulf*.

14 Namely, a harp like the replica, 'a trifle over fifteen inches high' (15 in. = 38.1 cm), first produced to elucidate the Sutton Hoo fragments, and referred to by Bessinger, p. 3; the second replica produced is 74.2 cm in length, (= 29¼ in), that is, almost twice the height of the first; see M. Bruce-Mitford, 'The Musical Instrument' (1983; see II[10]), p. 689. Everything Bessinger says about the sounds produced by the little harp has to be reconsidered because the new replica is different.

15 J. Nist, 'The Harp in *Beowulf*', in Creed's, *Old English Poetry* (1967; see II[12]), 42.

16 A footnote refers us to a paper of his: 'Textual Elements in the *Beowulf* Manuscript', *Papers of the Michigan Academy of Science, Arts, and Letters*, 42 (1957), 331-8. He does not refer us

continues to demand the metrical accompaniment of a functional, not decorative, harp.

A statement, similarly vague though it too asserts that the harp was used for accompaniment, is made by N. D. Isaacs at about the same time:[17]

All of this raises questions concerning the use of the harp. As Jess B. Bessinger ably demonstrated in the Old English Group meeting at MLA in 1960, playing on a harp reconstructed according to the specifications of Sutton Hoo fragments, a great latitude of accompanying procedures may have been open to Old English scops. Basically there has been an assumption of a one-strum-per-measure arrangement, but any number of pickin' [= plucking] and frailin' [= beating] designs are possible; and a four-measure line can easily accommodate six strums for two pairs of syncopated bars.

There is no need to give further details of speculations about the use of the harp in the original or modern recitation of *Beowulf*. The *Beowulf* harp is perhaps to be considered as the aural equivalent of the emperor's new clothes. In the words of D. A. Pearsall:[18]

but the plain fact is that we are lacking all kinds of evidence needed for more elaborate theorising. For instance, we have no idea how this poetry was delivered, and cannot assume that the mode of recitation described in *Beowulf*, in an idealised portrayal of the heroic age, is the mode of recitation of the poem itself. And even if we do assume that *Beowulf* was recited to the harp, we have no idea how the harp was used, whether to provide rhythmic background, melodic accompaniment, free arabesques, or to supply intermittent speech-rests.

There is less life than there used to be in the oral-formulaic theory; many have attacked it as extreme, especially when oral composition is insisted on. Formulas appearing in *Parallelstellen* can be introduced by a poet who composes as he writes down what he has put together. Thus L. D. Benson, in a paper of 1966, shows clearly how literary, how bookish, Old English formulaic verse may be.[19]

A. C. Watts has both lyre and harp in the title of her book of 1969, the first

to his book, *The Structure and Texture of Beowulf*, Universidade de São Paulo Faculdade de Filosofia, Ciêcias e Letras, No 229, Lingua e Literatura Inglêsa, I (1959), especially 'New Theory' pp. 93-102, and, on Cotton MS Vitellius A.xv, ch. viii 'Textual Elements in the Beowulf MS.'

[17] N. D. Isaacs, *Structural Pinciples in Old English Poetry* (Knoxville, Tennessee, 1968), 175. At the 1960 meeting of the Old English group of the Modern Language Association of America Bessinger's recital was combined with an early version of his paper (1967; see II[12]) from which I have quoted.

[18] Derek Pearsall, *Old English and Middle English Poetry*, The Routledge History of English Poetry, I (London, Henley on Thames, and Boston, Massachusetts: 1977), 16.

[19] 'The Literary Character of Anglo-Saxon Formulaic Poetry', *PMLA*, 81 (1966), 334-41.

two chapters of which give a good account of Milman Parry and Homeric scholarship, and of the application to Old English of what he thought true for Homer.[20] Her third chapter shows the insufficiency of the method used for Old English by followers of Parry, especially in their lack of precision in regarding Old English poetic formulas as strictly comparable with Homeric formulas. Throughout she draws on both *Beowulf* and *Elene* for a careful analysis of their formulas; her conclusions are firm, as in this statement (p. 196):

> If the formulaic analysis of Old English texts is not in itself sufficient witness to an oral-formulaic method of composition, the secondary evidence supplied by historical documents and critical analogy is too limited and con-tradictory to either support or condemn Magoun's theory. A consideration of Cynewulf's Latinity produces a strong argument for his literacy. It is tempting to ask, if Cynewulf could *write* formulae, could not the *Beowulf*-poet also?

There are, however, attempts at defining the term 'formula', whether or not used in oral composition, and of the relationship of the formula to the metrical unit, the half-line. They are well discussed in a survey by K. Reichl.[21] He takes for granted the existence of 'epic' in Old English, thus (p. 42), 'formulas and formulaic style in Old English (OE) epic poetry – in particular in the heroic epic *Beow.*'

Perhaps underlying this assumption is yet once more the less restricted German terminology, German *Epos* rather than English *epic*, as in an encyclo-paedia entry on the poem by T. Finkenstaedt:[22]

> Das altenglische Epos, seit Grundtvig 1808 nach seinem Helden benannt,[23] umfaßt 3182 alliterierende Langverse; es ist das einzige weltliche Gedicht in ae. Sprache von solchem Unfang.
>
> [The Old English epic, since 1808 named *Beowulf* after its hero,[23] comprises 3182 alliterative long lines; it is the only secular poem in the Old English language of such compass.]

The German term *Epos* is discussed in an encyclopaedia entry 'Epos' by H.

---

20 A. Chalmers Watts, *The Lyre and the Harp. A Comparative Reconsideration of Oral Tradition in Homer and Old English Epic Poetry*, YSE, 168 (1969).

21 K. Reichl, 'Old English: Formulaic Diction in Old English Epic Poetry', in A. T. Hatto and J. B. Hainsworth (eds), *Traditions of Heroic and Epic Poetry*, II Characteristics and Techniques (London, 1989), 42-70.

22 J. Hoops (ed. of the 1st edn, 1911-1919; see I[61]) *Reallexikon der Germanischen Altertums-kunde*, (2nd edn; Berlin and New York, 1968-), II/2-3 (1974), 337.

23 For Sharon Turner's use of the name of the poem in 1807, see I[55]. I do not know where Grundtvig used the title *Beowulf* as early as 1808; cf. R. W. Chambers, *Beowulf An Introduc-tion* (1921; see I[23]), 391:

> 1832 GRUNDTVIG, N. F. S. Nordens mythologi. Anden Udgave. Kiöbenhavn. (Pp. 571-94 give a summary of the Beowulf-stories. This was, of course, wanting in the first edit. of 1808.)

Beck, the General Editor of the new 'Hoops'. He is much concerned with the genesis of epic, and begins, ponderously, with the term itself:[24]

Epos

Der poetologische Terminus E[pos] wird einerseits in einem vorwiegend normativen (gattungssystematischen und fundamentalpoetischen) Sinne gebraucht, andererseits von einer hist[orischen] Werkbetrachtung her bestimmt. Im letzteren Sinne hat sich die E[pos]-Diskussion im Ger[manischen] ins Besondere am → Beowulf und → Nibelungenlied . . . entzündet.

[*Epos*

The poetological[25] [German] term *Epos* is used (*a*) in a mainly normative sense, within a system of literary kinds or genres, and fundamentally descriptive of the verse so designated; (*b*) it is determined within an historically conceived consideration of the poetic work. In the latter sense the discussion of Germanic *Epos* has been sparked off in connection especially with *Beowulf* and the *Nibelungenlied* . . .]

A similar use is found in connection with *Beowulf* in J. de Vries writing in German,[26] for example: 'Die Hauptfiguren des englischen Epos haben tatsächlich gelebt' [the principal characters of the English 'Epos' actually existed].

Fact and fiction

For a book published as recently as 1965, some of K. Sisam's literary concerns seem to me strikingly old-fashioned,[27] as if belonging to the literary scene before Heusler, Schücking and Tolkien. He still speculates about how best to distinguish 'Fiction and History' in the poem (pp. 51-2):

The borderland between fiction and history in *Beowulf* is a curious field for speculation. By 'history' here I mean little more than some stories or mentions of persons who lived and of things that happened. The heroic traditions known in England in the seventh and later centuries must have been discontinuous. They were distorted by the arts of storytellers as well as by faults of memory. Their subject-matter was not the development or decline of nations, but heroic characters or remarkable events which struck the imagination of poets and

---

[24] *Reallexikon* (2nd edn; see II[22]), VII/5-6 (1989), 423. The article has a good bibliography (p. 428), from which emerges Heusler's importance to more recent work on epic.

[25] I do not know what, if anything, *poetologisch* means beyond 'of the study of poetry'. G. Wahrig (ed.), *Das grosse deutsche Wörterbuch* (Gütersloh, 1966), characterizes *Poetologie*, s.v., as 'Poetik, Lehre von der Poesie' [poetics; the science of poetry]; and marks it with the unexplained abbreviation 'unz.', probably *unzählbar* 'uncountable', rather than *unziemlich* 'indecent', *unzüchtig* 'obscene', *unzulänglich* 'inadequate', or *unzulässig* 'inadmissible'.

[26] Jan de Vries, *Heldenlied und Heldensage*, Sammlung Dalp, lxxviii (Berne and Munich, 1961), 79. I have not seen the original Dutch version; de Vries translated it into German himself.

[27] *The Structure of* Beowulf (Oxford, 1965).

held their audiences over several generations. For most people without written records the past closes up behind their grandfathers' time. . . . In such conditions historical perspective, or a view of the course of history was unattainable.

This borderland is the more baffling because the distinction between fact and fiction is seldom clear, and because the poet has the art of giving verisimilitude to his stories.

One wonders, however, whether the poet was really striving for verisimilitude rather than for wonder in presenting Grendel and his mother, the dragon, and Beowulf himself with the hand-strength of thirty and with matchless endurance in swimming, as a boy contending with Breca and as a man traversing the multitudinous seas between Frisia and Geatland. Heusler's view that realism is not to be looked for in *Beowulf* is, therefore, in conflict with a natural modern wish to breathe realism into Beowulf's retreat from Frisia to Geatland (lines 2359b-62, 2367-8):

> Þonan Biowulf com
> 2360 sylfes cræfte, sundnytte dreah.
> Hæfde him on earme (ana) þritig
> hildegeatwa þa he to holme (st)ag. . . .
> Oferswam ða sioleða bigong sunu Ecgðeowes,
> earm anhaga eft to leodum.

[By his own strength Beowulf got away from there, performed an act of swimming. On his arm he alone had thirty battle-armours when he entered the sea. . . . The son of Ecgtheow swam across the expanse of the waters(?) back to the tribe, a forlorn and solitary man.]

F. C. Robinson's interpretation of these lines reduces Beowulf's amazing natatorial feat unnecessarily, and is, I think, unconvincing, especially in seeking in manuscript '[X]XX.' (of the thirty pieces of war-gear) a misplaced fit-number when the manuscript numbering runs correctly from 'XXXIII' to 'XXXIIII' at lines 2312 and 2391; but unconvincing also in not allowing the unique phrase *sundnytte dreah* and the verb *oferswimman*, not recorded again in English till Chaucer, to mean 'performed an act of swimming' and 'swam across', but to refer to some mode of marine locomotion other than natation, because elsewhere in Old and later English the subject of *to swim* can be a ship.[28]

---

[28] See F. C. Robinson, 'Beowulf's Retreat from Frisia: Some Textual Problems in ll. 2361-2362', *SP*, 62 (1965), 1-16. In the manuscript (fol. 182ᵛ) there is no trace of the word *ana* preceding [.X]XX. (expanded to *þritig*); the Thorkelin transcripts show that at the end of the eighteenth century the first X of XXX was still to be seen, where now only XX. remains [see K. Malone (ed.), *The Thorkelin Transcripts of Beowulf in Facsimile*, EEMF, I (Copenhagen, 1951), A p. 69, B p. 108a]. See also K. Malone, *Nowell Codex*, EEMF, XII (1963), 89/2 on fol. 185ᵛ [= 182ᵛ in the old foliation, still in use in *Beowulf* studies]. See also F. C. Robinson, 'Elements of the Marvellous in the Characterization of Beowulf: A Reconsideration of the

Another problem, historical or mythological depending on how one views the names of tribes distant in space or time from the Anglo-Saxon poet, arises in connection with the Geats. In the latter part (pp. 54-9) of Sisam's book, he shows how, whatever the poet may seem to be saying at lines 3019-20 about the maidens of that nation awaiting a grim life of exile now that their lord lies dead, the Geatish nation was not destroyed, but survived long after.

Who were the Geats? Older German scholars used to refer to them quite often by the related tribal name of the Goths. In a strange book, J. A. Leake regards them as the same as the Getae, failing to discuss the quantity of the stem-vowel, long in *Geatas* but short in *Getae*.[29] She is the latest to resurrect the Scythian myth. In doing so, she goes back to Aylett Sammes's chapter 'The Antiquity and Original of the Saxons', and she has an approving note about one of Sammes's sources, Robert Sheringham:[30]

> Using many of the same sources I have utilized, Sheringham soberly traces the Getes' fabulous past, arguing at length that they were the progenitors of the English.

She does not, however, go back to Grotius himself, Sheringham's source (pp. 198-9) for the identity of the Scythian, the Getic and the Gothic languages, nor forward to John Pinkerton with whom the Scythian myth also flourished, though he was no follower of Grotius:[31]

> Cluverius led the van, by asserting, on *his own* authority, that the *Gothi* were the *Gutones*, or *Gothones*, of Pomerellia, who went and ate up the Getæ, – because Cluverius was himself a native of Pomerellia . . .! Grotius followed, who asserted on *his own* authority that the Goths went from *Gothland* in Sweden, a name unknown till the Thirteenth, or Fourteenth century, and rising merely from some property of the country*, and ate up the Getæ, about three centuries before Christ – because Grotius was embassador from the Queen of Sweden to France, and bound . . . to do all in his power for the honour of that kingdom. Such infants are men of learning!
>
> > *Cluverius says it is called *Gudske*, and *Gudland*, and *Gulland*, from the *goodness* of the soil. But in Icelandic Sagas it is *Gotaland*, or *Gautaland*, *terra equorum*, and was probably so called from its horses, as was the isle Gotland. Ptolemy places *Gutæ* in Scandinavia, opposite the *Gutones* of Prussia, from whom they seem to have sprung.

Textual Evidence', in R. B. Burlin and E. B. Irving, Jr (eds), *Old English Studies in Honour of John C. Pope* (Toronto, 1974), 124-6, and notes 14-20. For Heusler's view on historicity in heroic poetry, see I[50].

29 J. A. Leake, *The Geats of* Beowulf (Madison, Milwaukee, and London, 1967).

30 A. Sammes, *Britannia Antiqua Illustrata: or, The Antiquities of Ancient Britain, Derived from the* Phoenicians (London, 1676), 411-67; R. Sheringham, *De Anglorum Gentis Origine Disceptatio* (Cambridge, 1670). Cf. J. A. Leake's note, *The Geats* (see II[29]), p. 173 note 37.

31 John Pinkerton, *A Dissertation on the Origin and Progress of the Scythians or Goths. Being an Introduction to the Ancient and Modern History of Europe* (London, 1787), 9. Hugo Grotius's work referred to is *Historia Gotthorum, Vandalorum, & Langobardorum* (Amsterdam, 1655); on the Scythians see 'Prolegomena', p. 8; on the Goths and Getae see Grotius's

It is all ludicrously confusing, with wild etymologies of etymologically obscure tribal names. According to these early scholars, everybody meets everybody else in the Crimea, whether banished like Ovid or migrated like the Goths whose descendants the Flemish diplomat Ogier Ghiselin Busbecq did indeed interview there in the 1560s.[32] It seems amazing that such ancient lore should have seemed to a scholar publishing her work in 1967 worth more than a dismissive mention.

A major departure in the literary reading of *Beowulf* is R. Frank's highly original view of the use made of historical elements in the poem; the hero, Beowulf of the Geats, is a creation by the poet, the New Man, who inhabits the world of historical and mythical kings and heroes of Germania, providing in his invented person the yardstick by which to measure them all:[33]

> The pleasure of recognition, of sharing in an erudite game, seems to have been as important to the Anglo-Saxons as to readers of Ovid or Milton. Germanic legend was something people had to know . . . if they wanted to be thought cultured. *Widsith* names some seventy kings and as many tribes in its 143 lines; *Deor*, in 42 lines, refers to five or six stories . . .; and *Beowulf*, in 3182 lines, draws on about twenty legends. The audience's memory, like a frame, shapes and gives meaning to the poet's often fleeting allusions.
>
> There was also the pleasure of surprise. All three poems introduce a fictive or new character into the known world of legend: Widsith, the far-travelled poet; Deor, the supplanted scop; and Beowulf, The Good Samaritan Geat. We follow each *novus homo* as he meets and mingles with the heroes of past times.

The sophisticated audience, or was it still primitive?

The audience of *Beowulf* has more often been thought lay than religious, regardless of whether or not the poet (of the version we have) was thought to be a cleric or a layman. Schücking thought it may have been written for the education of royal princes in the Danelaw, and attached that to a late date of composition, about AD 900.[34] Others are less specific about the audience; thus W. P. Ker

---

edition of Isidore of Seville's *Chronicon* in the same volume, pp. 730-2. The work by Philippus Cluverius (Philipp Clüver) referred to by Pinkerton is *Germania Antiqua* (Leiden, 1616); on the Scythians, see I, 22-3; on the Goths and Getae, see III, ch. xxxiv, 128-36.

[32] Augerius Gislenius Busbequius, *Legationis Turcicae epistolae quatuor* (Paris, 1589), epistola IV, p. 135. See, for the relevant literature, W. Streitberg, *Gotisches Elementarbuch* (5th and 6th edn; Heidelberg, 1920), 39-40, § 17.

[33] Roberta Frank, 'Germanic legend in Old English literature', in M. Godden and M. Lapidge (eds), *The Cambridge Companion to Old English Literature* (Cambridge, 1991), 88-106; the quotation is at pp. 97-8.

[34] L. L. Schücking, 'Wann entstand der Beowulf? Glossen, Zweifel und Fragen', *Beiträge*, 42 (1917), 347-410.

has a high regard for the audience of *Beowulf*, as fit to receive a noble poem, implicit in his low regard for the audience of Middle English verse:[35]

> the poem of *Beowulf* is unmistakably heroic and weighty. The thing itself is cheap; the moral and the spirit of it can only be matched among the noblest authors. It is not in the operations against Grendel, but in the humanities of the more leisurely interludes, the conversation of Beowulf and Hrothgar, and such things, that the poet truly asserts his power. It has often been pointed out how like the circumstances are in the welcome of Beowulf at Heorot and the reception of Ulysses in Phæacia. Hrothgar and his queen are not less gentle than Alcinous and Arete. There is nothing to compare with them in the Norse poems . . . . It is not common in any age; it is notably wanting in Middle English literature, because it is an aristocratic temper, secure of itself, and not imitable by the poets of an uncourtly language composing for a simple-minded audience.

Dorothy Whitelock's lectures on the audience (published in book-form)[36] brought greater precision to the connected ideas of 'the poet' and 'the audience': (p. 5) 'He was composing for Christians, whose conversion was neither partial nor superficial'; and more specifically (pp. 8-9):

> I would go further than claiming that the audience of *Beowulf* was thoroughly acquainted with the Christian religion. I believe that it was also accustomed to listen to Christian poetry. There is no general difficulty in the way of such an assumption, unless one wishes to date the poem very early indeed. Already when Bede was writing his *Historia Ecclesiastica*, which he tells us he finished in 731, there had been a number of poets who had followed Caedmon's example and composed religious poems in the traditional metre; and from *Beowulf* itself it can legitimately be gathered that it was not only ecclesiastics who listened to poems on religious themes.

And with reference to dating (p. 21): 'For a lay company to be so steeped in Christian doctrines, a considerable time must have elapsed since the acceptance of Christianity.' She does not think it was a reading public, but a listening audience, lay rather than religious therefore.[37] The assumption of a sophisticated audience alters the understanding of the poem; and indeed the very fact that the narrative proceeds in the poem in ways so far from straightforward can no longer be dismissed as the result of an unsophisticated poet producing some-

---

[35] *The Dark Ages* (1904), 253-4 (part of this passage is quoted by Tolkien, see I[84]).

[36] *The Audience of* Beowulf (1951; see I[45]).

[37] Though D. Whitelock does not refer to it, the view that 'Cædmonian' biblical paraphrase was earlier than *Beowulf* is central to Hertha Marquardt's article on the relative chronology of these poems, 'Zur Entstehung des Beowulf', *Anglia*, 64 (1940), 152-8. Earlier studies seeking to show that *Genesis* and *Exodus* influenced *Beowulf* are F. Klaeber's two articles, 'Die Ältere Genesis und der Beowulf', *EStn*, 42 (1910), 321-38, and 'Concerning the Relation between "Exodus" and "Beowulf" ', *MLN*, 33 (1918), 218-24.

thing of which one could truly say with W. P. Ker that 'the thing itself is cheap': not for such an audience. D. Whitelock's book clinched the long process by which *Beowulf* was removed from the Germanic Heroic Age and became the literary production of a sophisticated Christian poet catering for a sophisticated Christian audience, yet looked back to an ancient world which, in reality, both poet and audience had left behind.

Some scholars writing on *Beowulf* had not left that world behind, though they had to acknowledge the possibility that the poem was a product at least a little coloured by influences beyond the strict confines of heroic song and heroic legend; thus J. de Vries on our *Großepos* treating of *echt germanische Sagenstoffe* expressed in a way to remind him of *Hildebrandslied* (p. 83):[38]

Denn eines dürfen wir nie aus dem Auge verlieren. Der Beowulf möge einen Stoff enthalten, der von allen Seiten zusammengerafft zu sein scheint, er möge seine breit ausladende Art lateinischen Vorbildern verdanken, dennoch kann man nicht leugnen, daß er in einer alten heroischen Tradition der germanischen Stämme Englands verwurzelt ist. Darauf deuten nicht nur die eingefügten Episoden, die echt germanische Sagenstoffe behandeln. Das ergibt sich noch viel bestimmter aus dem poetischen Charakter des Dichtwerkes. Diese Art von Sprachbehandlung findet ein klassisch geschulter Mönch nicht in seinen lateinischen Vorbildern, und noch viel weniger fallen sie ihm von selbst ein. Die metrische Struktur des Verses stimmt vollkommen mit jener der deutschen und nordischen Epik überein. Das gilt ebenso von der Sprache mit ihrem festgeprägtem Formelschatz und ihrem typischen Stil der Gedankenvariation; diese erinnert uns unmittelbar an das fast gleichaltrige Hildebrandslied. Das Gedicht als Großepos mag also eine neue Schöpfung gewesen sein, es weist dennoch auf ältere Kurzlieder zurück, wie wir sie bei allen germanischen Völkern vorfinden und von denen wir nachgewiesen haben, daß sie mindestens bis in die Völkerwanderungszeit zurückreichen.

[For we must never lose sight of one thing. It may be that *Beowulf* contains material scraped together from all sides, as it seems, it may be that it owes its wide sweep to Latin models; yet it cannot be denied that it is rooted in an ancient heroic tradition of the Germanic tribes of England. Not only the inserted episodes treating of genuine Germanic legendary material indicate that; it is to be deduced with much greater certainty still from the poetic character of this verse composition. No monk trained in Classical scholarship would have found this kind of linguistic treatment in his Latin models, and even less could he have invented them independently. The metrical structure of the verse agrees perfectly with that of German and Norse epic. That applies equally to the fixed coinages of his formulaic hoard and to its typical style of thought-variation, the latter reminding us directly of the nearly contemporary *Hildebrandslied*. It may be, therefore, that considered as a whole, this extended epic verse composition was a new creation; nevertheless it refers back

---

[38] *Heldenlied und Heldensage* (1961; see II[26]).

to older short lays such as we find among all Germanic tribes; and, as we have demonstrated, these go back at least to the Age of Germanic Migrations.]

J. de Vries is a scholar so steeped in earlier ways that he cannot tear himself away from such preoccupations and predilections. Moreover, proof comes easily to him; he has proved to his own satisfaction that heroic short compositions go back to the Age of Migrations; he has found short heroic song in every one of the Germanic peoples – though one suspects that outside Scandinavia he depends heavily on *Hildebrandslied* and *The Battle of Finnsburh*, fragments both, and both more easily assigned to a poetic kind, the heroic lay, because fragmentary, and because the heroic lay flourishes more vigorously in the minds of Germanic scholars than the extant remains on which they operate warrant.[39] His notion of metrical structure was imprecise if he thought the metre of *Beowulf* agrees perfectly with that of Old High German and Old Saxon as well as Scandinavian alliterative verse. His method is the mere assertion of what he believes in, false or true.

By the 1960s de Vries sounded out of date; and so to some extent did Kenneth Sisam, a much better scholar of Old English literature who cannot really believe in the literary sophistication of the audience and, therefore, of the poet writing for such an audience: 'the plot is extended by a primitive method':[40]

> Whether or not delivery in instalments based on the three great fights was contemplated, the plot seems to have been built up to meet the demand for another story about the hero who destroyed Grendel. . . . So another story about the destroyer of Grendel suggested one where his marvellous strength and courage were pitted against monsters with which other brave men could not contend. Once the adventure with Grendel's mother had been added . . . the pattern was established. So, besides the primitive unity of a single hero, there is a second almost as primitive: the adventures are of the same kind.

And in similar vein (p. 8):

> [Heorot] was the ideal setting for a discursive heroic poem; and so long as the scene is laid in a royal hall, whether Hrothgar's or Hygelac's, the poet has no great difficulty of construction. Outside the hall his machinery is often clumsy.

Sisam is not among those readers of *Beowulf* who put their trust in the understanding of the audience (p. 9, and footnote 1):

---

[39] Cf. 'The Germanic "Heroic Lay" of Finnesburg', first published in E. G. Stanley, *Collection of Papers* (1987; see I[45]), 281-97.

[40] *The Structure of* Beowulf (1965; see II[27]), 2 and 5.

But the main audience would be the king's bodyguard .... These men were not chosen for intellectual qualities. They should not be thought of as learned in legendary history or allusion.[1] Bold rather than delicate effects would suit them best.

> [1] The knowledge of heroic legend to be expected from the audience should not be overrated. Some knew more than others. The essentials of some stories, such as those of Ingeld and Finnsburh, would be widely known. ... But enjoyment of poetry does not require the understanding of every allusion, and that degree of perfection is unlikely in a mixed audience.

Allegorical exegesis and other theological interpretations

A sophisticated allegorical reading would, of course, make greater demands on the audience than Sisam supposes. Indeed, some of the allusions suggested by learned exegetes might well have been beyond the poet's ken, let alone that of the audience.

Take the hart facing the hounds rather than plunge into the mere (lines 1368-72):[41]

> Ðeah þe hæðstapa   hundum geswenced,
> heorot hornum trum,   holtwudu sece,
> 1370 feorran geflymed,   ær he feorh seleð,
> aldor on ofre,   ær he in wille
> hafelan [hydan].

[Though the proud-antlered stag that roams the heath, hard pressed by hounds (and) put to flight from afar, may seek the trees of the forest, he will give up his existence, his life on the shore, rather than that he will (plunge) in [to hide] his head.]

Almost a hundred years ago Sarrazin felt that the hart seemed a little out of place in Germanic poetry, as did the depiction of landscape such as that of Grendel's mere, and several scholars sought a Virgilian source.[42] In such work all the Virgilian hunted and stricken deer are brought before us as connections are looked for between Virgil and the *Beowulf* poet, but even the closest of them (at *Aeneid* XII, 749-55) is not very close, seeing that, according to Virgil, the stag *could* not flee because of the water, but in *Beowulf* the stag *would* not flee into the water for fear of the supernatural aura of the place.

---

[41] For the *ær* ... *ær* construction, cf. E. G. Stanley, 'Old English *ær* Conjunction: "rather than" ', *N&Q*, 237 (1992), 11-3. For line 1372a the manuscript reads only *hafelan* followed by a mark of omission; the editors supply *hydan* 'to hide' or *beorgan* 'to save'.

[42] See G. Sarrazin, 'Die Hirsch-Halle', *Anglia*, 19 (1897), 379; F. Klaeber, 'Aeneis und Beowulf', *Archiv*, 126 (1911), 341-2; and T. B. Haber, *A Comparative Study of the* Beowulf *and the* Aeneid (Princeton, 1931), 92-3.

The exegete D. W. Robertson goes into patristics, 'higher meanings' he says (p. 32), for an understanding of the scene:[43]

> Certain attributes of the scene are extremely significant. In the first place, the pool is the dwelling of a giant, one of the generation of Cain. In Bede's *Hexaemeron* we find that the giants of Gen. 6.4 were 'terrenis concupiscentiis adhaerentes' (men who cling to fleshly lusts) and that although they were destroyed in the flood, they arose again thereafter. Figuratively, the generation of Cain is simply the generation of the unjust to which all those governed by cupidity belong. They are monsters because they have distorted or destroyed the Image of God within themselves. Babylon . . . traditionally began with Cain, and it is maintained on earth by his generation. We may say as much for the evil garden. Thus Grendel is the type of the militant heretic or worldly man, and his dwelling is appropriately in the waters which are the opposite of those which spring from the Rock of Christ.

This is hardly preferable to seeing Grendel and his mother as related to the trolls of the north, though trolls too show a concupiscible appetite. It seems all the more regrettable that the poet has created Grendel and his mother speechless, or they might have told us in words even more than is revealed (lines 1687-98) by a reading of the runes on the *scenn* of the giants' sword brought back from the mere. Only words, the poet's or those of figures in the poem or of an inscription reported in the poem, might have confirmed Robertson's allegorical reading; without such confirmation this exegesis seems no more than a reading into the poem.

A passage in the introduction to Klaeber's *Beowulf* is designed to lead us towards an interpretation of the hero Beowulf as the allegory of a Saviour, a saviour from monsters: the third monster, 'the dragon was in ecclesiastical tradition the recognized symbol of the archfiend':[44]

> That the victorious champion, who overcomes this group of monsters, is a decidedly unusual figure of very uncertain historical associations, has been pointed out before. The poet has raised him to the rank of a singularly spotless hero, a 'defending, protecting, redeeming being,' a truly ideal character. We might even feel inclined to recognize features of the Christian Savior in the destroyer of hellish fiends, the warrior brave and gentle, blameless in thought

---

43 D. W. Robertson, Jr, 'The Doctrine of Charity in Medieval Literary Gardens: A Topical Approach through Symbolism and Allegory', *Speculum*, 26 (1951), 24-49 [reprinted in L. E. Nicholson, *Anthology* (1963; see I[78]), 165-88]. I quote from p. 33, omitting an endnote reference, and adding the translation of the Latin from the reprinted version.

44 In all three editions; the first edition (1922), pp. li-lii, is worded, 'In fact, we need not hesitate to recognize features of the Christian Savior', which in the third edition (1936) has become (pp. l-li), 'We might even feel inclined to recognize features of the Christian Savior'. For the statement on the dragon as the archfiend, Klaeber adds a footnote referring to his important series of articles, 'Die christlichen Elemente im Beowulf' in *Anglia*, 35 and 36 (1912), this reference *Anglia*, 36, 188-9.

and deed, the king that dies for his people. Though delicately kept in the background, such a Christian interpretation of the main story on the part of the Anglo-Saxon author could not but give added strength and tone to the entire poem. It helps to explain one of the great puzzles of our epic. It would indeed be hard to understand why the poet contented himself with a plot of mere fabulous adventures so much inferior to the splendid heroic setting, unless the narrative derived a superior dignity from suggesting the most exalted hero-life known to Christians.

The last sentence quoted recalls an earlier statement by Klaeber, part of the summarization of his view, then novel, now universally accepted by *Beowulf* scholars, that the Christian elements are inseparable from the poem as we have it, and central to it:[45]

Der dichter würde eine solche einzigartige fabel überhaupt nicht gewählt haben, wäre dieselbe einer Christianisierung nicht so außerordentlich günstig gewesen.

[The poet would never have selected so singular a fable if it had not been so exceptionally suited to Christianization.]

Without adding much, M. B. McNamee agrees with Klaeber's allegorical interpretation:[46] 'Beowulf's conflict with the monsters comes closer to that of Adam with Satan in *Paradise Lost*.' In a wise reply, A. Bonjour praises Klaeber's relative restraint, and would go no further than Klaeber went in this direction:[47] 'la position de Friedrich Klaeber a paru, et peut encore paraître, comme fort avancée sinon extrémiste.' Once the possibility of allegory was raised it proved difficult to set limits to it. M. E. Goldsmith takes the *dryncfæt deore* of 'Elegy of the Last Survivor' to be part of the dragon's hoard, the *sincfæt* of line 2231; and she believes it to be nothing other than Adam's *poculum mortis*.[48] Again, an innocent reader may look in vain in the text for confirmation.

Alvin A. Lee reaches 'Heorot and the Guest-Hall of Eden Symbolic Metaphor and the Design of *Beowulf*' as the last of his essays applying allegorical exegesis to Old English poetry, exegesis that delves deep as he reads into the poem what he thinks concealed beneath its surface:[49]

---

[45] *Anglia*, 36 (1912; see II[44]), 195; cf. E. G. Stanley, *Paganism* (1964-1965; reprinted 1975; see I[2]); reprint, pp. 48 and 127 note 127.

[46] M. B. McNamee, '*Beowulf* An Allegory of Salvation', *JEGP*, 59 (1960), 190-207; reprinted in L. E. Nicholson, *Anthology* (1963; see I[78]), 331-52. I quote from the last paragraph of the article.

[47] '*Beowulf* et le démon de l'analogie', *Twelve* Beowulf *Papers 1940-1960*, Université de Neuchatel, Recueil de travaux publiés par la Faculté des Lettres, XXX (1962), 182.

[48] M. E. Goldsmith, *The Mode and Meaning of 'Beowulf'* (London, 1970), 255-6.

[49] A. A. Lee, *The Guest-Hall of Eden Four Essays on the Design of Old English Poetry* (New Haven and London, 1972), 181-2.

In the poet's use of *the myth of the Fall and the origin of fratricide,* he often specifically connects the Grendel kin with hell, which should make it easy to recognize the metaphorical structure barely concealed beneath the relatively slight surface realism of the poem. On one level of meaning, *Beowulf* can best be understood as a reworking of the same war between heaven and hell that emerges in its undisplaced mythical form in *Christ and Satan* and other poems. As in the Christian mythology, where demonic powers are assumed to have taken possession of the world shortly after the Creation, so in *Beowulf* a monster comes out of the mere and possesses the poem's *imago mundi,* Heorot. This necessitates a war between a heaven-sent champion and the monster, a war in which the champion's victory is a "cleansing" and a preliminary defeat of the feond on the earthly level, as in Christ's victory on the rood. But, again as in Christian story, the deliverer's victory in the world must be extended and consolidated by a further triumphant battle in the depths from which the demonic attacks have come. Whether the hell referred to in *Beowulf* is from Teutonic myth or, more plausibly, from a mixture of both does not alter the fact that the images of bondage, darkness, endless pain, joyless exile, fire, ice, wind, storm, and enmity against mankind, images associated with the monsters and their haunts, are the same ones found over and over again in the Old English poetic accounts of man apart from God. Nor does the fact that Grendel and his mother seem in some ways to be trolls from a different legendary background diminish the connotations they draw from Christian symbolism; it means only that they have this additional extension, as compared with a less poetically complex demon like the one tormenting Cynewulf's Juliana.

To a reader disinclined to follow A. A. Lee when he pries 'beneath the relatively slight surface realism of the poem', with the hopeful intention of finding 'the metaphorical structure barely concealed beneath' that realism, it may seem that 'this additional extension' is not that the monsters, Grendel and his mother as they assail the hall Heorot, are like trolls and Beowulf is like a hero set in this world, but that they are Germanic monsters and he is a Germanic hero, and that the 'additional extension' is what Lee reads into the poem by Christian mythological cryptology. I agree with E. B. Irving's account of the book; he too quotes (part of) the first sentence which I have quoted, and says of it:[50]

> One telltale sentence betrays the nature of Lee's bias. . . . How eager Lee seems in his desire to get to this concealed structure, and then to go on to equate Grendel with the standard devil of Christian theology. And how quickly he brushes aside the "slight surface realism" – by which he must mean the words of the story, all that we can know.

[50] E. B. Irving, Jr, *Rereading* Beowulf (Philadelphia, 1989), 9-10. The likelihood of allegorical and typological meanings in Old English biblical paraphrase is, of course, not to be denied; cf. pp. 97-8, below.

The 'hart' overtly present in the name of Heorot well demonstrates Lee's exegetical procedure.[51] Antler-adorned gables and the little stag of Sutton Hoo, now back on top of the 'sceptre' but when Lee wrote still on the 'standard', either way presumably a symbol of royalty, are both used to explain the name, but an explanation is also given 'in terms of scriptural association. We are referred to a passage in C. L. Wrenn's 'Sutton Hoo and *Beowulf* ':[52]

> It has been shown by Professor Karl Hauck in his important paper entitled "Herrschaftszeichen eines Wodanistischen Königstums[53]" that both the Sutton Hoo standard and the helmet and shield designs are in origin *signa sacra* or ritually significant pagan element in the cult of Woden. . . But at the same time the features of pagan warfare could be specifically Christian symbols – the "Vexilla Regis," the "Shield of Faith" and the "Helmet of Salvation." Thus the cult of Woden – so powerful in ancient Sweden whence the Geatas had come – is linked with Christian transitional art. For instance, too, the royal stag surmounting the standard-holder, which suggests the name Heorot of Hrothgar's hall, could at the same time symbolize the thirsting stag of Psalm 42 and the cult of an ancestral Woden.

The thirsting stag of the opening of Psalm 42 [Vulgate 41 (Roman and Gallican only)] sets Lee going. In the Doway translation the opening verses read:

> Euen as the harte desireth after the fountaines of waters: so doth my soule desire after thee ó God.
> My soule hath thirsted after God the strong liuing: when shal I come and appeare before the face of God?

This, according to Lee, takes us straight to the hart at Grendel's mere:

> if we remember that we are told later in *Beowulf* by the king of Heorot that the "hart strong in his antlers" will give up his life rather than enter the hellish mere (1368-1372), the possibility emerges that Hrothgar's mighty human hall

---

[51] *Guest-Hall of Eden* (1972; see II[49]), 180-2. This part of the essay goes back to an earlier version of it, 'Heorot and the "Guest-Hall" of Eden', *Mediaeval Scandinavia*, 2 (1969), 78-91, at 82-3. The article does not contain the long passage quoted above from the book.

[52] In R. W. Chambers, *Beowulf An Introduction* (3rd edn, 1959; see I[83]), 518.

[53] Wrenn has a footnote with a reference to K. Hauck, 'Herrschaftszeichen eines Wodanistischen Königstums', in Institut für fränkische Landesforschung an der Universität Erlangen, *Jahrbuch für fränkische Landesforschung*, 14 (1954) 'Festgabe Anton Ernstberger', 9-66.

See also R. Bruce-Mitford, Sutton Hoo (1975-1983); see II[10]), II (1978), ch. vii 'The Sceptre', especially pp. 370-7, and C. Hick's Appendix A 'A Note on the Provenance of the Sutton Hoo Stag', pp. 378-82; note p. 382:

> If, as has been suggested, it [the Sutton Hoo stag] was already regarded as a valuable possession and heirloom, it may have been deliberately mounted upon the similarly remarkable stone bar to serve as a totemic symbol of the ruling house. The name 'Heorot' for Hrothgar's hall also implies that the animal was then regarded as a symbol associated with royalty.

is imagined primarily as the earthly dwelling place of the human soul, both communal and individual.

'Primarily'? Surely not! The fountain of the Psalm and, by association with it, the stag in *Beowulf*, soon become baptismal symbols (pp. 209-10), without even the help from St Augustine that might have been expected. St Augustine provides the following exegesis on these verses:[54]

> Audi quid aliud est in cervo. Serpentes necat, & post serpentium interemtionem majori sitis inardescit, peremtis serpentibus ad fontes acrius currit.
>
> [Hear what else there is to the stag. He destroys serpents, and after the killing of serpents he is inflamed with greater thirst, having killed serpents he runs more keenly to the fountains.]

No doubt, without great effort and without any support from the text of the poem, this could have been turned to use in exegesis of *Beowulf*.

If one believes, as some have done and some may still do, that *Beowulf* was written at the time of Bede, would it be useful to read the poem, if not as if through the eyes of Bede, at least as if informed through his writings with his spirit? I wonder. In spite of every attempt to be guided by what used to be referred to as the historical imagination, most people at the end of the twentieth century read the poem as late twentieth-century readers. W. F. Bolton's attempt to read it as if he were Alcuin seems puzzling to me.[55] For example (p. 143):

> An Alcuinian reading . . . sees the first two fights no less as temptations than the last, and Beowulf's pagan limitations as leading to shortcomings that forebode the disaster of the goldhoard; so that his Christlike attributes serve to underline how he is unlike Christ, not how the gloom that surrounds him is tempered by these similarities.

Clearly, the various theological readings do not give us a single view. But the matter arouses a different form of puzzlement. To read *Beowulf* as if one were Alcuin, is that not like reading, say, *Hamlet* as if one were Bacon, or any other writer of any age as if one were a theologian or philosopher contemporary with the author? It may be helpful if the theologian or philosopher shares an identifiable interest with the poet. For example, Alcuin has an interest in Rhetoric, but, of course, he applies it to Latin writings only, and the *Beowulf* poet does not provide clear evidence of having applied to his vernacular poem anything directly or indirectly dependent on any Latin rhetorician. The connection

---

[54] See *Enarratio in Psalmus XLI*, in the Maurist *Augustinus Hipponensis Opera*, IV (Venice, 1730), col. 355.

[55] W. F. Bolton, *Alcuin and* Beowulf *An Eighth-Century View* (New Brunswick, 1978; London, 1979).

attempted by W. F. Bolton (p. 61) is quite unconvincing, and there is good sense in J. D. Niles's rejection of such an Alcuinian reading:[56]

> Altogether one thus finds little or no evidence that the poet knew Latin letters directly. The few possible instances of direct influence are counterbalanced by many examples of critics' strained efforts to pursue comparisons that prove weightless. While direct Latin influence on *Beowulf* cannot be ruled out, attempts to discover it have failed to establish a valid literary context for the poem.

It seems equally Quixotic, rather than a phenomenological revolution, to pretend that any reader at the end of the twentieth century could take in the poem as an Anglo-Saxon listener might have done, whether or not it is claimed that an Anglo-Saxon audience 'participated in a game of the imagination' with the poet or with someone reading aloud the poem, as J. D. Niles suggests (p. 206):

> When readers pick up *Beowulf* privately today and study it as it was never studied in Anglo-Saxon times, they can perhaps gain some additional insight into it by putting themselves in the place of original listeners, who did not have the text before them but entered an arena in which speaker and audience participated in a game of the imagination.

The art of the poem

More straightforward readings, such as are attempted in many lecture-series on *Beowulf*, seem more rewarding. An example is provided by E. B. Irving, with many passages quoted and translated.[57] Trying to put life into a poem as stern and ancient as *Beowulf* is not always easy; but to detect comedy or joviality where there appears to be very little is hardly a solution. Even if one is not inclined to see in Grendel all the theological and especially allegorical implications some exegetes have seen in him, it is difficult to find him 'comic' (p. 103):

> Grendel's intentions and predictions are so massively frustrated that the fight itself comes to have a distinctly comic quality. It is always the figure with the most elaborate and serious plans who makes the most comic character; even the prat-faller of farce must seem to be overflowing with intentions just before he tumbles.

Similarly, Beowulf's speech to Hrothgar (lines 1652-76) seems jovial to E. B.

---

[56] J. D. Niles, *Beowulf The Poem and Its Tradition* (Cambridge, Massachusetts, and London: 1983), 91. For the Anglo-Saxons' knowledge of Latin rhetoric, see two articles by J. J. Campbell, 'Learned Rhetoric in Old English Poetry', *MP*, 63 (1965-1966), 189-201, and 'Knowledge of Rhetorical Figures in Anglo-Saxon England', *JEGP*, 66 (1967), 1-20.

[57] E. B. Irving, Jr, *A Reading of* Beowulf (New Haven, 1968).

Irving (p. 127). In his more recent book, his rereading of the poem,[58] this aspect has been dropped.

Many *Beowulf* scholars have praised the art of the poem. Every analysis of detail reveals fresh excellencies. The structure of the narrative is no longer censured. A. G. Brodeur's book made a valuable contribution: *The Art of Beowulf*, partly based on earlier articles of his and on studies of Old English and Old Norse poetic expression, among which the kenning and variation are particularly significant.[59] The kenning had been well analysed before, especially in the work of H. Marquardt for Old English, R. Meissner for Scaldic verse, and, less fundamentally, by H. van der Merwe Scholtz comparing Anglo-Saxon with Old Norse poetic expression.[60] As early as 1889 R. M. Meyer had surveyed formulaic features of Germanic poetry in a major work.[61] Meyer does not, however, make a significant contribution to the study of *Beowulf*; what little he says is indebted to the superficial comparativist work of R. Heinzel, now quite out of date.[62]

The stylistic device of variation in Germanic alliterative poetry, which had been discussed in a monograph by W. Paetzel, was subjected to an interesting and detailed, well-systematized analysis by S. Colliander, but her subject is variation the Old Saxon *Heliand*, and her work throws light on other Germanic verse only indirectly since nothing other than *Heliand* is given by her more than a brief introductory mention.[63] A. G. Brodeur, therefore, cannot be said to have been the first in the field, even for *Beowulf*, and yet, following on from Tolkien's

---

[58] 1989; see II[50].

[59] A. G. Brodeur, *The Art of Beowulf* (Berkeley and Los Angeles, 1959). Cf. his articles, 'The Structure and Unity of *Beowulf*', *PMLA*, 68 (1953), 1183-95; 'Design for Terror in the Purging of Heorot', *JEGP*, 53 (1954), 503-13.

[60] Hertha Marquardt, *Die altenglischen Kenningar. Ein Beitrag zur Stilkunde altgermanischer Dichtung*, Schriften der Königsberger Gelehrten Gesellschaft, Geisteswissenschaftliche Klasse, 14th year, III (1938); R. Meissner, *Die Kenningar der Skalden. Ein Beitrag zur skaldischen Poetik*, Rheinische Beiträge zur germanischen Philologie und Volkskunde, i (1921); H. van der Merwe Scholtz, *The Kenning in Anglo-Saxon and Old Norse Poetry* (Utrecht doctoral dissertation, 1927).

[61] Richard M. Meyer, *Die altgermanische Poesie nach ihren formelhaften Elementen beschrieben* (Berlin, 1889).

[62] R. Heinzel, *Über den Stil der altgermanischen Poesie*, QF, X (1875). Some idea of how superficial Heinzel's criticism is may be gained from the fact that he devotes only eleven pages (his chapter 'Vergleiche und Umschreibungen', pp. 14-25) to all similes, kennings, poetic circumlocutions, etc., in all Germanic poetry, Scandinavian, Anglo-Saxon, Old Saxon and Old High German, including comparisons with Indian, Greek and Latin poetry of many ages. W. Bode ranges widely beyond Old English, with lists of kennings from the other Germanic languages, in his Strasburg doctoral thesis, *Die Kenningar in der angelsächsischen Dichtung mit Ausblicken auf andere Litteraturen* (Darmstadt and Leipzig, 1886); O. Krackow, *Die Nominalcomposita als Kunstmittel im altenglischen Epos* (Berlin, 1903), has statistics that are still usable.

[63] W. Paetzel, *Die Variation in der altgermanischen Alliterationspoesie*, Palaestra, XLVIII (1913); S. Colliander, *Der Parallelismus im Heliand* (Lund doctoral dissertation, 1912).

'The Monsters and the Critics', he is early in treating the poem primarily as a work of literature, the excellence of which needed to be demonstrated in detail.

The harmony in the poem of the poet's habit of mind with the traditional prosody, in the use of metrical types analysed within the half-line unit of verse and within the long line consisting of two half-lines alliterating with each other (but less frequently discussed within the syntactical unit of the sentence), was also discussed by Tolkien, whose statement about 'two halves of roughly equivalent phonetic weight' is, however, to be regarded as only an approximation designed to bring out the difference between Old English alliterative verse and 'regular' post-medieval English verse:[64]

> The very nature of Old English metre is often misjudged. In it there is no single rhythmic pattern progressing from the beginning of a line to the end, and repeated with variation in other lines. The lines do not go according to a tune. They are founded on a balance; an opposition of two halves of roughly equivalent phonetic weight, and significant content, which are more often rhythmically contrasted than similar. They are more like masonry than music. In this fundamental fact of poetic expression I think there is a parallel to the total structure of *Beowulf*. *Beowulf* is indeed the most successful Old English poem because in it the elements, language, metre, theme, structure, are all most nearly in harmony.

I have elsewhere attempted to trace the presumed associative imagination of the poet in the annexive syntax of the poem:[65]

> The excellence of the poem is in large measure due to the concord between the poet's mode of thinking and his mode of expression. An associative imagination works well in annexive syntax: each is the cause of the other's excellence. A the same time he is good with the smaller units, the words and formulas which all Anglo-Saxon poets had to handle. Perhaps there is a deeper reason why *Beowulf* is satisfactory. The Christian poet chose to write of the

---

[64] 'Monsters and Critics' (1936; see I[82]), 273. He attaches a note to 'equivalent' in the phrase 'two halves of roughly equivalent phonetic weight': 'Equivalent, but not necessarily *equal*, certainly not as such things may be measured by machines.' In fact, it is in the nature of Old English verse that the first half-line, but not the second, can sustain double alliteration required for some metrically heavy half-line units; see A. J. Bliss, *The Metre of Beowulf* (1st edn, Oxford, 1958; I refer throughout to the revised 2nd edn, 1967), Appendix C, Table II (pp. 123-7), showing in three columns the occurrence of each of his 'types': (1) in the first half-line with double alliteration, and (2) in the first half-line with single alliteration; (3) in the second half-line (where double alliteration does not occur). J. R. R. Tolkien's 'On Metre', in J. Clark Hall, *Beowulf and the Finnesburg Fragment A Translation into Modern English Prose* (completely revised edn by C. L. Wrenn; London, 1940, corrected 1950), pp. xxx-xxxvi, indicate clearly that Tolkien was fully conversant with metre, and in these pages explains the limits to the equivalence of the two halves of the long line (see p. xxx and footnote 3).

[65] '*Beowulf*', in E. G. Stanley (ed.), *Continuations and Beginnings: Studies in Old English Literature* (London, 1966), 104-41; reprinted in *Collection of Papers* (1987; see I[45]), 139-69. The quotation is at pp. 136-7 [= 167].

Germanic past. His ideal king is Beowulf the monster-slayer, whom he compared, not with Daniel, but with Sigemund, and contrasted, not with Saul, but with Heremod.

His success lies in that choice. The elements of Old English poetic diction, the words and the traditional phrases feel at home in the world which they first celebrated in song.

Parts of F. C. Robinson's monograph on *Beowulf* are similarly concerned with annexive syntax, or, in his terminology, 'the appositive style'.[66] The reader learns from the book that an understanding of the syntax of clause and sentence construction is not a pedantic inessential forced by philologists upon their more literary pupils, but a literary way of life nurtured on close reading.

The episodes and digressions of the poem had more usually occupied earlier scholars on account of their subject-matter, historical or mythical; but Tolkien had defended them, and their art, including the art that fits them into the narrative of the poem as a whole, was the subject of parts of A. G. Brodeur's book, as well as of a monograph by A. Bonjour.[67] The poet's narrative skill and the use in *Beowulf* of narrative devices, 'pace', 'focus' and 'point of view', for example, are compared with the Middle English Laȝamon's *Brut* in a monograph by H. Ringbom, and a Structuralist analysis of the poem was attempted, with interesting results, by T. A. Shippey.[68] In recent literary studies of the poem there may be a danger to think that whatever is is best. The faults in narrative art are seen to be virtues, and since I too proceed along that line of argument, I gladly defend and am glad that others defend the poem from superficial charges of want of narrative art of which I have listed some:[69]

> Though we may like the poem, we can see deficiencies in its narrative art: lack of steady advance; lack of narrative turning-point demanding resolution; lack of the critical point of the action. Is nothing left us for the demonstration by analysis of the *Beowulf* poet's narrative art?

The move away from the supposition of an epic ideal of which *Beowulf* falls short is welcome to anyone who has no faith in the doctrine of such an ideal, and does not believe that the poem is an epic in any useful sense of the term; as Tolkien says:[70]

---

66 Fred C. Robinson, Beowulf *and the Appositive Style* (Knoxville, 1985).

67 A. Bonjour, *The Digressions of* Beowulf, MÆ Monographs, V (1950). Similarly, J. A. Nist, 'The Structure of *Beowulf*', *Papers of the Michigan Academy of Science, Arts, and Letters*, XLIII (1958), 307-13, defends the art shown in the structure of the poem.

68 H. Ringbom, *Studies in the Narrative Technique of* Beowulf *and Lawman's* Brut, Acta Academiae Aboensis, ser. A Humaniora, 36/2 (1968); T. A. Shippey, 'The Fairy-Tale Structure of "Beowulf"', *N&Q*, 214 (1969), 2-11.

69 E. G. Stanley, 'The Narrative Art of *Beowulf*', in H. Bekker-Nielsen, P. Foote, A. Haarder, and A. M. Sørensen (eds), *Medieval Narrative: A Symposium* (Odense, 1979), 58-81, reprinted in *Collection of Papers* (1987; see I[45]), 177.

70 'Monsters and Critics' (1936; see I[82]), 275.

. . . in the centre we have an heroic figure of enlarged proportions.

Beowulf is not an 'epic', not even a magnified 'lay'. No terms borrowed from Greek or other literatures exactly fit: there is no reason why they should. Though if we must have a term, we should choose rather 'elegy'. It is an heroic-elegiac poem.

The elegiac elements of the poem had its place earlier in an important article by G. Ehrismann, as well as in a doctoral dissertation by M. A. O'Neill, whose work is difficult to obtain, and, no doubt at least in part for that reason, has not been as influential as it might.[71]

Celtic influences

The closeness of Anglo-Saxon monasticism to contemporary Irish monasticism makes it likely that a literate poet, such as the poet of *Beowulf* is now generally thought to have been, was subjected to Celtic influence. Over sixty years ago the suggestion was made that the theology of those monsters, Grendel's ancestors, who survived the flood may have been Irish in origin.[72] Of course, if the Irish connection is correct, the material derived from Irish monasticism is learned though recognizably Irish only because it is not Roman. More recently an attempt has been made by M. Puhvel to seek Irish origins for some of the main events in the central narrative of the poem, for example, the fight under water with Grendel's mother.[73] The Celtic tradition is rich in what are usually regarded as folk-tales, and many of the features thought to be Celtic by M. Puhvel are what are usually regarded as folk-tale elements. How far in time do they go back in Celtic narratives? How good is the evidence for dating them early enough to have influenced the composition of *Beowulf*? Some of the motifs are widely distributed, but a few appear to be rare enough for a Celtic connection to be an interesting speculation, though ultimately undemonstrable.

---

[71] G. Ehrismann, 'Religionsgeschichtliche Beiträge zum germanischen Frühchristentum', *Beiträge*, 35 (1909), 200-39; it is not confined to *Beowulf*, but deals with many aspects of the world as the spirit's exile, and surveys and traces to its origins the elegiac motifs in Old English poetry. I give some indication of the contents of the most substantial chapters in Sister Mary Angelica O'Neill, *Elegiac Elements in* Beowulf, Ph.D. dissertation of the Catholic University of America (Washington D.C., 1932), because it is not published if D. K. Fry, Beowulf *and* The Fight at Finnsburh *A Bibliography* (Charlottesville, Virginia, 1969), 137 no. 1600, is correct. Chapter i (pp. 1-26), 'Elegiac Character of *Beowulf*: A Historical Survey of the Question', is comprehensive, but does not sufficiently distinguish 'elegiac' from 'sad' and 'gefühlvoll'; chapter ii (pp. 27-72), 'A Critical Examination of the Elegiac Passages in *Beowulf*', lists fifty such passages; chapter iii (pp. 73-8) analyses their distribution.

[72] S. J. Crawford, 'Grendel's Descent from Cain', *MLR*, 23 (1928), 207-8; supplementing significantly O. F. Emerson's important 'Legends of Cain, Especially in Old and Middle English', *PMLA*, 21 (1906), 831-929.

[73] M. Puhvel, Beowulf *and the Celtic Tradition* (Waterloo, Ontario, 1979).

General critical introductions to the poem, and its treatment in literary histories

There is an endless succession of elementary introductions to Old English literature and to *Beowulf*. Originality will not be looked for in such works which present accepted views, often derived from the authors' lecture notes. Of course, in the last fifty years some of the stupidities of earlier introductions are no longer favoured, among them racial statements and insistence on racial continuity of the ideal warrior from their day to ours, such as about a hundred years ago Stopford A. Brooke reverted to in order to demonstrate the continuity of the English warlike spirit combined with gentleness.[74] Brooke saw a likeness to Beowulf in Lord Nelson (p. 29): 'Gentle like Nelson, he had Nelson's iron resoluteness.' And he detected in Wiglaf qualities which (p. 31)

> represent the ancient English ideal, the manhood which pleased the English folk even before they came to Britain; and . . . in all our history since Beowulf's time, for 1200 years or so, they have been repeated in the lives of the English warriors by land and sea whom we chiefly honour.

Perhaps not so many of the writers of recent introduction to *Beowulf* try to identify the characteristics of epic in the poem after Tolkien had ruled out the simple notion that *Beowulf* is an epic. Tolkien was not the first to insist that *Beowulf* should be read as it is, rather than as Germanic scholars and comparativists with a *penchant* for epic would have it in its original form. W. P. Ker saw it thus in the opening to a good chapter on the poem, about forty years before Tolkien's lecture, but Ker never doubted that *Beowulf* is an epic poem:[75]

> It is an extant book, whatever the history of its composition may have been; the book of the adventures of Beowulf, written out fair by two scribes in the tenth century; an epic poem, with a prologue at the beginning, and a judgment pronounced on the life of the hero at the end; a single book, considered as such by its transcribers, and making a claim to be so considered.

This is echoed by G. K. Anderson, whose account of the poem, first published in 1949, is often less persuasive than in this statement:[76]

> And so, to summarize, one may grant the pagan qualities of the original story; one may further assume that one or more bards contributed descriptive details, didactic passages, elegiac lays, some historical or legendary digressions,

---

[74] Stopford A. Brooke, *The History of Early English Literature* (London, 1892). For a similar view of the unchanging English national character, cf. E. Dale, *National Life and Character in the Mirror of Early English Literature* (Cambridge, 1907).

[75] W. P. Ker, *Epic and Romance. Essays on Medieval Literature* (London, 1897), 182-3.

[76] G. K. Anderson, *The Literature of the Anglo-Saxons* (1st edn, 1949; revised edn, 1966 from which I quote), 83.

until eventually a more gifted individual, known as the Beowulf Poet put the accumulated epic and lyric material down into his individualized concept much as we have it now. The Beowulf Poet may have composed the major part of the poem as it now exists – perhaps all of it – or he may only have transcribed the poem as he knew it from a predecessor or predecessors. But he is responsible for *Beowulf* as we understand it, and he composed it some time in the eighth or ninth century.

Some of the introductions are well written and present elegant expressions of interesting views. I like T. A. Shippey's brevity and wit:[77]

> I can now say no more than that many of the problems of *Beowulf* dissolve if one accepts it as the work of a literate man in a pre-literate society – one might say, a sort of Cædmon in reverse.

That seems wiser than the assumption of some scholars that the folk itself speaks formulaically through the mouth of the man who first sang our poem in days of yore, or of those other scholars who think our learned poet had behind his desk the well-indexed, well-thumbed Patrologia Latina (as far as it had got by the time he wrote).

Some of the introductions make good use of earlier criticism; thus K. H. Göller recalls Schücking's characterization of Beowulf in terms of the ideals of *mensura* and *sobrietas*, and adds:[78]

> Von der germanischen Kampfesraserei, die sich manchmal gar zum Blutrausch steigert, finden wir nichts im *Beowulf.*
>
> [There is nothing in *Beowulf* of Germanic battle-madness, which sometimes escalates to blood-frenzy.]

Many of the account of *Beowulf* in the histories of Old English literature add little to our understanding. But occasionally points of detail are presented which are clearly the result of a sensitive reading. Perhaps a reader must not ask if we have enough feel for Old English verse and syntax to be able to judge it, as does S. B. Greenfield on lines 1322-3:[79]

> And, on the most detailed stylistic level, we find such moments as that in which Beowulf comes, the morning after the celebration of Grendel's death, to ask whether Hrothgar has spent the night pleasantly.

---

[77] T. A. Shippey, *Beowulf*, Studies in English Literature, lxx (London, 1978), 59. I correct an obvious minor misprint.

[78] *Geschichte der altenglischen Literatur* (Berlin, 1971), 176. For Schücking on this subject, see I[78].

[79] S. B. Greenfield, *A Critical History of Old English Literature* (New York, 1965), 89; with some changes, revised edition, S. B. Greenfield and D. G. Calder, *A New Critical History of Old English Literature* (New York, 1986), 143, which I quote.

"Ne frin þu æfter sælum!   Sorh is geniwod
Denigea leodum.   Dead is Æschere,"

replies the king. ('Ask not of joy! Sorrow is renewed / among the Danes. Dead
is Ashere.') The opposition of joy and sorrow is suggested by the syntactic
break at the caesura, yet the alliterative connection of *sælum* and *sorh* under-
lies the confluence of the emotions.

Sensitivity in reading is easily assumed, yet the aptness of sensitive subtleties
less easily demonstrated. On what grounds does D. Pearsall detect 'embarrass-
ment' or 'impurity' in the last lines of the poem; why does he differentiate,
'Grendel is clearly evil, his mother slightly less so'?[80] Is it true, as M. Swanton
thinks,[81] that 'Of all the major characters mentioned in the poem, the hero is the
only one for whom we do not have some external corroboration'? What about
Wealhtheow or Hygd (not to mention Grendel's mother), or do the women not
count? The feminists will not like that. Grendel's mother is given the full
treatment as a character by J. Chance:[82] 'Grendel's Mother is presented as
husbandless and son-obsessed.'

Irony

Irony is often asserted in Old English verse, but its existence is not so easily
demonstrated. T. A. Shippey, writing of the Finn Episode in a section given the
title 'The ironic background',[83] wonders if we are to think 'That the *Finnsburg
Episode* was chosen from all other legends precisely to create the right kind of
ironic gap between its audience and that of *Beowulf*'. To weigh the relationship
of the inner audience at Heorot to the poet's own outer audience makes good
literary sense. We can see the larger patterns of irony in the poem; for example,
Wealhtheow, welcoming Beowulf as Hrothgar's son by adoption, expresses faith
in the loyalty of Hrothulf (lines 1180-7) just after the telling of the Finnsburh
Episode and the woes of Hildeburh, and we know from other sources of the
subsequent disloyalty of Hrothulf. When it comes to individual words, however,
we always have to ask ourselves if we understand the language well enough to
detect the kind of irony which we can detect easily in Modern English. Thus
when at line 1259 the poet calls Grendel's mother an *ides* we do not know what
exactly that word connotes. One remembers Jacob Grimm's handling of the
meanings of the word:[84]

---

[80] D. Pearsall, *Old English and Middle English Poetry* (1977; see II[18]), 8 and 9.
[81] M. Swanton, *English Literature before Chaucer* (London, 1987), 49.
[82] J. Chance, 'The Structural Unity of *Beowulf*. The Problem of Grendel's Mother', in H.
Damico and A. H. Olsen (eds), *New Readings on Women in Old English Literature* (Bloom-
ington and Indianapolis, 1990), 252.
[83] T. A. Shippey, *Old English Verse* (London, 1972), 35.
[84] Jacob Grimm, *Deutsche Mythologie* (2nd edn, 1844; see I[25]), 372.

das ahd. *itis* pl. *itisî*, alts. *ides*, pl. *idisî*, ags. *ides*, pl. *idesa* bedeutet femina überhaupt und kann von jungfrauen oder frauen, armen oder reichen gelten.

[Old High German *itis* (pl. *itisî*), Old Saxon *ides* (pl. *idisî*), Old English *ides* (pl. *idesa*) means 'woman' in general and can be used of virgins or women, socially low or high.]

with a footnote:

freolicu meovle = ides. cod. exon. 479, 2. veras und idesa oder eorlas und idesa stehn sich gegenüber, daselbst 176, 5. 432,2.

[*freolicu meowle* = *ides* (*Riddle* 61 lines 1-2), *weras* and *idesa* (*Guthlac B* line 1232) or *eorla* and *idesa* (*Riddle* 46 line 7) are antonyms.][85]

C. Fell, with unwarranted assurance, says of the use at *Beowulf* line 1259:[86] 'The poet calls her [Grendel's mother] *ides*, 'lady', which has suggested to some editors and translators that one proper meaning of *ides* is 'hag', but it is much more likely that the poet is using the word ironically to stress the unladylike qualities of his creation.'

The date of composition

For true literary history some chronology is essential. We should want to know, if possible, absolute dates, as we know for *Cædmon's Hymn* composed while Hild was abbess, or for *Bede's Death Song*, or for *The Battle of Maldon*, or for the *Chronicle* poems. We do not know the date of composition of *Beowulf*. A. S. Cook saw Aldfrith of Northumbria (AD 685-705) as the poet's patron;[87] the eighth century is generally favoured by those who consider an early date likely; K. S. Kiernan dates the composition in the eleventh century,[88] rather later than competent palaeographers date the *Beowulf* manuscript. A conference at Toronto, called to date the poem, found no scholarly consensus, though a surprising number of participants thought of a date no earlier than the reign of Alfred and no later than the reign of Athelstan.[89] The dates of the other poems in the great poetic codices are also not known. We cannot establish relative chronology of composition with any certainty. We cannot write a history of Old English verse as history is usually understood.

---

[85] In the translation I give references to ASPR instead of Grimm's references B. Thorpe (ed.), *Codex Exoniensis – A Collection of Anglo-Saxon Poetry, from a Manuscript in the Library of the Dean and Chapter of Exeter* (London, 1842).

[86] C. Fell, *Women in Anglo-Saxon England* (London, 1984), 29.

[87] A. S. Cook, 'The Possible Begetter of the Old English *Beowulf* and *Widsith*', *Transactions of the Connecticut Academy of Arts and Sciences*, XXV (1922), 281-346.

[88] K. S. Kiernan, Beowulf *and the* Beowulf *Manuscript* (New Brunswick, 1981), passim.

[89] C. Chase (ed.), *The Dating of Beowulf* (1981; see I[45]).

Silence, a great gift in a critic

Sometimes when one reads critics of Anglo-Saxon poetry, who have tried, one hopes, successfully, by their publications to justify their place in the harsh university world of the past half-century, one longs for those occasional flashes of silence, that, Sydney Smith tells us, made Macaulay's conversation perfectly delightful. Some years ago, the late John Crow of King's College, London, formulated Crow's Law: 'You mustn't say what you want to say till you know what you ought to know.' Silence is a valuable present from the critic to the reader when the critic's foundations are weak in scholarship and critical good sense seems out of reach,[90] and when the critic is not yet long enough dead to be – perhaps – interesting whatever he or she says.

[90] For a different opinion, see D. G. Calder, 'The Canons of Old English Criticism Revisited', *Old English Newsletter*, Subsidia, 15 'Twenty Years of the *Year's Work in Old English Studies*' (1989), 11-21, who when he refers to me (as far as I can tell in the onomastic confusion of his article – Stanley Greenfield or E. G. Stanley?), misrepresents me: my prerequisite for publication is not a great load of erudition, a burden heavier than some may wish to carry, but the small light of critical good sense which might enable the critic to distinguish 'any new insight', the critic's own or another's, from much new nonsense.

III

Uncertainties of the Date and Transmission
of *Beowulf*

Chronology

As in the first two chapters of this book, I begin with doubts about most studies of Old English poetry: doubt that we have the communion of informed taste necessary for literary criticism, and doubt that we have the factual knowledge of chronology of composition necessary for its history. In the first chapter some attempt was made to proceed through a hundred and fifty years of Literary History in chronological order; the second chapter, covering only fifty years abandoned chronological order; yet chronological order is more than a mere convenience. Writers on *Beowulf* are subject to the influence of earlier writers on the poem, and, if they are so fortunate, they may exert influence on those who come after them. Critical and scholarly fashions may flourish for a time, and then make way for a newer fashion. In the History of Scholarship as in Literary History, who writes what when is usually datable without any difficulty. Often it is known who read what, or who taught whom at which university.

The history of modern literatures, the subject of much Literary History, is also full of datable facts: births and deaths of poets and of their parents and siblings, the association with partners in friendship, love or marriage, first publication and later revision of a single work or of a succession of works, meeting this or that fellow writer, the reading of some book, journeys undertaken, political events, exploits in war, adventures in peace, and sickness borne. These and a host of other datable events or circumstances fill the biographies of literary figures and bestow some sense of direction, if not on the study of literature, certainly on literary biography.

The earliest period of English verse is that of the Anglo-Saxons. It runs from near the end of the seventh century to the century of the Norman Conquest, and perhaps a little later, four hundred years or so. As a rule, the dates of Anglo-Saxon poets and their compositions are unknown. The chronological study of Old English verse is impossible because it is impossible to establish a demonstrable chronology of composition for it. Writing a history of Old English poetry is strictly impossible. As we have seen, the date of composition of *Beowulf* is unknown, and in the last fifty years scholars have assumed or proposed dates of composition from the eighth to the eleventh centuries. *Beowulf*, therefore, cannot be fitted into a chronology. Those who have attempted to write a history of Old English poetry have spent much time on matters of chronology which for later periods of English verse can be dismissed quickly or taken for granted. Not only is there no agreement among those who write about Old English verse when most of what has survived was composed, no agreement at all about any of the longer poems and not even much agreement about the chronological relationship in which they stand to each other.[1]

That Old English verse survives at all is in each case a result of the operation of arbitrary chance. There is probably more scholarly consensus about the chronological relationship in which the longer poems stand to the small number of datable shorter poems, most of them occasional poems for which the occasion is datable: a continental monk recalling a proverb on the companionship in valiant action which Boniface (died 754) used to quote, or the song Cædmon was given in a dream when St Hild was abbess of Whitby (657-680), or the song Bede uttered on his deathbed (died 735), these are the earliest poems we have; and the poems contained in *The Anglo-Saxon Chronicle* which take as their subjects royal, political and martial events of various dates, from 937 to 1087, and *The Battle of Maldon* referring to an event of 991, these are among the latest Old English poems.[2] The great bulk of Old English verse is contained in a small number of major codices, the Junius Manuscript, the Vercelli Book, the Exeter Book, and the *Beowulf* Manuscript. The earliest short poems are usually thought earlier than any of the long poems, and most of the late datable poems are assigned to a date later than the dates usually assigned to most of the rest of Old English verse. As a result of our inability to date most of the verse we cannot always, when we suspect indebtedness of one poem to another, establish the direction of the debt, whether it is, say, from a secular poem to a religious poem, or whether, as is now thought a more likely relative chronology, some or much of the religious poetry we have from Anglo-Saxon times is earlier than some or much of the secular poetry.

This lack of scholarly consensus is not the result of academic factiousness. Of course, where the material itself allows of a wide range of opinion, no opinion demonstrably true and most opinions variously controvertible, scholars soon group themselves in accordance with opinion held or rejected. On the dating of

---

[1] Cf. pp. 49-51 and notes 36 and 37.

[2] For *A Proverb from Winfrid's Time*, *Cædmon's Hymn*, and *Bede's Death Song*, cf. E. G. Stanley, 'The Oldest English Poetry Now Extant', *Poetica*, 2 (Tokyo, 1974), 1-24 [reprinted in *A Collection of Papers* (1987; see I[45]), 115-38]. For these three, as well as for the other datable poems (including those in *The Anglo-Saxon Chronicle* and *The Battle of Maldon*), see also ASPR, VI. For facsimiles see F. C. Robinson and E. G. Stanley (eds), EEMF, XXIII (1991).

the manuscripts in which the poetry has come down to us there is certainty at least to within a scribe's life-span of, say, fifty years; and there is therefore a great measure of agreement, with Neil Ker's *Catalogue* the acknowledged authority.[3] From the *Catalogue* it emerges that writing of the four major codices falls within a relatively short period, in the fifty years around AD 1000. The Paris Psalter and the part of Corpus Christi College Cambridge MS 201 containing the verse are a little later, in the middle of the eleventh century. The badly damaged Cotton MS Otho A.vi, containing the Alfredian *Metres of Boethius*, is a little earlier, namely, the middle of the tenth century; the composition of the *Boethius* itself, in prose and verse, must go back to Alfred's reign, 871 to 899. For the other verse the distance in time between the date of composition of a poem and the date of the manuscript in which it is preserved is uncertain.

The distribution in time of manuscripts containing Anglo-Saxon is such that the distribution in time of the poetic manuscripts need not surprise us. In fact, of only 29 major manuscripts listed by Ker (p. xv) as 'written in the late tenth century and earlier' two are great poetic manuscripts, the Vercelli Book and the Exeter Book. Among major manuscripts listed by him (pp. xv-xviii) as 'written about 1000 and in the eleventh century', a total of over 130, we find the other manuscripts with substantial poetic pieces. That leaves only about another 30 to 35 major manuscripts, and there is very little verse in any of them, except for the datable short poems of the Peterborough Chronicle.

It is, therefore, not possible to infer on statistical grounds that the copying of Old English verse belongs to a peculiarly limited period of Anglo-Saxon book production. It is also not possible to infer from any evidence we have that the distance in time between the putative date of composition of a piece of verse and the date of the manuscript in which it has come down to us is greater than, on the whole, would be likely for prose. We are, however, so ignorant of the date of composition of very much Old English verse and of much Old English prose that even that negative statement is difficult to base on evidence, and it is best not to generalize pseudo-historically along such lines as may suggest themselves; namely, that much of the verse, perhaps including *Beowulf*, belongs to a period considerably earlier than that of most of the prose, or that the verse was first written down long after it was composed, longer than would in general be true of prose.

Being able to assign approximate dates to the poetic manuscripts is of little help towards arranging their verse contents in a chronological order of all extant Old English verse. If we had the knowledge to arrange Old English verse chronologically we should be better able to trace its course.

---

[3] N. R. Ker, *Catalogue of Manuscripts Containing Anglo-Saxon* (Oxford, 1957; reprinted with a supplement, 1990).

Good and bad Old English verse

The historical study of literature is, of course, not the only way, and we may, to use the well-worn phrase (ultimately St Jerome's), make a virtue of necessity, or better (borrowing pseudo-Quintilian's phrase on which Jerome probably modelled his)[4] we may find solace in our very need, by claiming that in the absence of historico-literary evidence we have nothing to distract us from a purer form of literary criticism, that based on the works themselves untrammelled by complications of literary history.

However, I have no faith in scholarly ignorance as grounds for critical comfort. We must remember that our lack of chronology for Old English verse may lay us open to quite fundamental errors of understanding which would seem to us intolerable for more familiar, later periods of English poetry with an established chronology of composition. For example, Wordsworth's sonnets cannot be divorced from the traditions of the sonnet form in English verse. Even if total grasp of the form in English from Wyatt's time to Wordsworth's may not be prerequisite to understand 'London, 1802' ('Milton, thou shouldst be living at this hour'), some knowledge of literary history is presupposed in Wordsworth's wording. For an understanding of Wordsworth's art in blank verse some knowledge of earlier blank verse, especially Milton's, is desirable, necessary even. Comparison and contrast give a special kind of pleasure to literary scholarship, involving the delight of recognizing the familiar recalled by the poet as well as the delight of surprise at the new the poet has created. It is a literary pleasure informed by a sense of the historical development of English verse.

Since for Old English verse we lack that sense of historical development, this book is different from an academic book (and I use 'academic' as a meliorative) such as one might wish to write or read for later periods of English verse. Throughout, I emphasize uncertainty of knowledge, both historical and linguistic.[5] Especially, I emphasize our difficulty when trying to develop a direct feel for Old English alliterative metre sufficient for us to sense prosodic subtleties that might distinguish late verse from early verse. I believe that we have that

---

4 See Jerome, *In Rufinum*, 3 n. 2: *Apologia adversus Rufinum*, in J. P. Migne (ed.), Patrologia Latina, XXIII (1845), col. 458, B, 'Quinpotius habeo gratiam, quod facis de necessitate virtutem'; cf. P. Lardet (ed.), Saint Jérôme, *Apologie contre Rufin*, Sources Chrétiennes, 303 (1983), 216-17, 'Quin potius habebo gratiam quod facis de necessitate uirtutem' [Je te saurais bien plutôt gré de ce que tu fais de nécessité vertu]. And see pseudo-Quintilian, *Declamationes*, 4, 10: G. Lehnert (ed.), M. Fabius Quintilianus, *Declamationes XIX maiores* (Lepzig: Teubner, 1905), 77 (IV. 10), 'faciamus, potius de fine remedium, de necessitate solacium.'

5 The impossibility of using what we know of the historical development of the Old English language for dating verse is demonstrated by Ashley Crandell Amos, *Linguistic Means of Determining the Dates of Old English Literary Texts*, Medieval Academy Books, 90 (Cambridge Massachusetts, 1980). On the difficulty of localizing Old English texts, see IV[86], below.

direct feel for verse from, say, *The Owl and the Nightingale* onwards, or, at least, from Chaucer's poetry onwards, poetry in which there is some regularity in the alternation of stressed and unstressed syllables. I parade unashamedly our ignorance of Old English shades of meaning in many cases; many subtle semantic shifts that must have come with time escape us wholly. Such historical and semantic information and metrical feeling are available to us increasingly for later periods, and are essential to us as academic readers of the verse of later periods, but are not available to us for Old English.

I do not mean to suggest that in tracing developments we should invest them with value-judgements. It is usually foolish to assert systematic and progressive improvement or deterioration in the peaks and troughs seen all along the line when individual poetic achievements are strung together into a chronological continuum; that is, to assert that as the tradition goes on its products become better and better, or worse and worse. For Middle English, better and better used often to be asserted, till the climax has been reached in Chaucer; and then worse and worse in the fifteenth century, though that facile view is no longer in favour now that the poetry of the century after Chaucer has been studied more carefully. For Old English, without genuine chronological information, it used often to be asserted, and the view still lingers, that earliest means best, and then worse and worse in quality: decline in poetic conception accompanied by decline in metrical accuracy. I think that such assertions are not merely worthless for Old English, but based on literary taste, that is, on nothing other than the asserter's preoccupations and predilections unencumbered by factual information about dates of composition and the known facts of prosody.

Though it is unwarranted to see the individual achievements of Old English poets in terms of peaks and troughs in a clear line of mapped-out historical development, it is possible and desirable to discern individual poetic achievements, to tell the good from the bad. To do so is one aim of this book, in the foreground, *Beowulf* as the measure of excellence in Old English poetry. It is necessarily an idiosyncratic book: one reader's reading of Old English verse, against a background of the poetry of later ages, read idiosyncratically and recalled haphazardly.

Anglo-Saxonists, as they pass judgement on the poems that form a valuable part of the literary stock-in-trade of their profession, may not always acknowledge frankly enough that, of the Old English verse now extant, a small proportion only is truly good even in their own, favourably predisposed opinion, and that, if they were more honest, they would have to admit that a somewhat larger proportion is rather indifferent literary art, if not downright bad. As I have said, by general consent *Beowulf*, the longest single poem extant, is good, but the metrical psalms of the Paris Psalter, a versified sequence considerably greater in total length than *Beowulf*, is very pedestrian versifying. Between these extremes far too much is praised, not in terms of academic interest – an academic can usually say something of interest (at least to professional colleagues) about writings that have failed to gain the doubtful accolade of 'critical acclaim', – but in terms of poetic excellence perceived as for later poetry; that is, in terms falsely assumed to be universally valid and, therefore, not needing analysis when applied to this distant material. Once, when I made this point, less forcefully, in fact, but on a public occasion, a fellow-Anglo-Saxonist rushed up to me to say that I was doing a great disservice to Anglo-Saxon studies by revealing that some of the writings extant were of poor quality, that that would make our enemies wish even more keenly to shut down our activity; nor was he pacified when I said that I should agree with that wish if we could not or would not, to the best of our ability, discriminate between good and bad in Old English literature.

The historical imagination

Sometimes, though probably less frequently in the last twenty-five years than earlier this century, 'the historical imagination' has been invoked to help us towards a discriminating reading of this ancient literature; as if, for example, one could read *Beowulf* with the eyes of a contemporary of the poet, a contemporary perhaps of Bede or Alcuin or Alfred.[6] For such a distant period of literature, reliance on the historical imagination may be even more of a self-delusion than for later periods. How far it works for them, for example, for the later Middle Ages or the Renaissance, may be left to the defence or attack of those of our colleagues who make the study of these later periods of literature their concern; and most of them would not wish to rely on such an historical imagination.

Leaving aside the special problem that, at least for the last four hundred years, every generation seems to have undervalued works regarded by them as having been overvalued by their parents and grandparent, the historical imagination probably works best as an evaluative agent the shorter the distance in time between the reader and the work read. In short, the historical imagination works best the less historical it is. I suspect that we cannot validly use the historical imagination to evaluate Old English literature: but the word 'validly' begs the question. Where are the absolutes when literary judgement is of a kind that only satisfies the judge? I do not know how to establish 'validity' of evaluation for Old English verse other than in terms of impressions formed unhistorically and subjectively, but with some knowledge of modes of expression in Old English and some awareness of our limitations as modern readers of this ancient material.

A modern reader has to be aware of his or her preoccupations and predilections. The kind of person who turns to Old English verse rather than to that of the last two hundred years is perhaps a reader inclined to think that old is beautiful, and so inclined also to think the oldest poetry is best. To a modernist,

6 Cf. p. 58.

all Old English is so old that it makes no difference if some of it is late Old English and some is early Old English. The Anglo-Saxonist similarly, though in the opposite direction, may let a predilection for the old guide any attempt at dating Old English verse of unknown date of composition: the better is thought the earlier, what seems the best may be dated the earliest.

Sometimes an Anglo-Saxonist so predisposed may get some relative chronology right for the wrong reason; but even then it must be remembered that 'right' for the relative chronology of Old English verse is usually undemonstrable, and may mean little more than conformable to what is generally held to be true by Anglo-Saxonists on the evidence available, cumulative evidence usually.

Complexity of transmission

Most scholars would agree that the excellent *Beowulf* is earlier than the pedestrian versified psalms of the Paris Psalter. They might seek to justify that opinion, but hardly by merely expressing their liking for the subject matter of *Beowulf* and the lack, in the psalms, of novelty for them. Perhaps they would justify it after considerations of metre, vocabulary and style. But more probably they would base their opinion on many signs of a complicated textual transmission as appears from the only text preserved in a manuscript of the late tenth or early eleventh century; whereas the text of the versified psalms seems, in spite of errors and corruptions, to have undergone a less complicated transmission till it was written down in a splendid manuscript of about the middle of the eleventh century, less splendid now than when it still had its 'ten or twelve sumptuous illustrations in colour', and was thought worthy of acquisition by so discriminating a collector as Jean Duc de Berry, and recorded as his in 1402.[7] The contrast in the appearance of the two manuscripts, the rather scruffy *Beowulf* manuscript (even before the damage it sustained in the fire of 1731 and the subsequent rebindings) and the much more elegant Paris Psalter, could correspond to the contrast in scribal care. If, as seems likely, the *Beowulf* manuscript of unknown provenance is the work of two scribes working in a less distinguished scriptorium than that (also unidentified) which produced the Paris Psalter, it could be argued that the difference in scribal care resulting in a difference in textual correctness need not be the result of *Beowulf* having passed through a longer succession of scribes than the versified psalms, but that it was copied by less careful scribes.

That, however, is not supported by the evidence of the other texts in the manuscript. The scribe who wrote the beginning of *Beowulf* ending in line 1939 also wrote three prose texts in which there is far less corruption, and the second

---

[7]   See J. Bromwich's account of the 'General History of the Manuscript', in the facsimile of the Paris Psalter, EEMF, VIII (1958), 11-12.

scribe who wrote *Beowulf* from the last word of line 1939 to the end also wrote *Judith*, and that too has far less textual corruption.[8] No doubt, the prose texts and *Judith* are easier syntax than *Beowulf*; but *Beowulf* also has many unusual linguistic features, including many words rare in Old English or unique to the poem. That is usually interpreted as a sign that it is an older text. Not everyone accepts that, and one lonely voice even dates the composition of the poem eleventh century.[9]

Bede's Death Song

On the other hand, if we did not know that the date of *Bede's Death Song* is early – we have it in early form and know the occasion when Bede uttered it, in 735 on his deathbed – and had to rely for dating on our subjective opinion of it, we might have been tempted to date it late: a Latinate period uncharacteristic of Old English poetry. An historian of Old English literature has stated such views and coupled them with what are probably expressions of dislike.[10] Reasons of dislike, and a feeling that Bede would have been too poorly on his deathbed to indulge in verse composition, or alternatively that the poem is too poor in quality for so great man as Bede at any time, have led some to think that Bede merely quoted the lines, which, therefore, would be even earlier in date of composition.[11] Another, even more absurd, reason that has been advanced 'for maintaining that Bede quoted the verses instead of composing them lies in the variety of these versions',[12] namely, the textual variants found in no fewer than thirty-five manuscripts in which it is recorded, both in non-West-Saxon (mainly Bede's own dialect, Northumbrian) in continental hands, the earliest of them being of the eleventh century, and West-Saxon in Insular hands none earlier than the middle of the twelfth century, and some by hands, both continental and Insular, as late as the sixteenth century.[13]

   Bede's Death Song may seem uncharacteristic of Old English poetry in sentence structure and perhaps in sentiment. The poem, *The Judgement Day II*, has a spring opening such as is common in Middle English poetry, but is uncharacteristic of the vernacular verse of the Anglo-Saxons. In fact, a late date

---

[8] See K. Sisam, 'The Beowulf Manuscript' and 'The Compilation of the Beowulf Manuscript', *Studies in the History of Old English Literature* (Oxford, 1953), 61-4 and 65-96. The prose texts were edited by S. Rypins, *Three Old English Prose Texts in MS. Cotton Vitellius A xv*, EETS, o.s. 161 (1924).

[9] See II[88].

[10] See A. Brandl, 'Die angelsächsische Literatur' (1908; see I[45]), 1032 [= 92]; cf. E. G. Stanley, 'The Oldest English Poetry' (1974; see III[2]), 131-2.

[11] See W. Bulst, 'Bedas Sterbelied', *ZfdA*, 75 (1938), 111-14.

[12] B. C. Williams (ed.), *Gnomic Poetry in Anglo-Saxon* (New York, 1914), 69. She thinks, however, that in sentiment *Bede's Death Song* is characteristic of Germanic thought: 'prudence and death, two favorite themes with Germanic folk, here come together.'

[13] See F. C. Robinson and E. G. Stanley, EEMF, XXIII (1991), pp. 19-20.

of composition is supported by such evidence as the language and versification of the poem, and probably also by the manuscript in which it is preserved.[14] The poem is a translation of Bede's Latin poem on the Day of Judgement, and that has the spring opening.[15] Is our knowledge of Old English literature really good enough to enable us to say that, if Bede himself – 'ut erat doctus in nostris carminibus' [for he was learned in our songs], says Cuthbert who witnessed his death[16] – or an Anglo-Saxon contemporary with him had made a translation of it into alliterative vernacular verse, such an early translation would not have kept the spring opening? We know too little for firm statements, such as the assertion that that would have been unlikely or impossible.

Transmission, oral and written, and manuscript pointing of verse

Unless they wrote it down in manuscript (or, rarely, incised verses in a short inscription)[17] we have no knowledge of anything the Anglo-Saxons may have composed by way of poetry. And we possess no manuscript that is thought to be in the hand of the poet.

It may be that some poets composed in their heads without at the same time holding a pen. That is likely to have been so in the case of King Alfred the Great, if he, as I believe, really was the author of the verse preface and epilogue to the translation of Gregory the Great's *Cura Pastoralis* and of the proem and metrical version of the Metres of Boethius; for in the early Middle Ages kings did not sully their hands with ink – scribes did that.[18] Before the Anglo-Saxons were taught literacy as part of the Christian missions to England emanating

---

[14] Corpus Christi College Cambridge 201A. The date of the manuscript, of the beginning of the eleventh century is not very late, but nothing in this part of the manuscript appears to be of a date earlier than the Benedictine Reform of the last quarter of the tenth century.

[15] There is also a prose version of part of the Old English translation; both versions are printed in parallel together with Bede's Latin poem by H. Löhe (ed.), *Be Dōmes Dæge*, BBzA, XXII (1907). Bede's 'De Die Iudicii' is edited in *Bedae Venerabilis Opera*, III-IV, Corpus Christianorum, ser. lat. CXXII, iii-iv (1955), 439-4. Cf. E. G. Stanley, 'The Oldest English Poetry' (1974; see III²), 133-5.

[16] See B. Colgrave and R. A. B. Mynors (eds), *Bede's Ecclesiastical History of the English People* (Oxford, 1969), 580, 'Epistola de obitu Bedae'; they translate the Latin, 'for he was familiar with English poetry'. Cf. E. V. K. Dobbie (ed.), *The Manuscripts of Cædmon's Hymn and Bede's Death Song With a Critical Text of the Epistola Cuthberti de obitu Bedæ*, Columbia University Studies in English and Comparative Literature, 128 (New York, 1937), 120 line 3, 121 line 2.

[17] The only Old English verse inscriptions known to us are those inscribed on the stone cross at Ruthwell and, probably related to it, on the silver of the the reliquary in the shape of a cross at Brussels, on the whalebone of the Franks Casket (in the British Museum and the Bargello in Florence), on a silver disc-brooch from Sutton, Isle of Ely (now in the British Museum), and a six-word posy on a gold finger-ring from Lancashire (now in the British Museum); as well as short commemorative inscriptions on six stone monuments. Cf. F. C. Robinson and E. G. Stanley, EEMF, XXIII (1991), nos 37-46.

[18] Cf. E. G. Stanley, 'King Alfred's Prefaces', *RES*, n.s. 39 (1988), 349-64.

from Ireland and Rome, that is, before the end of the sixth century, poets must have composed in their heads without at the same time writing down their poetry.

Speaking of the Germanic barbarians on the continent of his time, towards the end of the first century AD, nearly four centuries before the Germanic tribes had settled in England, Tacitus tells us that the peoples of Germania had song, and passed it on from singer to singer as if a form of oral history.[19] Obviously, it is in the nature of our evidence that we have no orally transmitted verse, and if we choose to believe that some of the verse that has come down to us in writing was composed orally and that it was first transmitted orally we go beyond what can be deduced from the material we have and, except for *A Proverb from Winfrid's Time* (perhaps), *Cædmon's Hymn*, and *Bede's Death Song*, contemporary statements about poetry we actually have.

If from recurrent poetic formulas in the extant verse it may seem that some of the mannerisms of oral poetry are to be found in our written material, we have no certain evidence that the mannerisms of oral composition do more than reflect by deliberate sophisticated art an oral stage of poetry. We have no evidence that the extant written verse in which such mannerisms occur does, in fact, itself go back to either preliterate Anglo-Saxon England (or even further back, to the preliterate Anglo-Saxon tribes still on the continent, that is, to a date before the middle of the fifth century). Moreover, we have no evidence that it goes back to oral composition by a singer within a literate, Christian England from the beginning of the seventh century onwards.

For an understanding of the poetic art of the Anglo-Saxons some attempt to analyse their poetic formulas is of value, and it sharpens the analysis if the concept 'poetic formula' is defined. To use that concept within a theory of oral-formulaic composition is too speculative for me when the theory is such that, using the written evidence we have, it can never be proved, and, equally, can never be refuted, though the prevalence of poetic formulas in verse translated from a Latin source should serve to make us wary.[20]

Scholars differ in their definitions of the concept 'poetic formula', but most are agreed that such a formula must be bounded by the limits of the half-line; and that metrical concept is not a modern invention (though the term is modern),[21] but has its origin in the punctuation of some of the manuscripts in which

---

19 See M. Winterbottom (ed.), in M. Winterbottom and R. M. Ogilvie (eds), *Cornelii Taciti opera minora* (Oxford, 1975), De origine et situ Germanorum, (p. 38) 2, 2: 'Celebrant carminibus antiquis, quod unum apud illos memoriae et annalium genus est, Tuistonem deum' [They celebrate in ancient songs, which is with them the only kind of recorded annals, a god Tuisto].

20 Cf. L. D. Benson, 'Literary Character' (1966; see II[19]).

21 Cf. R. W. Burchfield, 'The prosodic terminology of Anglo-Saxon scholars', in R. B. Burlin and E. B. Irving, Jr (eds), *Studies in Honour of J. C. Pope* (1974; see II[28]), 183. Cf. German *Halbvers* or *Halbzeile* and *Langzeile*, the terms used by K. Lachmann in 'Über althochdeutsche Betonung und Verskunst', the first part of which (read 21 April 1831) was published in

Old English verse has come down to us. The appearance of a manuscript page of verse is very much like the appearance of a manuscript page of prose as far as the use made of space is concerned. The Anglo-Saxons did not write out the verse in lines as now printed.[22] They wrote verse continuously, as we write prose. Division into half-lines conforms with the metrical pointing of some of the poetic manuscripts, marking off with some consistency the metrical units we call half-lines. The best-known example is the Junius Manuscript, but also, for example, the verse texts in and following the version of *The Anglo-Saxon Chronicle* contained in Cotton MS Tiberius B.i of the middle of the eleventh century.[23]

Modern scholars, from Christopher Rawlinson and George Hickes around 1700 onwards,[24] learnt what constituted a metrical unit in Anglo-Saxon verse

Abhandlungen aus dem Jahre 1832, Akademie der Wissenschaften zu Berlin, Historisch-philologische Klasse (1834), and reprinted in K. Müllenhoff (ed.), *Kleinere Schriften zur deutschen Philologie*, K. Lachmann, Kleinere Schriften, I (Berlin, 1876), 358-406, at 361 [= Abhandlungen, p. 238 (p. 4 of the separate)], with reference to Otfrid whose metre is not the Germanic alliterative line, but rhyming verse, see J. K. Bostock, *A Handbook of Old High German Literature* (2nd edn rev. by K. C. King and D. R. McLintock; Oxford, 1976), 322-6. Lachmann used the terms *Halbvers* or *Halbzeile* in contradistinction to *Langzeile*, the 'long line' consisting of two half-lines, in Otfrid bound by rhyme, in alliterative verse bound by alliteration. He had earlier used *Halbvers* and *Halbzeile* in his encyclopædia article 'Alliteration' in S. Ersch and S. G. Gruber, *Allgemeine Encyclopädie der Wissenschaften und Künste*, III (Leipzig, 1819), 166-7 [reprinted in *Kleinere Schriften* (1876; see above), 137-9]. The term *lange Zeile* 'long line' goes back to Jacob and Wilhelm Grimm's edition of *Hildebrandslied*, together with the general idea that Germanic poetry, including Old English poetry with a specimen of thirteen lines from *Judith*, should be edited in long lines: the Brothers Grimm (eds), *Hildebrand und Hadubrand und Weißenbrunner Gebet* (1812; see I[20]), 37.

22 An exception is *The Leiden Riddle*, which is written in long lines of verse by a continental scribe of the ninth or tenth century. It is a translation of a Latin riddle by Aldhelm, with two lines of Old English used to render one of Latin. Cf. M. B. Parkes, 'The manuscripts of the Leiden Riddle', *ASE*, 1 (1972), 207-17; N. R. Ker, *Catalogue* (1957; see III[3]), appendix no. 19.

23 For facsimiles, see F. C. Robinson and E. G. Stanley, EEMF, XXIII (1991), nos 14.1.4, 14.2.4, 14.3.4, 14.5.1, 14.6.1 (*Chronicle* poems); 16 (*The Menologium*); 17 (*Maxims II*). It is perhaps of some interest that Franciscus Junius, the first editor of the poems in Bodleian MS Junius 11, *Cædmonis Monachi Paraphrasis Poetica Genesios ac præcipuarum Sacræ Paginæ Historiarum . . .* (Amsterdam, 1655), not only retained the manuscipt pointing, but, on the evidence of his transcript of *The Menologium* and *Maxims II* in Bodleian MS Junius 67, seems to have had an interest in such pointing.

24 G. Hickes, *Thesaurus* (1703-1705, see I[10]), I, 177-221, 'De Poetica Anglo-Saxonum'; verse pieces are set out in half-lines, each ending with a point whether or not the manuscript from which it is taken is pointed as regularly. Often he follows earlier scholars; for example, Franciscus Junius, in his transcript of *The Metres of Boethius* [in Bodleian MS Junius 12; see the facsimile in F. C. Robinson and E. G. Stanley, EEMF, XXIII (1991), no. 5.21], pointed more regularly than in the manuscript, and Junius's pointing led the first editor to print the verse in half-lines each ending with a point, C. Rawlinson (ed.), *An. Manl. Sever. Boethii Consolationis Philosophiæ libri v. Anglo-Saxonice redditi ab Alfredo . . .* (Oxford, 1698). Rawlinson's arrangement in printed verse lines is exceptional; usually the early editions (and transcripts) wrote the verse continuously like prose, copying the manuscript pointing. Hickes, pp. 203-9, in editing *The Menologium* and *Maxims II*, setting it out in half-lines each ending

from that punctuation, and Hickes's discussion of the characteristics of Old English poetry is of historical interest still. Two further sources for the same information about metrical units, long lines the half-lines of which rhymed with each other and macaronic verse with a half-line in Old English followed by a half-line in Latin, were used by J. J. and W. D. Conybeare a little over a century later.[25]

The manuscripts use 'metrical' pointing also for some rhythmical prose; for example, the rhythmical parts of the second prose homily in the Vercelli Book are provided with such pointing, in contrast with the non-rhythmical parts of the same homily in the same manuscript, which are much more lightly pointed.[26] The Anglo-Saxons themselves must therefore have attached importance to the distinction, thus made apparent, between rhythmical and non-rhythmical discourse.

There are, however, many manuscripts both of Old English verse and prose in which the punctuation, guiding the reading neither in syntax nor in rhythm, but having marks of punctuation introduced unsystematically. *Beowulf* is punctuated in that way.[27] Metrical half-lines or long lines are not easily counted in poetic manuscripts, especially when the pointing is unsystematic. It seems absurd, therefore, to attempt numerological exegesis on them, as is done from time to time by those inclined that way, sometimes with reference to the golden section, sometimes to triangulation, and, where numbers are derived from the texts themselves, adjustments are entertained so that the textual reality may be helped towards the numerological ideal.[28]

with a point, more or less as in the manuscript where, of course, the poems are written like regularly punctuated prose, and were transcribed thus by Junius (see III[23]).

25 J. J. Conybeare, 'Observations on the Metre of Anglo-Saxon Poetry' and 'Further Observations . . .', *Archæologia*, xvii (1814), 257-66 and 267-74; reprinted in W. D. Conybeare (ed.), *Illustrations* (1826; see I[21]), pp. v-xv, xxvii-xxxv. William Daniel Conybeare added an edition of *The Riming Poem* and one further example of 'other instances of rime, not indeed used through an entire poem . . ., but occasionally introduced', pp. xvi-xxvi.

26 See E. G. Stanley, '*The Judgement of the Damned*, from Corpus Christi College Cambridge 201 and Other Manuscripts, and the Definition of Old English Verse' [first published in 1985, with subeditorial interference], reprinted in more acceptable form in *A Collection of Papers* (1987; see I[45]), 352-83, especially pp. 358-9.

27 Cf. E. G. Stanley, '*Beowulf*' (1966; see II[65]), reprinted in *A Collection of Papers*, pp. 150-2 [= 117-19], and 'Notes on Old English Poetry, iv, A long unit of Old English Verse and modern editorial punctuation: *Beowulf*, lines 864-917a', *LSE*, n.s. XX (1989), G. Barnes, S. Jensen, L. Jobling, and D. Lawton (eds), *Studies in Honour of H. L. Rogers*, 330-4.

     K. O'Brien O'Keeffe, *Visible Song: Transitional Literacy in Old English Verse*, Cambridge Studies in Anglo-Saxon England, 4 (Cambridge, 1990), strives to find reason in the punctuation and lineation of the Vercelli Book and Exeter Book (but not of the *Beowulf* Manuscript), but the conclusions based on her elaborate and careful study of the evidence are unconvincing.

28 See, for example, D. R. Howlett, 'Form and Genre in *Widsith*', *ESts*, 55 (1974), 505-11, 'The Structures of *The Wanderer* and *The Seafarer*', *StNeophil*, 47 (1975), 313-17, and other articles by the same. Similarly R. D. Stevick, 'Geometrical Design of the Old English *Andreas*', *Poetica*, 9 (Tokyo, 1978), 73-106; 'Mathematical Proportions and Symbolism in

The language of Old English verse

The Anglo-Saxons wrote their vernacular in a script, Insular script, derived from Irish practice (and in appearance similar to the lettering generally familiar now from its use on Irish coins and postage stamps); whereas for writing Latin the Anglo-Saxons, after about the middle of the tenth century, used a script, Caroline script, derived from continental practice.[29] In the macaronic poems, in which half-lines of Latin alternated with half-lines of English, the reader is able to separate the rhythmical half-line units because each unit is visually perceptible through the differing form of script used for the two languages.

The chief and most palpable obstacle to any evaluation of Old English verse is the linguistic change over the centuries that lie between the Anglo-Saxons and ourselves. It led step by step to increasing differences between their language and ours. When we read Chaucer, who comes about halfway between the earliest Old English now extant and ourselves, we are helped by our current, archaic spelling system which fits the language, roughly, of the century or two after the death of Chaucer (in 1400). Old English is so distant from Chaucer's language that the archaic nature of our orthography is of no real help.

Much of their poetry, chiefly because their language is so different from ours, is difficult enough to require translation by us word for word, construction by construction, if we are to understand it exactly. The alternative pedagogic method by which an attempt is made to familiarize oneself sufficiently with Old English to lead to the eventual understanding of Old English texts without the medium of translation works quite well for easy Old English verse or prose, but not for difficult texts, like *Beowulf*, or for difficulties in easier Old English texts; the divergent interpretations of difficult passages by different but equally experienced scholars shows that. The result of an act of translation, essential for difficult Old English, is that the reader's translated version into his or her own modern language, even when made for the reader and not necessarily in writing, becomes at the same time the reader's text and the reader's understanding of that text.

A modern reader has little direct sense of the sounds of Old English poetry, even after mastering the rules of scansion derived, without achieving a consensus, by modern scholars[30] from the practice of the poets without the aid of any contemporary treatise on vernacular versification (such as we have for Old

---

The Phoenix', *Viator*, 11 (1980), 95-121; and 'Two Notes on *Christ II*', in *LSE*, n.s. XX (1989; see III[27]), 293-309.

[29] See B. Bischoff (translated by D. Ó Cróinín and D. Ganz), *Latin Palaeography – Antiquity and the Middle Ages* (Cambridge, 1990), 83-92 and 112-18; cf. N. R. Ker, *Catalogue* (1957; III[3]), pp. xxv-xxvi.

[30] See ch. iv, especially pp. 120-1, below.

Icelandic in Snorri Sturluson's *Skaldskaparmal*).[31] Only a very small number of Anglo-Saxonists have ever been able to claim honestly that they feel the rhythms of Old English verse as many modern scholarly readers feel the rhythms of, for example, Chaucer's poetry or even the alliterative verse of *Sir Gawain and the Green Knight* or *Piers Plowman* in the fourteeenth century.

A modern reader never feels truly at home in the rhythm of Old English poetry, nor in the sounds of that language. Having mastered the chapter on pronunciation to be found in any Old English grammar, the modern reader, starting from the sounds of twentieth-century English, will never cease to regard much of what is to be learnt about Old English pronunciation as something un-English: so guttural, the long vowels undiphthongized, and almost all their diphthongs quite unlike any in Modern English. Having mastered later chapters in the grammar giving inflexions followed by an Old English syntax, perhaps supplemented by articles,[32] the reader will be made aware, perhaps painfully aware at first, that Old English is more highly inflected than Modern English, and that its structure is fundamentally un-English. The average length of Old English words are at a glance found to be longer than those of Modern English almost all the unstressed syllables of which (including inflexional endings) have been reduced to silence, and the prefix *ge-*, very common in Old English, has disappeared. As a result there are in Modern English many more monosyllabic lexical words, that is words bearing meaning, than there were monosyllabic lexical words in Old English. Lexical words in Old English bear stress (or were stressable) usually on the stem syllable, that syllable very often followed by an unstressed ending and not infrequently preceded by a prefix (usually unstressed, especially when the word is a verb).

Word-order, sentence structure and editorial punctuation

For an understanding of the poetic art of Old English verse, as exemplified well in *Beowulf*, prosody must be considered; but phonology and syntax is less central to such an understanding, and in the present section my concern is chiefly, and then only very briefly, with word-order and sentence structure.

A reader of Old English poetry has to learn this important fact about Old

---

31 A convenient translation is available in A. Faulkes, *Snorri Sturluson Edda*, Everyman Classic, 449 (London and Melbourne, 1987), 59-164.

32 The standard Old English grammars are: A. Campbell, *Old English Grammar* (Oxford, 1959; and later, corrected editions, that in paperback first in 1983), and K. Brunner, *Altenglische Grammatik nach der angelsächsischen Grammatik von Eduard Sievers* (3rd edn, Tübingen, 1965); the standard Old English syntax is B. Mitchell, *Old English Syntax* (Oxford, 1985), whose chapter ix deals with 'Element Order', and his chapter x with 'Some Problems Related to Poetry'. A good, brief introduction to Old English word-order and sentence structure is that by B. Mitchell, in B. Mitchell and F. C. Robinson, *A Guide to Old English* (4th edn, Oxford, 1986), part 1, V, i and ii (pp. 63-70, §§ 143-53).

English word-order, that there were marked differences between the usual word-order of late Old English prose and the freer word-order of Old English verse, as a result of which it is likely that an Anglo-Saxon would have felt the distinction between the two forms of discourse not merely to have been that verse is in short metrical units whereas prose is not (unless it is rhythmical prose), but also that most Old English verse manifests a greater degree of complexity in its word-order and sentence structure than most prose.

What is involved is easily exemplified by a piece of straightforward prose, the annal for the year 999 from the Abingdon Chronicle, British Library, Cotton MS Tiberius B.i.[33] In printing the annal I leave unlabelled elements of the clauses that have no role in establishing the order of subject, verb, object; the elements within each clause have been labelled by the following abbreviations:

S	= subject	I	= adverbial introduction
V	= finite verb	Cc	= coordinating conjunction
O	= object	Cs	= subordinating conjunction (incl. *þæt*)
inf	= infinitive	R	= relative pronoun

I V S , Cc V
Her com se here eft abutan in to Temese, & wendon þa up andlang Medwægan
In this year the army came back round into the Thames, and turned then up
along the Medway

, Cc V S , Cc S
& to Hrofeceastre, & com þa seo Centisce fyrd þar ongean, & hi ða þær fæste
and to Rochester, and the Kentish fyrd then came opposite there, and they then
stoutly

V . Cs S V ! Cc S V
togædere fengon. Ac wala þæt hi to raðe bugon & flugon! & þa Deniscan ahton
gave battle there. But alas that they too soon turned and fled! And the Danes
held

O , Cc V O , Cc V Cs S V ,
wælstowe geweald, & namon þa hors, & ridan swa hwider swa hi sylf woldon,
the field, *and they took horses then, and rode wheresoever they*
themselves wished,

---

[33] For the text, cf. M. Ashdown (ed.), *English and Norse Documents Relating to the Reign of Ethelred the Unready* (Cambridge, 1930), 44. Following D. Whitelock, in D. Whitelock (and others), *The Anglo-Saxon Chronicle A Revised Translation* (London, 1961), 84, I emend *ylcodon þa deman* of the manuscript to *þa ylcode man*. It has not proved possible to align the translation exactly; if that had been done the translation, over-literal as it is, would have had to depart even further from normal Modern English.

Cc   O   V   . I V   S
& forneah ealle Westkentingas fordydon & forheregodon. Ða rædde se cyning
and almost all West Kent they destroyed and ravaged. Then the king decided

                Cs S   V
wið his witan þæt man sceolde mid scypfyrde & eac mide landfyrde hym ongean
with his councillors decided that one ought to advance against them with both a
                                                        naval force and a land

    inf .   Cs   S   V   I V   S   , Cc
faran. Ac þa ða scipu gearwe wæron þa ylcode man[?] fram dæge to dæge, &
force. But when the ships were ready, then one delayed from day to day, and

    V   O   R   V , I Cs S   inf
swencte þæt earme folc þæt on ðam scipon læg, & a swa hit forðwerdre beon
oppressed the poor people who were on the ships, and ever as it ought to have
                                                                        been

    V   I V   S   , Cc I S V
sceolde swa wæs hit lætre fram anre tide to oþre,   & a hi leton
specially urgent so it was the more delayed from one hour to the next, and
                                                        always they let

                O   inf , Cc I S V   , Cc S V
heora feonda werod wexan,   & a man rymde fram þære sæ, & hi foron
their enemies' force increase, and always there was retreat away from the sea,
                                                        and they [the Danes] were

                .   I   V   S   O ,
æfre forð æfter. & þonne æt þam ende ne beheold hit nan þing, seo scypfyrding
always in pursuit. And then in the end it effected nothing, neither the naval force

ne seo landfyrding, buton folces geswinc & feos spylling & heora feonda
nor the land-force, except the distress of the nation and the waste of money and
                                                        the encouragement

forðbylding.
of their enemies.

The following points are the more important in determining word-order:

1. After an adverbial introduction the order is usually VS (but not after *a*
   'ever'.

2. After a subordinating conjunction the word-order is SV.
3. After a coordinating conjunction the usual main clause order is SV, but VS is found: *& com . . . seo . . . fyrd.*
4. The object usually follows the verb, or in VS order the subject; but the object can precede: *ealle Westkentingas fordydon & forheregodon.*
5. The infinitive usually goes to the end of the clause, but note *beon sceolde.*

The basic rule that a main clause introduced by an adverb or an adverbial phrase has VS order and that a subordinate clause has SV order is rarely broken. That rule leads very commonly to clauses constructed according to the following pattern (in the emended sentence): *Ac þa ða scipu gearwe wæron þa ylcode man.*[34]

Reasons for exceptional word-order readily suggest themselves: special emphasis, the need for clarity, the demands made by elaborate verbal complexities, long subject phrases or object phrases, the need to accommodate an elaborate adverbial element, and so forth. No matter how we explain each example, introducing our explanation with a modest 'presumably' or the like, it clearly emerges that, though Old English prose usually adheres to certain 'rules' of word-order, these 'rules' are not rigorously observed.

The word-order of verse is freer than that of prose, but on the whole follows the same 'rules'; 'greater freedom' is merely another way of expressing 'more violations of grammarians' rules'. Again, reasons for that greater freedom readily suggest themselves. They may be presumed to have been the result partly of the greater openness of verse to unusual effects of expressiveness; and partly the result of the exigencies of prosody, especially an observed tendency in verse, sometimes elevated to a 'law', Kuhn's Law of sentence particles (the first of Kuhn's two laws),[35] that unaccented words (other than clitics) must come either before the first stress or between the first and second stress of their clause.

---

[34] It may seem preferable to quote a sentence that has not been subjected to emendation in illustration of adverb followed by VS order in a main clause and conjunction followed by SV order in a subordinate clause. For example, from Alfred's preface to the *The Pastoral Care,* Bodleian MS Hatton 20 [see the facsimile, N. R. Ker (ed.), EEMF, VI (Copenhagen, 1956), fol. 1ᵛ, retaining the punctuation of the manuscript, but not its word-division]: *Ða ic ða ðis eall gemunde . ða gemunde ic eac hu ic geseah ær ðæm hit eall forhergod wære . & forbærned . hu ða ciricean giond eall Angelcynn stodon maðma & boca gefylde ?* [When I remembered all this, then I remembered also how I saw before it was all ravaged and destroyed by fire, how the churches throughout all England stood filled with treasures and books].

[35] See H. Kuhn, 'Zur Wortstellung und -betonung im Altgermanischen', *Beiträge,* 57 (1933), 1-109; reprinted in H. Kuhn, *Kleine Schriften,* I (Berlin, 1969), 18-103. A useful account of the major differences between prose and verse word-order is that by A. Campbell, 'Verse Influences in Old English Prose', in J. L. Rosier (ed.), *Philological Essays . . . in Honour of Herbert Dean Meritt* (The Hague and Paris, 1970), 93-8; see also the sections referred to in the index of B. Mitchell's *Syntax* (1985; see III³²), under 'poetry, OE: syntax, differences from prose'; and especially §§ 3944-7, § 3947 of interest in connection with Kuhn's Laws; on which see further: A. J. Bliss 'Auxiliary and verbal in *Beowulf*', *ASE,* 9 (1981), 157-82; K. Grinda, 'Pigeonholing Old English Poetry: Some Criteria of Metrical Style', *Anglia,* 102

In both prose and verse, therefore, word-order usually guides the reader, and originally also the listener if the reading was aloud to an audience, to distinguish between *þa* used as an the adverb ('then') and *þa* used as a conjunction ('when'), *þonne* used as an the adverb ('then') and *þonne* used as a conjunction ('when, whenever'), *swa* used as an the adverb ('so') and *swa* used as a conjunction ('as'). For when any such word, which can function as either adverb or subordinating conjunction, stands at the beginning of the clause, the adverb is followed by VS order, the conjunction by SV order.

But we must never allow our faith in grammar-rules to undermine our understanding of the obvious sense, especially when reading verse the word-order of which is freer than that of prose.[36] Thus in *Cædmon's Hymn* (lines 5-9) adverbial *tha* 'then' is used (in conjunction with the adverbs *aerist* 'first' and *æfter* 'thereafter, afterwards') with SV order:[37]

> He aerist scop   aelda barnū
> heben til hrofe,   haleg scepen;
> tha middungeard   moncynnæs uard,
> eci dryctin,   æfter tiadæ
> firum foldu,   frea allmectig.

[He first created for the children of mankind heaven as a roof, holy Creator; then the Guardian of mankind, the eternal Lord, thereafter established the world, the earth for humans, Lord almighty.]

The sequence *aerist . . . tha . . . æfter* reflects the first chapter of Genesis. It begins with the whole divine programme of creation, expressed in the opening words, 'In the beginning God created heauen and earth'. It goes on (vv. 7 and 8) to assign the creation of the firmament and God's naming of it, 'Heaven', to the second day. The disposition of 'the drie land' and God's naming of it, 'Earth', is assigned (vv. 9-10) to the third day. Here *tha* cannot be the conjunction meaning 'when'; it must be the adverb meaning 'then, thereupon'. The construction is made more complicated through the placing the object *middungeard* immediately after *tha*, and because the verb *tiadæ* is preceded and followed by the

---

(1984), 305-22; P. J. Lucas, 'On some Breaches of Kuhn's Law of Particles and *Genesis A* 2745', *PQ*, 64 (1985), 386-91; D. Donoghue, 'Word order and poetic style: auxiliary and verbal in *The Metres of Boethius*', *ASE*, 15 (1986), 167-96, and especially D. Donoghue, *Style in Old English Poetry The Test of the Auxiliary*, YSE, 196 (1987).

36 Excessive faith in grammar-rules mars the two books by S. O. Andrew, *Syntax and Style in Old English* (Cambridge, 1940; reprinted, New York, 1966), and *Postscript on* Beowulf (Cambridge, 1948; reprinted, New York, 1969). The books remain useful, provided allowance is made for a greater degree of freedom in the word-order of Old English texts, especially of verse texts, than Andrew thinks proper.

37 I quote the Northumbrian version added towards the end of the first half of the eighth century to the Moore MS, Cambridge University Library Kk.v.16; see E. V. K. Dobbie, *Cædmon's Hymn and Bede's Death Song* (1937; see III[16]), 13.

subject in variation, *moncynnæs uard, eci dryctin, . . . frea allmectig* so that the order of elements after *tha* is the exceptional OSSVS.

Such theological certainty, however, is rare; and in Old English verse it is often best to acknowledge that ambiguity of syntax is widely prevalent, especially in verse, with VS order when the finite verb is a function word (such as *is, wæs, mæg, sceal*) and the subject is a lexical word (that is, not a personal pronoun), and when the position in the clause of an object expressed by a lexical word may add further complexity. In many cases word-order is no sure guide; and it has rightly been argued that where both adverb and conjunction make sense, there was no problem for the Anglo-Saxons: the choice is our problem as we translate into our modern language from a language less conveniently compliant with the grammar-rules we have thought out for it than we should like to help modern editors to punctuate the text so as to make translation easier for us, though I believe that occasionally scansion, especially of light first half-lines with initial clusters of unstressed syllables, may help us in our struggle to identify the beginning of a major syntactical unit.[38] A good example in *Beowulf* of our inability to decide for certain if *þa* is an adverb or a conjunction comes at line 461b (singled out for demonstrating the uselessness of word-order by Schücking).[39] Klaeber has the following punctuation (and emendation to *Wedera*):

> Gesloh þin fæder   fæhðe mæste;
> 460   wearþ he Heaþolafe   to handbonan
> mid Wilfingum;   ða hine *Wede*ra cyn
> for herebrogan   habban ne mihte.

[Your father brought about very great hostilty by fighting; he came to be the hand-slayer of Heatholaf among the Wylfings; *then* the tribe of the Geats could not maintain him on account of the military threat.

Or:

---

[38] Cf. E. G. Stanley, 'Initial Clusters of Unstressed Syllables in Half-Lines of *Beowulf*', in M. Korhammer (ed.), *Words, Texts and Manuscripts. Studies in Anglo-Saxon Culture Presented to Helmut Gneuss . . .* (Cambridge, 1992), 272 and footnote 18.

[39] See the following discussions of the general problem: L. L. Schücking, *Satzverknüpfung* (1904; see I[74]), 108-16 (§ 66), a study which led to the excellent glossary entries for syntactically ambiguous function words in his revisions of M. Heyne (ed.), *Beowulf*, from the 8th edn (Paderborn, 1908) onwards; B. Mitchell, 'The Dangers of Disguise: Old English Texts in Modern Punctuation', *RES*, n.s. 31 (1980), 385-413 [reprinted in B. Mitchell, *On Old English – Selected Papers* (Oxford, 1988), 173-202, for verse pp. 183-200], and *Syntax* (1985; see III[32]) §§ 2536-50; F. C. Robinson, *Appositive Style* (1985; see II[66]), 18-19; D. Donoghue, *Style in Old English Poetry* (1987; see III[35]), 71-2; E. G. Stanley, 'Apo Koinou, Chiefly in *Beowulf*', in K. Grinda and C.-D. Wetzel (eds), *Anglo-Saxonica Beiträge zur Vor- und Frühgeschichte der englischen Sprache und zur Literatur der altenglischen Zeit Festschrift für Hans Schabram zum 65. Geburtstag* (Munich, 1993), 181-207.

> Your father brought about very great hostilty by fighting; he
> came to be the hand-slayer of Heatholaf among the Wylfings,
> *when* the tribe of the Geats could not maintain him on account
> of the military threat.]

In Modern English the difference may be made to seem great, but if the adverb *ða* has the sense 'then, at that time', a not uncommon sense of the word, the difference between it and the conjunction 'when, at which time' referring to a bygone period is less than if we translate *ða* into Modern English as 'thereupon' or 'at the very time that'.

When the adverb *her* begins a clause the word-order following it is usually VS, as in the opening of the *Chronicle* annal quoted: *Her com se here*; but occasionally the order is SV, as, for example, the first use in the annal for 986 also in the Abingdon Chronicle Cotton Tiberius B.i:[40]

> Her se cyning fordyde þæt bisceoprice æt Hrofeceastre. Her com ærest se
> micla yrfcwealm to Angelcyn.
>
> [In this year the king ravaged the diocese of Rochester. In this year the great
> murrain first came to England.]

SV order is found after *Her*, and is not a rare phenomenon: it is found also in the annals for 990 and 992.

In verse too, when an adverb like *her* opens its clause the usual word-order is VS. A glance at the concordances shows that. There are always exceptions, not many but sufficient in number for them to be regarded as support for the general contention that grammar-rules are not as strictly adhered to in verse as some grammarians suggest.[41] Thus in *Judith* line 177:

> Her ge magon sweotole,   sigerofe hæleð,
> leoda ræswan,   on ðæs laðestan
> hæðenes heaðorinces   heafod starin,
> Holofernus . . .,

and it is amusing to see the editor, A. S. Cook, in his accompanying, alliterative translation finding a more ancient-sounding word-order than the poet used:

> 'Here can ye clearly, conquering heroes,
> Leaders of legions, gaze on the loathsome
> Head of the heathen Holofernus . . .'[42]

---

40 See M. Ashdown, *English and Norse Documents* (1930; see III[33]), 40.
41 Cf. S. O. Andrew's two books; see III[36]).
42 A. S. Cook (ed.), *Judith An Old English Epic Fragment* (2nd edn; Boston, Massachusetts, 1904), 14-15. Cook leaves *heaðorinces* untranslated; his glossary gives 'warrior'.

In *Beowulf* too the usual order after initial *her* is VS; for example, line 1228: *Her is æghwylc eorl oþrum getrywe* [Here every man is true to the other].

An apparent exception occurs at lines 2053-4, where the adverbial introduction is *Nu her*:

> Nu her þara banena   byre nathwylces
> frætwum hremig   on flet gæð.

[Now here the son of some man among those slayers, exulting
in finery, steps forth on to the hall-floor.]

But the exception is only apparent. SV order is normal after initial adverbial *nu*,[43] as, for example, in *Beowulf* line 395: *Nu ge moton gangan in eowrum guðgetawum* [Now you may proceed in your war-equipment]. Exceptional VS order after adverbial *nu* does occur; for example, in the opening line of *An Exhortation to Christian Living*: *Nu lære ic þe swa man leofne sceal* [Now I instruct you, as one ought one's friend]. This is a late poem in Corpus Christi College Cambridge MS 201; but there is no reason for thinking that there was a late Old English change from SV to VS order after adverbial *nu*: it is always possible to devise some explanation, but none that suggests itself seems convincing. The metre of the poem is not so strict that any metrical explanation is required. *Beowulf* is metrically strict, and VS order after adverbial *nu* is readily explicable in line 2900 because it is a metrical requirement that all unaccented words must be placed together in the same unstressed position with *nu*:

> Nu is wilgeofa   Wedra leoda,
> dryhten Geata   deaðbedde fæst.

[Now the generous benefactor of the people of the Wederas,
the lord of the Geats lies held fast on his death-bed.]

Other examples with VS order after *nu* occur in *Andreas* lines 391 and 1425, and in the late, stanzaic poem *The Seasons for Fasting* line 134. *Christ II* lines 561-3 is notable, with the subject placed at the end of the clause, so that the elaborate description of the suffering inflicted on those who in the Harrowing of Hell fought for the devils (or, more probably, were devils) comes between the *Nu sind* opening of the clause and the subject phrase *deofla cempan*, as I attempt to imitate in my translation (in which 'they' is introduced because of the inflexible word-order of Modern English):

> Nu sind forcumene   ond in cwicsusle
> gehynde ond gehæfte,   in helle grund
> duguþum bidæled,   deofla cempan.

---

[43] As one might expect, SV order appears to be without exception after *nu* when the word acts as the subordinating conjunction corresponding to 'now that'.

[Now (they) are vanquished and in living torments humbled
and confined, in the pit of hell deprived of blessings, the
devils' warriors.]

The order VS after *nu* in *Christ III* lines 1489 is perhaps to be explained on the
grounds (familiar to us from Modern English) that it is desirable to place the
noun close to the relative clause qualifying it; Christ addresses in lines 1489-
92b one sinner, 'and nathless shall He mean all sinning folk', in Gollancz's
translation of the words introducing the speech:[44]

> Nu is swærra mid mec   þinra synna rod
> þe ic unwillum   on beom gefæstnad,
> þonne seo oþer wæs   þe ic ær gestag
> willum minum.

[Now lies more heavily on me the cross of thy sins on which I
am crucified unwillingly, than did that other one which I willingly ascended before.]

What is a modern reader to make of such Old English rules or word-order,
generally observed but sometimes disregarded for reasons easy to suggest and
impossible to prove? Is there in Old English verse a feeling in any way comparable with that experienced by a modern reader when faced with the archaism
of Cook's 'Here can ye clearly, conquering heroes, / Leaders of legions'? It
could not have been so for Anglo-Saxon readers. For them, after an introductory
adverb, VS order was so common that they cannot have felt any special recognition of a poetic heirloom when they departed from SV order more common after
her and *nu*. It could have given them no literary pleasure in the fond belief this
is the genuine thing in poetic style, as it seems to have given translators into
Modern English like Cook and Gollancz with their Wardour Street – that term
of abuse itself now archaic – 'Here can ye' and 'nathless shall He', which
almost a century later has the opposite effect on readers, who may well fail to
recognize poetic heirlooms in artful inversions, only a display of the translators'
poetastic insufficiencies: no elevation, only bombast. It is impossible for us to
recapture the *Sprachgefühl* of the Anglo-Saxons, what they might have felt for
their poetic language in contrast with what they may not have felt for their
unconsidered colloquial Old English.[45]

In early Middle English it seems that after *her* and *nu* both SV and VS order
was used, so that it is useless information for dating that in some late Old

---

[44] See the translation of lines 1376-8, by I. Gollancz (ed.), *The Exeter Book*, I, EETS, o.s. 104
(1895), 87.

[45] B. von Lindheim's 'Traces of Colloquial Speech in Old English', *Anglia*, 70 (1951), 22-42, is
a very good article, but not concerned with such features as word-order; it has no place in B.
Mitchell, *A Critical Bibliography of Old English Syntax to the End of 1984* (Oxford, 1990);
but is put to good use in A. Cameron, A. Kingsmill and A. C. Amos, *Old English Word
Studies: A Preliminary Author and Word Index*, Toronto Old English Series, 8 (1983), 102.

English poems, such as *The Seasons for Fasting* and *An Exhortation to Christian Living*, we find VS order: VS order is to be found also, as we have seen, in poems that are not to be regarded as late.[46]

Any attempt to recover the tone conveyed by VS order at various periods in the history of the language is difficult; it is clear that the greater frequency of VS order in former times has led to a predilection for it in writing Modern English verse or elevated prose, as if VS order were to be treasured as a grace-note. Since Chaucer comes half-way between us and Old English, his practice in verse is worth a glance. After *here* and *now* VS order is normal; for example:[47] 'Now wol I tellen of my ferthe housbonde', *The Wife of Bath's Prologue*, CT III (D) 480; and *The Merchant's Tale*, CT IV (E) 1330-1:

> Here may ye see, and here may ye preeue
> That wyf is mannes helpe and his confort.

The Wife's introduction to what she has to tell about her fourth husband may feel lower in sentiment than the Merchant's lines about woman as helpmeet for man, ironic though they are; but word-order does not in any way contribute to that feeling.

In the word-order of Modern English poetry some vestiges of that greater freedom have been and are available. Spenser and Milton were still in the tradition of VS order after *here* and *now* when they wrote 'Now is my Love all ready forth to come', *Epithalamion* line 110, or 'Here shalt thou sit incarnate, here shalt Reigne / Both God and Man', *Paradise Lost*, III, 315-16, and 'Now came still evening on', *Paradise Lost*, IV, 598; but also *Paradise Lost*, IV, 156-8:

---

[46] A serviceable sampling of Middle English usage, sufficient for a generalization about word-order after initial, adverbial *nou*, is provided by such concordances of Middle English verse and prose as concord function words like *now*: M. J. Preston (ed.), *A Concordance to the Middle English Shorter Poem*, Compendia, 6 (Leeds, 1975), s.vv. *nou*, *nov*, *now* [R. L. Greene (ed.), *The Early English Carols* (1st edn; Oxford, 1935), is only partially concorded with line quotations, and so also two less substantial anthologies, including C. Brown (ed.), *Religious Lyrics of the XVth Century* (Oxford, 1939)], *nowe*, *nu* and *nv*. In the poetry of Chaucer VS order seems to be the rule; but J. S. P. Tatlock and A. G. Kennedy, *A Concordance to the Complete Works of Geoffrey Chaucer* (Washington, 1927), do not provide a sufficient number of 'specimens' s.v. *Now*. In Gower SV order is highly exceptional; see J. D. Pickles and J. L. Dawson, *A Concordance to John Gower's* Confessio Amantis, Publications of the John Gower Society, I (Cambridge, 1987), s.v. *Now*. In late Middle English prose similarly, VS order is regular after *now*, if Malory is representative; see T. Kato, (ed.) *A Concordance to the Works of Sir Thomas Malory* (Tokyo, 1974), s.v. *now*.

[47] See L. D. Benson (general ed.), *The Riverside Chaucer* (Boston, 1987); and cf. P. G. Ruggiers (ed.), *The Canterbury Tales, A Facsimile and Transcription of the Hengwrt Manuscript*, A Variorum Edition of the Works of Geoffrey Chaucer, I (Norman, Oklahoma, 1979). *The Riverside Chaucer* (p. 155) follows the Ellesmere reading *heer by may* at *Merchant's Tale* 1330: *and heerby may ye preve*.

now gentle gales
Fanning thir odoriferous wings dispense
Native perfumes

and 'Here we may reign secure', *Paradise Lost*, I, 261.

Inversion in poetry led to the feeling that it is good for poetry, more elevated than the ordinary 'Here we may reign'. No doubt, metrical considerations played a part in the order chosen. In poetry, Old, Middle or Modern English, whenever choice is possible, metre plays a part in the decision.

Exploiting what little remains to be exploited of the Modern English inflexional system, Gray uses inversion daringly and elaborately in 'Elegy Written in a Country Churchyard', stanza ix:

The Boast of Heraldry, the Pomp of Pow'r,
And all that Beauty, all that Wealth e'er gave,
Awaits alike th'inevitable Hour.

Early publishers, printers or editors mistook Gray's subtle, but by the 1750s unidiomatic,[48] word-order, OVS, with fourfold object phrases at the beginning, and the verb *Awaits* by means of its final *s* proclaiming that its subject is singular, *th'inevitable hour* at the end of the sentence; and they changed *Awaits* to *Await*, so making nonsense of Gray's long-delayed subject which lies in wait for the *beau monde*, as a thief in the night.

Our perception of the word-order of Old English is filtered through our modern notions of what is natural for us in the English of the end of the twentieth century, and how we arrive at notions of what we rightly regard as archaic in Old English, and wrongly regard as artificial or poetic. In Old English VS order was part of a well-established, though not wholly inflexible system. In Modern English, as used in the heightened language often thought suitable for translating the poetry of English antiquity, that word-order is an

---

[48] For details of the text of the 'Elegy', see F. G. Stokes (ed.), *An Elegy Written in a Country Church Yard* (Oxford, 1929), 71. Quartos 1 to 8 read *Awaits*; but from 1754 onwards the quartos read *Await*, as does R. and J. Dodsley (eds), *Collection of Poems*, IV (London, 1755), the edition in *The Grave. A Poem by Robert Blair* (Edinburgh, 1761), Dodsley's *Poems by Mr. Gray. A New Edition* (London, 1768), and W. Mason's edition of *The Poems of Mr. Gray* (York, 1775; 2nd edn, London, 1775). See also R. Lonsdale (ed.), *The Poems of Thomas Gray, William Collins, Oliver Goldsmith* (London, 1969), 123-4.

That VS order after an adverbial introduction to the clause was regarded as archaic, and suitable therefore for archaizing imitation, is demonstrated by the pastiche biblical language of [Robert Dodsley's] *The Chronicle of the Kings of England. Written in the Manner of the Ancient Jewish Historians. By Nathan Ben Saddi* (London, 1740), for which see E. G. Stanley, 'Robert Dodsley's Archaizing Chaucer Allusion', *N&Q*, 237 (1992), 278-80. Dodsley indulges in many archaisms, including inversion, in his reference to Chaucer (p. 34), and nowhere else: 'In these Days lived thilk grete Poet, hight Geoffery Chaucere, the Fader of Inglis Poesie.' VS order must have been perceived by him as quintessentially archaic, as much so as *thilk* and *hight*, and so Dodsley did not introduce *there*, to produce more modern 'In these days there lived . . .'

affectation. To achieve it, use is often made of *nor* or *never* or *not at all* after which Modern English requires VS order still. Translators who would not stoop to an archaizing mode of expression can claim that by using these emphatic negatives they have availed themselves of the very limited means still current for varying word-order a little, not so much in imitation of the greater freedom of Old English, but as a reminder of that greater freedom which is very readily perceptible and and to some extent still imitable in Modern English.[49]

Old English sentence structure and Modern English punctuation; long and short sentences

Old English verse has a very varied sentence structure, and the *Beowulf* poet especially seems to have delighted in that variety. The poem has a high proportion of long sentences; but short sentences too are used, sometimes with obvious special effect. For example, three times in the poem virtually the same brief sentence sums up a prince: *þæt wæs god cyning* 'That was an excellent king', line 11 of Scyld, line 863 (with initial *ac* 'but then') of Hrothgar, line 2390 probably of Beowulf.[50] The preceding sentence is long: before 11b, either all of lines 4-11a or 7b-11a; before 2390b, 2387-90a; but somewhat shorter before 863b, 862-3a, probably just to establish the contrast expressed by *ac*.

The decisive and ironic wording of *Beowulf* line 754b *No þy ær fram meahte*, 'He could not [get] away any the sooner', constitutes a different form of summary. The reference is to Grendel's attack on Heorot: first (lines 702b-45a), the aggressor hoping for and enjoying the delights of cannibalistic feasting on some sleeping Dane; secondly (lines 745b-53a), coming upon Beowulf, awake and stronger than anyone Grendel had known; and lastly (lines 753b-4a), Grendel seized with fear: but (line 754b) it was too late to flee, *No þy ær fram meahte* – the climax summarized.

---

[49] Cf. E. G. Stanley, 'Translation from Old English: "The Garbaging War-Hawk," or, The Literal Materials from Which the Reader Can Re-create the Poem', in M. J. Carruthers and E. D. Kirk (eds), *Acts of Interpretation* – ... *Essays on Medieval and Renaissance Literature in Honor of E. Talbot Donaldson* (Norman, Oklahoma: 1982), 67-101 [reprinted in E. G. Stanley *A Collection of Papers* (1987; see I[55]), 83-114].

[50] Onela is referred to a few lines before (2382-4a) as

> þone selestan sæcyninga
> þara ðe in Swiorice sinc brytnade,
> mærne þeoden.

> [the best of maritime kings who distributed riches in the kingdom of Sweden, a renowned prince.]

But Beowulf has just been mentioned at line 2389b, and it is more likely therefore that *þæt wæs god cyning* (line 2390b) refers to him than to Onela. These words end the numbered section XXXIII, and the next section begins with the pronoun *Se* referring to Beowulf, who must be the *god cyning* of the preceding line.

Occasionally in *Beowulf* short sentences with a verb in the jussive ominously interrupt the flow of moral utterance;[51] as in line 1003b:

<blockquote>

　　　　　　　　No þæt yðe byð
　　　to befleonne　– fremme se þe wille! –
　　　ac gesecan sceal　sawlberendra
1005　nyde genydde,　niþða bearna,
　　　grundbuendra　gearwe stowe,
　　　þær his lichoma　legerbedde fæst
　　　swefeþ æfter symle.

</blockquote>

[That is never easy to flee from – let him try to achieve it who will! – but he must seek out the place made ready for soul-bearers, for the children of men, for earth's denizens, there where his body, held fast on a bed of rest, sleeps after the banquet.]

A similar jussive intrudes at line 2766b into the long description of the treasure seen by Wiglaf after it was freed from the dragon, forming a unit of discourse, though perhaps not a single sentence as that is perceived in Modern English:

<blockquote>

　　　　　　　　Geseah ða sigehreðig,　þa he bi sesse geong,
　　　　　　　　magoþegn modig　maððumsigla fealo,
　　　　　　　　gold glitnian　grunde getenge,
　　　　　　　　wundur on wealle,　ond þæs wyrmes denn,
2760　ealdes uhtflogan,　orcas stondan,
　　　fyrnmanna fatu,　feormendlease,
　　　hyrstum behrorene:　þær wæs helm monig
　　　eald ond omig,　earmbeaga fela
　　　searwum gesæled.　Sinc eaðe mæg,
2765　gold on grunde,　gumcynnes gehwone
　　　oferhigian　– hyde se ðe wylle! –
　　　swylce he siomian geseah　segn eallgylden
　　　heah ofer horde,　hondwundra mæst,
　　　gelocen leoðocræftum,　of ðam leoma stod
2770　þæt he þone grundwong　ongitan meahte
　　　wræte giondwlitan.

</blockquote>

[The brave young retainer, triumphant in victory, saw, as he went by the seat, many treasure-jewels, close to the ground gold glistening, on the wall things of wonder, and the lair of the dragon, of the old flyer at dawn, (saw) cups standing (there), the vessels of men of old now without burnishers, deprived of

---

51 Klaeber's edition emphasizes the intrusion by the use of dashes, both in this quotation and the next. I have followed Klaeber's use of dashes, though in other respects I have not followed Klaeber's punctuation exactly; for example, in the next quotation Klaeber has a dash at the end of line 2764a, and not at the beginning of 2766b where I have placed it.

their ornaments: there were many helmets, old and rusty, many
arm-rings skilfully wreathed. Treasure, gold on earth, can
easily overbear everyone of human race – let him hide it who
will! – so too he saw towering high above the hoard a standard
all of gold, the greatest of marvels made by hand, entwined by
skilful fingers, from which shone a light so bright that he
could comprehend the surface of the floor, gaze all over the
ornaments.]

Of course, short sentences introduced for special effect, are not confined to
Beowulf. Thus, near the end of *The Wanderer* a speaker, who has pondered this
dark life deeply, utters his gnomes in brief questions and exclamations, each a
half-line long, and, after some longer sentences (lines 95b-107, which I omit),
answers his gnomes in brief exclamations, each similarly a half-line long, ending with a summarizing sentence a whole line long (110). The editors separate
the half-line sentences of lines 108-9 (or even 108-10) by commas, and therefore they may not look like the separate sentences I take them to be in our
modern perception of what constitutes a sentence (lines 92-110):

    Hwær cwom mearg?   Hwær cwom mago?   Hwær cwom
                                 maþþumgyfa?
    Hwær cwom symbla gesetu?   Hwær sindon seledreamas?
    Eala beorht bune!   Eala byrnwiga!
95   Eala þeodnes þrym! ......
106 Eall is earfoðlic   eorþan rice.
    Onwendeð wyrda gesceaft   weoruld under heofonum.
    Her bið feoh læne.   Her bið freond læne.
    Her bið mon læne.   Her bið mæg læne.
110 Eal þis eorþan gesteal   idel weorþeð.

[Where has the steed gone? Where has the (young) man gone?
Where has the treasure-giver gone? Where have the banquet-
ing-seats gone? Where are the revelries of the hall? Alas, the
bright cup! Alas, the warrior in armour! Alas, the prince's
majesty! ...... All the realm of earth is full of hardship. The
course of ordainments brings change to the subcelestial world.
Here wealth shall perish. Here friend shall perish. Here man
and woman shall perish. Here kindred shall perish. All the
foundation of this earth shall become useless.]

Such occasional half-line sentences are not infrequent. But we see Old
English as punctuated by modern editors. At times they may prefer to end the
sentence preceding the half-line sentence with a colon or a semi-colon, both in
Modern English or Modern German editions. One example is enough. *Exodus*
line 300b reads *mere stille bad* [the sea stood still]. In the manuscript (Junius 11,
p. 158) the pointing marks off the half-lines as usual in the fairly consistent

manuscript pointing. The treatment of the caesural punctuation of line 300 in the major editions is as follows:[52]

Thorpe: text follows manuscript; translation ': *the* sea stood still.'
Bouterwek: text, semi-colon before, full stop after 300b; translation differs: '; das Meer verharrte still;'
Grein: text and translation, colon before, full stop after 300b.
Wülker: text retains Grein's punctuation.
Blackburn: text, comma before, full stop after 300b.
Krapp: text, full stop before and after 300b.
Irving: text, full stop before and after 300b.
Lucas: text, semi-colon before, full stop after 300b.
Tolkien: text, semi-colon before, full stop after 300b; translation: '. Still stood the sea.'

We are dealing with the simplest, shortest sentence unit in Old English verse; and even here there is no agreement, no consistency even (in both Bouterwek and Tolkien) between text and translation. Yet for Modern English and Modern German, sentence length, and therefore complexity of utterance, is in no small measure perceived as a reflexion of complexity of thought. Sometimes the brevity of the half-line verses has been used to characterize the manly vigour – or is it, 'reduced to its crudest form', warlike insensitivity? – of the poetry of the Anglo-Saxons: 'the short emphatic lines . . . ring like blows of hammers on an anvil';[53] 'a verse cadenced by the crashing blows of sword and axe';[54]

> the characteristic Anglo-Saxon rhythm. It is a formalized version of the rhythm of emphatic speech, derived originally from the rhythm of the heart and the rhythm of the breath. Reduced to its crudest form, it might be represented by
>
> *BANG. . .BANG : BANG. . .CRASH*[55]

The critics who comment so on the versification may be influenced by editorial punctuation: editorial clause units guide the reader into judgements of long or short, complex or simple. But look at Tolkien's translation; there, perhaps

[52] B. Thorpe, *Cædmon's Metrical Paraphrase of Parts of the Holy Scriptures . . . with and English Translation* (London, 1832), 197 line 2; K. W. Bouterwek, *Cædmon's . . . biblische Dichtungen*, (Gütersloh, 1849-1854), I, 122 line 3229, translation p. 253; C. W. M. Grein, *Bibliothek*, I (1857; see I[49]), 85, translation, *Dichtungen*, I (1857; see I[19]), 90; R. P. Wülker, (revision of Grein's) *Bibliothek*, II/2 (Leipzig, 1894), 460; F. A. Blackburn, *Exodus and Daniel* (Boston, Massachusetts, and London, 1907), 18; Krapp, ASPR, I (1931), 99; E. B. Irving, Jr, *The Old English Exodus*, YSE, 122 (1953), 56; P. J. Lucas, *Exodus* (London, 1977), 116; J. R. R. Tolkien, *The Old English* Exodus (ed. J. Turville-Petre; Oxford, 1981), 10, translation p. 26 line 261.
[53] J. R. Green, *A Short History of the English People* (London, 1874), 27.
[54] F. B. Gummere, *A Handbook of Poetics* (Boston, Massachusetts, 1885), 176.
[55] M. Alexander, *The Earliest English Poems* (first published in Penguin Classics, 1966; I quote: Berkeley and Los Angeles, 1970), 18.

because of the inversion, mainly because of the resulting stress on 'Still', the short sentence forms the fulcrum of stasis:

> Upon these words all the host arose, a mighty concourse of valiant men. Still stood the sea. There the companies uplifted their white shields and their ensigns upon the sand.

Tolkien's edition seems to me to accord less well with the Old English than his translation. In the manuscript (p. 158) the text has, as usual, no punctuation other than metrical pointing:

· æfter

> þam wordum · werod eall arás . modigra mæ[-]
> gen · mere stille bad · hofon here cyste . hwí[-]
> te linde . segnas on sande .

Punctuation is always editorial punctuation, and it matters in assessing subjectively, often in ill-founded generalizations, the individual poems and the whole of the poetry of the Anglo-Saxons.

Exodus lines 523-6 may contain the poet's suggestion that his poem can be read figurally. There is no need to give in full the history of editorial punctuation. Krapp in ASPR appears to be alone among major editors in beginning a new sentence with *Run bið gerecenod* at line 526. E. B. Irving, the next editor of the poem after Krapp, comments (p. 98, note on line 568 = Krapp 526):

> Krapp puts a stop after *cægon* and begins a new sentence with *rūn*. The phrase *gif onlūcan wile* he attaches to the end of the sentence beginning at 561b [= 519b]. This may have been suggested by the fact that *rūn* begins with a small capital in the MS, but it seems a less coherent reading.

Krapp attached importance to the occurrence in the manuscript of small capitals; he lists them in an appendix (for *Exodus*, ASPR I, p. xlii). There are 27 small capitals in the poem. Do they matter? Krapp (and other editors) ignore the capital in the following cases: *From* 54b, *Nymðe* 124a, *Wonn* 164a, *Gesittað* 563a; *Ne* 415a preceded in Grein and Grein-Wülker (their 414) by a colon, in Lucas by a semi-colon. Many of the small capitals in the manuscript open major units, both sentences and speeches. But even Krapp, who thought small capitals significant enough for his appendix, ignores them when they do not fit.

In Irving's edition of this passage (his lines 565-8) he follows Krapp having the sentence begin with *Dægword* (MS *dægweorc*) line 518b (= Irving 561b). Krapp began a new sentence with *Run* (line 526a); and Irving rejects that punctuation. In an article subsequent to his edition and containing material amounting to a revision of it,[56] Irving shows clearly how the lines are to be punctuated better, and how they are to be interpreted:

---

[56] E. B. Irving, Jr, 'New Notes on the Old English *Exodus*', *Anglia*, 90 (1972), 321.

522-6. This passage should be repunctuated with a full stop after *soðum wordum*, so that the next sentence begins with the *gif-clause*: "If the interpreter of life will unlock the ample good, etc., then the mystery will be solved."

By 'should be repunctuated' Irving means 'should not be punctuated as in my edition, but should be punctuated instead as follows'. In the next two notes Irving explains the passage further. First, that *lifes wealhstod* (line 523b) could well be connected with II Corinthians 3:6:

> qui et idoneos nos fecit ministros noui testamenti
> non litterae sed Spiritus
> littera enim occidit Spiritus autem uiuificat

> Who also hath made vs meete [A.V. 'able'] ministers of the new testament: not in the letter, but in the Spirit. For the letter killeth: but the Spirit quickeneth.

And secondly, that *Gastes cægon* is almost certainly a reference to the Holy Ghost, and that 'key' is a standard image in medieval typology, and, as *Dictionary of Old English* now clearly shows, not uncommon in Old English with the sense 'solution, means of understanding, the key to a mystery'.[57] In fact, the punctuation advocated by E. B. Irving is that of the passage in all the editions (other than Krapp's in ASPR and his own):[58]

> Gif onlucan wile   lifes wealhstod,
> beorht in breostum   banhuses weard,
> 525   ginfæsten god   Gastes cægon,
> run bið gerecenod,   ræd forð gæð.

[If the exegete of life, the guardian of the body bright within the breast,[59] will unlock the ample good with the keys of the (Holy) Spirit, (then) the mystery will be explained, wisdom will go forward.]

---

[57] Irving gives a reference to R. B. Burlin, *The Old English Advent: A Typological Commentary*, YSE, 168 (1968), 75, on the opening of the second antiphon, 'O clavis David', *Christ I* lines 18-49. See *DOE*, s.v. *cæg*, 1.b.1.

[58] See III[52]: Thorpe, p. 211 lines 6-13. Bouterwek, p. 130 lines 3451-4; translation, top of p. 258. Grein, p. 92, lines 522-5; translation, p. 96. Wülker, pp. 471-2, lines 522-5. Blackburn, p. 29. Lucas, pp. 142-3. Tolkien, pp. 16-17, lines 522-3; translation, p. 31, lines 447-51. Grein interprets *god* of line 525 (= his 524) as 'God'.

[59] H. Marquardt, *Kenningar* (1938; see II[60]), 150 (= 48 of separate) and cf. 200 (= 98), regards *banhuses weard* as a tripartite kenning, *banhus* 'bone-house, body, flesh', its *weard* 'guardian' perhaps the soul' or 'the intellect'; *DOE*, s.v. *bān-hūs*, a, gives the meaning of the phrase as 'the body's guardian, the mind'. The senses given in Tolkien's note on the lines (pp. 75-6) are interesting:

> 522-3. *lifes wealhstod . . . banhuses weard*: both refer to the soul. *Lifes* is used in the Biblical sense: what is vivifying and soul-nourishing; cf. *lifes word*, *Cri* 1392, *lifes snyttru*, *Guð* 163. The 'interpreter of life-giving

There is for almost every poetic text a long history of scholarship, with the result that for many problems of sentence structure, manifesting itself in editorial punctuation, a consensus has evolved. 'Repunctuation' may be an editor's change of mind: Irving in the new notes of 1972 no longer thinks as he did in the edition of 1953. There is every reason for applauding a scholar who changes his mind, thinks better of it – in the words of Pope or Swift (or of one of their friends), it 'is but saying, in other words, that he is wiser to day than he was yesterday'.[60] When the wording '523-6, repunctuated' is used, as it is by M. Godden,[61] to mean that these lines are not punctuated as in Krapp's philologically often insufficient, but now 'standard' ASPR edition, and are, in fact, punctuated as in the, in many ways more scholarly, editions both before and after Krapp's, the use of 'repunctuated' shows unawareness of the editorial tradition of punctuation, and unawareness perhaps that for poems, which in MS Junius 11 are pointed metrically, editorial punctuation is as necessary for modern understanding as for a poem transmitted as is *Beowulf* in a manuscript pointed seemingly at random. Modern punctuation is less of a necessity for a competent Anglo-Saxonist's understanding of well-punctuated Ælfrician manuscripts, so that the ultra-conservative decision to retain the manuscript pointing (taken in editing *The Catholic Homilies*)[62] would be even less defensible for *Exodus* or *Beowulf* or any other Old English poem, whether metrically pointed or not.

Languages differ in how their speakers, writers and readers regard complexity of sentence structure, and within a language both synchronically and

knowledge' refers to the intellective faculty of the soul. *Banhuses weard* is
the conscience, governor of the whole incarnate person.

The sense 'conscience' seems unlikely at *Exodus* lines 522-3, as it is not at *Beowulf* lines 1741-2: *se weard . . ., sawele hyrde* 'the guardian, the shepherd of the soul' [and cf. the early Middle English Text *Sawles Warde*, recently edited by S. T. R. O. d'Ardenne, *The Katherine Group edited from MS. Bodley 34* (Bibliothèque de la Faculté de Philosophie et Lettres de l'Université de Liège, CCXV (1977), 165-85). Tolkien can hardly make the soul, 'the body's guardian' also the conscience which is 'the soul's guardian'.

60 'Thoughts on Various Subjects', A. Pope and J. Swift (eds), *Miscellanies in Verse and Prose* (London, 1727), II *Miscellanies The Second Volume*, 340.

61 M. Godden, 'Biblical literature: the Old Testament', in M. Godden and M. Lapidge (eds), *The Cambridge Companion* (1991; see II[33]), 217.

62 See M. Godden (ed.), *Ælfric's Catholic Homilies, The Second Series, Text*, EETS, s.s. 5 (1979), p. xciv. The decision to reproduce manuscript punctuation in a modern edition of excellent Old English prose does not make for readability when no translation is provided – if it is hoped to win readers for the text. Charters are generally printed pseudo-diplomatically, with punctuation generally, and capitalization less commonly, as in the manuscript. C. Plummer's edition of J. Earle's *Two of the Saxon Chronicles Parallel* (Oxford, 1892) pursued the policy of reproducing manuscript spacing, but not manuscript punctuation or capitalization. For Ælfric, the excellent edition by J. C. Pope, *Homilies of Ælfric A Supplementary Collection*, EETS 259, 260 (1967-1968), set what might have been regarded and welcomed as the standard procedure for non-rhythmical prose for the *Alia Narratio de Euangelii Textu* at pp. 575-8 lines 203-51 (cf. Godden, pp. 217-19 lines 127-79). Pope explains his policy of printing the metrical prose in alliterative lines that look like long verse lines; and he explains

diachronically there is variation in how its speakers, writers and readers regard complexity of sentence structure. That applies to both verse and prose. Syntactical simplicity, that is, no greater complexity than seems called for to give expression to the ideas, is regarded as a virtue in twentieth-century English. Milton will not have shared that view when for the opening sentence of *Paradise Lost* his 'adventrous Song' soared 'with no middle flight' for sixteen lines before he reached the first full stop, though about half way through, at line 10, he had a colon followed by a capital letter. It is noticeable in German academic prose that many Germanists seem not to strive for brevity of sentence length, unlike most of their Anglist colleagues who have embraced the ideal of simplicity to which most English-speaking academics at least pay lip-service.

Some Old English poems show greater complexity of sentence structure than others. As punctuated in the ASPR edition of *The Dream of the Rood* there is no sentence longer than four lines before line 95; then longer sentences are to be found: 95-100, 103b-109, 117-21, 131b-44a (by far the longest sentence in the poem), 150-6. The preferable punctuation of lines 90-4 in other editions,[63] makes that passage one sentence of five lines. I believe that the poem is one integral unit, unlike the disintegrators of *The Dream of the Rood*. Yet they seem

his treatment of 'ordinary' (that is, non-rhythmical) prose in the introduction to the homily in which it occurs (pp. 188 and 566):

> The metrical lineation is editorial and the punctuation has been modernized throughout. Sentences, however, accord with the capitals and punctuation of the basic manuscript unless otherwise stated. In texts based on MS. U [Trinity College Cambridge MS B. 15. 34 (369)], which points with some regularity by metrical phrases or half-lines, erratic pointing as judged by my own lineation is noted in the apparatus. The capitals of proper and sacred names are modern: no manuscript normally uses capitals for this purpose . . .
>
> It may seem strange that Ælfric should insert an old composition, mainly in ordinary prose, into the midst of a homily written in his fully matured rhythmical style . . . It should be observed, however, that the *Alia Narratio* is partly rhythmical at several points where I have maintained the prose way of printing it, and so regularly rhythmical at the end [pp. 578-9 lines 252-76; cf. Godden, pp. 219-20 lines 179-97] that I have arranged it in metrical lines.

For the advocacy that Old English punctuation should be reproduced in modern editions without consideration for what the 'ordinary' modern reader (that is one who is not an experienced Anglo-Saxonist) may be used to and, will, therefore, find a help to understanding – misunderstanding, Mitchell thinks, see B. Mitchell, 'The Dangers of Disguise' (1980; see III[39]), reprinted in B. Mitchell, *On Old English* (1988; see III[39]), 176-83 'The presentation of prose texts for ordinary readers'. For a clear discussion of this notion, see D. Donoghue, *Style in Old English Poetry* (1987; see III[35]), 45-51, 92-9.

63 First punctuated thus by J. M. Kemble (ed.), *The Poetry of the Codex Vercellensis*, part II 'Elene and Minor Poems', Ælfric Society, No. 6 (London, 1856), 89, his lines 177-86. K. W. Bouterwek (ed.), *Cædmon*, I (1849-1854), p. clxxi (his lines 91-5), has a semi-colon before *swylce*, where the ASPR edition has a mark of exclamation. Bouterwek (p. clxxv) has the same punctuation in his translation. G. Stephens, *The Old-Northern Runic Monuments*, I (London and Copenhagen, 1867), 426, has a comma before *swylce* (his line 185) in the Old English, but a semi-colon in his rendering into Anglo-Saxonized Modern English.

to have overlooked this particular stylistic difference between lines 1-89 and 90-156.[64] It would, in any event, have been unconvincing as corroborative evidence of their case, since the change in style is likely to have been the result of the change in subject-matter which takes place at line 78 when the dream-vision has been told and the exercises of devotion arising from it begin.

No single measure of sentence length fits all occasions; and how sentence length or brevity is valued varies among individual speakers of a language as well as from language to language and, within a language, from age to age. Yet for Old English verse (and some prose, *Kunstprosa* especially) there is a different problem, well defined by H. Pilch and H. Tristram:[65] 'Die syntaktischen Verknüpfungen der altenglischen Dichtung und Kunstprosa sprengen den Rahmen des Satzes, wie ihn unsere grammatische Tradition festlegt' [The syntactic means of connecting clauses in Old English verse and *Kunstprosa* burst the limits of what our grammatical tradition defines as a sentence]. When, in Old English verse, short sentences follow each other without coordinating or subordinating conjunction can they together form a single unit, 'the sentence', of which they are constituent members, 'clauses'? By way of example, we may consider again *The Wanderer* lines 106-10:[66]

```
106   Eall is earfoðlic   eorþan rice.
      Onwendeð wyrda gesceaft   weoruld under heofonum.
      Her bið feoh læne.   Her bið freond læne.
      Her bið mon læne.   Her bið mæg læne.
110   Eal þis eorþan gesteal   idel weorþeð.
```

The *Eall is earfoðlic / eorþan rice* of line 106 is not merely echoed, but is answered by the *eal þis eorþan gesteal / idel weorþeð*: all this earth of ours is full of hardship now and shall become useless, a vanity. The four brief *Her bið ... læne* half-lines exemplify that single notion of universal mutability. Should we get it into one sentence, loosely constructed perhaps? In translation into Modern English we shall have to avoid full stops till we get to the end, adding 'and' when useful, and availing ourselves of the colon:

'All the realm of earth is full of hardship, and the course of ordainments brings change to the subcelestial world: here wealth shall perish, here friend shall perish, here man and woman shall perish, here kindred shall perish, and all the foundation of this earth shall become useless.'

---

[64] It is overlooked also in M. Swanton's account of 'Style and Structure', in his edition of *The Dream of the Rood* (Manchester, 1970), 61. He, in line with current thinking, believes in the unity of the poem as we have it, unlike B. Dickins and A. S. C. Ross (eds), *The Dream of the Rood* (London, 1934), especially p. 18.

[65] H. Pilch and H. Tristram, *Altenglische Literatur*, Anglistische Forschungen, 128 (Heidelberg, 1979), 99, § 2.24 'Satzverknüpfung'.

[66] See p. 95, above. On sentence structure and thought units, cf. pp. 61-2 and notes 65 and 66.

We have turned the unconnected structure (that is, the asyndetic parataxis)[67] of the Old English expression of one single thought into a grammatically connected Modern English expression equally one single thought. We may have been conditioned by our grammatical tradition to prefer the partial syndetic parataxis – two 'ands' (but also a colon together with four commas substituted for full stops, but still with asyndetic parataxis) – of this translation to the original: we have perhaps accommodated the single thought better within our grammatical conception, but by doing so we have neither improved the thought nor made its expression clearer.

Elsewhere,[68] I have discussed *Beowulf* lines 864-917, which I regard as a single sense-unit, but beyond the capacity of Modern English punctuation to hold as a single sentence: the *Hwilum* of line 864a, repeated by the *Hwilum* line 867b, is given a concluding response by the *Hwilum* of line 916a, and the whole is a celebration of Beowulf after his triumph over Grendel: the horse-racing inaugurated, the songs sung comparing him with Sigemund the dragon-slayer, contrasting him with Heremod the tyrant, and back to the horse-racing again, in fifty lines of verse. This is not a sentence as defined by our grammatical tradition. It has been suggested, in an excellent account of this phenomenon,[69] that *The Phoenix* lines 424-42 is another such sense unit, though in the ASPR edition it appears as four sentences. Some earlier editions and translations punctuated these 19 lines as two sentences, beginning a new sentence at line 437. The point is of some importance: if we regard it as one sentence, its opening is answered by the *swa* of 437b:

> Is þon gelicast,   þæs þe us leorneras
> 425   wordum secgað   ond writu cyþað,
> þisses fugles gefær . . .

[This bird's journey is, as scholars tell us in words and make known in writings, most like to that . . .]

>   swa ða foregengan,
> yldran usse,   anforleton
> þone wlitigan wong . . .

[as[70] those forefathers, our ancestors, renounced that lovely plain . . .]

---

67 See the discussion of that concept by B. Mitchell, *Syntax* (1985; see III[32]), § 1683; but the whole of his ch. v, 'Parataxis and the "Multiple Sentence" ', is relevant.
68 E. G. Stanley, '*Beowulf*' (1966; see II[65]), 121-4, reprinted in *A Collection of Papers* (1987; see I[45]), 154-6; and again, 'Notes on Old English Poetry' (1989; see III[27]), iv 'A long unit of Old English Verse and modern editorial punctuation: *Beowulf*, lines 864-917a', pp. 330-4.
69 B. Mitchell, *Syntax* (1985; see III[32]), §§ 1881, 3956. Cf. further, B. Mitchell, 'Dangers of Disguise' (1980; see III[39]), reprinted in B. Mitchell, *On Old English* (1988; see III[39]), 183-200, advocated a reformed system of punctuation with which I have little sympathy, though I admire the discussion leading up to it.
70 Word-order is no help in determining whether *swa* is conjunctive 'as' or adverbial 'thus', as is shown, for example, by the use at *The Phoenix* lines 350-1 where *Swa se gesæliga* . . .

In wording, this clear, logical connection is less close verbally than the repetition of *hwilum* in the *Beowulf* passage. The logical connection between lines 424 ff. and 437b ff. of *The Phoenix* does not depend on our modern punctuation. The difficulty is that our system of punctuation cannot, without strain, let the connection appear. The punctuation in the poetic manuscripts does not adequately show whether a subordinate clause comes after its principal clause, that is, it is 'right-branching' in a linguistic 'tree-diagram' (the usual order); or precedes its principal clause, that is, it is 'left-branching' (a much rarer order, though not uncommon for conditional clauses and clauses of manner or comparison, especially with correlative *swa . . . swa*).

After lines 1-5 of *The Wanderer* giving a description of the *anhaga* 'the solitary one' (referred to further in the third person, singular), two lines with initial *swa* describe a speaker, and are followed by a lonely traveller's complaining (in the first person, singular, used from lines 8 to 29a, and again from 58a). The passage is well known, as is the double problem which modern punctuation presents us with: for direct speech we now use inverted commas, and if lines 6-7 with initial *swa* refer back, that might indicate that the opening lines 1-5 are part of the speech that goes on from line 8; or lines 6-7 could perhaps refer forward only. In our grammatical tradition we need certainty so that we can punctuate properly. The punctuation of the Exeter Book is often very insufficient. At this point (fol. 76^v), however, the manuscript is more informative than is usual. Initial *OFT* is capitalized as for a new poem; the first mark of punctuation is a point at the end of our line 5, and *Swa* has an initial capital; the next mark of punctuation is a point at the end of our line 7, and *Oft* at the beginning of our line 8 has an initial capital. In the copious discussion these lines have received, modern critics suggest that in reading aloud or reciting an Anglo-Saxon would have made clear by vocal art what may seem obscure on the page. I am less impressed by arguments from unprovable – but now fashionable – orality than by the visuality of the page: *Oft ic* at line 8 leaps to the eye after the opening *OFT him* and in between lies the interrupting *Swa cwæð*. An Anglo-Saxon, who has not seen inverted commas used in his vernacular poetry, the visuality of the page in the best-written of the extant poetic codices may mean more when pondering the operation of divine grace as expressed in *The Wanderer* than how some *scop* or other may have camped it up:[71]

---

geneosað 'Thus the blessed one . . . visits' has *SWA* capitalized as opening a fit; it is very unlikely to form the opening subordinate clause of comparison or manner of a 'left-branching' sentence, with *fugelas cyrrað* beginning the principal clause, for which we should expect correlative *swa . . . swa*. See further B. Mitchell, *Syntax* (1985; see III^{32}), §§ 3267-70 'Swa adverb or conjunction', and § 3384.

[71] See the excellent discussion by B. Mitchell, 'Some Syntactical Problems in *The Wanderer*, ll. *Swa* line 6', *NM*, 69 (1968), 175-8 [reprinted in B. Mitchell, *On Old English* (1988; see III^{39}), 101-3]. I quote from p. 178 [= 103].

The Wanderer is more carefully pointed in the manuscript than many other poems; and the use of small capitals is not without interest. I. Gollancz, in his edition (1895; see III^{44}), 286, 288, 290 and 292, reproduces these features in general; cf. ASPR, III, *The Exeter Book*, p.

Since we cannot hear a *scop* perform and cannot interrogate a native speaker of Old English, we lack the vital clue of intonation. Hence we must be prepared to admit that there are some questions we can never answer, some problems we can never solve, some propositions we can never prove. This truth . . . is sadly in need of recognition by students of Old English language and by critics of Old English literature alike.

If we believe a little in the connected appearance of *OFT him* and *Oft ic*, may we make something of the fact that a large initial is found near the beginning in *Swa cwæð* at line 6 and then again near the end in *Swa cwæð* at line 111? I think not, because it is easy to make too much of too little in order to find support in a supposed factual observation for a subjective literary view – even in this poem which has in line 1 *him anhaga are gebideð* [the solitary one awaits for himself or experiences in himself grace or help or mercy], and in line 114 *Wel bið þam þe him are seceð* [It shall go well with him who seeks grace or mercy for himself]. The poem has come full circle, and in a subjective view the *Swa cwæð* of line 111 has given the answer to the opening: *The Wanderer* is a single utterance, but we cannot treat it as a single sentence, and must pockmark it with our modern punctuation.

The sentence structure of *The Battle of Maldon* has caused less discussion. A 'left-branching' sentence, lines 36-41, is well understood as such, and no one comments on the fact that it is, I believe, relatively rare in Old English verse for an initial subordinate clause to have an adjective clause as well as an object clause subordinate to it; there is no need for comment since the structure is quite clear:

> Gyf þu þat gerædest,   þe her ricost eart,
> þæt þu þine leoda   lysan wille,
> syllan sæmannum   on hyra sylfra dom
> feoh wið freode   and niman frið æt us,
> 40   we willaþ mid þam sceattum us[72]   to scype gangan,
> on flot feran,   and eow friþes healdan.

lxxix, for a list of the small capitals in the poem, including long \<i\> twice in line 12, once each in lines 22, 27, 44, 65, 84 (rightly ignored by Gollancz); and slightly longer \<f\> in *forþon* line 58. Small capitals come in more than one size. The larger size occurs in the following words only: \<ðõn\> (that is, *Ðonne*) 39 and 45, perhaps \<Ne\> lines 15 and 66a, \<Ongietan\> 73, \<Swa\> at lines 6 and 111, and \<Stondeð\> line 97. The initial \<s\> in \<Se\> line 88 is considerably smaller than that of \<Swa\> at lines 6 and 111, and of \<Stondeð\> at line 97.

72 Bodleian MS Rawlinson B. 203, fol. 7ᵛ, D. Casley's transcript of the poem from the original lost in the Cottonian fire of 1731, has a metrical point between *sceattū* and *us* [see the facsimile, F. C. Robinson and E. G. Stanley, EEMF, XXIII (1991), plate 15.2], correctly represented by T. Hearne (ed.), *Johannis . . . Glastoniensis Chronica sive Historia de Rebus Glastoniensibus* (Oxford, 1726), II, 571. D. Donoghue, *Style in Old English Poetry* (1987; see III³⁵), 197-8, seems right, however, to take *us* as the second stress of the first half-line, because, as he says, it avoids the breach of H. Kuhn's 'Law' of sentence particles, 'Wortstel-

[If you, who have the greatest wealth and authority here, determine that you are willing to redeem your people, giving money to the seamen at their own assessment in exchange for amity, and to make peace with us, we shall be willing to betake ourselves to the ships with the money, put to sea, and keep peace with you.]

There is no consensus on how best to analyse and, therefore, punctuate many passages of Old English verse. A good example of such editorial disagreement is *Daniel* lines 7b-21. The following eight editions have been used; and in the printed text below, at the end of each half-line, the marks of punctuation used by the editors are indicated by these sigla:[73]

T   =   Thorpe (1832) as inferred from the translation printed in parallel with the text in half-lines.
Bo =   Bouterwek (1854).
G   =   Grein (1857).
W   =   Wülker (1894) who in this passage virtually always follows Grein.
S   =   Schmidt (1907) who says that in this passage he follows Grein (but, in fact, follows Wülker).
Bl =   Blackburn (1907).
K   =   Krapp (1931).
F   =   Farrell (1974).

   [TBoKF./ GWS:/ Bl;]   Þæt wæs modig cyn, [TBoGWSBl,/
                       KF! *followed by new paragraph*]
þenden hie þy rice [*all zero*]   rædan moston, [*all*,]
burgum weoldon. [T:/ GWSBlF;/ Bo.]   Wæs him beorht wela
        [TBoGWS,/ Bl *zero*/ K./ F. *followed by new paragraph*]
10 þenden þæt folc mid him [*all zero*]   hiera fæder wære [*all zero*]
healdon woldon. [TBoGWS./ Bl;/ KF,]   Wæs him Hyrde god
        [TBoKWS 'good' *zero*/ BlKF 'God',]
heofonrices Weard, [*all*,]   halig Drihten, [*all*,]
wuldres Waldend, [TBoGWSBl,/ KF.]   se ðam werude geaf [*all zero*]
mod and mihte, [*all*,]   Metod alwihta, [BoGWSB, T;]

lung und -betonung' (1933; see III[35]), involved in taking *us* as the first word of the second half-line; but, in view of the relative lack of metrical strictness of the poem, there can be no certainty in such matters.

73 B. Thorpe, *Cædmon* (1832; see III[52]), 216 line 16 to 217 line 12; K. W. Bouterwek, *Cædmon*, (1849-1854; see III[52]), I, 133 (his lines 3525b-39); C. W. M. Grein, *Bibliothek*, (1857-1858; see I[49]), I/1 94; R. P. Wülker, *Bibliothek . . . begründet von . . . Grein*, II/2 (1894; see III[52]), 476-7; W. Schmidt, 'Die altenglischen Dichtungen "Daniel" und "Azarias" ', *BBzA*, XXIII (1907), 7; F. A. Blackburn, *Exodus and Daniel* (1907; see III[52]), 67; G. P. Krapp, ASPR, I (1931), 111; R. T. Farrell, *Daniel and Azarias* (London, 1974), 47-8. The punctuation (and capitalization) in the text printed here follows no single editor, but is as it seems best to me.

15 þæt hie oft fela folca [*all zero*]   feore gesceodon, [TBlKF, BoGWS
                                                                    zero]
    heriges helmum, [TGWSBlK, BoF *zero*]   þara þe him hold ne wæs,
                                                                [BoGWSBlKF,/ T;]
    oðþæt hie wlenco anwod [BoGWSBlKF,/ T;]   æt winþege
                                                            [BoGWSBlKF *zero*/ T,]
    deofoldædum [*all*,]   druncne geðohtas, [TBo,/ GWS:/ Bl;/ K./ F.
                                                            followed by new paragraph]
    þa hie æcræftas [*all zero*]   ane forleton, [*all*,]
20 Metodes mægenscipe, [TBo./ GWSBlK,/ F;]   swa no man scyle [*all*
                                                                    zero]
    his gastes lufan [*all zero*]   wið Gode dælan. [TBoWSBlK./ GF!]

As I have punctuated it, so I translate it:

That was a brave nation, for as long as they were allowed to rule the realm,
(and) governed the citadels. Their prosperity was bright for as long as the
nation was willing to keep their father's [Abraham's?, Noah's??] covenant with
Him. The Guardian of the heavenly kingdom was a good Shepherd to them,
the holy Lord, the Ruler of glory, who gave to that host spirit and power, the
Lord of all creatures, so that they often harmed mortally many a nation,
leaders of the army, (many a one) that was not well-disposed towards them,
until pride seized them at the wine-drinking in Satanic deeds, drunken
thoughts, when they abandoned the virtues of (God's) law, (abandoned) the
Lord's mightiness, as no one ought to sever his soul's love from God.

The ASPR punctuation (and emendation of *weoldon*, line 9a, to *wealdan*) leads
to quite another sentence structure:

That was a brave nation!
    For as long as they were allowed to rule the realm, [*wealdan*] to govern the
citadels, their prosperity was bright. For as long as the nation was willing to
keep their Father's covenant among themselves, God, the Guardian of the
heavenly kingdom, was a protector to them, the holy Lord, the Ruler of glory.
That One gave to that host spirit and power, the Lord of all creatures, so that
they often harmed mortally many a nation, leaders of the army, (many a one)
that was not well-disposed towards them, until pride seized them at the wine-
drinking in Satanic deeds, drunken thoughts. Then they abandoned the virtues
of (God's) law, (abandoned) the Lord's mightiness, as no one ought to sever his
soul's love from God.

I have little doubt that the tearing up of this passage into two paragraphs (three
by Farrell), three full stops and one mark of exclamation, (plus one semi-colon
added by Farrell at line 9a), is against the spirit of Old English poetic statements
in several ways, yet there is no way of proving it. Nothing is gained by counting
the numbers of editors who support a particular mark of punctuation indicative
of sentence division. Editors follow each other: Schmidt follows Wülker,

Wülker follows Grein, and Farrell follows Krapp. For Old English verse, experience may, with whatever degree of self-delusion, guide a reader, to accept or reject an editor's imposition of sentence structures. When they differ, Wülker usually seems to me better than Krapp, because Wülker understands Old English word-order better than Krapp, and Wülker is less inclined than Krapp to chop up the sentence paragraphs of Old English verse into the smallest units to which they can be reduced: the smaller units facilitate translation into Modern English. The problem such passages present to our understanding is mainly of what we can let a sentence do in our modern language and what is beyond the capacity of modern punctuation. The problem posed by *Beowulf* lines 864-917a, by *The Phoenix* lines 424 ff.–437b ff., and by the opening and, probably, also by the total structure of *The Wanderer* is different from the more local problem which the *The Wanderer* presents in lines 106-10, how to join up the little asyndetic clauses. But it is a difference, not in kind, only in size: capacity is all about size. Our modern language has lost the capacity to accommodate the largest Old English sense units as a single syntactical unit.

No selected passages can be regarded as typical of all Old English verse. Nevertheless, some generalizations can be made. First, about our preoccupations and predilections. I believe that we are likely to answer, yes, if we were asked whether we consider syndetic hypotaxis as a means of expressing complex ideas superior to asyndetic parataxis; and we might go further, and say that until a language has evolved syndetic hypotaxis its speakers and writers cannot achieve complex ideas. But no Old English poem is unrelieved parataxis, not even *The Rune Poem*, which one might be inclined to compare, as if the nearest thing we have in Old English, with a modern alphabet poem, such as:

> **A** was an apple-pie.
> **B** bit it.
> **C** cut it.[74]

In Old English, there is poetic art in varying syndetic hypotaxis with asyndeta, as we have seen in *Beowulf* line 1003b, *fremme se þe wille!*, and line 2766b, *hyde se ðe wylle!* In fact, *The Rune Poem* is not a string of asyndeta, and has received high praise from Wilhelm Grimm, too high perhaps:[75]

> Kenner der eddischen Lieder werden eine gewisse Verwandtschaft damit finden: jene eigenthümliche Anschauung einzelner Naturzustände, und den reichen, oft großartigen Ausdruck, der sich in mannigfachen Wendungen und immer von neuem anhebenden Bildern gefällt. Wie schön und wahr gefühlt ist die Beschreibung von Eis, Wasser und Tag.

---

[74] *The Rune Poem* must not be undervalued by forcing such a comparison on it; I agree with much of M. Halsall's defence of it in her *The Old English* Rune Poem: *a critical edition*, McMaster Old English Studies and Texts, 2 (Toronto, Buffalo and London, 1981), 61-3 'The Literary Achievement of the *Rune Poem*'. Her defence avoids Wilhelm Grimm's enthusiasm.

[75] I quote his general praise, *Ueber deutsche Runen* (Göttingen, 1821), 234-5, in the notes to his edited text and translation of the poem, pp. 217-33.

[Those who know the Eddaic songs will find a certain affinity with them: that characteristic perception of natural conditions, and the rich, often magnificent expression which delights in idiomatic variety and in imagery always conceived afresh. How beautifully and justly the description of ice, water and day is felt!]

Stanza xi, 'ice' (lines 29-31), is asyndetic; but stanza, xxi 'water' (lines 63-6), and stanza xxiv, 'day' (lines 74-6) are not. I give these three stanzas, the text (the rune replaced by the rune name), and under it a translation; next Wilhelm Grimm's translation as he prints it in half lines, and lastly a translation of Grimm's translation (without attempting to correct its errors):

[xi]   IS byþ oferceald, ungemetum slidor.
        Glisnaþ glæshluttur gimmum gelicust,
        Flor forste geworuht, fæger ansyne.

[Ice is excessively cold, immeasurably slippery. It glistens as clear as glass most like jewels, a floor made by frost beautiful in appearance.]

E i s ist überkalt,	[*Ice* is over-cold,
unmäßig glatt,	immeasurably slippery,
glänzt glashell,	glistens glass-clear
Edelsteinen ähnlich:	similar to gemstones:
Flur von Frost gewirkt,	land fashioned by frost,
lieblich anzusehen.	lovely to behold.]

[xxi]   LAGU byþ leodum langsum geþuht
        gif hi sculun neþan on nacan tealtum,
        and hi sæyþa swyþe bregaþ,
        and se brimhengest bridles ne gymeþ.

[Water seems tedious to people if they must venture forth in a heaving boat, and the waves of the sea much frighten them, and the ocean-steed takes little notice of the bridle.]

W a s s e r ist den Leuten	[*Water* is to people
beständiger Gedanke,	a constant thought,
wenn sie sollen nieden	if they must below
in Nachen schwanken,	sway to and fro in boats,
und die Seewellen	and the sea-waves
sie gewaltig schrecken,	terrify them mightily,
und das Meer-Roß	and the sea-steed
des Zügels nicht achtet.	does not heed the bridle.]

[xxiv] DÆG byþ Drihtnes sond deore mannum,
        mære Metodes leoht, myrgþ and tohiht
        eadgum and earmum, eallum brice.

[Day is a gift sent by the Lord dear to people, the glorious light of God, joy and hope to the prosperous and wretched, of use to all.]

T a g ist des Herrn Bote,
theuer den Menschen,
herrliches Licht Gottes,
Freude und Zuversicht
Reichen und Armen,
allen gedeihlich.

[*Day* is the messenger of the Lord,
dear to humans,
glorious light of God,
joy and confident hope
for rich and poor,
beneficial to all.]

Conjunctives

No single passage of Old English verse can regarded as typical of all Old English verse. It may be useful to look again at *Beowulf* lines 2756-71, printed above (p. 94). In these lines we can find the means of expressing complex ideas, and, indeed, *Beowulf* is generally considered a poem the well-expressed ideas of which are often far from simple; whereas *The Rune Poem* is not usually praised for complexity of ideas, not even in Wilhelm Grimm's admiration of stanzas xi, xxi and xxiv. The clause conjunctives (including the relative pronoun) used to achieve the complexity of the *Beowulf* passage are, together with adverbials: *ða . . . þa* 'then . . . when' (2756), [*þær* 'there' (2762b), *swylce* 'likewise' (2767a),] *of ðam* 'from which' (2769b), *þæt* '(so) that', giving one time clause, one adjective clause, and one result clause; and the adverbs *þær* and *swylce* introduce clauses, main clauses in the usual analysis, of place and manner.

There happen to be no noun clauses in this passage, though they do occur quite often, especially for reported speech after verbs of speaking. Noun clauses are usually introduced by *þæt*, which is sometimes preceded by a formal pronoun object of the verb of speaking, *þæt* (strictly 'that', but often better rendered by 'this', or better still, left untranslated in Modern English). That formal object is in apposition with the noun clause. Thus in *Beowulf* 942-5: *þæt secgan mæg . . . þæt hyre Ealdmetod este wære*. This short sentence is worth quoting in full because in it the poet achieves complexity by well-organized hypotaxis:

> Hwæt, þæt secgan mæg
> efne swa hwylc mægþa   swa ðone magan cende
> æfter gumcynnum,   gyf heo gyt lyfað,
> 945   þæt hyre Ealdmetod   este wære
> bearngebyrdo.

[Truly, whichever of women gave birth to that son in manhood can say this, if she is living still, that the ancient Lord has been gracious to her in child-bearing.]

This translation fails to reproduce the full complexity of the compound conjunctive *efne swa hwylc . . . swa*, for which there is no idiomatic word-for-word rendering in Modern English. Compound conjunctions are common in Old English, and we must remember that the antecedents of many little Modern

English conjunctions go back to earlier phrases, as if whittled down by constant use.[76] Examples of conjunctives include OE *æfter þæm þe* > MnE *after*, OE *eal swa* > MnE *as*, OE *þa hwile þe* > MnE *while*, OE *þy læs þe* > MnE *lest*; ME *bi cause* partly taken over and partly calqued on OF *par cause de* 'by reason of' > MnE *because*, ME *on* (or *of*) *lasse than* (cf. French *á moins que*).[77] It will not do to say that compound conjunctions are a sign of a less advanced language than simplex conjunctions; first, because 'advanced' of a language means 'most like mine', as opposed to 'barbarous' or 'unformed' which means, usually by false prediction, 'not yet like mine', or as opposed to 'decayed' or 'debased' meaning 'past the prime condition I recognize in my own language and in the languages of selected foreigners ancient and modern'. Secondly, to mention just one foreign language, French has gained precision by phrasal conjunctions such as *á moins que*, *de crainte que* and (written as one word) *quoique*; at the same time, French allows *que* on its own to stand for many complex conjunctions of which it forms the last part.

Achieving clarity in verse; stichic style and 'Bogenstil'

Partly because metrical phrasing gives some clarity to the half-line sense unit, a clarity reinforced by the skilful use of the device of variation (discussed in the next chapter), and partly because clusters of unstressed syllables come at the beginning of larger sense units,[78] Old English verse can deploy connected sense units, sentences more like paragraphs, of a length and complexity such as are not found in Old English prose, not even in Ælfric's alliterative prose. In considering Old English verse, though as modern readers we need the editorial help given by punctuation of the kind with which we are familiar, we should always remember how the text appears in the manuscripts: written continuously like prose, sometimes with metrical pointing, sometimes, as in the case of *Beowulf*, with very rudimentary punctuation, sometimes, as in the case of *The Wanderer*, with pointing and small and larger initial capitals giving some help, not always clear, towards an understanding of the syntactic structure of the largest units.

---

[76] The classic statement of the theory that words in frequent use may be whittled down without loss of intelligibility is W. Horn, *Sprachkörper und Sprachfunktion*, Palaestra, 135 (2nd edition, 1923), for conjunctions, especially pp. 99-105. For a more recent discussion of the formation of Old English conjunctives, see B. Mitchell, 'The Origin of Old English Conjunctions: Some Problems', *Trends in Linguistics, Studies and Monographs*, 23 J. Fisiak (ed.), Historical Syntax, 271-99 (Berlin, New York, and Amsterdam: 1984 [reprinted in B. Mitchell, *On Old English* (1988; see III[39]), 269-95].

[77] Cf. A. Tobler, *Vermischte Beiträge zur französischen Grammatik*, (Leipzig, 1902-12), III/1, 105, IV/1, 50, for the history of the conjunction in French.

[78] Cf. E. G. Stanley, 'Initial Clusters', in M. Korhammer (ed.), *Words, Texts and Manuscripts . . . H. Gneuss* (1992; III[38]), 263-84.

Our predilection may be for short sentences. In *Beowulf* lines 864-917, or *The Phoenix* lines 424-42, or the opening and, probably, also the total structure of *The Wanderer*, we are not dealing with a long complex sentence which, when clumsily handled, bears in German the term of abuse *Schachtelsatz* 'package sentence', a term which emphasizes the embedding common in long Modern German sentences. Long sentences with embedding are not uncommon in Old English; at p. 94, above, we looked at *Beowulf* lines 2756-71b with 2764b-66 embedded within it. But a structure like *Beowulf* 865-917, if considered a syntactic unit, is not like that. It is no mere *Schachtelsatz*: it is a Russian-doll sentence, with independent sentence-units within independent sentence-units. Lines 884b-913a form an independent double-unit within the larger structure, and within lines 884-913, lines 889b *ne wæs him Fitela mid* [Fitela was not with him], 897b *wyrm hat gemealt* [the dragon melted hot], and 900b *he þæs ær onðah* [he had prospered by that] are independent little sentence-units.

These little sentences occupy second half-lines. Is that chance? It seems not to be. Before line 884 we find in *Beowulf*: 11b *þæt wæs god cyning* [that was an excellent king], 18b *blæd wide sprang* [renown spread far and wide], 114b *he him þæs lean forgeald* [He gave them their due reward for that], 137b *wæs to fæst on þam* [he was too firmly in their grip], 269b *wes þu us larena god!* [be good to us in advice!], 343b *Beowulf is min nama* [my name is Beowulf], 359b *cuþe he duguðe þeaw* [he knew the etiquette of high courtliness], 423b *wean ahsodon* [they courted trouble], 455b *Gæð a wyrd swa hio scel!* [the fated outcome always goes as it must!], 469b *se wæs betera ðonne ic!* [He was better than I!], 472b *he me aþas swor* [he swore oaths to me], 548b *hreo wæron yþa* [the waves were fierce], 586b *no ic þæs gylpe* [I do not boast of that], 651b *Werod eall aras* [the entire host rose], 730b *Þa his mod ahlog* [Then his spirit laughed], 754b *no þy ær fram meahte* [he could not get away at all], 760b *fingras burston* [his fingers burst], 811b *he fag wið God* [he at war with God], 852b *þær him hel onfeng* [hell received him there]; but also 210a *Fyrst forð gewat* [Time went by], 316a *Mæl is me to feran* [It is time for me to go], 407a *Wæs þu, Hroþgar, hal!* [Hail to you, Hrothgar!], 767a *Dryhtsele dynede* [The lordly hall resounded]. This list follows Klaeber's punctuation; but it would not be difficult to reduce the number of examples by different punctuation. An easy example is 852b, where, in fact, *þær* could be interpreted as 'where', and the half-line would then be a subordinate clause, as in very many editions.

Such short sentences do seem to occur far more frequently as second half-lines than as first half-lines. They interrupt the movement of the sentences as the longer sentence units run on from metrical line to metrical line. Looking at almost any passage of *Beowulf*, it soon becomes apparent that clauses more often begin with the second half-line than the first, but that the larger units, paragraphs and fits, usually begin with the first half-line. That is why some of Klaeber's paragraph divisions, many beginning with *Þa* 'Then', not only look odd in his printed text, but seem at variance with the flow of the poetry; thus at lines 331b, 702b, 1008b, 1159b, 1306b, 1441b, 1709b, 1724b, 2069b, 2231b (but the manuscript damage makes it impossible to say how best to organize the flow of the passage), 2354b, 2379b, 2462b, 2591b, 2711b, [2792b,] 2845b, and 2910b.

The relationship of the metrical unit, the long line divided into two half-lines, to the sense units, sentences constructed from phrases and clauses, is fundamental for an understanding of the alliterative verse of the Anglo-Saxons. There are basically two styles: the style in which the sense-unit usually begins at the beginning of a long line and ends at the end of a long line; and the style in which the sense unit usually begins at the caesura that is, at the beginning of a second half-line, and ends at the caesura, that is, at the end of a first half-line. The former style is often called stichic (vaguely reminiscent of 'end-stopped' blank verse); the latter (recalling, but not strictly comparable with, enjambment) is given the name *Bogenstil* 'curve-style', perhaps better 'S-bend style', or *Hakenstil* 'hook-style', perhaps better 'S-hook style'.[79] Almost any passage of *Beowulf* could serve as an example of *Bogenstil*; thus lines 205-16:

205   Hæfde se goda   Geata leoda
cempan gecorone || þara þe he cenoste
findan mihte. || Fiftyna sum
sundwudu sohte, || secg wisade,
lagucræftig mon   landgemyrcu. ||
210   Fyrst forð gewat; || flota wæs on yðum,
bat under beorge. || Beornas gearwe
on stefn stigon. || Streamas wundon,
sund wið sande. || Secgas bæron
on bearm nacan   beorhte frætwe,
215   guðsearo geatolic. || Guman ut scufon,
weras on wilsið,   wudu bundenne. ||

[The excellent man had chosen warriors from the people of the Geats of the boldest he could find. With fourteen men he went to the wooden ship, the warrior, a sea-skilled man, led the way to the land's edge.

Time went by; the ship was on the waves, the vessel under the cliff. The men readily went aboard the prow. The currents eddied, the sea against the shore. The warriors bore bright armour, adorned battle-equipment, into the hold of the ship. Men shoved off the well-braced vessel, warriors on their wished-for voyage.]

---

[79] Cf. E. G. Stanley, 'Heroic Lay', in *A Collection of Papers* (1987; see II[39]), 288-9 footnote 24. There is an excellent discussion of the relationship of verse structure to sentence structure in E. Sievers, *Altgermanische Metrik* (Halle, 1893), § 30; I follow Sievers in using *Beowulf* lines 205-16 to demonstrate what *Bogenstil* is (but I have not followed his punctuation, nor that of any one of the editions). Sievers does not use that term, which is A. Heusler's, and is most fully discussed by Heusler, 'Heliand, Liedstil und Epenstil', *ZfdA*, 57 (1920). 1-48 [reprinted in *Kleine Schriften* (1969; see I[50]), 517-65], especially II. Der freie Zeilenstil und seine Auflösung.

The pattern is one of S-bends, but each S laid flat and back-to-front:

Stichic style is less frequent in Old English; and poems are not uniformly stichic even when stichic style preponderates. Thus *The Battle of Finnsburh* lines 13-23:

> Ða aras mænig goldhladen ðegn,   gyrde hine his swurde. ||
> Ða to dura eodon   drihtlice cempan,
> 15 Sigeferð and Eaha,   hyra sword getugon,
> and æt oþrum durum   Ordlaf and Guþlaf, ||
> and Hengest sylf   hwearf him on laste. ||
> Ða gyt Garulf   Guðere styrode
> ðæt he swa freolic feorh   forman siþe
> 20 to ðære healle durum   hyrsta ne bær*e*,
> nu hyt niþa heard   anyman wolde; ||
> ac he frægn ofer eal   undearninga,
> deormod hæleaþ,   hwa ða duru heolde.

[Then many a gold-adorned retainer rose, girded on his sword. Then Sigeferth and Eahha, noble warriors, went to one doorway, drew their swords, and Ordlaf and Guthlaf (were) at the other doorway, and Hengest in person followed them. Then further Garulf urged on Guthhere[80] that he, a life so noble, should not at the first occasion bear armour to the door of the hall, now that one valiant in battles wished to take it. He, however, a brave-spirited warrior, asked openly above it all who held that doorway.]

It does not seem that the poet of *The Battle of Finnsburh* created stichic verse because his poetry is much simpler in sense and sentence structure than *Beowulf*. *Maxims II*, though even simpler in sense and sentence structure, is in *Bogenstil*, monotonously so at times; for example, in the *sceal* sentences of lines 16-41:

> Ellen sceal on eorle. || Ecg sceal wið hellme
> hilde gebidan. || Hafuc sceal on glofe
> wilde gewunian. || Wulf sceal on bearowe,

---

[80] Guthhere is usually considered the subject, Garulf the object, and emendations are often embarked on to achieve that; but the matter is irrelevant for the present purpose. On the whole, I believe the word-order favours the interpretation that Garulf is the subject [but cf. B. Mitchell, *Syntax* (1985; see III³²), §§ 11 and 3944], yet it is Garulf who gets killed at line 31; cf. J. Hill (ed.), *Old English Minor Heroic Poems*, Durham and St. Andrews Medieval Texts, 4 (1983), 85, s. Garulf.

         ear*m* anhaga. || Eofor sceal on holte
20   toðmægenes trum. || Til sceal on eðle
         domes wyrcean. || Daroð sceal on handa,
         gar golde fah. || Gim sceal on hringe
         standan steap and geap. || Stream sceal on yðum
         mecgan mereflode. || Mæst sceal on ceole,
25   segelgyrd seomian. || Sweord sceal on bearme,
         drihtlic isern. || Draca sceal on hlæwe,
         frod, frætwum wlanc. || Fisc sceal on wætere
         cynren cennan. || Cyning sceal on healle
         beagas dælan. || Bera sceal on hæðe,
30   eald ond egesfull. || Ea of dune sceal
         flodgræg feran. || Fyrd sceal ætsomne,
         tirfæstra getrum. || Treow sceal on eorle,
         wisdom on were. || Wudu sceal on foldan
         blædum blowan. || Beorh sceal on eorþan
35   grene standan. || God sceal on heofenum,
         dæda Demend. || Duru sceal on healle,
         rum recedes muð. || Rand sceal on scylde,
         fæst fingra gebeorh. || Fugel uppe sceal
         lacan on lyfte. || Leax sceal on wæle
40   mid sceote scriðan. || Scur sceal on heofenum,
         winde geblanden   in þas woruld cuman. ||

[Courage must dwell in the man. The sword must experience battle against the helmet. The fierce hawk must perch on the glove. The wolf, wretched and solitary, must be in the forest. The boar, strong through might of tusks, must be in the wood. The virtuous must strive for glory in the homeland. The lance must be held in the hand, the spear gold-adorned. The jewel, high and broad, must stand out on a ring. The current must stir the sea-flood in waves. The mast and the sailyard must be fixed on a ship. The sword, the glorious steel, must lie in the lap. The dragon, old, proud of his treasure, must lie in a barrow. The fish must bring forth its own kind in the water. The king must distribute treasure-rings in the hall. The bear must inhabit the heath, old and terrifying. The river must run down in a grey flood. The army must keep together, a comradeship intent on glory. Loyalty must dwell in the warrior, wisdom in the man. The wood must flourish in blossoms on earth. The mound must rise green on the land. God has his right abode in heaven, the Judge of deeds. The door, the building's wide mouth, must be set in the hall. The boss, the firm protection of fingers, must be set on the shield. The bird must disport itself high up in the air. The salmon with the trout must glide on its way in the ocean. The shower must be in the sky, must come into this world when stirred by the wind.]

IV

Some Metrical Considerations, Poetic Diction and Ornamentation

Essential differences between Old English prose and verse

We have no manual written by an Anglo-Saxon to tell us what was required in metre for an Old English poem. That some Anglo-Saxons were interested in Latin metres appears from Bede's *De metrica arte*, written while he was still a deacon, yet no statement survives by any Anglo-Saxon on the technical requirements of vernacular verse, nothing contemporary, or at least near contemporary when the tradition was to some extent alive, as is the case with Snorri Sturluson; the first (known to us) to write on the subject was George Hickes in the *Thesaurus* of 1705.[1]

If we try to define Old English verse so as to distinguish it from Old English prose, more particularly from Old English rhythmical prose, we must look away from any notions of imaginative quality, if such innocent notions still survive, as they did when F. J. E. Raby began his characterization of Bede's *De metrica arte* with 'His was not a poetical nature'.[2] The vernacular verse of the Anglo-Saxons requires regular alliteration within a restricted range of rhythmical patterns and makes use of diction not found in prose. These are the three essential ingredients:[3]

---

[1] *Skáldskaparmál*, in F. Jónsson (ed.), *Edda Snorra Sturlusonar*, 78-212 (Copenhagen, 1931); cf. A. Faulkes's translation (1987; see III[31]). G. Hickes, *Thesaurus* (1703-1705; see I[10]), I, 177-221.

[2] F. J. E. Raby, *A History of Christian-Latin Poetry from the Beginnings to the Close of the Middle Ages* (Oxford, 1927), 146. For more sympathetic considerations of Bede's metrical textbook, in the standard surveys of medieval Latin literature from which Raby might have learnt, see A. Ebert, *Allgemeine Geschichte der Literatur des Mittelalters im Abendlande bis zum Beginne des XI. Jahrhunderts* (2nd edn; Leipzig, 1889), I, 648-9, and M. Manitius, *Geschichte der lateinischen Literatur des Mittelalters*, in I. von Müller (ed.), Handbuch der klassischen Altertums-Wissenschaft, IX/2, vol. I (Munich, 1911), 74-5.

[3] See pp. 78-9 and n. 21, above, for the terms 'half-line' and 'long line', and for the history of printing verse in long lines. See p. 61 and n. 64, above, for some of the differences between the first and the second half-line.

1. RHYTHM. Old English poetry is rhythmical discourse, the unit of which is, as we have seen in the preceding chapter, the half-line. The variety of rhythmical patterns is limited, and the versifyers, with varying degrees of strictness, do not stray in rhythmical inventiveness beyond these limits.

2. ALLITERATION. As we have seen in the preceding chapter, two adjacent half-lines share in alliteration to form the alliterative long line. The alliterative syllables are those most strongly emphasized in what we believe to be the normal Old English system of stress. The number of alliterating syllables is limited to two in the first half-line, one in the second half-line. Because of this difference, the two halves of the long line are not equivalent in syllabic weight. The single alliterating syllable of the second half-line must come on the first stressed syllable; the half-line contains a second stressed syllable which does not share in the alliteration of the line.

3. DICTION. Some of the words (and a small number of longer locutions, including some syntactical contructions) used by the poets are not found in Old English outside rhythmical, alliterative discourse. In Middle English (and early Scottish verse, as well as to a very limited extent in early Modern English) a significant proportion of this diction, with ancestors in the poetic vocabulary of the Anglo-Saxons, is confined to the alliterative poetry of these later periods.

Rhythmical prose

There are in Old English, as also in early Middle English, several kinds of rhythmical prose, some with alliteration.[4] No neat borderline separates verse from prose; and in an age when verse was not written in verse lines, but continuously like prose,[5] no authorial intention is to be discerned in the manuscript testimony of the texts themselves. Heightened emotion was given rhythmical expression in prose of many periods of the English language. In Modern

---

4   For non-alliterative Old English prose, see A. McIntosh, 'Wulfstan's Prose', *PBA*, XXXV (1949), 109-42 [reprinted in E. G. Stanley (ed.), *British Academy Papers* (1990; see I[6]), 111-44; cf. D. Bethurum, 'Wulfstan', in E. G. Stanley (ed.), *Continuations and Beginnings* (1966; see II[65]), especially pp. 229-35. The best account of Ælfric's alliterative prose is that by J. C. Pope, in *Homilies of Ælfric* (1967-1968; see III[62]), I, Introduction, ch. 5 'Ælfric's Rhythmical Prose', 105-36. For the borderland of Old English verse and prose, cf. E. G. Stanley (ed.), *The Judgement of the Damned* (1985. With improvements 1987; see III[26]). For early Middle English rhythmical prose, alliterative with varying regularity, see B. Millett, 'The Saints' Lives of the Katherine Group and the Alliterative Tradition', *JEGP*, 87 (1988), 16-34; cf. B. Millett, ' "Hali Meiðhad", "Sawles Warde", and the Continuity of English Prose', in E. G. Stanley and D. Gray (eds), *Five Hundred Years of Words and Sounds A Festschrift for Eric Dobson* (Cambridge, 1983), 100-8, B. Millett and J. Wogan-Browne (eds), *Medieval English Prose for Women Selections from the Katherine Group and* Ancrene Wisse (Oxford, 1990), pp. xxxiv-xxxviii, and G. Shepherd (ed.) *Ancrene Wisse Parts Six and Seven* (London and Edinburgh, 1959), pp. lxvi-lxxiii.
5   Almost without exception; see p. 79 n. 22, above.

English literature, one thinks of Lady Wishfort addressing Waitwell, disguised as Sir Rowland in the hope of winning him to matrimony, for such is *The Way of the World*;[6] and of Dickens's ingenuous, yet skilful, grieving rhythms at the death of Little Nell:[7]

> For she was dead.
> No sleep so beautiful and calm,
> so free from trace of pain,
> so fair to look upon.
> She seemed a creature
> fresh from the hand of God,
> and waiting for the breath of life;
> not one who had lived
> and suffered death.
> Her couch was dressed with
> here and there
> some winter berries
> and green leaves,
> gathered in a spot
> she had been used to favour.
> "When I die,
> put near me something
> that loved the light,
> and had the sky above it
> always."
> Those were her words.

It is likely that in Old English similarly, as also in the other early West Germanic languages,[8] heightened emotions, including feelings aroused in prayer or in contemplating Judgement Day and eternal rewards and punishments, led to tighter prose rhythms to give expression to them. In a book on the poetry of the Anglo-Saxons there is not space to deal at length with their rhythmical prose too; but I give one example in Old English since this may be regarded as evidence of a link between feelings deeply moved and poetry, though all I have in mind is some regularity of rhythm which is a technical requirement of Old English verse, not the result of an overflow of emotion on the part of an Anglo-Saxon. The annal for AD 1011 in *The Anglo-Saxon*

---

[6] See E. G. Stanley, '*The Judgement of the Damned*' (1985. With improvements, 1987; see III²⁶), 370-2.

[7] Charles Dickens, *The Old Curiosity Shop*, ch. lxxi, *ad finem*. I have arranged in rhythmical lines the passage printed as ordinary prose, in the edition in weekly parts: the last part of *Master Humphrey's Clock*, No. 44, Saturday, 30 January 1841, ch. LXXI, p. 209.

[8] For similarities between the rhythmical prose of the older continental West Germanic languages and that in Old English, see E. G. Stanley, 'Alliterative Ornament and Alliterative Rhythmical Discourse in Old High German and Old Frisian Compared with Similar Manifestations in Old English', *Beiträge*, 106 (Tübingen, 1984), 184-217.

Chronicle[9] recounts, in a manner that may be found affecting even now nearly a thousand years later, how Archbishop Ælfheah was taken prisoner at Canterbury by the Danes, who, violent in their drunken feasting, slew him after he had been held for seven months in shameful captivity. The chronicler gives expression to the hostage-taking, exceptionally, in rhythmic prose. Some editors print the rhythmical passage in long lines as if it were verse; but I print it in phrases (of half-line length) because there is no alliteration, and several of the phrases do not give good metre, much like Dickens's rhythmic prose:

> Wæs ða ræpling
> se ðe ær wæs heafod
> Angelkynnes
> ond Cristendomes.
> Þær man mihte ða geseon yrmðe
> þær man oft ær geseah blisse
> on þære earman byrig,
> þanon com ærest
> Cristendom ond blis
> for Gode ond for worulde.

[Then was he captive who had been head of English Christendom. There misery was to be seen then where often before happiness was seen in that wretched city, from where Christianity and bliss first came in Church and State.][10]

On the whole, I do not believe that the annalist strayed into rhythmical utterance inadvertently, so moved that he could not help it. There was too much rhythmical prose about by 1011 for inadvertency in such matters. At a time when much verse seems no longer to have been produced, Ælfric and Wulfstan wrote their different kinds of rhythmical prose for various purposes. In Medieval Latin, rhythmical prose had a long pedigree, and some relationship of vernacular rhythmical prose to Latin models, with ornamental features including alliteration and rhyme, is likely, but difficult to demonstrate; and, since alliteration and rhythm in vernacular prose seem to have closer affinity to

---

9 I quote the Abingdon Chronicle, British Library MS Cotton Tiberius B.i. The manuscript is more heavily pointed for these lines (and for the Chronicle poems) than for non-rhythmical prose. For the text, see D. Whitelock (ed.), *Sweet's Anglo-Saxon Reader in Verse and Prose* (Oxford, 1967, and reprints), 94-6. Cf. D. H. Farmer, *The Oxford Dictionary of Saints* (Oxford, 1978, and corrected reprints), s. Alphege.

10 In some respects my translation is not literal. I believe *Angelkynnes ond Cristendomes* constitutes an hendiadys, and therefore do not translate it literally 'of the English people and of Christendom'. The phrase *for Gode ond for worulde* could well mean 'in the eyes of God and the world', but it is a phrase not uncommon in homiletic prose, especially the prose of Archbishop Wulfstan of York, Ælfheah's contemporary; see D. Whitelock (ed.), *Sermo Lupi ad Anglos* (3rd edn; London, 1963 and corrected reprints), 55 line 72, and glossary s.v. *God*: '*for Gode & for worulde*, in matters of Church and State 72.' For *þanon com ærest* other manuscripts read *þanon us com ærest* 'from where first came to us'.

alliteration and rhythm in vernacular poetry than to the ornaments and rhythms in Latin *Kunstprosa*, both these traditions are likely to have contributed to Old English rhythmical prose.[11] It is not impossible, likely even but we lack contemporary evidence, that the Anglo-Saxon masters of rhythmical prose, Ælfric and Wulfstan, derived much of their prosodic art from the vernacular tradition in verse and prose, but their practice may have gained support and assurance of legitimacy within a Christian orthodoxy from Latin *Kunstprosa*, at a time from which, most probably as a result of the Benedictine Reform of the last quarter of the tenth century, longer vernacular poems on Christian themes do not survive and may not have been allowed to be written. That would accord well with Ælfric's dropping his use of *Dryhten* as a *nomen sacrum*, a word originally secular and heroic in application to the leader of a warlike band.[12]

A prose writer as syntactically complex as Ælfric is likely to have been conscious of the clarity that could be achieved (even in manuscripts with only rudimentary punctuation, like the *Beowulf* manuscript) in long and complicated Old English syntactical verse units of sentence length and longer, because of the regularity of metrical phrasing, in each phrase the most important lexical item (or items) brought into prominence by alliteration. Yet a man of his grammatical bent, and centrally placed in the movement of Benedictine Reform,[13] is unlikely

---

[11] Any reference to the voluminous scholarship of Greek and Latin *Kunstprosa*, Classical, Medieval and Renaissance, must begin with E. Norden, *Die antike Kunstprosa vom VI. Jahrhundert v. Chr. bis in die Zeit der Renaissance* (Leipzig, 1898; reprinted Leipzig and Berlin, 1915-1918); see his index (s.vv. Alliteration, *cursus* orationis, Hendiadyoin, Reim, Worte, Wortspiel, etc.) for the relevant discussion. Other treatments of the subject include: W. Meyer, *Gesammelte Abhandlungen zur mittellateinischen Rhythmik*, II (Berlin, 1905), 'Die rhythmische lateinische Prosa', 236-86 (402-3); K. Polheim, *Die lateinische Reimprosa* (Berlin, 1925), especially pp. ix-xx, 'Reim und Kursus' 55-87, and 'Angelsachsen und Iren' 309-20; and, less directly concerned with Anglo-Saxon authors, T. Janson, *Prose Rhythm in Medieval Latin from the 9th to the 13th Centuries*, Studia Latina Stockholmiensia, 20 (1975).

Cf. J. Kuryłowicz, *Die sprachlichen Grundlagen der altgermanischen Metrik* (Innsbruck, 1970); S. M. Kuhn, 'Cursus in Old English: Rhetorical Ornament or Linguistic Phenomenon?', *Speculum*, 47 (1972), 188-206 [reprinted in S. M. Kuhn, *Studies in the Language & Poetics of Anglo-Saxon England* (Ann Arbor, 1984), 167-85]; M. R. Godden, 'Aelfric & the Vernacular Prose Tradition', in P. E. Szarmach and B. F. Huppé (eds), *The Old English Homily and its Background* (Albany, New York, 1978), 99-117, especially 109-10 and note 34 with references to two earlier studies, that by G. H. Gerould, 'Abbot Ælfric's Rhythmic Prose', *MP*, 22 (1924-1925), 353-66 [deriving Ælfric's rhythmical prose from Latin examples, now generally rejected; cf. J. C. Pope, *Homilies of Ælfric* (1967-1968; see III[62]), I, 108-9; and D. Bethurum, 'The Form of Ælfric's *Lives of Saints*', *SP*, 29 (1932), 515-33 (setting Ælfric's rhythmical prose within the vernacular tradition)]. See also the references at p. 116 n. 4, above.

[12] See M. R. Godden, 'Ælfric's Changing Vocabulary', *ESts*, 61 (1980), 206-23. Cf. E. G. Stanley, 'New Formulas for Old: *Cædmon's Hymn*', forthcoming in *Germania Latina*, II (Groningen, 1994). Much is made of the warlike origins of the word *dryhten*, and its later dissociation from warfare, by D. H. Green, *The Carolingian Lord* (Cambridge, 1965), part two, *truhtin*.

[13] For the linguistic implications, see H. Gneuss, 'The origin of Standard Old English and Æthelwold's school at Winchester', *ASE*, 1 (1972), 63-83; W. Hofstetter, *Winchester und der*

to have developed his kind of *Kunstprosa* if nothing at all like it had existed in Christian Latin writings.

The metre of Old English verse: basic facts known securely, and some reasonable inferences

Some basic facts underlie discussion of Old English versification and metrical theories. Of these facts some are apparent from the poetic manuscripts, others have been inferred from the texts by analysis, usually helped by statistics:[14]

1. Metrical pointing in the manuscripts and macaronic verse allow the modern reader to discern metrical half-lines. That evidence serves as a basis for the editorial division of all verse, however pointed, into long lines consisting of pairs of alliterating half-lines.
2. We know, because of the system of stress in English and closely related languages, which syllable in words of more than one syllable the stress must fall: usually the stem-syllable, but in mominal compounds, often the prefix (other than *ge-*). We surmise that in nominal compounds, including names, both elements are stressed.
3. We know which classes of words are always stressed: nominals and non-finite parts of verbs; and we know which classes of words are normally unstressed: most function words.
4. We know that inflexional syllables are not silent, though always unstressed; and we surmise that final *-e* may be elided before an initial vowel of the next word in the same half-line.
5. We can see where there is alliteration, and we can deduce how it works in binding two half-lines into a long line. We can see that there is a minimum length for the half-line, four syllables. At least one syllable must be stressed and alliterate in the first half-line; usually the first half-line has two stressed syllables of which the first must and the second may alliterate. Two syllables must be stressed in the second half-line, and the first stress must alliterate.

---

spätaltenglische Sprachgebrauch, Münchener Universitäts-Schriften, Philosophische Fakultät, Texte und Untersuchungen zur Englischen Philologie, 14 (1987).

[14] On 'half-line', 'resolution, resolve', and other terms used, see R. W. Burchfield, 'Prosodic Terminology' (1974; see III[21]). On the division of Old English into half-lines and printing in long lines, also see III[21]; cf. 'Initial Clusters of Unstressed Syllables' (1992; see III[38]).

Point 8. states the principles of resolution too simply. In fact, resolution does not take place in the second stress of a relatively rare metrical pattern, in *Beowulf* highly exceptional; for example, *Beowulf* line 1828b *hwilum dydon* [did at times], *Exodus* line 391b *tempel Gode* [tempel to God], *Genesis* line 1553a *folc geludon* [nations are descended], *Daniel* line 735b and *Genesis* line 1818a *Drihtne gecoren* [chosen by the Lord], *Riddle* 27 line 14a *mægene binumen* [deprived of strength], *Riddle* 93 line 12a *strong on stæpe* [strong of step]. This important exception to the principle of resolution is discussed by H. Schabram, '*The Seasons for Fasting* 206f. Mit einem Beitrag zur ae. Metrik', in W. Iser and H. Schabram (eds), *Britannica Festschrift für Hermann M. Flasdieck* (Heidelberg, 1960), 221-40.

In the count of syllables it is to be noted that in the manuscripts some words, originally of two syllables, have been contracted to appear as monosyllables, and the original uncontracted form may be required metrically.

6. Half-lines with more than two stresses often have two alliterative syllables: some patterns of heavy stress call for double alliteration; and, since double alliteration cannot occur in the second half-line, such heavy patterns can occur only as first half-lines.

7. We can see that clusters of unstressed syllables usually occur once only in each clause, namely at its beginning.

8. We can see that at the end of the half-line at most one single unstressed syllable occurs, unless the preceding stressed syllable is metrically short and that short stressed syllable is not preceded immediately by a long stressed syllable. A short stressed syllable followed in the same word by an unstressed syllable is the metrical equivalent of a long syllable: the stress is said to be 'resolved'. A resolved stress may be followed by an unstressed syllable at the end of the half-line.

9. It follows that the length of stressed syllables is significant. A stressed syllables is metrically long when it contains a long vowel or ends in one or more consonants which close the syllable (that is the consonant must end the word or be the first of a cluster of two or more consonants). All stressed monosyllabic words (or monosyllabic stem-syllables in words preceded by an unstressed prefix) are metrically long.

The rest is more speculative inference or pure theory.

The Common Germanic origins of alliterative verse

As regards the early history, the proto-history even, of Old English versification, it is highly probable that alliterative verse was not the invention of the Anglo-Saxons after they settled to England in the middle of the fifth century. They must have composed alliterative verse while still in their continental homes: but none of that survives.

Other Germanic peoples on the continent and in Scandinavia had alliterative verse, though none now extant is earlier than that of the Anglo-Saxons.[15] The

---

[15] The inscription on the Golden Horn of Gallehus is thought to be no later than the beginning of the fifth century, and is usually regarded as the earliest known alliterative line. The language of the inscription is generally accepted as Norse of the earliest recorded period. Cf. K. Düwel, *Runenkunde* (Stuttgart, 1968), 28; W. Krause (and H. Jahnkuhn), *Die Runeninschriften im älteren Futhark*, Abhandlungen der Akademie der Wissenschaften in Göttingen, Philologisch-Historische Klasse, 3rd series, 65 (1966), 97-103. Gallehus, where the horn with the inscription was found, is near the larger village of Møgeltønder, on Jutland just north of the Danish-German frontier, in the land of the Angles, and it has been asserted, unconvincingly, that the language is proto-Anglian; see G. Baesecke, *Vorgeschichte* (1940; see I[85]), 111-12, 143, and 152 (the Angle king Offa spoke the language of the Horn of

West Germanic tribes most closely related to the Anglo-Saxons, especially the Old Saxons (who, unlike the Anglo-Saxons, their continental neighbours, did not emigrate to Britain but stayed in what is now northern Germany), also had Christian alliterative verse of which two poems are extant, namely, *Heliand* and fragments of *Genesis*.[16] There are connections between both these poems and England: one of the two most nearly complete manuscripts of *Heliand* is of Anglo-Saxon scriptorial workmanship of the later tenth century; and the Old Saxon *Genesis* is translated in the Old English *Genesis B*.[17] It is possible that Old Saxon alliterative verse is influenced by the Old English alliterative, Christian verse which Anglo-Saxon missionaries and the Anglo-Saxon religious who followed them may have brought with them and may have given to the continental religious houses. If the Old Saxons had, as is usually believed, their own tradition of alliterative poetry, its adaptation for Christian use is likely to have been the result of contact with Anglo-Saxon Christianity. On the other hand, that England is the recipient in the tenth century is certainly shown by the inclusion in *Genesis* of an interpolation translated (later than the composition of *Genesis A*) from an Old Saxon poem, and is shown also by the Caligula MS of *Heliand*

Gallehus!). Its alliteration depends on names, as in many inscriptions and lists of kings; cf. J. de Vries, *Altnordische Literaturgeschichte*, 2nd edn, in (H. Paul), Grundriss der germanischen Philologie (3rd edn, ed. W. Betz: Berlin, 1964), I, 13-15; Baesecke, *Vorgeschichte*, p. 313. *Beowulf* line 61 is often adduced for alliteration on names:

> Heorogar ond Hroðgar   ond Halga til

[Heorogar and Hrothgar and the good Halga].

Or may one, in this connection, think of the alliteration in *Widsith* line 35 [without opening the can of worms in R. W. Chambers (ed.), *Widsith* (1912; see I[35]), 84-92, and 202 note on the line, and K. Malone (ed.), *Widsith* (1936; see I[45]), 21-3, cf. 2nd edn (1962; see I[45]), 39-40]? –

> Offa weold Ongle,   Alewih Denum

[Offa ruled Angle, Alewih the Danes].

16 For the language of the poems (and often also the language of some smaller texts, of Low German origin till about 1150) the term 'Old Saxon' is in general use and corresponds to German *altsächsisch*. The term 'Old Low German', corresponding to *altniederdeutsch*, is used for the group of early North German dialects, including Old Saxon but not necessarily the language of the Saxon tribe only; the term is sometimes preferred to Old Saxon when the point is being made that it is not certain if the language of a particular text is strictly that of the Old Saxon tribe.

The standard edition of the Old Saxon poetic texts is that by E. Sievers, *Heliand* (Halle, 1878; reissued with an appendix including the Prague fragment of *Heliand* and the Vatican fragments of *Heliand* and *Genesis*, edited by E. Schröder; Halle and Berlin, 1935).

17 See R. Priebsch, *The Heliand Manuscript Cotton Caligula A. VII in the British Museum* (Oxford, 1925). The Old Saxon origin of the Old English *Genesis* lines 235-851 was demonstrated by E. Sievers, *Der Heliand und die angelsächsische Genesis* (Halle, 1875), and confirmed by the discovery of the Old Saxon fragments in the Vatican, published by K. Zangemeister and W. Braune, 'Bruchstücke der altsächsischen Bibeldichtung aus der Bibliotheca Palatina', *Neue Heidelberger Jahrbücher*, 4 (1894), 205-94 (also published separately, without plates).

which was 'produced in Southern England at some centre in touch with the Benedictine reform movement of the tenth century'.[18]

The amount of alliterative verse from the Old High German area is small, and what little there is differs from Old English alliterative verse in being metrically less strict; Old Saxon alliterative metre has many half-lines of greater length than occur in Old English (except very rarely), but it has also many shorter half-lines similar to ordinary Old English verse. Metrically, though less tight perhaps than Old English, there is systematic regularity which is absent from Old High German alliterative metre. Old High German alliterative verse includes the secular poem *Hildebrandslied*, (under seventy lines long), and much valued by those who wish for evidence of the heroic world of Germania before it was lost to Christianity; and it is therefore perhaps overvalued by them.[19] Yet even if we regard that as an error to be avoided, this single fragmentary piece must provide evidence for the existence of early German heroic poetry, not exactly *Volkspoesie*. It must provide also the basis for any evaluation of indigenous West Germanic poetic art on the continent and, less aesthetically, how Old High German alliterative metre in general resembled, but in detail differed from, the metres of *Beowulf* (3182 lines long) and *Heliand* (almost 6000 lines long). The metaphor, drawn by A. Ebert from Comparative Anatomy, may be

---

[18] F. Wormald, 'Decorated Initials in English MSS. from A.D. 900 to 1100', *Archaeologia*, XCI (1945), 120; the relevant section (pp. 119-21) is 'Initials from the Middle of the Tenth Century to about the year 1000', Wormald's 'Type I', 'distinguished . . . by the use of a complete creature to form the whole or part of a letter' and 'certainly derived from the same sort of creatures found in the Junius Psalter' of the first half of the tenth century, perhaps from Winchester [cf. N. R. Ker, *Catalogue* (1957; see III³), no. 335]. For the importance of Anglo-Saxon Benedictines in the foundation history of monasteries in Germania, see W. Levison, *England and the Continent in the Eighth Century* (Oxford, 1946), 103. Contacts between England and monastic houses at Werden and Essen in the territory of the Old Saxons are well documented by R. Drögereit, *Werden und der Heliand* (Essen, 1951), though it would be unwise to regard Werden as more than one possible place of origin of *Heliand*, among several; cf. J. K. Bostock, *Handbook*, revised by K. C. King and D. R. McLintock (1976; see III²¹), 179, in an excellent account (pp. 168-86, on the metre 305-19) of the poem. Athelstan's relations with the continent included in 930 the marriage of his sister Edith to that son Otto of the Emperor Henry I, the Fowler, who became Otto I, the Great. Bearing gifts from Athelstan, Bishop Coenwald of Worcester visited many continental monasteries, including St Gall with its library and archives well preserved to this day, so that information survives about Coenwald's embassy; see D. Whitelock, M. Brett and C. N. L. Brooke, *Councils & Synods with Other Documents Relating to the English Church* (Oxford, 1981), I, 40-3, no. 10. That document has been valued as important by historians, from C. P. Cooper onwards [see his *Report on Rymer's Foedera*, Appendix A (for the Record Commission, printed in 1836 and distributed to Members of the Commission and selected scholars in 1837), 84]. Cf. K. Leyser, 'Die Ottonen und Wessex', *Frühmittelalterliche Studien*, 17 (1983), 73-97. For contacts between England and Germany at the end of the century, see also J. Campbell, 'England, France, Flanders and Germany in the Reign of Ethelred II: Some Comparisons and Connections', in D. Hill (ed.), *Ethelred the Unready. Papers from the Millenary Conference*, British Archaeological Reports, British Series, 59 (1978), 255-70, reprinted in J. Campbell, *Essays in Anglo-Saxon History* (London and Ronceverte, 1986), 191-207 (especially pp. 195-7).

[19] Cf. the remarks of the Brothers Grimm (1812; see I²⁰), quoted above, p. 10.

applicable, but the presumed certainty that the outcome of such anatomical reconstruction would, for the earliest German poetry, lead to the King of Beasts, the Lion, may be significant in revealing Ebert's preoccupations and predilections and his insufficient awareness of how much had to be hypothesized:[20]

> Viel später als in England beginnt in Deutschland eine Literatur in nationaler Sprache sich zu entwickeln. Und doch ging ihr eine alte, vielleicht auch reiche Volkspoesie voraus, die auch bereits einen nicht geringen Grad ästhetischer Reife erlangt hatte, wie uns ein einziges, und nicht einmal vollständig erhaltenes Gedicht, das wohl Ende des achten Jahrhunderts aufgezeichnet wurde, beweist. Es ist die Klaue aus der wir den Löwen erkennen; um so mehr verdient es eine genauere Betrachtung: ich meine das H i l d e b r a n d s l i e d .

> [Vernacular literature began to develop in Germany much later than in England. And yet folk-poetry, ancient and perhaps rich also, had preceded it, which had already achieved no small measure of aesthetic maturity, as is demonstrated to us by one single, not even completely preserved poem, probably written down at the end of the eighth century. This is the claw in which we recognize the lion; it deserves our close scrutiny all the more. I refer to *Hildebrandslied*.]

If we try and reconstruct a metrical system from *Hildebrandslied* we obtain something very irregular, judged by the standards of *Beowulf*, a very high proportion of lines with only one stress and a very high proportion of lines longer than is usual in *Beowulf* (though perhaps to be comprehended in the concept of hypermetric lines), as well as many examples of lines with alliteration 'irregular' by Old English standards.[21]

Some presumably ancient, Eddaic metres, though preserved in manuscripts of a period much later than Old English, have close affinities to the alliterative

---

[20] A. Ebert, *Allgemeine Geschichte* (1887-1889; see IV²), III, 97.

[21] See the acccount in J. K. Bostock's *Handbook*, revised by K. C. King and D. R. McLintock (1976; see III²¹), 319-22. The vehemence of E. Sievers in controversy on Germanic metre together with his strenuous advocacy (till he was converted to *Schallanalyse*) of his own system of scansion, for example, in *Altgermanische Metrik* (1893; see III⁷⁹), §§ 3, 124-37 and 139, has led many scholars to follow him in scanning Old High German verse like *Beowulf*, yet his system is not flexible enough to accommodate within it what he finds: in *Hildebrandslied* he condemns many lines as of doubtful regularity, at least one line arouses his suspicion that it is prose, and several others are quite irregular. *Muspilli* (§ 130) is lacunose and contains prose sentences, and *Wessobrunner Gebet* and the *Merseburg Zaubersprüche* (§§ 137, 138) are no more regular. The much more open description of the metre of *Hildebrandslied* (with mention of *Wessobrunner Gebet* and *Muspilli*) by Karl Lachmann ['Über das Hildebrandslied', *Abhandlungen der Akademie der Wissenschaften zu Berlin aus dem Jahre 1833* (Berlin, 1835), 123-62, especially 128-31; reprinted in K. Müllenhoff (ed.), *Karl Lachmann, Kleinere Schriften*, I (1876; see III²¹), especially 413-17], does not, as he says [pp. 129-30 (= 414)], amount to the regular system he claims for it, with four lifts to each 'regular' half-line, giving eight for the long line, and also 'regular' half-lines of only two lifts; he himself acknowledges that such an open system may easily degenerate. Cf. E. G. Stanley, 'Alliterative Rhythmical Discourse' (1984; see IV⁸).

metre found most strictly used in *Beowulf*, and are regarded as Scandinavian developments of Germanic alliterative metre, such as found in the West Germanic languages, including Old English.[22] The existence of related forms of alliterative verse in so many Germanic dialects makes it likely that, in spite of frequent and continual contacts over many centuries between England and the continent and England and Scandinavia, no Germanic nation gave or received from any other this form of verse. That alliterative verse, not all identical in metrical detail, is found in the several ancient Germanic literatures leads to the inference that alliterative verse is a shared Germanic form, and in England, therefore, a part of the Germanic heritage of the Anglo-Saxons. It is possible, however, that Christian alliterative poetry such as, according to Bede, Cædmon was the first to sing, was an English export to the continent. For the Scandinavian verse closest in metrical form to Old English verse, English influence is not usually invoked; though Scandinavian influence has been invoked often to explain the stanzaic form of *Deor* and *Wulf and Eadwacer*,[23] but not, as far as I know, to explain the stanzaic form of *The Seasons for Fasting*.

It is demonstrable that Old English verse is metrically more exact than the comparable verse of the continental peoples closest to the Anglo-Saxons linguistically. Perhaps this metrical exactness is the result of monastic interest in Latin versification, and Bede's *De metrica arte* might be thought to exemplify and foster that interest; but since on the continent too Bede's treatise was widely

---

[22] See Sievers, *Altgermanische Metrik* (1893; see III[79]) §§ 32-58. A. Heusler, *Deutsche Versgeschichte*, I, in H. Paul (ed.), Grundriss der germanischen Philologie, VIII/1 (3rd edn; Berlin 1925), §§ 271-313. The Eddaic metres are given names and provided with examples by Snorri Sturluson in *Háttatal*; see F. Jónsson (ed.), *Edda Snorra Sturlusonar* (1931; see IV[1]), 213-52. For an excellent, brief account, with a valuable bibliography, see Klaus von See, *Germanische Verskunst* (Stuttgart, 1967), 56-60.

[23] The suggestion made by Sir C. Ball, 'Inconsistencies in the Main Runic Inscriptions on the Ruthwell Cross', in A. Bammesberger (ed.), *Old English Runes and their Continental Background*, AF, 217 (1991), 113-15, that the verse inscription forms verse in (unequal) stanzas is unconvincing:

> the standard Old English verse line is indeed the 'Caedmonian line', and . . . previously – and no doubt in some places for a time thereafter – other metrical possibilities co-existed. These might have included stanzaic forms and various mixtures of the three line-types: unsupported half-lines, normal (Caedmonian) lines and hypermetric lines. The poem on the Ruthwell Cross, is a unique relic of an alternative poetic tradition. Stanzaic verse is also found in Old Norse.

The opening *Ondgeredæ hinæ* is, as is obvious metrically, part of the following half-line (as in *The Dream of the Rood* line 39a); and before each of the other, metrically very different single half-lines (corresponding to *The Dream of the Rood* lines 44b, 56b and 62b) '. . .' is an acknowledgement that there is an omission, which could be of an even or an odd number of half-lines in each case.

A. J. Bliss, 'The Origin and Structure of the Old English Hypermetric Line', *N&Q*, 217 (1972), 242-8, explains some Old English hypermetric lines as related to the Scandinavian *ljóðaháttr*, and believes they go back to a common ancestry. In Old English this relatively rare kind of lines is more common in the *Maxims* than in other verse.

disseminated in the monasteries, and there was a similar interest in Latin versification, it is not a safe inference to connect Old English metrical exactness with
Anglo-Saxon monastic interest in metrics.[24] Probably we can go no further than
to say that most Old English verse is metrically exact; but some is less exact,
and not all of the metrically less exact verse is to be securely assigned to a late
date of composition, for example, *The Battle of Finnsburh*.

Systems of scansion

It is not my purpose to review the several systems of scansion available for
Germanic verse and, specifically, for Old English verse, or to promote one of
these systems of scansion. Several systems have been devised, and some are
widely used.[25] Some of the most recent studies, particularly those by G. Russom
and C. B. Kendall, draw on a greater number of quantifiable, observable characteristics than Sievers did and are well founded on the linguistics of Old English
poetry, thus shedding clear light on insufficiencies in Sievers's system, so that
they are likely to lead even further away from the imposition of Sievers's 'types'
on Germanic verse than we had been led by such masters of metrics as Heusler,
Pope and Bliss.

In weighing the value of systems of scansion, the first question to ask is, what
do we hope to gain from scanning Old English verse? Do we wish to develop a
sensitive reading skill? Or do we intend to find out what the Anglo-Saxons
themselves did when writing verse, in order that we, perhaps as editors of their

---

[24] Cf. A. Campbell, 'The Old English Epic Style', in N. Davis and C. L. Wrenn, *English and
Medieval Studies Presented to J. R. R. Tolkien* (London, 1962), 16 note 1:

> I differ from him [H. Kuhn] in believing that the Old English monastic
> poets represent an advance on the pre-literate poets in their attention to this
> matter [the observance of 'Kuhn's Laws'], and to some other refinements.
> Kuhn regards *Beowulf* as the most archaic Germanic poetry because it
> keeps his laws best. I would rather think that *Beowulf* (and similar English
> book epics) represent a tightening up of these laws.

[25] For an illuminating account of some of the more important of them, see J. C. Pope, *The
Rhythm of Beowulf* (New Haven 1942; revised edn; 1966), pp. ix-xxiii, 6-37. Pope's own
theory and practice are important; and his 'Appendix: Catalogue of Rhythmic Variation in the
Normal Verses of *Beowulf*', together with his line index to the catalogue is immensely useful.
Of importance too is A. J. Bliss, *The Metre of Beowulf* (1967; see II[64]). E. Sievers set out his
system most fully in 'Zur Rhythmik des germanischen Alliterationsverses', *Beiträge*, 10
(1885), 209-314, 451-545; 12 (1886), 454-82. Other studies include: E. Neuner, *Über
ein- und dreihebige Halbverse in der altenglischen alliterierenden Poesie* (Berlin doctoral
dissertation, 1920); A. Heusler, *Deutsche Versgeschichte* (1925; see IV[22]); T. Cable, *The
Meter and Melody of* Beowulf, Illinois Studies in Language and Literature, 64 (Urbana,
Chicago and London, 1974). Two recent books are important: G. Russom, *Old English Meter
and Linguistic Theory* (Cambridge, 1987); C. B. Kendall, *The Metrical Grammar of* Beowulf, Cambridge Studies in Anglo-Saxon England, 5 (1991). H. Kuhn's 'Laws', as enunci-
ated in 'Wortstellung und -betonung' (1933; see III[35]), have been increasingly influential.

verse and, especially, as emenders of extant manuscript readings, may have the assurance that we are creating nothing that goes against Old English metrical practice?

If the aim is to read the verse well, we must deal, to our own satisfaction as readers or reciters, with the striking variety in length of their half-lines: a half-line in a poem as 'regular' as *Beowulf* may be as short as line 100a *eadiglice* [happily], or as long as (or even longer than) line 722b *syþðan he hire folmum æthran* [when he touched it with (his) hands]; we must deal with a long line as short as line 566,

> be yðlafe   uppe lægon
>
> [were lying high by the shore],

or as long as (or even longer than) line 595,

> ac he hafað onfunden   þæt he þa fæhðe ne þearf
>
> [but he has discovered that he need not [*onsittan* 'be terrified of'] that enmity].

Did the Anglo-Saxons in their recitation allow equal time to lines of such different length? If so, they must have drawn out the short and gabbled the long half-lines to increase the former and reduce the latter till they occupied one standard measure of time for each half-line (that is, in the jargon of the subject, to make them 'isochronous'); or they must have had 'rests', to use the musical term, before, after, or during their shorter half-lines to make them isochronous with their longer half-lines, perhaps combined with drawing out or gabbling. We use rests for special emphasis in verse or prose.[26] Did the Anglo-Saxons too? We know nothing of Old English patterns of intonation; but if they did, they could not have introduced rests to achieve isochronism for each half-line without producing false emphases. Heusler, who believed in isochronism of the half-line, simply denied the possibility that the ancient poets availed themselves of the occasional special emphasis of a syllable, citing examples in Modern

---

[26] Cf. D. Abercrombie, 'Some functions of silent stress', in A. J. Aitken, A. McIntosh and H. Pálsson (eds), *Edinburgh Studies in English and Scots* (London, 1971), 147-56. A. J. Bliss, *Metre of Beowulf* (1967; see II[64]), 24 note 2, quotes with approval Daniel Jones's characterization of stress:

> Stresses are essentially subjective activities of the speaker. A strongly stressed syllable, for instance, is one which he consciously utters with greater effort than other neighbouring syllables in the word or sentence.

I presume that applies to the occasional, exceptional stress discussed below in connection with alliterating *þæm* and *þysses* in *Beowulf* line 197 (and similarly 790 and 806), *me* in line 563b, and *þy* in line 1797. Abercrombie's 'silent stress' is a refinement: special emphasis can be produced in Modern English not only by greater effort giving loudness, but also by preceding silence, as if by an effort of vocal inertia (if one insists on regarding it in terms of effort).

German verse in which, in his reading, the regular alternation of stress and
unstress remains while special sense stress elevates a normally unstressed syllable, in his example a function word (*Formwort*), in the dip to momentary
emphasis (*Augenblicksnachdruck*, or *Augenblicksiktus*) without converting the
dip to a lift:[27]

> Mit der Annahme emphatischer Augenblicksikten muß man bei der alten
> Dichtung zurückhalten!
>
> [You have to restrain yourself from the assumption that the ancient poetry too
> had special, momentary emphases.]

That is true in so far as we can see how in Old English poetry a function word
when stressed exceptionally is elevated to a lift from its normal place in the dip;
for example the alliterating words *þæm* and *þysses* in line 197 (and similarly
790 and 806), *me* in line 563b,[28] and *þy* in line 1797:

> on þæm dæge   þysses lifes
> [on that particular day of this life here],
>
> manfordædlan,   þæt hie me þegon
> [the evil-doers, that they partook of *me*],
>
> þegnes þearfe   swylce þy dogore
> [a retainer's need, such as at *that* time].

But Heusler knew nothing of 'silent stress' by means of a rest, or he would have
been more cautious about introducing so many rests into his system.

J. C. Pope is far more cautious in his use of rests. He introduces rests to
establish the isochronism of each of the 'members' ('feet' in much metrical
terminology) of which usually two make up a half-line, but in some lines,
especially where there are several more unstressed syllables than is usual, there
may be an additional foot, each of equal measure. That equality is produced by
rests or by slower or quicker reading, as required. As Bliss has shown in his
critique of Sievers's system, a centrally weak part of it is the assumption of
members ('feet') which are often not coincident with the word-division found in
the half-line, the bars separating the feet often cut words in two.[29] We cannot
know whether the Anglo-Saxons themselves thought that isochronism of

---

[27] *Deutsche Versgeschichte* (1925; see IV[22]), I, 59 § 69.

[28] Cf. E. G. Stanley, 'Notes on Old English Poetry, III 'The irony of the situation expressed by
the exceptional metrical stress of *Beowulf* line 563b', (1989; III[27]), 329-30.

[29] See A. J. Bliss, *Metre of Beowulf* (1967; see II[64]), 36-9; T. Cable, *Meter and Melody* (1974;
see IV[25]), 10; especially G. Russom, *Meter and Linguistic Theory* (1987; see IV[25]), 15-19.
The work of J. Kuryłowicz treats this metrical feature well in his interesting discussions of
metre as an area of Linguistics: 'Latin and Germanic metre', *English and Germanic Studies*,
2 (1948-1949), 34-8; *Die sprachlichen Grundlagen* (1970; see IV[11]); *Metrik und Sprach-
geschichte* (Warsaw, 1974).

metrical units was a requirement; and if it was, we cannot know whether it forced isochronism on each 'foot', on the half-line (the most likely, if such a Procrustean régime is to be hypothesized at all), or on the long line. It is certain, however, that any reader who now recites Modern English verse sensitively is instinctively inclined in reading Old English verse to produce the isochronism to which the reader is attuned through what is customary in post-medieval verse. It need not have been so with an Anglo-Saxon reading vernacular verse. As T. Cable has said,[30] 'At least three critics of Pope's system have pointed out that the only contemporary music of which we have detailed knowledge, Gregorian chant, has nothing like the isochronous measures that Pope describes.' Whether or not Gregorian chant throws light on vernacular verse, the principle of Occam's razor should make one hesitate to introduce into an explanation of how Old English scansion works the hypothesis of isochronism which seems unnecessary as well as undemonstrable. The problem is, however, important: the sound of poetry and of its rhythms matters. We want our reading of their verse to sound, in the first place, good to us. Good to us need not sound good to the Anglo-Saxons if they could hear us aloud, stumbling through their verse; yet since we cannot hope to satisfy their ears, we can only seek to please ourselves and our audience, if anyone can be found to listen to us reading *Beowulf* aloud.

We have to content ourselves with metrical theories based on systematic description of what the Anglo-Saxons have left us on the cold page, without complicating a deducible system by attempting to indulge the sensibility of readers attuned to modern verse. There is not a hope of gaining credence for our system, by pretending that we have recovered for ourselves the warm lips of an Anglo-Saxon's live reading of Old English verse.[31]

---

[30] *Meter and Melody* (1974; see IV[25]), 16; p. 19 note 29 names the three critics: P. F. Baum, A. J. Bliss and J. Taglicht.

[31] The healthy rejection by scholars of the dogmas of *Schallanalyse* to the enunciation of which Sievers devoted the last twenty years of his life shows that there are limits to scholarly credence even when a very great scholar tries to impose his responses in reading aloud upon the verse (and prose) as if they were a necessary part of it. Cf. P. Ganz, 'Eduard Sievers', *Beiträge*, 100 (Tübingen, 1978), especially 65-85. Sievers's understanding of *Schallanalyse* is set out, without reference to Old English, in 'Über ein neues Hilfsmittel philologischer Kritik', in E. Sievers, *Rhythmisch-melodische Studien* (Heidelberg, 1912), 78-111; his teaching is summarized by him in 'Ziele und Wege der Schallanalyse', in *Stand und Aufgaben der Sprachwissenschaft. Festschrift für Wilhelm Streitberg* (Heidelberg, 1924), 65-111. Applications to Old English discourse include: *Metrische Studien IV. Die altschwedischen Upplandslagh nebst Proben formverwandter germanischer Sagdichtung*, Abhandlungen der philologisch-historischen Klasse der Königlich Sächsischen Akademie der Wissenschaften, XXXV/1-2 (1918-1919); 'Zum Widsith', in M. Förster and K. Wildhagen (eds), *Texte und Forschungen zur englischen Kulturgeschichte Festgabe für Felix Liebermann* (Halle, 1921), 1-19; 'Zu Cynewulf', in *Neusprachliche Studien. Festgabe Karl Luick . . .*, supplement to *Die neueren Sprachen*, 33 (1925), 60-81; *Zur englischen Lautgeschichte kritische Untersuchungen*, Abhandlungen der philologisch-historischen Klasse der Sächsischen Akademie der Wissenschaften, XL/1 (1928); 'Cædmon und Genesis', in festschrift for M. Förster (1929; see I[58]), 57-84. On *The Dream of the Rood*, see H. Bütow (ed.), *Das altenglische "Traum-*

When we edit verse, printing it in half-lines and long lines and imposing modern word-division (and the compound formation our grammatical tradition thinks right for Old English), punctuation and capitalization, we are sometimes obliged to emend to make sense, and may sometimes feel the urge to improve the metre of the text transmitted in what we may believe to be a faulty manuscript reading. We must make sure in such cases that we get our emended lines to accord with the practice of the Old English poets as far as we can establish that practice.

Eduard Sievers's system, as refined and modified by H. Kuhn and A. J. Bliss, and as catalogued by Sievers himself and by J. C. Pope in the appendix to *The Rhythm of Beowulf* and indexed by Bliss according to his system, provides a good start. Yet I believe its days are numbered. Though no single system emerges from G. Russom and C. B. Kendall, together they show that more factors must be taken into consideration than Sievers knew of in 1885 to 1893. With the help of the computer it is possible now to feed in a vast amount of detailed information: where the syllables come and what constitutes a syllable, whether they are stressed, half-stressed (if that concept survives to shape a new metrical system), or unstressed, on what word-classes stress falls, how the word-divisions run, how compounding of stressed lexical elements and of unstressed morphemes works, how phrases go, where alliteration comes within a clause as well as within a line and also the half-line preceding a line,[32] the incidence of double alliteration, cross alliteration, and the possibility of transverse alliteration; and of special interest, how metrical patterns may be related to the syntactical organization of longer sense units, clauses, sentences, paragraphs (in our grammatical tradition). No one has ever thought that Old English versification is a settled subject; but perhaps it may be worth predicting that with the aid of the computer it will be, if not settled, certainly greatly advanced early in the next century. Whatever system is evolved on the basis of such a complicated, multifactorial data base, it must be simple enough for the poets to carry in their heads. It is well to recall Henry Sweet on the subject; he was wrong in regarding Sievers's classification of 'types' based on imposed feet (and with some elements regarded as anacrustic) as not a theory, but a statement of statistical facts; but he was right in what is implied in his statement, that a good metrical theory, however complicated, must describe a practice which versifiers can learn:[33]

> In the section on metre I have tried to give a clear abstract of Sievers' views
> . . ., which I feel obliged to accept, in spite of the adverse criticism of

---

gesicht vom Kreuz", AF, 78 (1935), 176-85; on *Beowulf*, see T. Westphalen, *Beowulf 3150-55 Textkritik und Editionsgeschichte* (Munich, 1967), 124-32 and plates III and IV.

[32] See A. S. C. Ross, 'Philological Probability Problems', *Journal of the Royal Statistical Society*, series B, 12 (1950), 19-41.

[33] H. Sweet (ed.), *An Anglo-Saxon Reader in Prose and Verse*, preface to seventh edition, 1894, quoted from the ninth edition (revised by C. T. Onions; Oxford, 1922), pp. xi-xii.

Lawrence . . ., Heath . . ., and others. These critics seem to forget that Sievers' classification of the Old-English metrical forms into types is not a theory, but a statement of facts, and that the complexity and irregularity to which they object is a fact, not a theory. The truth is that we know very little of the details of the versification of most languages; and it is possible that if our modern English metres, for instance, were analyzed in the same thorough way in which Sievers has analyzed the Old-English metres, we should have a difficulty in realizing that a modern poet could carry such a complicated scheme in his head.

Alas, we do not know how the Anglo-Saxon poets learnt their craft. There must have been more than instinctive feeling to composing Old English verse. We do not know even what sensitive Anglo-Saxons would have thought good or bad; we only hope that their taste might coincide with ours. The fuller, metrical computer analysis of verse would, no doubt, show further differences in the practice of individual poems. Differences have been demonstrated by the existing analyses; and it is likely that the same method of fuller metrical analysis would show more fundamental differences between Old English, Old Saxon, Old High German and Old Icelandic alliterative verse than Sievers accepted for his analysis of an art of versification grounded on a Common Germanic heritage.[34]

Some points of detail in Old English versification. Late verse and the alliteration of <c> and <g>

Alliteration provides one of the very few linguistic means of determining the dates of composition of some Old English poems. Letters <c> and <g>, when standing initially in a syllable, can be pronounced either as velar stop, that is /k/ and /g/; or <c> can be a palatal affricate /tʃ/, and <g> the palatal semi-vowel /j/. Which it is depends on the sound following <c> or <g>, and in the case of <g> the pronunciation also depends on the origin of the initial sound it stands for. Throughout most of the history of Old English verse /k/ and /tʃ/ alliterate with each other;[35] thus *Beowulf* line 1851:

---

[34] For metrical differences between Old English poems, see, for example, J. Roberts, 'A Metrical Examination of the Poems *Guthlac A* and *Guthlac B*', *Proceedings of the Royal Irish Academy*, LXXI, C, 4 (1971), 91-137; P. J. Lucas, 'Some Aspects of *Genesis B* as Old English Verse', *Proceedings of the Royal Irish Academy*, LXXXVIII, C, 6 (1988), 143-78. For Old Saxon (and Old High German, in so far as its limited amount of alliterative discourse can be securely regarded as verse) some of the discussions earlier than, and not all dismissed by Sievers and some of the discussions by those who did not accept Sievers may be found valuable again. Among the former, considered valuable by Sievers, is M. Rieger, 'Die alt- und angelsächsische Verskunst', *ZfdPh*, 7 (1876), 1-64. A metrical study of *Heliand* based on Sievers's system is F. Kauffmann, 'Die Rhythmik des Heliand', *Beiträge*, 12 (1887), 283-355.

[35] But no longer in the verse of Corpus Christi College Cambridge MS 201 and Bodleian MS Junius 121; in the latter /k/ and /tʃ/ do not alliterate even in *Fragments of Psalms*, perhaps not

to geceosenne   cyning ænigne

[any one to choose as (their) king],

and *The Death of Edgar* (MS Cotton Tiberius B.i) line 11:

to cynerice,   cild unwexen

[to the kingdom, a child ungrown].[36]

Towards the end of the Old English period there are no examples of /g/ alliterating with /j/, a frequent occurrence in earlier verse; for example *Beowulf* line 13:

geong in geardum,   þone Gode sende

[young in the courts, whom God sent],

and still frequently in the versified psalms.

It is thought, even by many who do not subscribe to the oral-formulaic theory, that early poems are nearer to the oral tradition which may be presumed to precede and underlie the extant bookish verse. To sustain such a view phonetic considerations have been brought to bear: vowels alliterate promiscuously because they were at one time preceded by a glottal catch, and the alliteration of

by chance, since /g/ and /j/ alliterate in Psalms 24:6, 34:2, 89:19, 102:5, and 140:2; and /g/ and /j/ alliterate often in the versified psalms of the Paris Psalter the text of which is close to that of *Fragments*, while alliteration of /k/ and /tʃ/ is relatively rare: Psalms 67:24, 5; perhaps 82:8, 4; 84:5, 3; 98:7, 1; perhaps 105:17, 1; 106:3, 4, 106:31, 1; 113:16, 1; 114:7, 1; 117:5, 1; perhaps 119:5, 4; 121:3, 2; 146:10, 3; to which may be added a very small number of double alliteration of /k/ and /tʃ/, which could be interpreted as single alliteration on /k/. 'Relatively rare' here means probably no more than that, when the versifier could think of nothing better, alliteration of /k/ and /tʃ/ was a possibility, but it was not so useful as alliteration of /g/ and /j/, for example for *God* and *gōd* with *georne* and *gearwe* in the versifier's characteristically feeble style.

[36] Cf. A. C. Amos, *Linguistic Means of Determining the Dates* (1980; see III[5]), 100-2.

D. Whitelock and others, *Chronicle . . . Translation* (1961; see III[33]), 77 note 2, says of the annal for 975, 'in alliterative metre of a quality to make one glad that the chroniclers mainly used prose'. She seems hard on the chronicler. By what standard are we judging the occasional poems which the chronicler included in his annals of the events of the time? A. Campbell (ed.), *The Battle of Brunanburh* (London, 1938), 42, like other competent Anglo-Saxonists in every period of scholarship before and after him, discusses the canons of criticism; Campbell comprehends the poem on the king's death in 975 in his praise of *The Battle of Brunanburh* celebrating the victory of 937:

Who the poet was it is impossible to say. His work, like that of the writers of the other panegyrics, was probably known at court, and hence became known to the writers of the *Chronicle* continuations . . . His work is the natural product of his age, an age of national triumph, antiquarian interest, and literary enthusiasm.

The antiquarian interest of the poem on 975 may show itself in the alliteration of /k/ and /tʃ/; but in none of these late poems can it be shown that /g/ and /j/ alliterate; see Campbell, *Brunanburh*, p. 33 and note 1.

/g/ with /j/ as also of /k/ with /tʃ/ looks back to an age before palatalization had taken place (though /j/ from /g/ by palatalization, as in *geard* 'court, enclosure', is to be distinguished from /j/ of Proto-Germanic origin, as in *gear* 'gear'). These, however, are early sound-changes; and, since late verse does not show alliteration of /g/ with /j/, it appears rather that the poets became more conscious of accuracy of sounds towards the end of the period than they had been at the dawn of English poetry.

The implications may, however, be different from this, on the face of it, not implausible view. The inherited alliterative system[37] is likely to have been exact in origin, and yet in both Old English and Old Saxon verse there is good evidence that /g/ and Proto-Germanic /j/ alliterate with each other as if they had always done so (but probably not in Old High German, and certainly not in Old Icelandic);[38] for example, *Beowulf* line 854:

> swylce geong manig   of gomenwaþe
>
> [also many a young one from the joyful journey],

and *Heliand* line 5716:

> uuas im glau gumo,   iungro Cristes
>
> [he was a wise man, a disciple of Christ].

On purely theoretical grounds it is unlikely that imperfect consonantal alliteration should go back to an early, preliterate period, a time when we would expect exactness in the sounds of alliteration. The traditional wording of Germanic poetry is likely to have led to the accepted habitual use of alliterative couplings that had been exact, but some of which ceased to be exact after palatalization, /k/ with /tʃ/ and /g/ with /j/. I presume that at that point such couplings, no longer exact, legitimized the similarly inexact alliteration of /g/ with /j/ in words with initial <g> derived from either Proto-Germanic /g/ or /j/.

---

[37] Very good accounts of that system in all the languages are by A. Heusler, 'Stabreim', in J. Hoops (ed.), *Reallexikon*, IV/3 (1918; see I[61]), 231-40, especially 'Lautliche Beschaffenheit' §§ 26-8; and his *Deutsche Versgeschichte* (1925; see IV[22]), 92-115, especially §§ 114-21.

[38] In Old Norse initial Germanic /j/ is lost; see A. Noreen, *Altisländische Grammatik* (4th edn; Halle, 1923), § 231. In southern dialects of Old High German initial /g/ is unvoiced; see J. Schatz, *Althochdeutsche Grammatik* (Göttingen, 1927), § 231. Other than to regard the alliteration and other prosodic features of the Strasburg charm to stanch blood as altogether too inconsistent for any deduction to be safe, I do not know how to interpret the alliteration of <g> and <j> in the opening lines [for the text, see E. v. Steinmeyer (ed.), *Die kleineren althochdeutschen Sprachdenkmäler* (Berlin, 1916), no. LXVIII; for the sense, cf. J. K. Bostock, *Handbook*, revised by K. C. King and D. R. McLintock (1976; see III[21]), 40]:

> Genzan unde Iordan   keiken sament sozzon;
> to uersoz Genzan   Iordane te situn.
>
> [Genzan and Jordan went together to shoot; then Genzan
> shot and wounded Jordan's side.]

This is presumably the stage to which the body of poetry preserved in the great codices looks back in its alliterative practice. In the course of the tenth century the tradition was broken, presumably at about the same time as the writing of Old English verse ceased to be practised. The alliterative licence of coupling /k/ with /tʃ/ and /g/ with /j/ was partly or wholly discontinued: that is, the discontinuance of the alliterative licence was caused by the break in the traditional art of vernacular versifying and constitutes evidence for the break.

In *The Battle of Maldon* /g/ and /j/ no longer alliterate.[39] If they did alliterate there would be double alliteration in line 192, a metrical irregularity very rarely found:

> Godwine and Godwig   guþe ne gymdon

[Godwine and Godwig did not care for battle].

The apparent other case, line 32, has been explained satisfactorily as transverse alliteration by E. V. Gordon:

> þæt ge þisne garræs   mid gafole forgyldon

[that you were to repay this onslaught of spears with tribute].

Transverse alliteration and cross-alliteration; enjambment of alliteration

In many Old English poems, transverse alliteration, that is alliteration of the pattern yx|xy, is rare and uncertain. In *Beowulf*, only line 2615 provides an example certain beyond any doubt:

> *b*runfagne **h**elm,   **h**ringde *b*yrnan

[The brown(?)-coloured helmet, the corslet made of rings].

Several other lines, however, have transverse alliteration though less certainly, since transverse alliteration in these lines depends on the status of the possible

---

[39] See E. V. Gordon (ed.), *The Battle of Maldon* (London, 1937), 44 note on line 32, for the explanation that there is transverse alliteration, *ge* and the stem of *forgyldon* alliterating on /j/, and *garræs* and *guþe* alliterating on /g/. Cf. the references in note 36, above. See also D. G. Scragg (ed.), *The Battle of Maldon* (Manchester, 1981), 29-31, and 52-3 notes 134-48, for remarks on the metre of the poem (but cf. p. 137 n. 45, below). Only in line 76 do /k/ and /tʃ/ seem to alliterate, provided that the etymology of Ceola is that of the name element *ceol-* 'ship', as is likely. Line 91 could alliterate either on /tʃ/ *ceallian* 'to call' with *ceald* 'cold', or on /k/ **callian* with *cald*; and cf. E. G. Stanley, 'Old English -*calla, ceallian*', in D. A. Pearsall and R. A. Waldron (eds), *Medieval Literature and Civilization Studies in Memory of G. N. Garmonsway* (London, 1969), 94-9, especially p. 98 (and cf. p. 160 n. 89, below).

first alliterative syllable: for example, in line 1728 *hwilum* would have to be regarded as a word weighty enough to bear alliteration:[40]

> *H*wilum he on lufan   læteð *h*worfan
>
> [At times He allows to wander in joy].

Transverse alliteration is perhaps ornamental rather than essential in many of the cases in *Beowulf* where it has been thought to occur.[41] The percentage of such lines in *Beowulf* is 0.72%. In *The Battle of Maldon* transverse alliteration occurs relatively more frequently, twice as often as in *Beowulf*.[42]

---

[40] Cf. E. G. Stanley, 'Some observations on the A3 lines in *Beowulf*', in R. B. Burlin and E. B. Irving, Jr (eds) *Studies in Honour of J. C. Pope* (1974; see II[28]), 139-64, especially p. 148. Cf. p. 120 n. 14, above, for stress on the unresolved, short penultimate syllable, that is, the stem-syllable of *lufan*.

[41] J. C. Pope, *Rhythm of Beowulf* (1966; see IV[25]), lists the following 23 lines of *Beowulf* as having transverse alliteration [I give the patterns under which he lists the lines, all of them (except line 2615) patterns within Sievers's type A3, namely, a first half-line with one alliterative stress only, and that on the penultimate syllable (or, if resolved, antepenultimate syllable) of the half-line which ends with an unstressed syllable]: A.66.a. 535, 1573, 1892, 1933, 2158, 3058, 3164; A.70.a. 1482, 1535, 1721, 1826, 2337, 2406, 2973, 3180; A.77.a. 1184; A.78.a. ?2377; A.80.a. 2020; A.83.a. 2053; A.90.a. 47, 1732; A.106.a. 1728; E.1.d. 2615. By a circular agument, once transverse alliteration is recognized, as it is by most metrists in line 1728 (Pope's pattern A.106.a), the first half-line could be said to belong to type A3 no longer: it now has two stressed syllables both participating in alliteration, the second (*lufan*) alliterating with the first alliterative stress of the second half-line, that is, with the head-stave (*læteð*), and the first stress (*Hwilum*) alliterating with the second stress of the second half-line (*hworfan*); the second stress of the second half-line does not normally alliterate (other than in transverse or cross-alliteration).

In the *Chronicle* poems the incidence of transverse alliteration is low too, perhaps *The Battle of Brunanburh* line 57 [cf. A. Campbell (ed.), *Brunanburh* (1938; see IV[36]), 32], but that is perhaps less certain:

> Swilce þa gebroþer   begen ætsamne
>
> [Likewise the brothers both together].

Cf. *Beowulf* line 1482, however:

> swylce þu ða madmas   þe þu me sealdest
>
> [Likewise you [*onsend* 'send out'] those treasures which
> you have given to me].

Pope regards that *Beowulf* line as having transverse alliteration. Perhaps it is exceptional in having the pronoun *me* as its head-stave; cf. line 2490 without transverse alliteration, and line 563 where I believe stress on *me* is ironic [see p. 128 and n. 28, above; and E. G. Stanley, 'Notes on Old English Poetry, III 'The irony of the situation expressed by the exceptional metrical stress of *Beowulf* line 563b', (1989; III[27]), 329-30].

[42] In E. V. Gordon (ed.), *Maldon* (1937; see IV[39]), 44 note on line 32, he lists by way of examples lines 32, 34, 50, 159, 189, 314. Some of these are questionable examples. In line 50 it would involve alliteration of /s/ with /sp/, but /sp/ alliterates only with /sp/ in Old English verse (including *The Battle of Maldon* lines 34, 137), but cf. the rhyming line 271 with alliteration of /st/ with /s/. In line 314 alliteration on initial *her* of the first half-line (usually unstressed) cannot be paralleled in that position; but in the second half-line initial *her* alliterates not infrequently, especially in late verse. Also doubtful, and not counted among lines with transverse alliteration by anyone, are lines 75 (on *h* of *wigheardne* in addition to

Cross-alliteration occurs more frequently than transverse alliteration.[43] In *Beowulf* cross-alliteration is common, much more common than transverse alliteration of which, as we have just seen, there is only one absolutely certain example, line 2615, and that is uniquely an E line in Sievers's system, all other possible lines with transverse alliteration are type A3.

The term 'enjambment of alliteration' refers to the common feature of Old English verse which allows the last stress of a second half-line, which is outside the alliteration of its own long line, to seem to participate in the alliteration of the following line, as if to announce the alliteration confirmed by the following head-stave, that is, the first stressed syllable of the second half-line.[44] *Beowulf* lines 88b-90 present a double example, unusual in that the last stress of line 88 participates also in cross-alliteration:

> þæt he dogora gehwam dream gehyrde
> hludne in healle. Þær wæs hearpan sweg,
> swutol sang scopes. Sægde se þe cuþe

[. . . that every day he might hear revelry loud in the hall. There was harp-music, the bard's clear song. He who knew told . . .]

---

double alliteration!), and 92 (on [*h*] of *Bryht*[*h*]*elmes* in addition to double alliteration!); other lines would involve usually unstressed words in transverse alliteration: 93, 151, 167, 197, 198, 205, 289. In line 32 it would mean that an alliterative stress falls on the pronoun *ge*; for *Beowulf* line 395 where *ge* might be thought to share in the alliteration, J. C. Pope does not consider this possibility (though he discusses the problem under the pattern to which the first half-line belongs, p. 266, A.70.b.; and though he allows transverse alliteration to fall on *wit* in line 535, p. 264, A.66.a.). In *The Battle of Maldon* line 86 it would involve transverse alliteration of /g/ with /j/, and in line 56 in addition *ge* may not be strong enough to bear alliteration. Cf. D. G. Scragg (ed.), *Maldon* (1981; see IV[39]), 53 note 139. This leaves lines 34, 159, 189, together with the doubtful 314, or an incidence of 1.23%; 1.54% if line 32 is included, as it probably should be: double the incidence found in *Beowulf*.

[43] E. V. Gordon (ed.) *Maldon* (1937; see IV[39]), 44 note on line 32, lists 'the pattern *abab* in 24, 63, 68, 98, 255, 285, 318, 320, &c.'. In fact, line 170 may provide a further example. Cf. D. G. Scragg (ed.), *Maldon* (1981; see IV[39]), 53 note 139. The following probably *not*: 102, 130 (if *up* takes precedence in stress of its verb immediately following, as is usual), 262, 279 (in addition to double alliteration), 311; with cross-alliteration of /k/ and /tʃ/, 256; he does not comment on the problematic alliteration of lines 29.

I do not know if it is possible to have cross-alliteration in addition to double alliteration. There are examples in *Beowulf*; thus line 33 with vocalic alliteration and perhaps also cross-alliteration on /f/:

> isig ond utfus æþelinges fær

[ice-covered and eager to depart, a prince's vessel].

[44] The term 'enjambment of alliteration' is from A. Campbell (ed.), *Brunanburh* (1938; see IV[36]), 32. The fullest account of the feature is that by A. S. C. Ross, 'Philological Probability Problems' (1950; see IV[32]). Examples in the first hundred lines of *Beowulf* are lines 15b-16 (if the last stress of 15b is correctly supplied as beginning with), 22b-23, 36b-7, 55b-56 (if, as is likely, the adverb *ellor* takes precedence of the finite verb *hwearf*), 81b-82, 88b-9, 89b-90, 92b-3.

Similar examples are found in other poems; thus *Exodus* lines 47b-9:

> druron deofolgyld.   Dæg wæs *mære*
> ofer **m**iddangeard   þa seo **m**engeo *for.*
> Swa þæs **f**æsten dreah   **f**ela missera

[. . . idols fell. The day was famous throughout the world when
that multitude departed. Thus [*Egypta folc* 'the people of the
Egyptians'] endured constraint (?) by that for many a year . . .]

The Battle of Maldon occasionally has two lines alliterating on the same letter,
interestingly so in lines 29-30 which are heightened both by unusual double
alliteration in the second half-line, 29b, the pivot of the sequence, and parono-
mastically enveloped in the preterite plural and infinitive of *sendan*, homo-
phones by this time but not homographs in this text:[45]

>   Me sendon to þe   sæmen snelle,
> 30   heton ðe secgan   þæt þu most sendan raðe

[Bold sea-warriors sent me to you commanding to say to you
that you must send quickly . . .].

Enjambment of alliteration is relatively rarer in *The Battle of Maldon* than in
Beowulf.[46] *Beowulf* gives the impression that literary effects, including metrical
effects, are achieved by a deliberate poetic art; less so in *The Battle of Maldon*.
Beowulf also gives the impression that it is written more tightly and elaborately
than *The Battle of Maldon*. It is hard to present the evidence that leads to these
impressions; complex statistical analysis would be required. Without that

---

45 For example, *The Battle of Maldon* lines 29-30, 69-70, 81-2, 110-11, 148-9, 180-1, 276-7,
290-1, 302-3.
   D. G. Scragg (ed.), *Maldon* (1981; see IV[39]), 52 note 136, seems to be deaf to the
alliterative and paronomastic play of lines 29-30, and so ventures (p. 69) the uncomprehend-
ing comment on *snelle*, 'The word does not alliterate (as Pope, p. 102, wrongly states).' The
reference is to a correct note in J. C. Pope's edition of the poem in *Seven Old English Poems*
(Indianapolis and New York, 1966; this note unchanged in the 2nd edn, New York and
London, 1981), 102 footnote 13. That /sn/ alliterates with /s/ in late (as well as early) verse is
demonstrated by *The Capture of the Five Boroughs* line 1, *A Prayer* line 36, and *Instructions
for Christians* line 73, as well as by many lines of the somewhat earlier *The Meters of
Boethius* and *Solomon and Saturn*.
   As F. Klaeber (ed.), *Beowulf* (3rd edn, p. lxx note 3) says, a succession of two lines
alliterating on the same letter is relatively rare in *Beowulf*, and lines 897-9 provide a unique
example of three lines alliterating on the same letter.
46 Certainly, *The Battle of Maldon* lines 82b-83, 117b-18, 125b-26, 173-4, 213-14, 223-4,
257-8, 271-2, 303-4. Perhaps, lines 44b-45, but 45 is one of three lines in the poem where the
alliteration falls on the second stressed syllable of the second half-line; the other lines are 75
(perhaps with a kind of cross-alliteration involving *haten*), and 288. Lines 94b-95 appears to
provide an example of enjambment of alliteration, but the alliteration on /w/ announced by
wat (94b) is continued as the only alliteration of lines 95-7, and in the cross-alliteration of
line 98; similarly, the alliteration on vowels announced by *eodon* of line 229b is continued in
lines 230-1.

demonstration, these impressions amount to little more than the assertion that
Beowulf and *Exodus* are better poems than *The Battle of Maldon*, and that
quality appears also, as far as we can judge, in the technical skill of metre. But
there is some skill, and some handling, new, as far as we can tell, in the
development of alliterative poetry towards the end of the Anglo-Saxon period:
lines 29-30 show that.

The alliteration of *Durham*, a poem only 21 lines long, composed in the early
twelfth century, is not without interest. Alliteration continued over two and three
lines occurs in lines 6-7 (on /w/) and 12-14 (on vowels chiefly of names);
enjambment of alliteration in lines 3b-4, 10b-11, and 14b-15. Triple alliteration
on /b/ occurs in line 15a, and double alliteration in all first half-lines except 4a,
6a, 9a, 10a, 11a, 19a;[47] but the only example of cross alliteration, and it is not
certain, is in line 13 (in addition to double alliteration):

> **Ea**dberch and **Ea**d*fri*ð,   æðele ge*f*eres
> [Eadbeorht and Eadfrith, noble companions].

I doubt if the dispraise for what the little piece says together with the praise
usually given to it for how it says it (it is, mistakenly, supposed to preserve many
of the technical features of Old English versification)[48] means much: it is
unprofitable to expect that as poetry the lines written about *Durham* should
affect the reader as he may be affected by 'Lines written above Tintern Abbey'.
In much mild praise, words like 'unexpectedly' or 'surprisingly' colour the
evaluation. We must remember the causes of such surprise, the unfulfilled,
mistaken expectations based on notions of decline in technical skill as the Old
English period ends and before the Middle English period has got into its stride.
Whatever the preoccupations and predilections of critics, it is best not to feel
surprise that these preoccupations and predilections have led to misconceptions;
or, if one does feel surprised it may be wiser not to says so.

Possible onomatopoetic effects in Old English verse

As far as we can tell, Old English alliterative verse does not use alliteration for
onomatopoetic effects. Some Middle English alliterative verse does; for
example, *Sir Gawain and the Green Knight* lines 746-7 may seek to use allitera-

---

[47] There is no alliteration at all in line 16b, but the reading *gecheðe* (variant *gicheðe*) is corrupt.
[48] For example, C. L. Wrenn, *A Study of Old English Literature* (London, 1967), 191: 'Yet the
interest of *Durham* is chiefly historical, for though unexpectedly well written technically in
the traditional style, it lacks poetic merit of any other kind.' That this is not 'unexpectedly
well written technically in the traditional style,' that there has, in fact, been great change, not
only in the principles of alliteration mentioned by me, but especially in terms of Sievers's
types, is well demonstrated by T. Cable, *The English Alliterative Tradition* (Philadelphia,
1991), 52-7.

tion to convey a little of the piping of the little birds in the cold of winter, but it seems not the use of alliterative /p/ so much as the use of /i/ and /i:/ in no fewer than six of the nine stressed syllables of the two lines that produces much of that effect:

> With mony bryddez vnblyþe vpon bare twyges
> Þat pitosly þer piped for pyne of þe colde.

[with many unhappy little birds on the bare twigs that peeped there pitifully because of the agony of the cold.]

Certainly, *Sir Gawain and the Green Knight* has onomatopoeia for the noise of grinding the axe in lines 2201-4, in which I find the exclamation *quat* or *what* untranslatable, yet its triple use contributes essentially to the sound-effect:

> Quat, hit clatered in þe clyff as hit cleue schulde,
> As one vpon a gryndelston hade grounden a syþe.
> What, hit wharred & whette as water at a mulle.
> What, hit rusched & ronge rawþe to here.

[It clattered in the crag as if that were to split, as if someone were grinding a scythe on a grindstone. It whirred and ground round like water at a mill. It made a noise of rushing and ringing grievous to hear.]

The alliteration of the exclamation derived from Old English *hwæt* is on /k/ or /xw/ (perhaps voiceless /ʍ/), and unlike the Old English word, in Middle English it shares in the alliteration (though not in the last line quoted).

Though Old English verse seems not to have used alliteration for onomato-poetic effects, it did occasionally produce such effects by other means; for example, the internal rhyme of *Flod blod gewod*, used in *Exodus* line 463b:

> Þær ær wegas lagon
> mere modgode,   mægen wæs adrenced,
> 460 streamas stodon. Storm up gewat
> heah to heofonum, herewopa mæst:
> laðe cyrmdon, lyft up geswearc
> fægum stæfnum. Flod blod gewod.
> Randbyrig wæron rofene, rodor swipode
> 465 meredeaða mæst, modige swulton,
> cyningas on corðre.

[Where paths had lain before, the ocean raged, the mighty army was drowned, the waters towered up. The storm rose high to the heavens, the greatest of weepings from an army: the hated foemen cried out, the air above grew dark with doomed voices. Blood entered the flood. The ramparts were broken, the sky lashed down the greatest of ocean-deaths, the proud perished, kings amidst their retinue.]

One editor, J. R. R. Tolkien, singles out for special execration, '*Flod blod gewod*: the noisy exaggeration is a specimen in little of the faulty handling of this scene'; to another, P. J. Lucas, 'in a descriptive *tour de force* such as lines 447-87 the tempo is increased to produce a breathless staccato-like effect.'[49]

Whose criticism is to be trusted? By what criteria are they judging, or is there only one measure for the poetry of all periods in all languages? Can we or the editors know how Anglo-Saxon ears would have received the passage and within it *Flod blod gewod*, Tolkien's 'intolerable deal of gore'? Not having their ears on our heads, we must trust our own ears and recognize them as ears of the late twentieth century, in general disinclined to gladness at the cries of armies drowning; deaf to typology, not in spirit so ready to know the danger of our Enemy in the Pharaonic hosts, not so ready, therefore, to rejoice with devout thanksgiving at that bloody drowning in a sea through which we had walked dry-shod at Pasch. The Anglo-Saxon poet's unusual sound-effects, the thuds of line 463b, are to draw attention to the occasion, which typologically is none other than the institution of the Eucharist: in salvation-history no occasion is grander. Or is that reading too much into too little? – 'Im Auslegen seyd frisch und munter!' etc.

The sound-effects of *Exodus* line 463b are not onomatopoetic. Perhaps *Beowulf* line 1881 is onomatopoetic, but not in its use of alliteration:

> 1880   Him Beowulf þanan,
> guðrinc goldwlanc   græsmoldan træd
> since hremig.

> [Beowulf departing, a battle-hero gold-adorned, trod the greensward, exulting in treasure.]

Line 1881 is unique in the poem in that all but one syllable, the unstressed ending of *græsmoldan*, carry stress. These are not hypermetric but normal half-lines; in Sievers's system the scansion looks thus:

$$A2ab \ \angle \ \backslash | \angle \ \backslash \ \| \ \angle \ \backslash \times | \angle \ E1$$

Another 'A2ab' half-line with double alliteration is line 1719a combined with a type B second half-line:

> breosthord blodhreow;   nallas beagas geaf
> [blood-thirsty hidden thought; not at all did he give rings]

---

[49] J. R. R. Tolkien (ed.) *Exodus* (ed. by J. Turville-Petre, 1981; see III[52]), 71; and P. J. Lucas (ed.), *Exodus* (1977; see III[52]), 45. Lucas draws attention to F. C. Robinson. *Lexicography and Literary Criticism: A Caveat*, in J. L. Rosier (ed.), *Philological Essays . . . in Honour of H. D. Meritt* (1970; see III[35]), 106 and footnote 20, for the interpretation of lines 462b-463a which I follow in my translation.

the scansion of which is in Sievers's system:[50]

$$\text{A2ab} \; / \; \backslash \, | \, / \; \backslash \; \| \times \times / \, | \times / \; \text{B}$$

In reading the passage containing line 1881 aloud and in hearing it read, even a modern reader and a modern audience can notice an unusual density of stresses, an effect not experienced in the passage containing line 1719.

Let us look at the context of line 1881. The passage comes at the end of the tearful leave-taking from Hrothgar as the footsteps by Beowulf and his fourteen are heard outside and away by the aged king within. Is the poet hoping to make us too hear their manly tread in the heavy metrical weighting of the line? I wonder: in our deafness to the nuances of Old English verse, it is marvellous for us to notice any of its sound-effects, and they have to be strident to make any impression on us. Yes, there probably is something there, but whether we have identified its rhythm correctly and interpreted it as an Anglo-Saxon might have interpreted it, who is to say?

Anacrusis and other initial unstressed syllables in a half-line; hypermetric lines; a half-line of only one syllable

The terms for initial unstressed syllables in a half-line of alliterative verse are various, and the place of one or more unstressed syllables either inside or outside the metre of the half-line is variously regarded by metrists. For syllables considered to be outside the metre of the half-line the term 'anacrusis' is widely used.[51] As applied to Old English prosody, 'anacrusis' suffers from a defect, not terminological but conceptual. *OED* s.v. *Anacrusis* quotes as its definition, 'A syllable at the beginning of a Verse before the just Rhythm.'[52] A minor point to be noted in passing is that Old English verse, and even more Old Saxon verse, has not infrequently more than one syllable in anacrusis, so that the definition has to be altered to read: 'One or more syllables at the beginning of a Verse before the just Rhythm.'

---

[50] The division into feet of the second half line imposes a metrical boundary not coincident with the word-boundary, and $\times \times \,| \; / \times \backslash$ or $\times \times \; | \; / \times \; | \, /$ seem preferable scansions, abandoning Sievers at one of his weakest points.

[51] For the terminology, see R. W. Burchfield, 'Prosodic Terminology' (1974; see III[21]), 171-202, s.vv. *anacrusis, extrametric, prelude*, and *upbeat*. The German term is *Auftakt*, and, less commonly, *Aufschlag* but that is chiefly in use for the analogous feature in music. English 'upbeat' translates the German term; perhaps *upbeat* is best avoided now in view of its colloquial extension, chiefly adjectival. The problems of anacrusis are well discussed by T. Cable, *Meter and Melody* (1974; see IV[25]), 32-44; and by G. Russom, *Meter and Linguistic Theory* (1987; see IV[25]), 33-8. For some of these problems, cf. D. Donoghue, 'On the Classification of b-Verses with Anacrusis in *Beowulf* and *Andreas*', *N&Q*, 232 (1987), 1-5.

[52] *OED*'s definition is from B. H. Kennedy, *The Public School Latin Grammar* (London, 1871; and reprints, 1874, etc.), 528 § 260 n. *C.* (a).

The trouble with the concept is, however, more deep-seated. If we accept Sievers's system *tout court*, anacrusis cannot exist in half-lines beginning with unstress, namely, his type B × ∕ | × ∕ and his type C × ∕ | ∕ ×. In fact, the initial unstressed position of types B and C is more often occupied by two or more unstressed syllables than by one: 'the just Rhythm' of types B and C could therefore be said to comprehend anacrusis. If we do not accept Sievers's system in its entirety, doubts in anacrusis take us further still. Under type B we find, as scanned by Sievers, line 518b: *Þa hine on morgentid* [then in the morning . . . him], × × × × ∕ | × ∕ with the foot-boundary not coincident with the word-boundary, so that × × × × | ∕ × | ∕ or perhaps more in keeping with the stress-system of nominal compounds × × × × | ∕ × \. Or one might argue for × × × | × ∕ × \, if one regards the preposition *on* as a proclitic comparable with a prefix. Similar problems of Sievers's foot-boundary conflicting with Old English word-boundaries arise in his type C; for example, line 243a *mid scipherge* [with a ship-army] × ∕ | ∕ ×, not perhaps unlikely if one regards *mid* as a proclitic, or one might argue for × | ∕ \ × as more 'natural' Old English, more 'natural' perhaps than taking *mid* as a proclitic. But 'natural' is an unsustainable concept for a dead language with such malleable scansion that metrists cannot agree how best to analyse it.

The matter looks worse if Old Saxon verse is considered a parallel.[53] The many examples of longer anacrusis at the beginning and multisyllabic dip in the middle of *Heliand* long lines present a striking contrast with the sparingness of unstressed syllables in *Beowulf* lines. Anacrusis can go up to ten syllables in *Heliand* and dips of similar length occur initially in types B and C, in B sometimes combined with multisyllabic second dip. Long anacrusis combined with multisyllabic dips occur in half-lines of type A. These features look excessive, hypertrophic (as Heusler calls them), to anyone used to Old English rather than Old Saxon verse. No theory has accommodated them, perhaps no theorist has understood them. In addition to the half-lines with long anacrusis and with dips of many syllables, *Heliand* has many hypermetric lines, not always distinguishable from hypertrophic 'normal' lines,[54] providing a further kind of lines longer than is usual in Old English.

Of course, it could be argued that Old Saxon poetry is verse without metre or, at least, verse outside the metrics of Old English, and therefore quite irrelevant. That goes too far, I think. The mere fact that Old English has hypermetric lines[55]

---

[53] See A. Heusler, 'Heliand, Liedstil und Epenstil' (1920; see III[79]), especially V 'Das Wachsen der Senkungen und Auftakte', pp. 541-8 (= 24-31). The standard discussion of the metre of *Heliand* according to Sievers's system is F. Kauffmann, 'Rhythmik des Heliand' (1887; see IV[34]).

[54] Cf. E. Sievers, *Altgermanische Metrik* (1893; see III[79]), §§ 120-3; Sievers corrects, according to his system, Kauffmann's scansion of hypermetric lines which, as Sievers noted, are wrongly scanned though Kauffmann thought he was using Sievers's scansion.

[55] A. J. Bliss, *Metre of Beowulf* (1958, 2nd edn 1967; see II[64]) 162-8, lists, and scans according to his system, all Old English hypermetric lines, including those in *Beowulf* (over twenty

(as does Old Saxon, often using lines longer and looser than anything in Old English) may indicate that longer units, their scansion not fully understood and their purpose obscure, were a feature of Germanic alliterative verse. Hypertrophic and hypermetric lines differ in that the former have no syllables participating as stresses in the scansion of the line, the latter do.

The relationship between the verse in the two languages is important for an understanding of these longer lines. If the original system was as found in Old English (without long anacrusis, and with only a relatively small number of dips consisting of very many syllables (other than in initial position at the beginning of larger sense units, often in 'light' half-lines, that is, half-lines with only one stress like Sievers type A3),[56] then Old Saxon verse must be the end of the development, which Heusler charted as a scale: its first step is the alliterative verse in the *Edda*; its second step, close to the *Edda*, in spirit rather than in metrics presumably, the verse of *The Battle of Finnsburh* and *Hildebrandslied*; its third step, the Old English 'epics'; and its fourth step, finally, *Heliand*.[57] In fact, the metrical peculiarities do not lead to Heusler's neat progression, from 'das nordische heidnische Heldenlied', the Norse pagan heroic song of the *Edda*, via the unbookish-looking secular heroic fragments, to the Old English 'book-epics', and lastly to *Heliand*. *The Battle of Finnsburh* is metrically less exact than most Old English long poems;[58] and *Hildebrandslied* is even less metrically tight, much closer therefore to *Heliand*.

The importance of the metre of *Heliand* for an understanding of Old English poetry lies in the interpretation of varieties of Germanic metre. It teaches us how little we know of them. For metrists of Old English, *Beowulf* is, very properly, the measure: we think it good. We cannot, therefore, look with special favour on the metrical imprecision of *Hildebrandslied*, imprecise, that is, by the standards of *Beowulf*. We are unlikely to sense in its poetry the voice of original declamation, belonging to a period when the Germanic Heroic Age was, if not still the poet's own age, then at least in very recent memory. Brought up on the metre of *Beowulf*, we, at the end of the twentieth century, could not look with disdain at some metrically exact saint's life, say *Guthlac B*, because we smell monastic lucubration in its metrical precision: that precision distinguishes our *Beowulf*, but not their *Heliand*.

We do not know how to accommodate the strings of unstressed syllables that come initially and medially so often in *Heliand* long lines, and our understanding of hypermetric lines in Old English and in Old Saxon verse is insecure. There are lines in *Hildebrandslied* that, without vigorous emendation (now unfashionable), look remarkably like prose. Therefore, we should be reluctant to

half-lines, mainly paired in hypermetric long lines); part II of J. C. Pope's *Rhythm of Beowulf* (1942, 2nd edn 1966; see IV[25]), 97-158, is a new theory of hypermetric lines.

[56] See E. G. Stanley, 'Initial Clusters of Unstressed Syllables' (1992; see III[38]).

[57] A. Heusler, 'Heliand, Liedstil und Epenstil' (1920; see III[79]), 559 (= 42).

[58] Cf. F. Klaeber (ed.), *Beowulf* (3rd edn, 1936), 237-8, for a concise account of the metre of *The Battle of Finnsburh*.

pass value judgements on Germanic poetry on the basis of metrical exactness alone. Critics of Old High German poetry have never done that for *Hildebrands-lied*. *Heliand* has not fared so well.

It looks as if in one place in Old English poetry an attempt may have been made by a versifier to play self-consciously with the length of the half-line. The second half of line 77 in *The Riming Poem* consists of only one syllable:

> oþþæt beoþ þa ban   an
> [till the bones remain – only].

The most recent editor of the poem attractively explains the line in its context, which is that the body lies in its grave, food for worms, and the final word of the line, *an* 'only, alone', metrically wrong, according to every system of scansion, is right in sense: 'this representation of the final reduced state of man, beyond even the devouring worms, by a half-line reduced almost to nothing'.[59] Not all the Old English poets, it seems, were unswervingly obedient to the most obvious rules of scansion created for them by the prosodic martinets who, about a thousand years after them, analysed their metre.

Rhyme

Striking to a modern reader, accustomed to rhyming verse but after the briefest acquaintance with Old English poetry no longer expecting it in Old English, is the use in Old English verse of rhyme.[60] It is not infrequent as an occasional ornament, both within the line, as in *Exodus* line 463b *Flod blod gewod*, *Andreas* line 1587a *brimrad gebad* [the sea-path stood still], and, more commonly, with the two half-lines of a long line rhyming, as in *Cædmon's Hymn* line 7 (St Petersburg MS):

> tha middingard,   moncynnæs uard
> [Then the earth, the Guardian of mankind . . .].

Similarly *Beowulf* line 1014:

> fylle gefægon;   fægere geþægon
> [rejoiced in the feast; partook with relish].

---

[59] O. D. Macrae-Gibson (ed.), *The Old English Riming Poem* (Cambridge, 1983), 54 note on line 77.

[60] For a history of rhyming in English verse from *Cædmon's Hymn* to Chaucer, see E. G. Stanley, 'Rhymes in English Medieval Verse: from Old English to Middle English', in E. D. Kennedy, R. Waldron and J. S. Wittig (eds), *Medieval English Studies presented to George Kane* (Wolfeboro, New Hampshire, and Woodbridge, Suffolk, 1988), 19-54; rhymes in Old English, pp. 19-38, 53-4.

In one passage of *Exodus* the final words of three lines form a spaced-out rhyming sequence: lines 476 (*geneop*, perhaps to be emended to *gehneop* 'pulled down'), 478 (*hweop* 'threatened'), and 481 (*sweop* 'rushed').

In a small number of poems rhymes are used consistently, either throughout, in *The Riming Poem*, or as a special feature, for example, in the passage of *Elene* (after the *finit* of line 1235) in which Cynewulf introduces himself, lines 1236-50, leading to his name in runes in lines 1257-69. Rhyme is used in some late poems in *The Anglo-Saxon Chronicle*; for example, in the annal for 1036 in Cotton MSS Tiberius B.i and Tiberius B.iv, and in the assessment of William the Conqueror in *The Peterborough Chronicle* annal for 1087.

In some poems, alliterative metre, not always as exact as strict metrists might like to see, is combined with jingling. The unsolved *Riddle 28* is a good example of verse constructed on prosodic principles other than the usual; thus the failure of line 2 to alliterate, the jingles of lines 2-6 and 8b, as well as the inaccurate rhyme *bruceð* (line 10a) with *spriceð* (line 10b), at the end of the riddle (of which the end, lines 9-13, is not quoted, because it presents too many obscurities):

> Biþ foldan dæl   fægre gegierwed
> mid þy heardestan   ond mid þy scearpestan
> ond mid þy grymmestan   gumena gestreona,
> corfen, sworfen,   cyrred, þyrred
> 5   bunden, wunden,   blæced, wæced,
> frætwed, geatwed,   feorran læded
> to durum dryhta.   Dream bið in innan
> cwicra wihta,   clengeð, lengeð,
>
> . . .

[Part of the earth is beautifully appointed with the hardest and with the sharpest and with the grimmest of the treasures of men, cut, rubbed, turned, dried, bound, rolled, bleached, weakened, adorned, fitted out, conveyed from afar to the doors of men. Within is the merry sound of living creatures, it is prolonged, it lingers, . . .]

Poetic diction

Some Old English words, both uncompounded and compounded, are confined to verse. Many of these poetic words occur frequently. With a dead language, for which the reader has no secure *Sprachgefühl*, the recognition of a poeticism depends on distribution. There is 16⅔ times as much prose as verse.[61] It follows

---

[61] I am informed by *The Dictionary of Old English*, Toronto, that there are about 3,000,000 words of prose and about 180,000 words of verse in Old English. For the statistical problem, see A. S. C. Ross's discussion (p. 386 note 1), in E. G. Stanley, 'Studies in the Prosaic

that if a word occurs half a dozen times in prose but never in verse, it does not mean that if we had much more verse it might not have occurred in it: one would need far more occurrences in prose, fifty or a hundred, perhaps, for the absence in verse to be significant. If, however, a word occurs only a few times in the language, and each occurrence is in verse, that is significant – unless, of course, the word involves a subject so rarely treated in prose that its absence in prose must be put down to the fact that there was no call for it to be used. For example, the word *hos* occurs once only in the language, *Beowulf* line 924b *mægþa hose* [a retinue of maidens]. Retinues are usually of men, and for that *dryht* and *gedryht* is used, both words virtually confined to poetry.[62] In prose the Anglo-Saxons used the word *geferscipe* for 'retinue (of men)', and that is used in the abstract sense 'fellowship' in *Guthlac* line 1258.[63] Though the word *hos* occurs once only, we may perhaps presume that it is a poetic word like *dryht* and *gedryht*, but that deduction is speculative.

The example teaches us that some senses of a word may be poetic, others confined to prose. The word *dom* 'judgement', in the Christian writings in verse and prose extant in such preponderance, is often used with reference to 'the Last Judgement'. The sense 'glory, fame, victory' is very rare indeed in prose, but common in poetry.

An anecdote may not be irrelevant. From time to time I receive letters of inquiry, often hoping for agreement with a view expressed by the inquirer. Some time ago I had an inquiry from a clergyman, telling me how sad it is that *Doomsday* is redolent of *doom* when it should be full of joy. In my reply I showed no contempt for a clerk in orders who, as I uncharitably imagined, is so deeply sunk in pastoral concern that he does not know where to go to establish the meaning of a fundamental English term in eschatology; and I confined myself to saying, *doomsday* means no more than 'Judgement Day', and has meant that since Anglo-Saxon times. I stuck firmly to the line, *dom* means 'judgement', and I resisted the temptation of preaching to him that the connotations of *Doomsday* were such, that he might be released from the doom and gloom of his mistaken lexical view, and that he might sally forth into realized

---

Vocabulary of Old English Verse', *NM*, 72 (1971), 385-418. The figures of words of prose (roughly 2,250,000) and verse (perhaps a little less than 250,000) given by me (pp. 385-6) were the result of a rough count, and have proved to be an underestimate for prose and an overestimate for verse, so that Ross's statistics have to be revised.

[62] Cf. the exceptional prose use in the West Saxon Gospels, John 2:8, of *drihte ealdor* rendering the Joannine *architriclinus* Rhemes 'the cheefe steward', Authorized Version 'the gouernour of the feast'; and note the exception plural use in Aldhelm glosses of *gedrihtu* for *elementa* 'the elements of nature'.

[63] So also three times, always abstract, in *The Metres of Boethius*, 11 lines 47, 82 and 94. The prose *Boethius* uses the word in its concrete sense 'retinue'; and it also uses the word in its abstract sense, but not, perhaps by chance, in the prose passages corresponding to the verse. See W. J. Sedgefield (ed.), *King Alfred's Old English Version of Boethius De Consolatione Philosophiae* (Oxford, 1899), 49-50 and 167-9.

eschatology, or, if not that, that he might trip it merrily to the burden of the late Middle English carol:[64]

> Gay, gay, gay, gay,
> Think on drydful domisday.

The Old English evidence is, however, more complicated than my simple reply suggested, though that does not apply to normal prose usage of OE *domesdæg*. If in verse *dom* means 'glory' as well as 'judgement', how do we understand the use of *domdæg*[65] in line 1636 of *Christ III*, lines 1634-8? –

> Þonne þa gecorenan   fore Crist berað
> 1635   beorhte frætwe,   hyra blæd leofað
> æt domdæge,   agan dream mid Gode
> liþes lifes,   þæs þe alyfed biþ
> haligra gehwam   on heofonrice.

[When the chosen shall carry gleaming treasures into Christ's presence, their prosperity shall live at Judgement Day, to have the joy of serene life with God which will be vouchsafed to each of the holy ones in the kingdom of heaven.]

'Judgement Day' would fit; but in verse especially *dom* often means 'glory': and here quite clearly the Day of Judgement is also a day of glory for God's chosen, a day of *dream*, that is, of jubilation.[66] In prose that sense of *dom* is rare; the clearest prose example quoted in the entry for the word in *The Dictionary of Old English* (sense 11) is from Ælfric's 'Passio Machabeorum':[67]

> And heora geferan fundon þæt feoh on heora bosmum · and cwædon þæt God sylf geswutelode heora unriht · and heredon Godes dom þe heora digle geopenode.

[And their companions found that treasure in their bosoms, and said that God himself had made manifest their sin, and praised the glory of God who had laid bare their secrets.]

It would be possible to find in this use by Ælfric other shades of meaning, Skeat translates 'and praised God's doom'; but probably it is closest to the sense 'glory' found most often in poetry. Whether Ælfric thought that by using that sense he was enriching his alliterative language is something we cannot answer.

---

[64] See R. L. Greene (ed.), *The Early English Carols* (2nd edn; Oxford, 1977), no. 329.

[65] The form *domdæg* is not confined to verse, and the sense 'Judgement Day' is usually assigned to it as for the far more common *domesdæg*. Both words occur rendering *dies iudicii*.

[66] Cf. K. Ostheeren, *Studien zum Begriff der "Freude" und seinen Ausdrucksmitteln in altenglischen Texten* (Berlin doctoral dissertation, 1964), 114-16.

[67] W. W. Skeat (ed.), *Aelfric's Lives of Saints*, II, EETS, o.s. 94 (1890), 96, XXV lines 465-7.

In prose the word *fær* occurs with the meaning 'movement'; the sense 'vessel' is found in verse only. The neuter word *feoht* 'fight' is found both in verse and in prose, the feminine *feohte* has the same meaning, but occurs in verse only. The usual word for 'day' in both verse and prose is *dæg*; *The Dictionary of Old English* says there are about 9,100 occurrences. The word *dogor* also meaning 'day' is much rarer, about 50 occurrences, and a high proportion of them in verse. The usual word for 'human being', either 'man' or 'woman' is *mon(n* or *man(n*, dative singular and nominative and accusative plural, *men(n*. Much rarer, weak *monna* or *manna* is used most often in the accusative plural in verse and prose (*monnan, mannan*) [Anglian (prose only) *monno, monnu, monne*].[68] Again, the weak forms occur disproportionately often in verse. One might like to know what led speakers of Old English to use one form rather than the other. For *dogor* metrical considerations may have played a part: its stem is long because the stem-vowel is long; and, obviously, both *dogor* and weak *monna* are dissyllabic but *dæg* and *mon(n* are monosyllabic. Did these rarer forms have different overtones from those of the usual words? Besides Modern German *Mann* 'man', nominative and accusative plural *Männer* (the normal form), there survives in literary use the weak plural *Mannen*. A reliable dictionary says:[69]

Zur Bezeichnung von 'Kriegern, Dienern, Gefolge' ist historisierend der veraltete Plural *Mannen* noch geläufig.

[The archaic plural *Mannen* is still in historicizing use to designate 'warriors, retainers, retinue'.]

We lack the detailed knowledge, the feel for the language, to describe in similar terms Old English usage of shades of meaning, rare forms, rare words, poeticisms. For the living language we can tell, not for a dead language undescribed by its speakers.

A well-known complication involving poetic usage is that *eorl* has two senses. In poetry it means 'man, warrior', in prose it denotes a rank of the Scandinavian nobility corresponding to the Anglo-Saxon rank of *ealdorman*. Thus in *The Anglo-Saxon Chronicle* (Parker MS) the annal 871 gives the rank *aldorman* to the English Æthelwulf, and we are told also that King Alfred fought 'against a group of (Scandinavian) nobles of the rank of *eorl* ', that is, *wiþ þara eorla getruman*, and the slain earls are named: *Sidroc eorl se alda* [Earl Sidroc the Elder], *Sidroc eorl se gioncga* [Earl Sidroc the Younger], *Osbearn eorl, Fræna eorl*, and *Hareld eorl*. In *Chronicle* verse, from *The Battle of Brunanburh* line 1, in the annal for 937,

Æþelstan cyning,   eorla dryhten

[King Athelstan, lord of men]

---

[68] For the Anglian forms especially, see A. S. C. Ross, *Studies in the Accidence of the Lindisfarne Gospels* (Leeds, 1937), 83-4.

[69] W. Pfeifer, *Etymologisches Wörterbuch des Deutschen* (Berlin, 1989), 1059.

to *The Death of Edward* line 31b, in the annal for 1065, where the English king Harold is called (in the dative) *æþelum eorle* [the noble man], who unlike his father and elder brother never had the rank of *eorl*, that word having supplanted *ealdorman* in prose usage earlier in the eleventh century.[70] In *The Battle of Maldon* line 218 Eal(h)helm, the ealdorman of Central Mercia from 940 to 951,[71] is referred to as *wis ealdorman woruldgesælig* ['a wise ealdorman prosperous in the world']. In the first half of the eleventh century *eorl* had not supplanted the title *ealdorman*, so that any English noble of that important rank is likely to be referred to by that title or by none. The use in verse of the word is not simple. In the plural, both *Andreas* and *Daniel* use it; *Andreas*, in Christ's speech line 608, uses it to denote the secular nobles sitting in council with ecclesiastical dignitaries witnessing Christ's ministry on earth, perhaps reflecting conditions in Anglo-Saxon England; *Daniel*, line 684, uses the word to mean 'princes, nobles' less precisely. It is also used (to render *princeps* whenever the Latin is close) in the versified Psalms of the Paris Psalter. We therefore cannot say why in *The Battle of Maldon* Byrhtnoth, the ealdorman of Essex, is referred to as *eorl*; we simply do not know what overtones the word might have had in the last decade of the tenth century, the most likely date of composition; and we have no evidence to date the composition late on the grounds that, in prose *eorl* did not supplant *ealdorman* as a title for an English noble of that rank till about 1020. But then, in prose the Anglo-Saxons did not use *eorl* other than for a Scandinavian noble of that rank. Datable diplomatic evidence is irrelevant for dating poetic usage.

Some editors of verse mark the poetic words with an obelisk † in the glossary to their text, Klaeber's *Beowulf* is an excellent example, and he has refinements, such as marking as poetic specific senses of words found in other senses in prose also. He uses the double obelisk ‡ for words found in *Beowulf* only, and he gives exceptional prose uses for what are mainly poetic words. Many of the poetic words are nouns and adjectives, often involving warfare and the deeds of men, many are compounds; but there also verbs, and a few other parts of speech.[72] When *The Dictionary of Old English* is complete we shall have a much more detailed knowledge of what the Anglo-Saxons did in verse only and what they did in prose only; but we shall never know why they did it.

---

[70] See F. E. Harmer, *Anglo-Saxon Writs* (Manchester, 1952), 48; H. R. Loyn, 'The Term *Ealdorman* in the Translations Prepared at the Time of King Alfred', *EHR*, 68 (1953), 513-25. Cf. J. McKinnell, 'On the Date of *The Battle of Maldon*', *MÆ*, 44 (1975), 121-36; D. G. Scragg (ed.), *Maldon* (1981; see IV[39]), 26-7.

[71] See C. R. Hart, *The Early Charters of Northern England and the North Midlands* (Leicester, 1975), 328-9. Cf. M. A. L. Locherbie-Cameron, 'Ælfwine's Kinsmen and *The Battle of Maldon*', *N&Q*, 223 (1978), 486-7.

[72] They are well discussed in the appendices to A. G. Brodeur's *Art of Beowulf* (1959; see II[59]), and see other relevant literature listed at p. 60 notes 60, 61 and 62.

Poetic compounds

Poetic compounds, both nouns and adjectives, are a special feature of Old English verse. From the beginning of the literary study of the language these compounds were clearly perceived as a glory of Anglo-Saxon poetry, happy in invention and use like those of Greek itself, happier even (though how is one to judge that?), and more frequent.[73]

In the extant verse many of the compounds occur once only. Some of these *hapax legomena* seem peculiarly expressive in their context, and so perhaps are nonce-coinages in which a poet shows his resourcefulness. This is an aspect of Old English verse much discussed by the critics. We should, however, remind ourselves that what seems to us such a visually striking feature of their verse because of the length of many of these compounds as we print them (usually unhyphenated, following Modern German practice) almost always appears in the manuscripts written by the Anglo-Saxon scribes themselves with the two elements separate. In compounds consisting of an adjective followed by a noun we can tell only when the adjective is uninflected that we may be dealing with a different linguistic structure from the ordinary sequence of adjective followed by noun. In such cases we may perhaps be justified in supposing that the Anglo-Saxons too might have thought the structure unusual.

For example, in the editions *Beowulf* line 853 has *ealdgesiðas* 'old companions, tried retainers', but reads *eald ge siðas* in the manuscript. We think it a compound because, if it were not, we should expect *ealde gesiðas* or *þa ealdan gesiðas*. Similar adjective-plus-noun compounds are *widwegas* 'distant ways or regions' occurring in several poems including *Beowulf* lines 840 and 1704; it is not found in the singular. To establish a compound is not always easy. *Genesis A* line 156a is part of the account of the Second Day, giving the reasons for the division of land and water:

155   Næron Metode ða gyta
        widlond ne wegas nytte,   ac stod bewrigen fæste
        folde mid flode.

[Spacious lands and regions were then still useless to the Lord, but the earth remained firmly covered with water.]

The manuscript reads *wid* [new line] *lond · ne wegas nytte ·* and there is every reason for regarding *widlond* a compound, but there is every reason also for

---

[73] Cf. Meric Casaubon, *De Quatuor Linguis Commentationis, Pars prior* (London, 1650), 217: 'Superest de compositis verbis in quibus Germanicam linguam ad Græcæ fœlicitatem proximè accedere, passiva observatio est.' Similarly, G. Hickes, *Institutiones Grammaticæ Anglo-Saxonicæ, et Moeso-Gothicæ* (Oxford, 1689), 10: 'Et ut linguarum nulla magis gaudet, ita nulla (ne Græcâ quidem exceptâ) in componendis nominibus est felicior quàm Anglosaxonica'; and cf. G. Hickes, *Thesaurus* (1703-1705, see I[10]), I, 9, virtually the same wording.

thinking the first element *wid* does duty again as the first element of the compound *widwegas* with *wid* understood, just as in Modern English we understand 'spacious' as qualifying both 'lands' and 'regions', and in Modern German that could be shown by having a hyphen before the second noun element; Grein's translation 'nicht / weites Land und Wege nutzbar'[74] could be brought visibly closer to the Old English by translating (overliterally, and coining compounds) 'Weitland und -wege' or perhaps (less elegantly, I think – but closer probably to the Old English) 'Weitländer [*or* Weitlande] und -wege'.

A related problem is presented by *Beowulf* line 1546a, in the manuscript *brad brún ecg*, in the editions emended to *brad ond brunecg* in line with *The Battle of Maldon* line 163a, *brad and bruneccg* [broad and with brown (gleaming?) edge].[75] In both poems *brad (ond) brunec(c)g* qualifies the preceding weapontype, *seax* in *Beowulf* and *bill* in *The Battle of Maldon*. In *The Battle of Maldon* line 15a most editors print *bord & brad swurd* [shield and broad sword], but E. V. K. Dobbie in the ASPR edition has *bradswurd* as a compound;[76] **bradecg*, however, does not occur, though adjectival compounds with second element *-ecg* are not uncommon in verse, and most of them are similarly used: *brun-*, *heard-* (*Beowulf* lines 1288, 1490), *scir-* (*Metrical Charm 11* line 28, figurative of St Luke as sword), *stið-* (*Riddle 93* line 20), *styl-* (*Beowulf* line 1533), and *twy-* (Paris Psalter, Psalm 73:5 line 2, 'two-edged' but used as a substantive).

---

74 C. W. M. Grein, *Dichtungen der Angelsachsen* (1857-1859; see I[19]), I, 5.

75 E. von Schaubert (ed.), *Beowulf*, part 2 'Kommentar' (1961; see I[77]), 98, has a good note. W. F. Bolton's revision of C. L. Wrenn's edition of *Beowulf* (London, 1973), 156, does not emend; he has no note on the half-line.

76 The reason is that *swurd* does not alliterate; but the adjective immediately preceding the noun it qualifies is stressed more strongly than the noun, which therefore alliterates in a second half-line (for example, *Beowulf* line 11b), and need not in a first half-line (for example, *Beowulf* line 16a). Dobbie's compound *bradswurd* in the ASPR edition follows a suggestion by F. Holthausen, 'Zur altenglischen Literatur. IX', *Anglia Beiblatt*, 21 (1910), 13. In the same article, pp. 12-13, he advocates that in *The Riming Poem* lines 62-4 the following compounds should be read: *flahmah, flanman, baldald, wræcfæc*, and *wrapað*, of which only *flahmah* and *wræcfæc* have been widely accepted by the editors. Lines 61-5, rhyming on *-it[d/þ]e[a]þ*, are difficult, and, without believing that Holthausen is right in all five cases, I offer a violently emended text with my unliteral translation using all his compounds without confidence in them or in my own readings and interpretations, or in the readings and interpretations of the many editions, dictionaries, and articles which I have consulted and from which I have taken many suggestions:

> Wencyn gewiteð,   wælgar sliteð,
> flahmah fliteþ,   flanman hwiteþ,
> borgsorg biteð,   baldald þwiteþ,
> wræcfæc wriþað,   wrapað smiteþ,
> 65 singryn sidað,   scærafearo glideþ.

[Hoped-for kin goes away. Killing spear cuts deep. The insidious evil one is in contention. Arrow-crime sharpens (the weapon). Surety-worry (or debt-worry) bites. The brave old one takes to paring down. Time of banishment fetters. Angry oath pollutes. Mighty snare opens wide. Shears' movement glides.]

Beowulf 1533a reads in the manuscript *stið & styl ecg* and refers to *wundenmæl* 'sword with curved markings' line 1531, and the half-line is usually rendered 'firm and steel-edged'. In view of the use of *stiðecg* in *Riddle 93* lines 19b-20a *þeah mec heard bite / stiðecg style* [though the hard-edged steel were to bite into me], it is possible that the *Beowulf* use is better represented by *stið- & styl-ecg*.

In listing such examples I do not intend to find fault with editors. As with punctuation, so with word-division and compounding we are forcing into our modern grammatical system a very different scribal record. In the last half-century or so English, especially American English, has witnessed a decline in the use of the hyphen. Modern German still compounds firmly. Yet even Klaeber in the glossary to his edition of *Beowulf* s.v. *wēl-þungen* 'accomplished, excellent', adds 'or *wēl þungen*?'. The combination *wel geþungen* occurs in *The Death of Edward* (1065) line 9. If the perception of what a compound is can change in the course of the twentieth century, if Modern German is different in this respect from Modern English, we cannot be sure that we understand how the Anglo-Saxons perceived adjectival compounds, and we may not be sure about substantival compounds.

Here then might be a baby deserving to be thrown out with the bath-water. I think not. Let this baby be: two heavy stresses joined, such as occur when adjective and noun stand contiguously and without any grammatical inflexion at the end of the adjective, is a poetic compound. We must, however, always remember that the Anglo-Saxons are likely to have 'heard' compounding in terms of stresses and lack of inflexion, whereas we see it on the printed page in verbal contiguity usually unhyphenated.

Verbs less prominent than nouns and adjectives in Old English verse

The poetic diction of the Anglo-Saxons, words confined to verse, consists more often of nouns and adjectives, especially nominal compounds, than of verbs and there are very few adverbs confined to verse: the nouns and adjectives, that is, the *nomina*, preponderate. That is in keeping with the high nominal density of Old English verse, which is in turn an effect of the system of stress in the language, and that system governs alliterative metre. We may contrast our general impression of stasis based on high nominal density and relative paucity of verbs in Old English verse with our general impression of movement and action based on the greater and more varied use made of verbs by many Middle English and Modern English poets.

A rare example of movement achieved less by verbs than by nouns occurs in *Judith* lines 159-66, especially 163-6:

> Þa wurdon bliðe   burhsittende,
> 160 syððan hi gehyrdon   hu seo halige spræc
>   ofer heanne weall.   Here wæs on lustum.

Wið þæs fæstengeates folc onette,
weras wif somod, wornum ond heapum,
ðreatum ond ðrymmum þrungon ond urnon
165 ongean ða þeodnes mægð þusendmælum,
ealde ge geonge.

[The citizens rejoiced as soon as they heard how the saint
spoke over the high wall. The army was filled with joy; the
people hastened towards the fortress-gate, both men and
women, in multitudes and swarms, in throngs and troops they
jostled and ran, old and young in their thousands, towards the
handmaiden of the Lord.]

Here is action, and, though there are verbs of motion in haste (*onettan, þringan, irnan*), most of the sense of urgency is achieved by an unusually dense massing of *nomina* (in the nominative and in the instrumental plural), reflecting the tumultuous rushing of the joyful Israelites towards the victorious Judith. That unusual feature is combined with the normal use in Old English of phrases like *weorþan bliðe* for 'rejoice' and *wesan on luste* for 'exult', each with the sense and stress in the *nomen* in syntactical combination with an auxiliary verb.

There are a few other locutions in common use in verse, and confined to verse. For example, the advance of warriors is described in terms of their carrying arms forward. In *Beowulf* alone this circumlocution occurs six times: lines 291b-92a *Gewitaþ forð beran / wæpen ond gewædu* [Advance, bearing forward weapons and armour!], in this use, not to war but to Hrothgar's court to offer help; and similarly (but to the fight), line 2539 with *hiorosercean* 'coats of mail', line 2653 with *rondas* 'shields', line 2661 with *wigheafolan* 'helmets', line 2754-5 with *hringnet* 'corslet' and *brogdne beadusercean* 'interlocked coat of mail', and line 2850 with *scyldas* 'shields'. Such locutions too lead to a greater use of nouns for weapons than would be used in Modern English for going into battle. The effect is of stasis, perhaps also of stateliness.

The heavy dependence of alliterative verse on *nomina* is not confined to the verse of the Anglo-Saxons, and we may again turn to *Heliand* for comparison. In a versified life of Christ there is not much opportunity for deploying the devices of Germanic battle-poetry; but there is a moment in the account of St Peter in wrath at the arrest of Jesus, striking off Malchus' ear. The Gospel has (John 18:10):[77]

Simon Peter therefore hauing a sword, drewe it out: and smote the seruant of the high priest: & cut of his right eare. And the name of the seruant was Malchus.

Heliand turns that into lines 4865-82:

---

[77] The name Malchus is given only by John, in the gospel for Good Friday. Cf. Matthew 26:51, Mark 14:47, Luke 22:50.

4865   Tho gibolgan uuard
         snel suerdthegan   Simon Petrus:
         uuel imu innan hugi,   that he ni mahte enig uuord sprekan;
         so harm uuard imu an is hertan   that man is herron thar
         binden uuelde.   Tho he gibolgan geng,
4870   suido thristmod thegan,   for is thiodan standen,
         hard for is herron.   Ni uuas imu is hugi tuifli,
         bloth*i* an is breostun,   ac he is bil atoh,
         suerd bi sidu,   *slog* imu togegnes
         an thene furiston fiund   folmo crafto,
4875   that tho Malchus uuard   makeas aggiun
         an thea suidaron half   suerdu gimalod.
         Thiu hlust uuard imu forhauuan: he uuard an that hobid uund,
         that imu herudrorag   hlear endi ore
         beniuundun brast.   Blod aftar sprang,
4880   uuell fan uundun.   Tho uuas an is uuangun scard
         the furisto thero fiundo.   Tho stod that folc an rum:
         andredun im thes billes biti.

[Then Simon Peter, the bold swordsman, was enraged: his
spirit was roused within him so that he could not speak one
word; so sore he felt at heart that they wished to bind his Lord
there. When enraged he came, [4870] the very bold-hearted
man, and stood before his Lord, the valiant one, before his
Liege. there was no doubt in his mind, no fear in his breast, but
he drew his blade, the sword by his side, struck out with the
strength of his hands towards him, into the foremost enemy,
[4875] so that then with the sword's edges Malchus was
marked on his right side with the blade. His sense of hearing
was cut to pieces, his head was wounded so that his cheek and
ear, bloody with the sword, were gashed in cut-wounds. Next,
blood spurted out, [4880] surged from the wounds. Then the
foremost of those enemies had his cheeks injured; then the
people fell back: they feared the bite of that sword.]

In this passage there are many points of similarity with Old English battle-
poetry. A number of Old Saxon words are probably poetic only, but not all of
them have cognates in Old English: *simplicia* like *bil* 'sword', *folm* 'hand', *hige*
'mind', *maki* 'sword', *thiodan* 'Lord'; and compounds like *beniuunda* 'cut-
wounds' (no Old English cognate), *herudrorag* 'sword-bloody' cf. Old English
heorodreorig, *suerdthegan* 'swordsman' (no Old English cognate), and *thristmod* 'bold-hearted' (no Old English cognate). The metre of *Heliand* is less tight
than that of most Old English verse (though less so in this passage of the poem
than in many others), but it is still dependent on nouns and adjectives which
seem to tower above the scatter of unstressed syllables, slightly so in line 4877:

         Thiu *hlust* uuard imu for*hau*uan: he uuard an that *h*obid *uund* and much more so in line 4884b (with *quad he* probably extrametrical):

> *skarp* an *sked*ia: 'Ef ik uuid thesa *sco*la *uuel*di,' quad he
>
> [. . . the sharp one into the scabbard: 'If I were to wish [to do battle] with this host,' he said,]

where the finite verb *uueldi*[78] takes the second stress.

Middle English alliterative verse is different. The system of *nomina* having precedence of finite verbs in stress and alliteration does not survive into Middle English, and my impression is that, as a result perhaps, there is greater expressiveness in the verbs used in Middle English, and that verbs play a more prominent role in the alliteration of Middle English.[79] For example, chosen more or less at random, is *The Wars of Alexander*, 964-71:[80]

> Þan was þe wale king wrath, as wondir ware ellis,
> 965 Braydis him vp fra þe borde & a brand clekis,
> Airid toward Alexsandire & ames him to strike;
> Bot þan him failis þe feete or he first wenys.
> He stakirs, he stumbils, & stande he ne miȝt,
> Bot ay fundirs & fallis as he ferde ware.
> 970 Þe fastir forward him he faris, þe fastir he snapirs;
> Quat was þe cause of þe case, þat knawis oure Lorde!

[Then the excellent king grew angry – it would have been a marvel otherwise! – gets up from the table and seizes a sword; he advanced towards Alexander, and takes aim to strike him; but then his feet fail him before he even knows what to think. He staggers, he stumbles, and he could not stand, but keeps on floundering and falling as if he were afraid. The more vigorously he advances forwards, the more vigorously he staggers. The Lord alone knows what was the cause of all this!]

The Anglian colouring of Old English verse

An overwhelmingly greater number of the surviving manuscripts of Old English are written in the West Saxon dialect than in any other. In the later Anglo-Saxon

---

[78] 1st sg. preterite subjunctive of *willan* 'to wish'. In Old English too, stress, especially the non-alliterating second stress of the second half-line, frequently falls on a finite verb.

[79] Cf. *Sir Gawain and the Green Knight*, lines 2201-4, quoted p. 139, above. It is noteworthy, however, that the index of words significantly discussed by M. Borroff, *Sir Gawain and the Green Knight, A Stylistic and Metrical Study*, Yale Studies in English, 152 (1962), 283-9, includes relatively few verbs. An analysis of alliterative formulas, on the other hand, includes many in which verbs play a part; see J. Fuhrmann, *Die alliterierenden Sprachformeln in Morris' Early English Alliterative Poems und im Sir Gawayne and the Green Knight* (Kiel doctoral dissertation; Hamburg, 1886).

[80] H. N. Duggan and T. Turville-Petre (eds), *The Wars of Alexander*, EETS, s.s. 10 (1989), 28. In the quotation the two emendations of this edition are not accepted.

period, to which belong most of the manuscripts containing Old English verse (as well as most of the manuscripts containing prose only), West Saxon was written not only in Wessex itself, but also outside the borders of Wessex. In not a few cases we can deduce, usually from cumulative linguistic evidence, that the poems contained in the great codices and some of the poems transmitted outside the great codices were not originally written in West Saxon, but further north, in Anglian (either Mercian or Northumbrian). A number of words, and a greater number of phonological forms of words, are thought to be Anglian rather than West Saxon, a supposition based in varying degree on statistical probability; and these words and forms occur in texts written in what seems on the whole West Saxon and are preserved in manuscripts thought to be of West Saxon or Kentish provenance.

The matter is complicated as soon as we get a mixture of forms. The Introduction of Klaeber's third edition of *Beowulf* has a section (pp. lxxxviii-lxxxix) 'Language, Manuscript § 24. Mixture of forms', summarizing and explaining the complexity that he had dealt with in preceding sections. This is the opening paragraph (from which I omit the valuable examples and the detailing footnotes, some of which I use below):

> How can this mixture of forms, early and late, West Saxon, Northumbrian, Mercian, Kentish, Saxon patois be accounted for? The interesting supposition that an artificial, conventional standard, a sort of compromise dialect had come into use as the acknowledged medium for the composition of Anglo-Saxon poetry, can be accepted only in regard to the continued employment of ancient forms (archaisms) and of certain Anglian elements firmly embedded in the vocabulary of early Anglian poetry. . . . But the significant coexistence in the manuscript of different forms of one and the same word, without any inherent principle of distribution being recognizable, points plainly to a checkered history of the written text as the chief factor in bringing about the unnatural medley of spellings. The only extant manuscript of *Beowulf* was written some two and a half centuries after the probable date of composition and was, of course, copied from a previous copy. It is perfectly safe to assert that the text was copied a number of times, and that scribes of heterogeneous dialectal habits and different individual peculiarities had a share in that work. Although the exact history of the various linguistic and orthographic strata cannot be recovered, the principal landmarks are still plainly discernible.

There is much to admire here, not least the clarity of Klaeber's reasoning; but there is also much to doubt. 'Saxon patois' assumes a pristine West Saxon orthographic purity to which none of the extant early West Saxon texts bears witness.[81] 'The continued employment of ancient forms (archaisms)' which led

---

[81] See R. M. Hogg, 'On the impossibility of Old English dialectology', in D. Kastovsky and G. Bauer (eds), *Luick Revisited* (Tübingen, 1988), 183-203; on the term 'Saxon patois', see in the same volume, E. G. Stanley, 'Karl Luick's "Man schrieb wie man sprach" and English

C. L. Wrenn to abandon caution, as he contemplated what he read as *wun[d]ini golde* at *Beowulf* line 1382, and so 'deduce that a written form of *Beowulf* existed little later than the middle of the eighth century', and to pay little heed to K. Sisam's clear demolition of this deduction.[82] In Klaeber's paragraph, 'the vocabulary of early Anglian poetry', presumably refers to more than the five early Northumbrian poems, *Cædmon's Hymn*, *Bede's Death Song*, *The Leiden Riddle*, and the Ruthwell Cross and Franks Casket inscriptions, but we are not told to which others. 'The unnatural medley of spellings', where 'natural' may mean acceptable, in an Anglo-Saxon scribe, to a Neo-Grammarian rigorously trained in Germany. 'Some two and a half centuries' would be halved by those who see the probable date of composition in the fifty years around 900. 'The principal landmarks' in the linguistic history of the text no longer seem 'plainly discernible'.

The most exact scholar to devote himself to the 'Dialect Origins of the Earlier Old English Verse' was Kenneth Sisam, and his conclusions are not to be lightly dismissed as a game.[83] He, like Klaeber, recognized that some sporadic spellings are probably late, though, equally sporadically, they occur also in very early texts: the <u> of *hliuade* line 1799, for example, which might be compared with *wiue* in Rushworth Mercian of the tenth century.[84]

Klaeber (p. lxxi, § 1) lists as 'distinctly early West Saxon' *hiera* line 1164, *gieste* line 2560, and (more complicated, and quite inconclusive, because confusion with the numeral 'six' has to be invoked) *siex* 'short sword' line 2904; as

---

historical philology', 311-34, especially pp. 319-20 on K. Bülbring's use of 'andere sächsische Patois' and K. Luick's 'strengwestsächsisch'.

[82] C. L. Wrenn (ed.), *Beowulf With the Finnesburg Fragment* (London, 1953), p. 17, and cf. pp. 9, 21 footnote 2, 34-5, 130, 210, and 302 s.v. *windan*. See K. Sisam, 'Notes on Old English Poetry: The Authority of Old English Poetical Manuscripts', *RES*, 22 (1946), 257-68 (p. 263 footnote 1), reprinted in his *Studies* (1953; see III[8]), 29-44 (p. 36 footnote 1); for further references to discussion of the reading, see E. von Schaubert (ed.), *Beowulf*, part 2 'Kommentar' (1961; see I[77]), 94.

[83] *Studies* (1953; see III[8]) 119-39. He was not given to intellectual play, 'Gedankenspiel' is the word used of Sisam's distinguished study in K. Grinda's rejection of W. Busse's interesting and refreshing *Altenglische Literatur und ihre Geschichte. Zur Kritik des gegenwärtigen Deutungssystems* (Düsseldorf, 1987), in a review-article, *Indogermanische Forschungen*, 96 (1991), 203-17. Sisam saw the faults of a philological method that pretends to certainty about dialectal origins of texts written in a country the early linguistic history of which is largely obscure, so that we cannot even tell for the second part of Cotton MS Vitellius A.xv if it is the product of a provincial centre or of a scriptorium in London (see Sisam's 'The Compilation of the Beowulf Manuscript', *Studies*, 65-96, that is, not one of the great Benedictine scriptoria. The consensus of scholars brought up in the same philological tradition failed to impress Sisam.

[84] See *Studies*, p. 85 footnote 1; the similar spellings with <u> in the early glossaries are most conveniently set out in H. M. Chadwick, 'Studies in Old English', *Transactions of the Cambridge Philological Society*, 4 (1899), 236-7 [= 144-5 of separate]. Cf. E. M. Brown, *The Language of the Rushworth Gloss to . . . Matthew*, II (Göttingen, 1892), 23 § 16.

well as *niehstan* line 2511.[85] He draws attention to verb forms regarded as archaic *hafu* line 2523 and *fullæstu* line 2668, but elsewhere (§ 23, 2 and 5) grants the possibility that they are Anglian; and for the further possible archaism *fæðmię* line 2652 his note on line 1981 indicates that the two scribes of the extant text were careless in some details of spelling to which anyone brought up as a Neo-Grammarian would attach importance: but the scribes, alas, were no Neo-Grammarians. The mixture of East Mercian (or is it West Mercian?)[86] and West Saxon in Farmon's part of the Rushworth Gospels (Matthew, the beginning of Mark, and three verses of John) shows such spellings to be features in the work of scribes not successfully disciplined in some great late West Saxon or Kentish scriptorium, but certainly not exclusively early features.

The mere fact that we cannot prove Rushworth Mercian to be East or West, from West Yorkshire or from Herefordshire, shows how ignorant we are of Old English dialectology. Well over a century of doctoral dissertations and *Habilitationsschriften* (with their, usually, reliable surveys of observable features, laboriously assembled, followed by, usually, unreliable conclusions, *Ergebnisse*) has

---

[85] From the two Toronto microfiche concordances of Old English, we can see at a glance the distribution of the spelling <hiera>: once in each of three of the poetic codices, Junius, Vercelli (plus 8 times in the prose), and *Beowulf* line 1164 (plus 3 times in the prose); it comes once in *Solomon and Saturn*; once (prose) in Corpus Christi College Cambridge MS 41; 6 times (prose, always the same homily) in Bodleian MSS Junius 85 and 86; once a variant reading in *The Distichs of Cato*; twice in the Codex Wintoniensis, once in Heming's Cartulary, once in the Liber Vitae of Hyde, once in Chronicle D in the annal for 1001, once in the Vespasian Psalter and once in the Eadwine Psalter; and very frequently in early West Saxon. Nothing can be deduced from the single occurrence of <hiera> in *Beowulf*.

After /j/ the spelling <ie> is much more widely distributed than <ie> spellings of *hira*, *heora*. From <gie-> nothing can be deduced of an early West Saxon stratum in the transmission of the text of *Beowulf*, though it is common in early West Saxon. Cf. Sisam, 'The Exeter Book', in *Studies* (1953; see III[8]), 98 and 102; Sisam rightly calls <ie> 'characteristic Early West Saxon', and shows that the distribution of <gie> is not identical with the distribution of <ie> after other consonants.

The spelling <niehst-> is much rarer, there is an occurrence in *Genesis A*, but otherwise it is mainly West Saxon, especially early West Saxon, and Canterbury too, with <niextan> 3 times in Bodleian MS Hatton 76A (Ælfric's *Admonitio*) as well as 4 times in the Eadwine Psalter.

[86] 1. East Mercian, written at Harewood about eight miles north of Leeds according to the more widely accepted view, first advanced by J. A. H. Murray, 'The Rushworth Glosses', *Academy*, 6 (1874), 561-2 (more generally, on Farmon's 'southernizing' into his 'Southhumbrian' the gloss of the Lindisfarne Gospels), and an unsigned article by Murray, 'The Anglo-Saxon Gospels', *The Athenæum*, 3 April 1875, 451-3 (quite specifically, that Farmon and Owun, the two glossators of the Rushworth Gospels, were of 'the Monastery of Harwood in the West Riding of Yorkshire'). 2. West Mercian, written at Harewood about 5½ miles west north west of Ross on Wye, advanced with question marks by M. Förster, *Der Flußname Themse und seine Sippe*, Sitzungsberichte der Bayerischen Akademie der Wissenschaften, Philosophisch-historische Abteilung 1941, vol. I, 473(-4) note 4.

See also P. Bibire and A. S. C. Ross, 'The Differences Between Lindisfarne and Rushworth Two', *N&Q*, 226 (1981), 98-116, especially p. 99; cf. E. G. Stanley, 'Karl Luick's "Man schrieb wie man sprach" ' (1988; see IV[81]), 321, and R. M. Hogg, 'On the impossibility of Old English dialectology' (1988; see IV[81]), 186-7.

shaped a species of philological scholarship in which lack of commonsense and absence of doubt in the customary linguistic analysis led and still lead to 'results' of doubtful value, the next generation of scholars building on the speculations of those who went before them as if such speculative *Ergebnisse* could form a sound foundation. The brilliance of Max Förster's assertion that Harewood near Ross on Wye could be the provenance of Rushworth Mercian is not that it is right, but that it dares to question established views, and that it cannot be proved wrong. The most we can say is that, if it is right, Rushworth Mercian does not include a very striking feature of Vespasian Psalter Mercian, <ea> in words like *feadur* (genitive and dative singular of the word for 'father'), *ðorhfearað* ('pertransibun[t]', '[they] shal passe'), but then the Mercian origin of the Vespasian Psalter gloss is not beyond all doubt.[87]

There is good reason for being suspicious of weighty conclusions of provenance and stages in textual transmission drawn from a sprinkling of occasional spellings given prominence because they are exceptional as shown by single-text philological analyses. When, however, in one manuscript some spelling peculiarities occur in one text only or in one group of texts only, analysis of the spellings of the whole manuscript may well reveal results. That is why Sisam's analysis of the prose and verse texts in the *Beowulf* manuscript (Cotton Vitellius A.xv B) is valuable; as was A. S. Napier's analysis of Bodleian MS Hatton 116 showing that the homily on the life of St Chad is different in dialect from the rest; and D. G. Scragg's analysis of the groups of texts in the Vercelli MS showing linguistic features shared by members within the group but different (or differently distributed) from features of other groups.[88]

These phonological pedantries matter because even in the great poetic codices, all four of them written in the south, some words forming part of Old English poetic diction always or often appear in spellings thought to reflect Anglian dialects associated with Mercian and Northumbrian further north. We do not know the reason for this 'Anglian colouring' of poetry copied in more southerly centres. Anglian *cald* is used occasionally in place of West Saxon

---

[87] See E. M. Brown, *Die Sprache der Rushworth Glossen* (Göttingen, 1891), 30 § 14, for second fronting see pp. 15-16 § 2; R. Zeuner, *Die Sprache des kentischen Psalters (Vespasian A. I.)* (Halle, 1881), 28-32; K. Brunner, *Altenglische Grammatik nach . . . Sievers* (1965; see III[32]), 83-5 § 109. For the possibility that the Vespasian Psalter may not be Mercian, see R. M. Wilson, 'The Provenance of the Vespasian Psalter Gloss: The Linguistic Evidence', in P. A. M. Clemoes (ed.), *The Anglo-Saxons Studies . . . Presented to Bruce Dickins* (Cambridge, 1959), 292-310. It is a matter of weighing not wholly unambiguous evidence: probably the generally accepted view that the gloss is West Mercian is preferable to the assumption of Kentish origins; but not so clearly as appears from A. Campbell's dismissal of the possibility of Kentish origins in the introduction to D. H. Wright's edition of the facsimile, *The Vespasian Psalter British Museum Cotton Vespasian A. I*, EEMF, XIV (1967), 'The Glosses', pp. 85-90 Language.

[88] K. Sisam, *Studies* (1953; see III[8]), 65-96; A. S. Napier, 'Ein altenglisches Leben des heiligen Chad', *Anglia*, 10 (1888), 131-54; D. G. Scragg, 'The compilation of the Vercelli Book', *ASE*, 2 (1973), 189-207.

ceald 'cold'; the difference is not merely of the vowel, but *cald* has <c> pronounced /k/ whereas *ceald* has <c> pronounced /tʃ/. In King Alfred's free rendering of Boethius' *Consolation* into prose he has in ch. xxi:[89] *on sumera hit bið wearm & on wintra ceald* [in summer it is warm and in winter cold]. He turns that into the verse of *Metre* 11 lines 59-61a:

> Winter bringeð   [we]der [un]gemet cald,
> 60   swifte windas.   [Sumor æft]er cymeð,
> wearm gewide[ru].
>
> [Winter brings very cold weather, swift winds. Summer fol-
> lows, warm weather.]

The scribe of the prose has *ceald*, the scribe of the verse has *cald*, in this poem composed by the West Saxon king and copied by a West Saxon scribe. As usual, we do not know the history of the textual transmission, but there is nothing to suggest that there is any intervening non-West-Saxon stage. The Anglian form *cald* was regarded as the form suitable for West Saxon verse.

The spelling of *waldend* 'ruler, the Lord' is similarly a spelling thought right for verse: 9 times in *The Metres of Boethius*, and 4 times *wealdend*; but forms of the verb *wealdan* 'to rule', which in verse is not usually given the Anglian spelling with <a> for West Saxon <ea>, is 7 times recorded with <a> and 5 times with <ea> in *The Metres of Boethius*.

Anglian *ælda* (gen. pl.), *ældum* (dat. pl.), also with <e> for <æ>, and West Saxon *ylda*, *yldum*, at *Elene* line 521 *ilda*, 'humans' is confined to verse. The form *ælda* occurs as early as *Cædmon's Hymn*[90] and as late as *The Seasons for Fasting* in forms of the phrase *ælda bearn* 'the children of mankind'. It is probably of Christian Latin origin as presented by the frequent biblical

---

89   W. J. Sedgefield (ed.), *King Alfred's Boethius* (1899; see IV[63]), for the prose version p. 49, for the verse version p. 168. Both the prose and the verse are preserved only in post-Alfredian manuscripts, the prose for this quotation) is from the twelfth-century Bodleian MS Bodley 180, the verse is from Cotton MS Otho A. vi of the middle of the tenth century [sup-plemented from Junius's transcript in Bodleian MS Junius 12]; cf. F. C. Robinson and E. G. Stanley (eds), EEMF, XXIII (1991), plates 5.12.3.1 and 5.12.3.2. Cf. E. G. Stanley, 'Spell-ings of the *Waldend* Group', in E. B. Atwood and A. A. Hill (eds), *Studies in Language Literature and Culture of the Middle Ages and Later* for R. Willard (Austin, Texas, 1969), 38-69; and see especially A. Lutz, 'Spellings of the *waldend* group – again', *ASE*, 13 (1984), 51-64. Cf. E. G. Stanley, 'Old English "-calla", "ceallian" ' (1969; see IV[39]), 94-9; the alliteration of *The Battle of Maldon* line 91 is more complicated than I then thought if, as I now believe /k/ and /tʃ/ do not alliterate in this poem, so that the <a> for /ea/ spelling in *cald* is to be looked upon as a mistaken, scribal poeticization, or, better, the spelling <ea> in *ceallian* is to be looked upon as a mistaken, scribal West-Saxonization, regardless of whether the word is indigenous, as I believe, or a Scandinavian loanword.

90   In some of the Northumbrian texts of *Cædmon's Hymn* and in almost all the West Saxon texts the original, variously spelt *aelda barnum* (West Saxon *ylda bearnum*) is replaced by *eorðan bearnum* (variously spelt); cf. F. C. Robinson and E. G. Stanley (eds), EEMF, XXIII (1991), plates 2.1 to 2.21; and E. V. K. Dobbie (ed.). *Cædmon's Hymn and Bede's Death Song* (1937; see III[16]), 43-8.

expression, for example, in Psalm 13:2 *Dominus de caelo prospexit super filios hominum* 'Our Lord hath looked forth from heauen vpon the children of men'; the phrase is not only English, for *Heliand* has *eldibarn* frequently, nor explicitly Christian in every application, for the *Edda* has *alda bornom* in *Vǫluspa* 20, 11.[91]

The form *mece* 'sword' is almost certainly Anglian, and not West Saxon, which should have the form *mæce*; but that is found only in rendering the fish-name *mugil* (or *mugilis*) 'mullet' (though the Anglo-Saxons may not have identified Latin *mugil* with mullet), variant spelling *mæcefisc*, twice in the same manuscript.[92] It is one of a number of poetic words that are not West Saxon in form. Some of these words have <ea> (in some words beside <a>), and that <ea> is characteristic of the dialect of the Vespasian Psalter, probably West Mercian:[93] *beadu* 'battle, war', *eafora* 'son', *eafoþ* 'strength, might', *eatol* 'terrible' (but the more common *atol* is not confined to verse), *heafolan* 'head' (<ea> does not occur in uninflected forms), *heafu* 'seas' (*Beowulf* line 1862, emended from *hea þu*), and *heaþo-* 'war'.

A dialect so specific as Vespasian Psalter Mercian, for this is an important feature the dialect of the Psalter does not share with Kentish, seems an odd choice for the linguistic colouring of poetry. A general northernism might be explicable as a language less influenced by the scriptorial prescriptions introduced in the later tenth century by the ascendant Benedictine Reform. One thinks of late medieval and post-medieval balladry for which the dialect of the

---

[91] G. Neckel (ed.), *Edda* (4th edn revised by H. Kuhn; Heidelberg, 1962), 5. Cf. J. W. Rankin, 'A Study of the Kennings in Anglo-Saxon Poetry', *JEGP*, 9 (1910), 65-8, listing and discussing *bearn-* compounds and phrases, and suggesting Christian Latin origin for *aelda barnum* and related phrases. For the use in Icelandic, cf. H. de Boor, 'Die religiöse Sprache der Vǫluspá und verwandter Denkmäler', in W. H. Vogt and H. Spethmann (eds), *Deutsche Islandforschung 1930*, I Kultur ed. W. H. Vogt, Veröffentlichungen der Schleswig-Holsteinischen Universitätsgesellschaft, 28/1 (Breslau, 1930), 73-9, who avers strenuously that Christian influence on Old Icelandic combinations like *Huna bornum* (*Atlaqviða* 27, 12) is unthinkable; but since both the generalized, Christian-looking *alda bornum* and the particular combination with first element a tribal name, *Huna bornum*, seems excessively rare, one can only marvel at de Boor's assurance. Till quite recently in Germanic scholarship, including that of Old Icelandic, when the direction of influence from pagan to Christian or Christian to pagan has been under discussion, the supposed factuality has often been the child of wishing. It is noteworthy that combinations like *Beowulf* lines 1141 *Eotena bearn* and 2184 *Geata bearn*, and *The Metres of Boethius* 1 line 34 *Romwara bearn*, are conspicuously less common than the Hebraisms of the type of *The Kentish Hymn* line 26 *bearn Is'rae'la*, and very much less common than the renderings and derivatives of *filii hominum*, no doubt as a result of the preponderance of religious texts in Old English. But a distribution of this kind does not invite assurance that Christian influence on the combination of *bearn* with Germanic tribal names (only the two in *Beowulf* are recorded in Old English) is unthinkable.

[92] See J. Zupitza (ed.), *Ælfrics Grammatik und Glossar* (Berlin, 1880), 39 note on line 1 and 308 note on line 5, variant readings in Cotton MS Julius A.ii of the Middle of the eleventh century; cf. J. J. Köhler, *Die altenglischen Fischnamen*, AF, 21 (also Heidelberg doctoral dissertation, both 1906), 58-9.

[93] See p. 159 n. 87, above. For other, less certain examples, see Klaeber's *Beowulf* (3rd edn, 1936), p. lxxviii § 12.

Scottish Border seemed the correct linguistic costume, so that the antiquary Robert Jamieson, one of Sir Walter Scott's circle, chose a timeless Scottish, rather than standard English, as his medium for translation of foreign, medieval chivalric literature:[94]

> Having cultivated an intimate acquaintance with the Scottish language in all its stages, so far back as any monuments of it remain, he [the translator speaking of himself in the third person] might be supposed to have some confidence in his use of it. If in his translations he has blended the dialects of different ages, he has at least endeavoured to do judiciously what his subject seemed to require of him, in order to preserve as entire as possible, in every particular, the costume of his originals. This is one of the strongest features of resemblance between the Northern and Scottish Ballads, in which there is found a phraseology which has long been obsolete in both countries, and many terms not understood by those who recite them, and for the meaning of which we must refer to the Norse or Islandic of the eighth and ninth centuries.

Of course, this analogy is imperfect. Jamieson was a Scot, and Edinburgh was his own linguistic and literary centre; his forays were into time, and not into a strange dialect area. The linguistic booty he brought back was not from distant places but from earlier strata of his own dialect. We learn also that those Scottish singers who, in the early nineteenth century, recited the ballads no longer understood the obsolete terms in their phraseology.

The scribes to whom we are indebted for the transmission of the poetry of the Anglo-Saxons may similarly not always have fully understood terms that were not in ordinary use in southern speech, either because they are of the north, or because they were obsolescent or obsolete. Obsolescence and obsoleteness are linguistic qualities which, in a dead language, we can infer only seldom, from rarity of usage perhaps or from a contemporary explanation indicating an expectation of unintelligibleness.

The linguistic costume of Anglo-Saxon poetry does not consist only in rare words, perhaps northern in origin or northern in phonology. Morphology too may be involved. In Anglian most verbs have in the 2nd and 3rd person present indicative unsyncopated forms, that is, forms a syllable longer than in West Saxon and Kentish where they are syncopated. In verse the additional syllable is sometimes required for scansion; and in King Alfred's *The Metres of Boethius* we find unsyncopated verb-forms, where a West Saxon might have been expected to use syncopated forms (though, in fact, Alfred is not a consistent user

---

[94] R. Jamieson, 'Popular Heroic and Romantic Ballads, translated from the Northern Languages', in [H. Weber, R. Jamieson and Walter Scott], *Illustrations of Northern Antiquities, from the earlier Teutonic and Scandinavian Romances* (Edinburgh, 1814), 257-430 [cf. J. G. Lockhart, *Memoirs of the Life of Sir Walter Scott, Bart.*, III (Edinburgh and London, 1837), ch. iii, 114-15]. The quotation, Jamieson's defence of his choice of Scottish, is from *Northern Antiquities*, p. 246.

of either syncopated forms for prose or unsyncopated forms for verse).[95] Alfred composes first the following short passage in prose (ch. iv):

> & þa tunglu þu gedest þe gehyrsume, & þa sunnan þu gedest þæt heo mid heore beorhtan sciman þa þeostro adwæscð þære sweartan nihte.

[and the stars thou dost make obedient to thee, and the sun thou dost cause that with his bright radiance he suppresses the darkness of the black night.]

He turns that freely into verse, *Metre* 4 lines 4b-7, using two unsyncopated verb-forms, *genedest* '(thou) dost compel' and *adwæsceð* 'suppresses', both needed for the metre of their half-lines (the corresponding prose passage has syncopated *adwæscð*, and no equivalent of *genedest*):

> & ðurh ðine halige miht
> 5 tunglu genedest   þæt hi ðe to herað.
> Swylce seo sunne   sweartra nihta
> ðiostro adwæsceð   þurh ðine meht.

[and through thy sacred might thou dost compel the stars that they obey thee. Likewise the sun suppresses the dark of black nights through thy might.]

Extant Old English poetry and the Germanic Heroic Age

The extant Old English verse is so preponderantly religious that we, as modern readers, are in danger of singling out for special admiration all secularities. Yet many poetic words may indeed have had their origin in poetic descriptions, celebrations even, of manly virtue, the art of war, and life at court or hall. *Beowulf* is a secular poem, so that its rich poetic vocabulary seems to have retained its original secular force. This is shown in the following words in the poem which in Klaeber's glossary (for reasons of space, I confine myself to words beginning with a, æ, and b) are marked as wholly or mainly poetic, or as *hapax legomena*:[96]

> *a-bredwian* 'kill', *a-breotan* 'kill', *ge)æfnan* 'perform, do', *æg-weard* 'watch by the sea', *æht* 'pursuit', *æl-fylce* 'foreign army', *æsc-holt* 'spear', *æsc-wiga* '(spear-)warrior', *æt-græpe* 'aggressive', *æt-windan* 'flee away', *ag-læca* 'fierce warrior', *and-rysno* 'courtesy', *and-saca* 'adversary', *an-hydig* 'resol-

---

95 See E. Sievers, 'Rhythmik des germanischen Alliterationsverses. II' (1885; see IV[25]), 465-71; cf. E. Krämer, *Die altenglischen Metra des Boetius*, BBzA, VIII (1902), 19. For the text, see W. J. Sedgefield (ed.), *King Alfred's Boethius* (1899; see IV[63]), prose p. 10 lines 3-5, verse p. 155. For comparable verb-forms of *Beowulf*, see Klaeber's 3rd edn (1936), pp. lxxxvi-lxxxviii § 23.

96 The meanings given are not identical with those provided by Klaeber in his glossary, and to some extent the meanings given here emphasize martial connotations.

ute', *ar* 'messenger, herald', *ar-stafas* 'grace, favour', *a-swebban* 'kill', *að-sweord* 'oath', *bat-weard* 'boat-guard', *beado* 'battle', *beado-grima* '(visored) helmet', *beado-hrægl* 'battle-armour', *beado-leoma* 'bright sword', *beado-mece* 'battle-sword', *beado-rinc* 'warrior', *beadu-folm* '(warlike) hand', *beadu-lac* 'sport of war', *beadu-rof* 'famous in warlike deeds', *beadu-run* 'declaration of war', *beadu-scearp* 'battle sharp', *beadu-scrud* 'battle-armour', *beadu-serce* 'battle-armour', *beag-gyfa* 'ring-giving liege-lord', *beag-hroden* 'ring-adorned', *beah-hord* 'treasure-hoard', *beah-sele* 'hall (in which treasure is given)', *beah-ðegu* 'receiving of rings', *beah-wriða* 'ring-band', *bealdian* 'show oneself brave', *bealdor* 'prince', *bealo* (noun and adjective) 'evil', *bealo-cwealm* 'baleful death', *bealo-hycgende* 'intending destruction', *bealo-hydig* 'intending destruction', *bealo-nið* 'pernicious enmity', *be-gylpan* 'exult', *ben(n)* 'wound', *benc-sweg* 'convivial noise', *benc-þel* 'bench-plank', *ben-geat* 'wound-opening', *beod-geneat* 'table-companion', *beorn* 'man, warrior', *beorn-cyning* 'warrior-king', *beor-scealc* 'beer-drinker, feaster', *beor-sele* 'banquet-hall', *beor-þegu* 'partaking of beer', *beot-word* 'word of avowing, challenge', *be-timbran* 'complete a building', *be-wægnan* 'offer', *be-wennan* 'entertain', *big-folc* 'neighbouring tribe', *bil(l)* 'sword', *blodegian* 'make bloody', *blod-fag* 'blood-stained', *bolgen-mod* 'enraged', *bon-gar* 'deadly spear', *bord* 'shield', *bord-hæbbend(e)* 'shield-bearer', *bord-hreoða* 'shield-cover, phalanx', *bord-rand* 'shield', *bord-weal(l)* 'shield-cover, protecting shield', *bord-wudu* 'shield (made of wood), *brego* 'chief, lord', *brego-rof* 'preeminent in valour, of princely fame', *brego-stol* '(a prince's) throne', *breost-gewæde* 'coat of mail', *breost-net* 'corselet', *brim-liðend(e)* 'seafarer', *brim-wisa* 'sea-leader', *brogden-mæl* 'sword with ornamented blade', *brun-ecg* 'with brown [or shining?] edge', *brun-fag* 'brown [or shining?]', *bryd-bur* 'lady's chamber', *brytta* 'distributor', *burh-loca* 'castle', *burh-stede* 'castle-court', *burh-wela* 'wealth of a castle', *byre* 'son, boy', *byrn-wiga* 'man in armour'.

Perhaps the high frequency in *Beowulf* of poetic words and rare compounds (many of them *hapax legomena*) is the result of the poetic language of the Anglo-Saxons being deployed in this poem in a world like the heroic world it first celebrated in song.[97] No doubt, the poet's excellence shows itself in his use of the poetic language available to him. To put it the other way round, his good sense shows itself in his choice of a heroic subject which allows him to deploy this poetic language. When he used the traditional, poetic words *beorn*, *hæle* or *secg*, for example, we can translate them as 'hero' if we wish, but that may well be overdoing it. It is probably better to translate them as 'warrior' or simply by the much paler 'man'; for in this poem the *beornas*, *hæleð* and *secgas* are fighters one and all. That the word *hæle* has no connotations of greater valour than *beorn* or *secg* is shown by the use at line 2224, *hæleða bearna* 'of the children of men' (one of the generalizing phrases for 'mankind'. This is a much damaged area of the manuscript, but it is clear that the man referred to, the one

---

[97] Cf. E. G. Stanley, '*Beowulf*' (1966; see II[65]), 167-9.

who removes the cup from the dragon is not singled out for heroism by the poet. Another unheroic use occurs when Holofernes' soldiery are called *hæleð* in *Judith* 247a, though irony could be invoked since in this part of the poem Holofernes' men seem to be mocked by the poet, and though irony in Old English is often difficult to prove, it seems not unlikely in the phrase *slegefæge hæleð* with the rhyming adjective, merrily as it seems, proclaiming the heroes' end, lines 246b-50a:[98]

> Þa ic ædre gefrægn
> slegefæge hæleð   slæpe tobredon
> ond wið þæs bealofullan   burgeteldes
> werigferhðe   hwearfum þringan,
> 250   Holofernus.

[Then I heard the warriors, about to meet a violent end, quickly shake off sleep and, weary-hearted, press forward in crowds towards the residential pavilion of that man full of evil, Holofernes.]

Etymology is often misleading in semantics: the Old English word has as its German congener *Held* 'hero'. That fact combined with the importance of German scholarship of Old English has led to the Old English *hæle* also being translated 'hero', rather than 'warrior' in a poem where they fight, or as 'man' in a poem where they do not. In Old English, the word for 'male human' is *wæpnedman(n)*, and *wæpned*, the etymological sense of which is 'bearing weapons', comes to mean 'male' qualifying *man(n)* which means 'person' of either sex; *wæpnedcyn(n)* is 'manly nature'. This usage is in contrast with *wifman(n)* 'womanly person; woman', *wifcyn(n)* 'the female sex, womankind; women'.

The sense of *wæpnedman(n)* is well exmplified in the use in *Genesis A* line 919, God's angry speech to Eve after the Fall, and by implication to all womankind, lines 919-22a:

> Wend þe from wynne.   Þu scealt wæpnedmen
> 920   wesan on gewealde   mid weres egsan
> hearde genearwad,   hean þrowian
> þinra dæda gedwild.

[Abandon joy. Under man's domination must you be, cruelly

---

[98] Cf. B. J. Timmer (ed.), *Judith* (London, 1952), 13, a discussion of grimly ironical and humorous effect, with a reference to his article 'Irony in Old English Poetry', *ESts*, 24 (1942), 171-5. These lines have several difficulties, of which the most important is that line 249a has *weras ferhðe* in the manuscript; of the emendations proposed, *werigferhðe* is perhaps the best. It involves alliteration with *hwearfum* on *w*, explained by E. Sievers, *Altgermanische Metrik* (1893; see III[79]), 37 footnote 1, as on *wearf*, a doublet of *hwearf* (cf. the similar alliteration of the Old Saxon cognate *huarf* on *w* in *Heliand* line 4467, and also of *hwearfum* at *Guthlac* line 263).

constrained in fear of (your) husband, abject you must suffer
for the error of your deeds.]

Benjamin Thorpe in his translation of 1832 rendered *wæpnedmen . . . on gewealde* correctly as 'to man . . . in subjection', but C. W. M. Grein in 1857
rendered it nonsensically 'in des Bewaffneten Macht' [in the power of the armed
man].[99] In *Beowulf* line 1284 the weaker war-terror of the woman, Grendel's
mother, is contrasted with the stronger terror of the male Grendel, though
Beowulf had a harder time of it with her than he had with him, lines 1282-7:

> Grendles modor.   Wæs se gryre læssa
> efne swa micle   swa bið mægþa cræft,
> wiggryre wifes,   be wæpnedmen,
> 1285 þonne heoru bunden,   hamere geþuren,
> sweord swate fah   swin ofer helme
> ecgum dyhtig   andweard scireð.

[. . . Grendel's mother. (Her) terror was less by even so much
as is women's strength, a female's war-terror, compared with
that of a man, whenever the bound sword, hammer-forged, the
blade, with edges excellent, stained with blood, cuts against
the boar-image above the helmet.]

This is warlike; yet even here *wæpnedman(n)* is used to signal the stronger sex,
not that that sex bears arms. The use in *Genesis* refers to humanity's only
non-martial age before Cain had found our first murder-weapon in a not so
peaceful-looking cudgel, if the drawing in MS Junius 11 has got it right.[100]
    When we find *hæleð* (a form of *hæle*) used in *The Dream of the Rood* line 39

---

99 See B. Thorpe (ed.), *Cædmon* (1832; see III[52]), 56, and C. W. M. Grein, *Dichtungen* (1957;
see I[19]), I, 27. K. W. Bouterwek (ed), *Cædmon* (1849-1854; see III[52]), I, 211, has, similar to
Thorpe, 'in deines Ehemannes Gewalt'. Thorpe was, in fact, following E. Lye and O.
Manning (eds), *Dictionarium Saxonico et Gothico-Latinum* (London, 1772), s.v. *Wæpned
bearn*: 'Wæpned-men wesan on gewealde. Viri (tui) esse sub dominio' (with a reference to
the Cædmonian *Genesis*); W. Somner in the first proper Anglo-Saxon dictionary, *Dictionarium Saxonico-Latino-Anglicum* (Oxford, 1659), s.vv. *wæpen, wæpen-wifestre, wæpman,
wæpned, wæpned-bearn, wæpned-cyn, wæpnedlic lim,* and *wæpned-mon,* shows that he
clearly understood that in many Old English words the etymological sense of 'weapon' is
forgotten in the primary reference to the male sex.
100 See Sir I. Gollancz's facsimile of the Junius Manuscript (1927), p. 49. The bible does not tell
us what murder-weapon Cain used. The use of the Samsonian jaw-bone of an ass as Cain's
weapon also may have originated among the Anglo-Saxons; cf. Meyer Schapiro, 'Cain's
Jaw-Bone that Did the First Murder', *Art Bulletin*, 24 (1942), 210-11. Cf. C. R. Dodwell and
P. Clemoes (eds), *The Old English Illustrated Hexateuch British Museum Cotton Claudius
B. IV*, EEMF, XVIII (1974), 19, 65, and fol. 8ᵛ. For a possible Irish connection, see A.
Breeze, 'Cain's Jawbone, Ireland, and the Prose *Solomon and Saturn*', *N&Q*, 237 (1992),
433-6. For the depiction of Cain's use of the jaw-bone of an ass in a fourteenth-century
English book (now British Library MS Addit. 47682), cf. W. O. Hassall (ed.), *The Holkham
Bible Picture Book* (London, 1954), 67-8 and fol. 5ᵛ. Hassall, p. 68, conveniently sums up
the supposed Anglo-Saxon connection, in which a supposed animal myth combines with a

there is no linguistic reason for reading into the word anything more warlike than 'man', lines 39-43:

> Ongyrede hine þa geong hæleð, þæt wæs God ælmihtig,
> 40 strang ond stiðmod. Gestah he on gealgan heanne,
> modig on manigra gesyhðe þa he wolde mancyn lysan.
> Bifode ic þa me se beorn ymbclypte. Ne dorste ic hwæðre
>   bugan to eorðan,
> feallan to foldan sceatum, ac ic sceolde fæste standan.

[Then the young man, strong and resolute, divested himself: that was Almighty God. He ascended on to the high gallows, valiant in the sight of many when he wished to redeem mankind. I [the Cross] trembled when that man embraced me. However, I dared not sink to the ground, fall to the surface of the earth, but I had to stand firm.]

If there are memories of a hero's life in this account, they reside in *stiðmod* and *modig*, and not in the unspecific *hæleð* and *beorn*; and of these four words, perhaps by chance, only *modig* occurs on the Ruthwell Cross inscription too. There is valour in Christ's act of Incarnation to achieve the Redemption of mankind, and the Passion may well have been perceived not so much in terms of Christ's human suffering (as it was and is perceived in later ages). Even so, to give to Christ in the poem 'the heroic status of the warrior-Lord'[101] is the result of reading heroic connotations into Old English poetic words that do not bear them as simply as some who write on the heroic elements of the poem seem to think. Perhaps these heroic elements retain traces of the 'spirit and color' concordant with the heroizing perception induced by George Stephens's wild rendering of 1867:[102]

> The translation is in my manner, in the metre of the original. And I have preserved many of the characteristical old words – as is my wunt. Without these not only would the version have been mechanically inferior, but it would have lost much of its spirit and color. As it is, we see and feel, from the terminology as well as the style, that everything is Old-Northern, imbued with the Gothic strength. And the effect is accordingly very striking and very fine.

possible etymology of the name Grendel (or perhaps *Beowulf* line 742a misunderstood) to become a fact:

> Meyer Schapiro . . . believes that the story originated partly in a vernacular play on Old English words and partly in a Saxon conception of an animal's jaw as an emblem of violence. This is typified by Grendel (who is called a descendant of Cain in *Beowulf*) crunching the bones of his victims.

101 Thus M. Swanton (ed.), *The Dream of the Rood* (1970; see III[64]), 71.
102 G. Stephens, *Runic Monuments*, I (1866-1867; see III[63]), 405-32 (the translation is at p. 424, his comment on it pp. 430-1); cf. III (London, Edinburgh and Copenhagen, 1884), 430-4.

This is Stephens's rendering of lines 39-43 (with *Bever* explained as 'To tremble, quake'):

> 'For the grapple then girded him youthful hero,
> lo! the man was God Almighty!
> Strong of heart and steady-minded
> stept he on the lofty gallows;
> fearless, spite that crowd of faces,
> free and save man's tribes he would there.
> Bever'd I and shook when that baron claspt me,
> but dar'd I not bow me earthward,
> fall a-fieldward mote I nowise,
> 'twas my duty – to stand fast!'

Some critics, not infrequently with Baldr in mind, have re-paganized the Christian poem, and magnifying the heroic aspect which they have read into it, make the poem enshrine the comitatus society of the Germanic Heroic Age, and make it anticipate the Christ-Knight of the later Middle Ages.[103] Anglo-Saxonists dwell on lines 37b-38a of the poem, and see the Cross as Christ's liegeman who could have struck down Christ's enemies; in Brandl's words, 'Gott ist der milde Scharführer, das Kreuz sein treuer Gefolgsmann, der ihm die Gegner erschlagen möchte' [God is the gentle squadron-leader, the Cross his loyal liegeman who would have liked to strike dead for him his adversaries]. Not surprisingly, for an Instrument of the Passion, the Cross is subservient to the will of God, inert except that here it speaks in wonderful prosopopoeia. Yet so predominant in criticism is the magnification of the heroic element in the poem that the character

---

103 Typical of the extensive 'literature' of the subject are: F. Hammerich (I use the German translation by A. Michelsen), *Älteste christliche Epik der Angelsachsen, Deutschen und Nordländer. Ein Beitrag zur Kirchengeschichte* (Gütersloh, 1874), 75-104. With interest also in liturgical motifs, A. Brandl, 'Zum ags. Gedichte "Traumgesicht vom Kreuze Christi" ', *Sitzungsberichte der Preußischen Akademie der Wissenschaften*, Philosophisch-historische Klasse, 1905, 716-23 [reprinted in A. Brandl, *Forschungen und Charakteristiken* (Berlin and Leipzig, 1936), 28-35], see especially the final paragraph (from which I quote, above), expressing pleasure at 'der reiche Einschlag des germanischen Gefolgschaftswesens, durch den der sehr fremdartige Stoff für die alten Nordhumbrer hier nationalisiert wird' [the rich element of the Germanic comitatus society by means of which the very foreign material is here nationalized for the Old Northumbrians], and cf. Brandl, 'Die angelsächsische Literatur' (1908; see I[45]), 1031 (= 91 of separate); R. Woolf, 'Doctrinal Influences on *The Dream of the Rood*', *MÆ*, 27 (1958), 137-53. Cf. also S. B. Greenfield and D. G. Calder, *New Critical History* (1986; see II[79]), chapter vii 'Christ as Poetic Hero', for example, p. 196: 'Stripping Himself for battle – again an unusual feature, but one within patristic tradition', in fact, somewhat toned down from S. B. Greenfield's *Critical History* (1965; see II[79]), 138; but both versions agree that the Cross is presenting 'itself as a loyal retainer in the epic mode' (whatever the 'epic mode' may be in this short poem; presumably, 'as befits a retainer in heroic society').

of the Cross easily comes to life as one of the two *dramatis personae* of the poem, Christ and Rood, and is endowed with heroic volition by a critic:[104]

> ... Rood comes to understand the incredible situation in which he has been placed. To the extent (a large extent) that he partakes of the role of hero, he must now endure the hardest fate a hero can suffer: to be blocked completely from taking any action. Action is the natural mode of the hero's being and his essential definition. To be thus blocked from it is to feel great pain. Familiar examples from *Beowulf* are King Hrothgar seething with helpless anger under Grendel's unrelenting attacks on his hall, or Hengest enduring the long winter in a foreign hall, prevented for a time by complex circumstances from avenging his king's death. Rood can neither defend his king nor avenge his death. Worse yet, unimaginably terrible, God his king has ordered him to be an accomplice, chief agent even, in the very torture and murder of God: Rood is given the technical term 'bana' ('bane,' or 'slayer') in line 66.

Unimaginably terrible indeed, and in the poem hardly a hint of it. Moreover, the technical term *bana* is misunderstood as 'accomplice in a murder' instead of 'instrument of a killing': 'agent' or 'slayer' is acceptable for a word that, applied to the instrument or weapon of juridical or martial killing, bears no implication of guilt, whereas *accomplice* is a sharer in guilt.

Generations of writers on Old English poetry, towards the end of the last century and early in this century, devoted themselves to searching in the Christian literature for antiquities, customs and views of the Germanic Heroic Age. I have elsewhere discussed at length some of their endeavours,[105] and will only quote again F. Brincker on *Judith* because he draws attention to Jacob Grimm and A. F. C. Vilmar as the founding fathers of this tradition which, it seems, still has some life left in it:[106]

> Besonders gerühmt wird die Geschicklichkeit des Dichters, die Quelle zu behandeln und seine Kunst, den biblischen Stoff in ein echt germanisches Gewand zu kleiden. Bekanntlich besingt die angelsächsische Epik nur fremde Helden und Heldenthaten, so daß man von einem Nationalepos im eigentlichen Sinne nicht reden kann. Judith aber darf man mit gewissem Rechte ein Nationalepos nennen, so stark tritt das germanische Gepräge der Dichtung

---

[104] E. B. Irving, Jr, 'Crucifixion Witnessed, or Dramatic Interaction in *The Dream of the Rood*. in P. R. Brown, G. R. Crampton and F. C. Robinson (eds), *Modes of Interpretation in Old English Literature Essays in Honour of Stanley B. Greenfield* (Toronto, 1986), 106.

[105] *The Search for Anglo-Saxon Paganism* (1964-1965, reprinted 1975; see I²), especially, 'The Search for Germanic Antiquities', pp. 67-82.

[106] F. Brincker, *Germanische Altertümer in dem angelsächsischen Gedichte "Judith"* (school-programme, Hamburg, 1898), 5. Brincker refers to A. S. Cook (ed.), *Judith: An Old English Epic Fragment* (Boston, 1888; 2nd edn, 1904; cf. III⁴²); J. Grimm (ed.), *Andreas und Elene* (1840; see I¹⁵); and A. F. C. Vilmar, *Deutsche altertümer im Hêliand als einkleidung der evangelischen Geschichte. Beiträge zur erklärung des altsächsischen Hêliand und zur innern geschichte der einführung des christentums in Deutschland* (school-programme, Marburg, 1845; reprinted, Marburg, 1862).

hervor. Nur die Fabel ist hebräisch, und auch sie ist nach germanischem
Geschmack vielfach umgestaltet; alles andere ist rein germanisch. Die Stadt
Bethulia erscheint uns als eine angelsächsische Burg, die Assyrer sowohl wie
die Hebräer sind germanische Krieger, Judith und ihre Dienerin sind germanische Frauen und Christinnen. Germanisches Leben, germanische Anschau-
ungen, germanische Sitten treten uns in allen Teilen des Gedichts entgegen, so
daß Cook in der Einleitung zu seiner Ausgabe (S. X) mit Recht sagt: "It is
Hebraic in incident and outline, Germanic in execution, sentiment, coloring,
and all that constitutes the life of a poem." Wenn Jacob Grimm in seiner
Ausgabe von Andreas und Elene, besonders aber Vilmar in seiner berühmten
Untersuchung über die deutschen Altertümer im Heliand . . . uns gelehrt hat,
in den Liedern unserer Altvordern Fundgruben für die deutsche Kulturgeschichte zu sehen, so dürfen wir mit Recht die angelsächsische Judith als
eine solche Fundstätte bezeichnen. Natürlich muß man in einem Gedicht von
verhältnismäßig so geringem Umfange kein vollständiges Bild germanischen
Lebens erwarten, wie es vielleicht der Heliand und Beowulf bieten; doch
finden wir in den 350 Langzeilen bei genauerer Betrachtung sehr viel, das uns
einen Einblick in das Leben der alten Angelsachsen thun läßt, auf ihre Vorstel-
lungen und Sitten anspielt.

[Singled out for special praise is the poet's skill in his treatment of the
source and his art in clothing the biblical material in genuine Germanic garb.
As is well known, the Anglo-Saxon epic poems sing only of foreign heroes
and heroic deeds, so that it is impossible to speak of a national epic *sensu
stricto*. We may, however, call *Judith* a national epic with some degree of
justice, since the poem is so strongly stamped with a Germanic impress. Only
the story is Hebraic, and even that is often altered to suit Germanic taste:
everything else is purely Germanic. The city of Bethulia is represented to us as
an Anglo-Saxon stronghold, the Assyrians as well as the Hebrews are
Germanic warriors, Judith and her maid are Germanic women and Christians.
Germanic life, Germanic views and Germanic customs appear before us in
every part of the poem, so that Cook in the introduction to his edition says
with justice, 'It is Hebraic in incident and outline, Germanic in execution,
sentiment, coloring, and all that constitutes the life of a poem.' If Jacob
Grimm, in his edition of *Andreas und Elene*, and especially Vilmar in his
famous investigation of the Germanic antiquities in *Heliand* . . . have taught us
to look upon the poetry of our forefathers as store-houses rich in source
materials for the history of Germanic culture, we may rightly call *Judith* such a
store-house. Of course, a complete picture of Germanic life, such as *Beowulf*
and *Heliand* perhaps give, is not to be expected from a poem of such relatively
slight compass; yet on closer inspection we find in the 350 lines of *Judith* very
much that lets us gain some insight into the life of the ancient Anglo-Saxons,
very much that alludes to their views and customs.]

In the event, what Brincker finds in *Judith*, as do many others in investiga-
tions similar in direction but applied to other Old English poems, is mainly a
linguistic costume. As the Anglo-Saxons wrote of their own England, so they
wrote of distant Palestine (or of whatever other country bible-story or hagio-

graphy might lead them to), the same words and concepts, and the language that seems at home in the world of Beowulf, a hero from as near as we can get to the Anglo-Saxons' Heroic Age, served them again for the newly perceived glories of the bible or hagiography. The language that had been used in what was for them too the heroic past was still used by them in their Christian present – often, in the Old English usage we know best, probably their coenobitic present with its hopes of an eternal future as they contemplate that greater banquet of longlasting joys better than, if the Germanic world of *Beowulf* is an example, the unceasing strife and the occasional joyful moments of feasting in the hall.

Around the year 1950, an important controversy engulfed Linguistics in the Soviet Union: the serious essentials of it hardly matter now, but an analogy of Joseph Stalin's sticks in my memory, a humorous, witty analogy to language perceived as reflecting the society of its speakers. Stalin mocked those comrades who, at the time of the 1917 Revolution and shortly after, were reluctant to go on using the trams that had served to carry bourgeois passengers in Tsarist times. The Russian language, so Stalin suggested, is like those trams: it has not changed much in spite of the Revolution, and you just have to go on using it, adapting it as best you can in changing circumstances. So it must have been with the English language at the time of the Conversion and the centuries that followed. The new religion introduced new connotations into old words; and we, as we try to understand these words, do wrong to insist on what we believe to be pristine meanings, as we hanker after a lost world of heroes in a Germania largely of modern invention where heroes join in the merry banquet of life around their chief, looking forward to a Wagnerian Valhalla where fighting never ceases and brave wounds are ever repaired better than under even the National Health Service.

Old English colour words and the limits of our understanding

The Old English vocabulary of colour, both in prose and verse, has served generations of contributors to Anglo-Saxon studies, in theses and articles, in books even, as a paradigm of our double-dyed ignorance. For many words we can barely grasp denotations, and connotations are beyond hope of recovery. We do not know how to translate such words consistently because Anglo-Saxon usage is based on perceptions different from ours. The very wish to find consistent equations of their perception as expressed in their words with our perceptions as expressed in our words leads to comment on what was found impossible to resolve. For words like *brun, fealu, græg, hwit*, there are some twenty to thirty studies (some of them only incidentally concerned with this group of words), of which that by G. König well summarizes the problem in its very title: 'Terms for colour, shine and brightness in Old English;[107] and even the attempt

---

107 G. König, *Die Bezeichnungen für Farbe, Glanz, und Helligkeit im Altenglischen* (Mainz

to translate the German title into English brings to mind several alternatives for 'shine' and 'brightness', some perhaps more suitable. As arms and armour, horses, the sea and the sky irradiate and reflect light of differing wave-lengths it is insolubly puzzling that they had not all the words for colours which we think apparent to every eye (unless of course colour-blind), and that instead they seem to distinguish rather the degree of brightness as reflected or irradiated. It cannot be true, as has been suggested,[108] that the Anglo-Saxons were simply unaware of the riches of colour. In the greatest scriptoria colours were highly prized and a wide range of pigments was used in the production of important codices, as the work of H. Roosen-Runge and A. E. A. Werner on the pigments used in the Lindisfarne Gospels amply shows.[109] Anglo-Saxon embroidery made subtle use of colours, though little survives.[110] Even if not many Anglo-Saxons saw these treasures, there is enough colour all around, so that the lack of linguistic specificity is not likely to have been the result of a lack of experience. One does not need a colour chart to see colours; as Goethe says in his history of the science of colours:[111]

Nirgends fehlte das Material zum Färben. Die Fruchtsäfte, fast jede Feuchtigkeit außer dem reinen Wasser, das Blut der Thiere, alles ist gefärbt; so auch die Metallkalke, besonders des überall vorhandenen Eisens. Mehrere verfaulte Pflanzen geben einen entschiedenen Färbestoff, dergestalt daß der Schlick an seichten Stellen großer Flüsse als Farbematerial benutzt werden konnte.

Jedes Beflecken ist eine Art von Färben, und die augenblickliche Mittheilung konnte jeder bemerken, der eine rothe Beere zerdrückte.

[Materials for dyeing were lacking nowhere. Fruit-juices, almost every kind of moisture except pure water, the blood of animals, are all coloured; similarly, metallic oxides, especially iron oxide which occurs everywhere. Several

---

dissertation, 1957). Studies up to about 1982 are comprehensively listed in A. Cameron, A. Kingsmill, and A. C. Amos, *Word Studies* (1983; see III[45]). See also J. Tischler, 'Farbe und Färben', § 1: Sprachliches, in [J. Hoops], *Reallexikon* (2nd edn, 1968-; see II[22]), 8, 1-2 (1991), 206-16.

[108] N. F. Barley, 'Old English colour classification: where do matters stand?', *ASE*, 3 (1974), 21:

The Anglo-Saxons had neither colour charts nor a large range of dyes. For them, colours were attributes of objects and had not reached the level of abstraction that they have in our own society.

[109] See T. D. Kendrick, T. J. Brown, R. L. S. Bruce-Mitford, H. Roosen-Runge, A. S. C. Ross, E. G. Stanley, and A. E. A. Werner, *Evangeliorum quattuor Codex Lindisfarnensis*, II/1 (Olten and Lausanne, 1960), H. Roosen-Runge, and A. E. A. Werner 'The Pigments and Medium of the Lindisfarne Gospels', pp. 263-77.

[110] See, for example, E. Plenderleith, 'The Stole and Maniples (a) The Technique', in C. F. Battiscombe (ed.), *The Relics of Saint Cuthbert* (for the Dean and Chapter of Durham Cathedral, 1956), 375-96; and M. Budny and D. Tweddle, 'The Maaseik embroideries', *ASE*, 13 (1984), 65-96.

[111] *Goethe's Werke*, Vollständige Ausgabe letzter Hand, LIII = Nachgelassene Werke, XIII (Stuttgart and Tübingen, 1833), *Geschichte der Farbenlehre*, part I, Von den Griechen und Römern bis auf Newton: Zur Geschichte der Urzeit, 11.

decayed plants yield a distinctive pigment, in such a way that silt in shallow places of great rivers could be used as a dye.

All staining is a kind of dyeing, and the instant diffusion (of the dye) was to be observed by anyone who squashed a red berry.]

To us the essence of the rainbow is the radiance of the colours of the spectrum displayed in perfect shape, so that Aldhelm's bookish enigma V, Rainbow, whatever its other subtleties may be, seems concerned with inessentials: it is poor on the colours, singling out from the seven of the spectrum only *ruber*, apparently 'red' but perhaps including 'orange' adjacent to red in the spectrum (though that analysis is unlikely to have been available linguistically to the Anglo-Saxons).[112]

To perceive colours as we do is sometimes regarded as a sign of an advanced stage in the development of civilization, where, of course, we come high, and whoever is or was unlike us must therefore be at least a little lower. W. E. Gladstone, midway in his great political career, wrote interestingly of colour in the third volume of his studies on Homer.[113] Gladstone (pp. 483-4) saw that the poetic riches of Homer do not lie in the expression of perceptions of colours; especially, that he lacked the perception of the colours of the spectrum. As a general rule, Homer was vague and indeterminate on colour. To what is this lack of precision to be ascribed? 1. To his reputed blindness? 2. To some defect in his or his countrymen's organization of colours? Or 3., 'are we to reject altogether the idea of defect, and to treat his use of colour as one conceived in the spirit which, with even the most perfect knowledge, would properly belong to his art?' He regards 2. the likely reason, that Homer and his contemporaries so much lacked a systematic grasp of colours, the seven of the spectrum together with white and black that give us our modern scheme. He comments on Homer's single colour description of Iris, not exactly Aldhelm's *ruber*, but (1) *porphyrén* 'dark with a hue of crimson', and (2) like a *drákon* 'dragon, snake', which is *kyáneos* 'dark with a hue of deep blue or indigo', and it leads Gladstone to conclude (p. 488):

It seems easy to comprehend that the eye may require a familiarity with an ordered system of colours, as the condition of its being able closely to appreciate any one among them.

I conclude, then, that the organ of colour and its impressions were but partially developed among the Greeks of the heroic age.

One wonders. Does the perception of an individual colour really depend on

---

112 M. de Marco (ed.), *Collectiones aenigmatum merovingicae aetatis*, Corpus Christianorum, ser. lat. cxxxiii (1968), No. V [the translation is by J. H. Pitman, first published in his *The Riddles of Aldhelm*, YSE, 67 (1925)]; cf. E. von Erhardt-Siebold, *Die lateinischen Rätsel der Angelsachsen*, AF, 61 (1925), 245-6.

113 *Studies on Homer and the Homeric Age* (Oxford, 1858), III, iv (Aoidos: Some Points of the Poetry of Homer), section iv 'Homer's Perceptions and Use of Colour', 457-99.

familiarity with a system of colours, namely, that of the spectrum? Gladstone goes on to discuss Aristotle's systematic philosophy of colour, and believes it to be close to theories of light of his own times (pp. 495-6):

> This condition of the philosophy of colour, so many centuries after Homer . . . may assist in explaining to us the undeveloped state of Homer's perceptions of this particular department.
>
> There appears to be a remarkable contrast between such undigested ideas, and the solidity, truth, and firmness of the remains of colour that have come down to us from the ancients. The explanation, I suppose, is, that those, who had to make practical use of colour, did not wait for the construction of a philosophy, but added to their apparatus from time to time all substances which, having come within their knowledge, were found to produce results satisfactory and improving to the eye. And even so Homer, though his organ was little trained in the discrimination of colours, and though he founded himself mainly upon mere modifications of light apart from its decomposition, yet has made very bold and effective use of these limited materials. His figures in no case jar, while they never fail to strike. Nor are we to suppose that we see in this department an exception to that comparative profusion of power which marks his endowments in general, and that he bore, in the particular point, a crippled nature; but rather that we are to learn that the perceptions so easy and familiar to us are the results of a slow traditionary growth in knowledge and in the training of the human organ, which commenced long before we took our place in the succession of mankind. We exemplify, even in this apparently simple matter, the old proverbial saying: 'The dwarf sees further than the giant, for he is lifted on the giant's shoulders.'

To an Anglo-Saxonist the Homeric similarity with our colour problem is pleasing. Whether we regard *Beowulf* as epic or not, that our poet is not alone in failing to include the joys of colour among the riches of poetic expression is comforting: he erred with Homer – he erred with Homer as seen by a great man who was the contemporary of the founders of modern Germanic scholarship. Perhaps also comforting, but uncomfortably so, at once humiliating and inspiring, is the energetic care with which Gladstone treated the subject, trying to seek an answer to the problem that a poet as excellent as Homer should have treated each colour, not within a colour theory comprehending all colours, but, like Old English usage, as epithetically attached to a particular manifestation of the colour: the sea, a horse, a piece of armour, to give typical examples from *Beowulf* rather than from *The Iliad* or *The Odyssey*. It is of little importance whether Gladstone's views on colour in Homer seem dated as does his belief in a single philosophy of colours; and it is of no importance at all that the actual applications of colour words are not the same in Homer as in Old English (though some correspondences are surprisingly close): what does matter is that a mind accustomed 'Th'applause of list'ning senates to command' should seek to understand Homer from within his works, and should with humility see himself and his age as comparable to a dwarf carried high and so gifted with wider vision because borne on the shoulders of the giants who came before.

The four occurrences of the word *fealu* in *Beowulf* (lines 865, 916, 1950, 2165) may be used to illustrate the problem. We are dealing with a hue or a shade, cf. the Modern German cognates (the sense of which happens to be relevant) *fahl* 'pale, pallid, wan', *falb* 'yellowish, dun-coloured'; we are not dealing with a determinate colour. There is no point in precision, in trying to establish where on a scale from yellow to brown *fealu* might be placed. At line 865 *fealwe mearas*, horses of this colour; at line 916 horses (colours not specified) engage in races on *fealwe strǣte*, on a road of this colour; at line 1950 the princess is sent forth *ofer fealone flod*, across a sea of that colour; and at line 2165 four horses are described as *ǣppelfealuwe*, the word comes only here, 'dappled' perhaps, or should one think of apple colours?

Was the poetic vocabulary of Old English obsolescent; was the art of coining compounds for poetry a dying art?

Some of the words of Old English poetry are rare; in *Beowulf*, for example, we find some *simplicia* that occur nowhere else in Old English; thus *berian* to clear away', *hos* 'troop (of attendants)', *hrine* 'rime-covered', *wala* (MS *walan*) part of a helmet. Some of the words in Old English prose too are very rare, and that is true of late texts as well as of early texts. In some cases we can elicit the meaning of a very rare word by reference to the related Germanic languages where a cognate of the Old English word may exist. For words unique in the language we cannot, of course, say for certain if they belonged to the poetic vocabulary only, even if the single occurrence is in verse. If the word is rare in Old English but occurs also in later English and has no cognate in the related Germanic languages it is possible that it is a new word in the language. Is the opposite true? Is it true that the rare words of Old English poetry were obsolescent in Anglo-Saxon times? Some must have been, on the general grounds that languages do not retain all words throughout their history. The history of the English language is no exception in this respect.

It is clear, however, that certain features of Old English poetic diction, especially the frequent use of compounds, remained a characteristic of the language of Middle English alliterative verse, preeminently of the language of Laȝamon's *Brut* (of the thirteenth century or perhaps a little earlier).[114] Laȝamon has a vocabulary of his own, often based on, or in seeming imitation of, the vocabulary of Old English poetry, both *simplicia* and especially poetic

---

[114] Cf. E. G. Stanley, 'The Date of Laȝamon's *Brut*', *N&Q*, 213 (1968), 85-8, 'Laȝamon's Antiquarian Sentiments', *MÆ*, 38 (1969), 23-37. The date must be after the death of Henry II in 1189; see G. L. Brook and R. F. Leslie (eds), *Laȝamon: Brut*, I, EETS, 250 (1963), lines 22-3 of the Prologue in Cotton MS Caligula A.ix.

compounds. Some of his words do not occur in the Old English poetry known to us, but, of course, we cannot say if La3amon had or had not read them in Old English verse available to him but no longer extant now. Some words known in English first from the poetry of the Anglo-Saxons, for example, *beorn* 'warrior' and *secg* 'man', survived into late alliterative verse, and even into the poetry of the sixteenth century. The habit of compounding is most pronounced in La3amon among Middle English poets; for example, he has a large group of compounds with *leod-* 'people-, national' as first element, not one of which goes back to Old English poetry now extant, yet all of them redolent of of Old English poetry in manner of compounding. Vestiges of Old English poetic diction are easily traced in the poetic diction of Middle English alliterative verse, for example, in *Sir Gawain and the Green Knight* or in *The Wars of Alexander*, as the following brief quotations show. *Sir Gawain and the Green Knight* lines 822-5, the arrival of Sir Gawain at the Castle of Hautdesert, with *seggez* 'men' and *buurne* 'warrior, knight':

> Sere seggez hym sesed by sadel quel he ly3t,
> And syþen stabeled his stede stif men inno3e.
> Kny3tez and swyerez comen doun þenne
> 825 For to bryng þis buurne wyth blys into halle.

[Several men seized hold of his saddle while he dismounted, and many bold men then put his horse in the stables. Next, knights and esquires came down in order to lead this warrior into hall with joy.]

The Wars of Alexander lines 2260-3, again with *seggis* 'men' and *bernes* 'warriors':[115]

> 2260 Þan takis þe kyng *his* kni3tis, vm[c]lapis þe wallis,
> Settis vpon a saute on sidis eno3e.
> Bot for þe cite was vnsure, þe seggis within
> Mi3t no3t þe braidis abide of bernes enarmed.

[Then the king leads his knights, invests the walls, and attacks on many wall-sides. But, the city not being secure enough, the men inside could not withstand the sudden assaults of warriors fully armed.]

The ballads too have vestiges of the Old English poetic vocabulary. For example, in *The Battle of Otterburn* (referring to the battle of 1388) stanza 5: 'Then spake a berne vpon the bent', with *berne* from Old English *beorn*, but *bent* does not go back to Old English literary usage, and the survival of Old English poetic words seems not to have depended on the use of these words in

---

[115] Ed. by H. N. Duggan and T. Turville-Petre (1989; see IV[80]); again, in the quotation not all the editors' emendations have been accepted.

set poetic phrases. As late as Tottel's *Miscellany* of 1557 descendants occur of *beorn* and *secg* together with alliterative collocations not attested before Middle English, namely, in 'The death of Zoroas', by Nicholas Grimald (born *c.* 1519, died *c.* 1562):[116]

> Of his right hand desirous to be slayn,
> The boldest beurn, and worthiest in the feeld:
> . . .
> Wherwith a hole route came of souldiours stern,
> And all in peeces hewed the silly seg.

Clearly, the words peculiar to Old English alliterative verse were not all dying out at the end of the Anglo-Saxon period. The process was one of gradual change; details of scansion, of diction and of figurative ornament changed slowly. Yet the habit of composing alliterative verse in language enriched by features confined to it seems to have been continuous, though our evidence for it in Middle English is better in the fourteenth century than earlier, giving an appearance of revival, probably a false appearance. Alliterative collocations changed, and not many such collocations involving native words, in Old English confined to verse, have a continuous history beyond the fourteenth century.

It is a mistaken notion, therefore, to regard the poetic vocabulary of Old English as consisting as a rule of obsolescent words that had become quite obsolete in prose and in the speech of the Anglo-Saxons. Though, no doubt, some rare *simplicia* occurring in verse were obsolescent, most poetic *simplicia* and compounds were widely current in the poetry of the Anglo-Saxons, and some of them remained widely current and well understood in the alliterative poetry of Middle English.

As early as 1840 Jacob Grimm, while he took the poetic vocabulary of the Anglo-Saxons to be obsolescent, recognized that it seemed nevertheless unserviceable for relative dating of the verse, largely, he thought, because the Anglo-Saxons developed a fairly uniform style of poetry which they employed throughout the Christian period from the seventh into the tenth century (though not in *The Metres of Boethius*, nor in the versified psalms which are probably later than the verse Grimm had in mind):[117]

> die poesie will nicht ihrer vergangenheit entsagen, zugleich aber der gegenwart huldigen. Man begreift, dass sich vom siebenten jahrhundert bis ins zehnte ein ziemlich fester stil der dichtkunst bildete und erhielt, der ohne der christlichen ansicht zu widerstreben noch manche gewohnheiten des heidenthums in sich trug. Wie wir das gedicht von Beóvulf besitzen, scheint es mir bald nach dem beginn des achten jh. aus der hand seines letzten umdichters

---

[116] See H. E. Rollins (ed.), *Tottel's Miscellany* (Cambridge, Massachusetts, 1965), No. 165 (p. 116 line 30, p. 117 line 32).

[117] J. Grimm (ed.), *Andreas und Elene* (1840; see I[15]), p. xlvii.

hervorgegangen, und ich stehe nicht an, für die abfassung von Andreas und Elene auf allen fall ungefähr die nemliche zeit in anspruch zu nehmen. Der cædmonischen genesis traue ich aber kein höheres alter zu. . . . In form und sprache . . . geben diese vier gedichte entschiedne verwandtschaft kund und es hält nicht schwer, ihrem stil den des zehnten jh. aus der metrischen bearbeitung der psalmen oder selbst schon der gedichte des Boethius gegenüber zu stellen.

. . . Mich dünkt, Andreas und Elene zeigen verhältnismässig eine gleich grosse, ihrem geringern umfange nach eine fast grössere zahl alter, seltner, in der gewöhnlichen ags. sprache bereits abgekommner wörter als Beóvulf und Cædmon.

[Poetry will not renounce its past, but at the same time will pay homage to the present. It is to be understood that from the seventh century into the tenth a fairly constant style of poetic art was evolved and maintained, which without resisting the Christian view still bore within it many habits of paganism. *Beowulf*, in the form in which we have that poem, seems to me to be the product of its last recaster soon after the beginning of the eighth century, and I have no hesitation to enlist in any case approximately the same time for the composition of *Andreas* and *Elene*. I do not trust the Cædmonian *Genesis* to be of greater age. . . . In literary form and language . . . these four poems manifest a decided relationship, and it will not be difficult to contrast their style with that of the metrical version of the psalms or even with that already of *The Metres of Boethius*.

. . . It seems to me that *Andreas* and *Elene* manifest an equally great number relatively, in view of their shorter length almost a greater number of ancient, rare words than *Beowulf* and *Genesis*, words which in ordinary Anglo-Saxon speech had by then passed into disuse.]

It is a fact also that the datable late verse of the Anglo-Saxons, in the *Anglo-Saxon Chronicle* and in *The Battle of Maldon*, continues to manifest a rich variety of poetic compounds, some not found before. Some of the words from this datable late poetry occur nowhere else in Old English, and many of these words are of considerable interest as poetic compounds.[118] That we should not regard these unique occurrences as late coinages necessarily, but as part of a wider, less recent tradition is shown by *The Coronation of Edgar* line 14 *wintergetæl* 'number of years', a compound which occurs nowhere else in Old English,[119] but a cognate is extant in Old Saxon poetry at *Heliand* (Munich MS)

---

[118] Cf. E. G. Stanley, 'Old English Poetic Diction and the Interpretation of *The Wanderer, The Seafarer,* and *The Penitent's Prayer*', *Anglia*, 73 (1956), 413-56, reprinted in *A Collection of Papers* (1987; see I⁴⁵), 261(-2) note 35.

[119] The word occurs in three manuscripts, Cotton Tiberius B.i *winter getæles*, Parker and Cotton Tiberius A.vi *winter geteles*. A relevant usage occurs three lines earlier in the poem:

tyn hund wintra   geteled rimes

[ten hundred years counted in numbers].

Cf. also *wintergerim* (*Elene* line 654, *The Metres of Boethius* 28 line 27), synonymous with line 725, in Herod's speech, planning the Slaughter of the Innocents in the knowledge of the the age of the Infant Christ, lines 724-7:

> 'Nu ic is aldar can,
> 725   uuet is uuintergitalu,   nu ic giuuinnan mag
> that he obar thesaro erdu   ald ni uuirdit
> her undar thesum heriscepi.'

['Now that I know his age, know his number of years, now I can bring it about that he shall not grow old upon this earth here under my dominion.']

Other unique compounds occurring only in the datable late verse are:

The Battle of Brunanburh: *arhwæt* 'eager for glory' 73, *bilgesleht* 'sword-battle' 45, *cumbolgehnast* 'clash of banners' 49, *ealdorlang* 'life-long, everlasting' 3, *garmitting* 'meeting of spears' 50, *guðhafoc* 'war-hawk, ?eagle, ?raven' 64, *hasupada* 'dun-coated one' [Parker MS *hasewan padan*] 62, *heapolind* '(linden) war-shield' 6, *hereflema* 'fugitive soldier' 23, *mylenscearp* '(?grind-stone-)sharp' 24, *scipflota* 'seafarer' 11, *wælfeld* 'field of slaughter' 51.

The Capture of the Five Boroughs: *hæfteclomm* 'binding fetter' 10.

The Coronation of Edgar: *niðweorc* 'warlike deed' 18.

The Death of Edgar: *cræftgleaw* 'wise in skills' 32.

William the Conqueror (Peterborough Chronicle, 1087): *deorfrið* 'game reserve'.[120]

The Battle of Maldon: *æschere* (probably) 'raiding army carried by ash-wood ship', or (perhaps) 'spear-bearing army' 69 [cf. the proper name in *Beowulf*], *beaduræs* 'onslaught of battle' 111, *bricgweard* 'bridge-guard, defender of the causeway' 85, *brimman* 'seaman' 49 and 295, *easteð* 'river-bank' 63, *færsceaða* 'sudden ravager' 142, *fealohilte* 'pale-hilted, ?gold-hilted' 166, *feolheard* 'hard as a file' 108, *feorhhus* 'abode of the soul' 297, *forþgeorn* 'keen to go forward' 281, *garræs* 'spear-attack' 32, *hringloca* 'ring-integument, ring-mail armour' 145, *wihaga* 'battle-hedge, shield-wall' 102, *woruldgesælig* 'prosperous in this world' 219.[121]

---

wintergetæl (sometimes rendered 'date' at *Elene* line 654). Uncompounded collocations, like *wintra (ge)rim*, are more frequent.

120 See B. J. Whiting (ed.), 'The Rime of King William', in T. A. Kirby and H. B. Woolf (eds), *Philologica: The [Kemp] Malone Anniversary Studies* (Baltimore, 1949), 94 line 13; cf. La3amon's *Brut* line 720: *Forboden he haueð his deor-frið* [he has closed his game-park].

121 The following words in *The Battle of Maldon* are also worthy of note because *hapax legomena*, but they may well not be part of the Old English poetic vocabulary: the compound verb *forwegan* 'to carry off' 228, the denominative verb *lytegian* 'to use guile' (cf. Old English *lytig* and early Middle English *luti3* 'cunning') 86, the frequentative verb *stemnettan* '?to stand firm' 122, and the negated past participle *unbefohten* 'without offering battle' 57 and the negated adjective *unorne* 'simple' 256.

    Since *stemn* and *stefn* are doublets [see K. Luick, F. Wild and H. Koziol, *Historische Grammatik der englischen Sprache*, I/2 (Leipzig, 1929-40), §§ 621, 4, 681; A. Campbell,

Beowulf and *Exodus* are rightly regarded as among Old English poems that best exemplify what good poets can achieve in the skilful deployment of a varied vocabulary, including many compounds. In choosing the datable late poems for my exemplification I do not wish to disparage the undatable poems, but to provide material at variance with a Neo-Romantic assumption which may still be widely held: that in the pagan period the art of poetic compounding flourished, and that in late Old English, though new formations many of them based on Latin came into the language to express religious and ecclesiastical concepts, skill in the ancient art of poetic compounding decreased. From the concluding statement by Otto Krackow, the author of one of the better monographs on Old English poetic compounds, we gather that a decline in the art of using poetic compounds was diligently looked for, and found in *The Battle of Maldon* (mistakenly, I think, but as expected by Krackow), yet not found in *Judith*, to Krackow's surprise, seeing that the material is biblical, and worse still perhaps, the protagonist is a woman:[122]

> Für die Chronologie der Dichtungen ergibt sich aus den vorliegenden Untersuchungen nichts. Die Begriffe, die umschrieben werden, sind ganz allgemeiner Natur, noch mehr die Glieder, aus denen sie gebildet werden. Sie sind nicht durch den Zeitpunkt, in dem das Denkmal entstand, charakterisiert, sonder fast ausschliesslich durch die Tradition, den Charakter des Stoffs, besonders aber durch die Individualität des Dichters. So hat der Verfasser der Ju[dith] zahlreiche C[om]p[osita], obgleich der Stoff – christlich, ein Weib Heldin – von einem a[lt]e[nglischen] Dichter wenige erwarten liesse; der Dichter des By[rhtnoth] aber, der sich ganz im Milieu des Heldenepos bewegte, hat kein Interesse mehr für das alte Kunstmittel.

> [From the present investigation no results relevant to the chronology of the poems emerge. The concepts expressed by periphrastic compounds are of a quite general nature, even more so the elements of which they are composed. They are not defined by the point in time when the literary monument came into being, but almost exclusively by the tradition, by the subject matter, and most of all by the individuality of the poet. Thus the author of *Judith* has numerous compounds though the subject matter – Christian, and a woman the heroine – would have led one to expect few compounds from an Old English poet. The poet of *The Battle of Maldon*, however, who moved entirely in the

---

Old English Grammar (1959; see III[32]), § 484], *stemnettan* appears to be related to early Middle English *steventen*, found only in St Katherine; see S. T. R. O. d'Ardenne (ed.), *The Katherine Group* (1977; see III[59]), 33 = fol. 8ʳ line 5 *hwi studgi ȝe nu & steuentiŏ se stille?* [why are you perplexed and remain so speechless?]; cf. J. Harris, '*Stemnettan: Battle of Maldon*, line 122a', *PQ*, 5 (1976), 113-17, would interpret both the Old English and the Middle English use as 'to stop (talking)', but, as D. G. Scragg (ed.), *Maldon* (1981; see IV[39]), 76, says, 'this does not seem to fit the context as well as Sweet's "stand firm".'

   Unnegated *bifohten* occurs once in *Riddle 3* line 32; Old Frisian *bifiuchta* is quite common, Old High German *bifehtan* is rare. In Middle English, *unorn* is not uncommon in both verse and prose.

[122] O. Krackow, *Die Nominalcomposita* (1903; see II[62]), 79.

world of heroic epic, no longer has any interest in the ancient device [of compounds] in poetic art.]

A year later, an editor of *The Battle of Maldon* and the Chronicle poems has hardly a good word to say of the latter:[123] 'Even the longest and best written of their number, the *Battle of Brunanburh*, is but a simulacrum, a ghost of the older epos; the others are not even ghosts, they are caricatures.' In some recent critical writings the Chronicle poems fare no better; a few lines (24-8) of *The Death of Edgar* are quoted because the passage 'illustrates the mechanical piling up of the older poetic formulas with little regard for specificity of meaning'.[124]

Figurative devices in Old English verse: perceptions of reality and their expression in simile and kenning

It is sometimes asserted that the Anglo-Saxons did not avail themselves of extended similes in their poetry. That is not so.[125] Many of the religious poems of the Anglo-Saxons make good use of simile. An exceptionally fine simile is introduced by King Alfred when he turns his prose version of Boethius' *De Consolatione Philosophiae*, Book III, Met. 9 into verse, adding a new idea (namely, a figure derived from a scholium) to God's establishing the earth firmly in its central place, *The Metres of Boethius* 20 lines 169-75:[126]

> Þæm anlicost   þe on æge bið,
> 170   gioleca on middan;   glideð hwæðre
> æg ymbutan.   Swa stent eall weoruld
> stille on tille,   streamas ymbutan
> lagufloda gelac,   lyfte and tungla,
> and sio scire scell   scriðeð ymbutan
> 175   dogora gehwilce,   dyde lange swa.

---

[123] W. J. Sedgefield (ed.), *The Battle of Maldon and Short Poems from the Saxon Chronicle* (Boston, Massachusetts, 1904), p. ix.

[124] S. B. Greenfield, *Critical History* (1965; see II[79]), 189, repeated in S. B. Greenfield and D. G. Calder, *New Critical History* (1986; see II[79]), 248. There is a grudging word of praise of line 28

> ofer hwæles eðel,   hama bereafod

setting up an unconvincing contrastive juxtaposition between the whale's habitat, the last of four kennings for the sea, and the loss of home of Earl Oslac, achieved by translating the line as 'over the whale's home, deprived of [his] homes': 'the last line is effective in its contrast of home with homelessness.'

[125] Cf. E. G. Stanley, 'Poetic Diction' (1956; see IV[118]), reprinted in E. G. Stanley, *A Collection of Papers* (1987; see I[45]), 235-7, 244.

[126] See W. J. Sedgefield (ed.), *King Alfred's Boethius* (1899; see IV[63]), 81 and 182. The simile is derived from the scholia found in some Boethius manuscripts; see Sedgefield, p. xxxiii: 'Caelum et terram mareque in modum ovi dicunt figurari'; cf. K. Otten, *König Alfreds Boethius*, StePh, n.s. 3 (Tübingen, 1964), 137 note 34. Cf. E. G. Stanley, 'Notes on Old English Poetry', v, Turning prose into verse, (1989; see III[27]), 234-7.

[It is most like to what is in an egg, the yolk in the middle; the
egg, however, glides all round it. Thus all the world stands still
in its fixed place, with the seas around it, the play of the
water-floods, the air and the stars, and the luminous shell takes
its course around it every day, as it has done since long ago.]

Another long simile compares the renewal of the flesh of the Phoenix with
fruit gathered in at harvest-time and producing, through the nature of the seed,
the new life in spring; *The Phoenix* lines 240-59:

```
240              Þonne bræd weorþeð
         eal edniwe,   eft acenned
         synnum asundrad;   sumes onlice
         swa mon to ondleofne   eorðan wæsmas
         on hærfeste   ham gelædeð,
245      wiste wynsume,   ær wintres cyme
         on rypes timan,   þy læs hi renes scur
         awyrde under wolcnum,   þær hi wraðe metað,
         fodorþege gefeon,   þonne forst and snaw
         mid ofermægne   eorþan þeccað
250      wintergewædum.   Of þam wæstmum sceal
         eorla eadwela   eft alædan
         þurh cornes gecynd   þe ær clæne bið
         sæd onsawen   þonne sunnan glæm
         on lenctenne   lifes tacen
255      weceð, woruldgestreon,   þæt þa wæstmas beoð
         þurh agne gecynd   eft acende,
         foldan frætwe:   swa se fugel weorþeð,
         gomel æfter gearum,   geong edniwe,
         flæsce bifongen.
```

[Then the incinerated flesh[127] is all renewed, born again freed
from sins, somewhat alike as mankind for sustenance at har-
vest brings home the fruits of the earth, delightful food, before
onset of winter at reaping time, lest a rain-shower destroy them
beneath the clouds, where they [mankind] find help, the delight of sustenance, whenever frost and snow cover the earth
with very great might in the raiments of winter. From those
fruits the prosperity of men is destined to re-emerge through
the nature of grain which is sown previously as a clean seed

---

[127] Old English *bræd* occurs only here. It is usually explained with reference to Old High
German *brat*; cf. the editions. E. Karg-Gasterstädt and T. Frings (eds), *Althochdeutsches
Wörterbuch* (Berlin, 1952), s.v., shows that this may have the same sense as its doublet Old
High German *brato* (cf. the Old English cognate *bræde*), 'roast meat'. Perhaps the unsuit-
ably comestible overtones of the more common form led the poet to use the rare doublet. I
translate it 'incinerated flesh' to avoid 'roast meat'.

when in spring the sun's radiance awakens the pledges of life,
treasure on earth, so that the fruits through their own nature
are reborn, adornments of earth: so that bird, old in the reckon-
ing of years, shall be young anew, clothed with flesh.]

    This simile is not derived immediately from the source, the Lactantian *De Ave Phoenice*, where the incinerated remains of the Phoenix are related to a seed, *et effectum seminis instar habet* [and the result has the form of a seed (line 100)], but that is rendered in the Old English poem by *æples gelicnes* [the likeness of an apple (line 230)]. It looks, therefore, as if the Old English poet has remembered the notion of the seed to use in an expansion of the original, a similitude based on corporeal rebirth, the dead Phoenix's flesh seedlike – and Christ-like – rises to new life.

    That Christian writings should contain somewhere a passage of which the Old English poem might seem a reminiscence is not to be wondered at: birds of heaven, death of the flesh, and seedlike resurrection to life are caught in a Gregorian similitude in his *Expositio* of Job 28:21, *volucres quoque caeli latet* [is kept close also from the birds of heaven]:[128]

    At contra in bono volucres poni solent, sicut in Evangelio Dominus cùm similitudinem regni cælestis ex grano sinapis denuntiaret, dixit: [Lucas 13:18-19] *Cui simile est regnum Dei, & cui simile æstimabo illud? Simile est grano sinapis, quod acceptum homo misit in hortum suum, & crevit, & factum est in arborem magnam, & volucrem cæli requieverunt in ramis ejus.* Ipse quippe est granum sinapis, qui in horti sepultura plantatus, arbor magna surrexit. Granum namque fuit cùm moreretur, arbor cùm resurgeret. Granum per humilitatem carnis, arbor per potentiam majestatis. Granum, quia [Isaias 53:2] *vidimus eum, & non erat aspectus:* arbor autem, quia [Psalmus 44:3] *speciosus forma præ filiis hominum.*

    [But on the other hand, 'the birds of heaven' are wont to be put in a good sense, as in the Gospel, when he was declaring a likeness of the kingdom of heaven by comparison with a grain of mustard seed, the Lord said [Luke 13:18-19], *Wherevnto is the kingdom of God like, and wherevnto shal I esteeme it like? It is like to a mustard seede, which a man tooke and cast into his garden, and it grew: and became a great tree, and the foules of the aire rested in the boughes thereof.* For he is himself a grain of mustard seed, who, when he was planted in the burial place of the garden, rose up a great tree. For he was a grain while, on the one hand, he died, but a tree while, on the other hand, he rose again. A grain, through the abasement of the flesh; a tree through the mightiness of his majesty. A grain, because [Isaie 53:2], *we haue sene him,*

---

[128] *Moralia in Iob*, XIX, 3; in the Maurist edition, *Opera* (Paris, 1705), I, col. 604. The Gospel reference to the parable is given as Mattheus 13:31-2, but the text is Lucas 13:18-19; cf. *Morals on the Book of Job, by S. Gregory the Great*, Library of the Fathers of the Holy Catholic Church (Oxford, 1845), II, 395.

and there was no sightlines; but a tree, because [Psalm 44:3], Thou art *Goodly of beautie aboue the sonnes of men.*]

The Phoenix is, I think, an intellectually astute poem: it seems to assume figural interpretation though it does not parade it. I do not believe that the passage quoted from the *Moralia* should be listed among firm *fontes Anglo-saxonum latini* specifically for *The Phoenix*; nor would I, with reference to these lines of the poem, claim more for Gregory's similitudinous interpretation of the seed than that, on the evidence of his poem, the Old English poet would have understood Gregory well.

What is more, though extensive similes and similitudes, allegories even, are not uncommon in the extant Old English poetry, the traditional scholarly view is surely right: these are Latinate, Christian imports, though perhaps readily accommodated within literary English because of the likely pre-existence of a native linguistic template of comparison, with *swa*, *gelice* or *gelicost* at its centre. Examples are numerous; the following has an obvious source in the Bible, but is extended by the device of variation: Daniel 3:36 has: '. . . promising that thou wouldest multiplie their seede as the starres of heauen, and as the sand that is in the sea shore.' This is expanded in *Daniel* lines 315-24 corresponding to *Azarias* lines 32-41,[129] which I quote:

>   Þu him gehete   þurh hleoþorcwidas
>   þæt þu hyra fromcynn   on fyrndagum
>   ycan wolde   þæt hit æfter him
> 35   on cyneryce   cenned wurde,
>   yced on eorþan   þæt swa unrime
>   had to hebban,   swa heofonsteorran
>   bugað bradne hwearft   oð brimflodas,
>   swa waroþa sond   ymb sealt wæter,
> 40   yþe geond eargrund: þæt swa unrime
>   ymb wintra hwearft   weorðan scolde.

[Thou didst promise them through spoken words that thou wouldst increase their progeny in days far off so that after them it should multiply into a kingdom, increased on earth to raise (its) condition, so countless as the celestial stars describe (their) broad circuit down to the sea-floods, (so countless) as the sands of the shores around salt waters, waves throughout the ocean-deep: that it was to be so countless in the process of years.]

This is as bookish an example as I know in Old English verse; but the basic, reiterated linguistic template is simple: *swa unrime (swa)*.

---

[129] The crux of *Daniel*, lines 320-4, requires several emendation to produce tolerable sense, as the editions show. *Azarias*, lines 37-41, is also difficult, but if a somewhat unidiomatic translation (such as I give) is permissible, some sense can be made to appear from it.

Another bookish example, again based on the Bible, is not reiterative. Matthew 13:43 has: 'Then shal the iust shine as the sunne, in the kingdom of their father.' It is quoted in *Christ and Satan* lines 306-8:

> 'Soðfæste men   sunnan gelice
> fægre gefrætewod   in heora fæder rice
> scinað in sceldbyrig.'

['Just men and women splendidly adorned will shine like the sun in the kingdom of their father within the defenced city.']

The familiar short simile of *Beowulf* lines 217-18[130] is, of course, less book-ish; and that has led commentators to believe that this is an example of the Germanic simile proper, and not a Latin import, not a Christian sophistication:

> Gewat þa ofer wægholm   winde gefysed
> flota famiheals   fugle gelicost.

[Then impelled by the wind across the billowy sea the ship went forth its neck foamy most like a bird.]

It is noteworthy, however, that the use of the near-zoomorphic *famiheals*, with *heals* 'neck' (a dead metaphor in Germanic for 'prow of a ship',[131] here brought back to life by the two-word simile that follows it) prepares us for the compari-son. It is less simple than it seems at first sight. A simpler bird simile occurs in the versified psalms; Psalm 102:5 has: *renouabitur sicut aquilae iuuentus tua* [thy youth shal be re[ne]wed as the eagles], rendered in the Paris Psalter:[132]

> eart þu edneowe   earne gelicast,
> on geogoðe nu   gleaw geworden.

[Thou art renewed most like to an eagle, become wise in youth now.]

It is impossible to say if the superlative construction (*gelicost*) is indigenous, but it seems likely since, as in Old English, similes in Old Saxon can be expressed with either positive *gilik* or superlative *gilikost*. How common short or long similes were before the influence of Christian Latinity it is, of course, impossible to say.

---

130 So also *Andreas* line 497.
131 That a ship is compared with a bird, and can be described as *fami(g)heals* 'foamy-necked' or *wundenhals* 'with sinuous neck' (as at *Beowulf* lines 218 and 1909, and 298) may not be unconnected with the existence of ships' prows in the shape of a bird's head and neck; cf. R. Bruce-Mitford, 'Ships' Figure-Heads of the Migration Period', in his *Aspects of Anglo-Saxon Archaeology. Sutton Hoo and Other Discoveries* (London, 1974), 175-87.
132 All three Latin Psalter versions have *renovabitur* 'shall be renewed'; Doway's 'rewed' is an error. Except for minor orthographic differences, *Fragments of Psalms* 102:5 is the same as the Paris Psalter, but with *gleaw* which I have adopted (instead of Paris Psalter *gleawe*).

Undoubtedly, the kenning was an indigenous figure. Discussion must proceed from the detailed account by Snorri Sturluson of kennings and related figures in Icelandic.[133] For application to Old English verse, it is important to note that the figures discussed by Snorri sometimes have Christian referents. The literature of the subject is voluminous, and the following remarks attempt neither a full survey of the Old English material, such as is available in the excellent book by H. Marquardt, nor a theoretical discussion of the concepts *kenning*, *heiti* and *fornafn*, such as is available in the several fundamental discussions, in the first place, of skaldic figures.[134] The kenning is a periphrasis for a proper or common noun expressed by a nominal compound or phrase consisting of at least two elements. The word is Icelandic, and its etymological meaning is 'knowing', perhaps 'recognition',[135] that is, the descriptive periphrasis allows the reader or hearer to recognize the subject of the kenning, sometimes helped by the device of variation which may present the referent more clearly or provide a synonym helpful for understanding.

It might be thought that *wægholm* 'the billowy sea' at line 217 introducing the little *Beowulf* simile is a kenning. I think not; the compound is too clear a term for the sea to be a kenning. In Old English verse, *holm* standing alone means 'the sea', and *wæg* means 'wave'. A kenning, as I understand the term, requires of the reader or hearer an imaginitive leap to recognize the referent: *wægholm* does not require that leap of the imagination. The phrase *flota famiheals* is not a kenning either; the word *flota* alone means 'ship' in verse (some other senses are found in prose, 'fleet', 'crew' or 'sailor', are probably irrelevant for verse usage). In *The Whale* line 7, the whale is described as *fyrnstreama geflota* 'the floating one of the ancient seas', usually emended to *fyr[ge]nstreama geflota* 'the floating one of the ocean-streams'. It is the only use of *geflota*, and probably *flota* was not used because it had lost its etymologi-

---

133 For editions and translations, see III[31] and IV[1] and IV[22]. Snorri, born 1179 and died 1241, is, of course, later than Anglo-Saxon England; and Old Icelandic poetry is very different from Old English poetry. Snorri's categorization of poetic figures is nevertheless relevant because it shows a profoundly self-conscious understanding of the arts of expression of a literature some parts of which go back to an early period – though expert scholarly statements about which parts and back to what time have to be treated with caution by Anglo-Saxonists aware of the wildly divergent views rampant in the dating of Old English verse.

134 For H. Marquardt's *Kenningar* (1938), R. Meissner's *Die Kenningar der Skalden* (1921), and H. van der Merwe Scholtz's *The Kenning in Anglo-Saxon and Old Norse Poetry* (1927), see II[60]. Cf. also W. Mohr, *Kenningstudien, Beiträge zur Stilgeschichte der altgermanischen Dichtung*, Tübinger germanistische Arbeiten, XIX (= Sonderreihe, Studien zur nordischen Philologie, II), 1933, with some references to Old English verse. The poetic language of *Beowulf* is particularly well discussed in an appendix, 'The Varieties of Poetic Appellations', and A. G. Brodeur, *Art of Beowulf* (1959; see II[59]), 247-53.

I owe to Professor Roberta Frank (Toronto) references to two important recent studies of the kenning in skaldic verse and Snorri's terminology: E. Marold, *Kenningkunst, Ein Beitrag zu einer Poetik der Skaldendichtung*, QF, 204, n.s. 80 (1983), with an excellent chapter 'Die Definition der Kenning und ihr Typeninventar', pp. 24-36; and M. Clunies Ross, *Skáldskaparmál*, The Viking Collection, 4 (Odense, 1987).

135 See M. Clunies Ross, *Skáldskaparmál* (1987; see IV[134]), 53-61.

cal sense 'floater, the floating one', and just meant 'ship', inappropriate for a whale. If, however, the etymological sense still inheres in *flota*, then *flota famiheals* would be a kenning, because the epithet *famiheals* allows the reader or hearer to recognize what kind of 'floater' it is – not, for example, a whale, and probably not a duck either, though *heals* 'neck, prow' could apply to a duck.

There are circumlocutions other than kennings in Old English verse (cf. p. 153, above); and they form a characteristic element of the poetry. For example, 'to advance' (of warriors) is 'to bear arms and armour (forward)', as in *Exodus* line 219 *beran beorht searo* [to bear shining armour], *Beowulf* lines 231-2 *beran . . . beorhte randas,* | *fyrdsearu fuslicu* [to carry shining shields, armour in readiness], *Beowulf* lines 291-2 *Gewitaþ forð beran* | *wæpen ond gewædu* [Go and bear forward weapons and armour], *The Battle of Maldon* lines 12-13 *ongan þa forð beran* | *gar to guþe* [did[136] then bear forward (his) spear to battle]. There are in Old English circumlocutions for 'to live' and 'to die'. For example, *The Seafarer* line 27-8 *se þe ah lifes wyn* | *gebiden* [who has experienced the joy of life (that is, who has lived in joy)]; *Genesis* lines 1608-10 (with *breosta hord* a kenning for [Japhet's] soul, made explicit in the variation *gast*):

> oð þæt breosta hord,
> gast ellorfus,   gangan sceolde
> 1610   to Godes dome.

[until the treasure of (his) breast, his spirit eager to depart, had to go to the judgement of God.]

Beowulf lines 851-2 *feorh alegde,* | *hæþene sawle* [he gave up life, his heathen soul].

There are several kennings for 'spirit, soul' in Old English verse:[137] *breosta hord* is found also at *Christ III* line 1072, varied in line 1073 by *feores frætwe* [the ornament of life (or the treasure of life)]; but *feorh* 'life' comes to mean 'the principle of life, the soul' in Old English Christian usage, so that *feores frætwe* may be too explicit to be considered a kenning. That 'soul' is meant for the phrase, even if not necessarily for the word, is made clear by *sawle* in line 1074,

---

[136] It seems that *onginnan* may be used in Old English verse, much as Middle English *gan* (or *gon*; and cf. chiefly Northern *can*, *MED* s.v. *can*, v.) as what *MED* s.v. *ginnen* 3.b. defines thus: 'As a weak [i.e. 'feeble, meaningless'] auxiliary used with infinitives to form phrases denoting actions or events as occurring (rather than as beginning to occur): do, did.' In *The Battle of Maldon* the verb is used eight times with infinitives (and never as a lexical verb), and it seems to have lost most, perhaps all, of its inceptive quality. D. Scragg's translation 'he set off then to carry his spear to the fray', in D. Scragg (ed.), *The Battle of Maldon AD 991* (Oxford, 1991), 19, may indicate unawareness of this late Old English (and Middle English) usage; *onginnan* with an infinitive never means 'to set off', even where some inceptive quality is thought to inhere in a particular use.

[137] Cf. H. Marquardt, *Kenningar* (1938; see II[60]), 199 [= 97].

in the same sentence as I punctuate the passage, and not in the next sentence (as lines 1069-75 are punctuated in most editions):[138]

> Ðonne weoroda mæst   fore Waldende,
> 1070   ece ond edgeong,   andweard gæð
> neode ond nyde   bi noman gehatne,
> berað breosta hord   fore bearn Godes,
> feores frætwe,   wile fæder eahtan
> hu gesunde suna   sawle bringen
> 1075   of þam eðle   þe hi on lifdon.

[When the greatest of hosts, eternal and made young again, will go before the Lord into his presence by express desire and force [each] called by name, will bear the treasures of their breast before the Son of God, the ornaments of life, (then) the Father will observe how healthful his sons may bring their souls from the country in which they had lived.]

The same elements of this kenning as occur in the genitival phrase are combined in the compound *breosthord*; but in Hrothgar's 'sermon', using many of the same ingredients to describe the tyranny of Heremod at *Beowulf* lines 1718-19, there seems to be no explicit reference to the Christian notion of the soul, *Hwæþere him on ferhþe greow | breosthord blodreow* [However, in his mind grew bloodthirsty inmost thoughts]; yet a translation, 'However, in his soul grew a bloodthirsty inmost spirit', could not be regarded as wrong, though it may be forcing a more theological sense on to the lines than appears to me to be suggested by the words. If only we understood the overtones better!

The compound as used to introduce Beowulf's dying speech (*Beowulf* lines 2791-2) cannot stand for 'soul': *oð þæt wordes ord | breosthord þurhbræc* [until the first word broke through the mind]. This use is a metaphor of many strands, and the kenning *breosthord* for 'mind' as the enclosure of pent speech breaking through as the dying man gives utterance in pain is perhaps the least striking part of it. Amusingly, and I think doubly right rather than doubly wrong, Bosworth-Toller's *Anglo-Saxon Dictionary* treats the metaphor in conflicting ways. S.v. *ord*, there is no mention that it is to be taken as anything other than literally: '*ord*, I. *a point*, (a) of a weapon', though sense III is given as 'beginning', and though, s.v. *word* sense III, 'speech, language, words', the striking phrase *wordes ord* (with internal rhyme) is translated as 'the first word'. The breaking through turns the *ord* into the point of a weapon; and the kenning that is pierced is the *breosthord*, the seat of the emotions. In the sad passage describing the impression made by bird-song on a sensitive spirit, *The Seafarer* lines 53-5, *breosthord* is rendered 'heart' or 'breast' in most translations:

[138] The translation by I. Gollancz (ed.), *The Exeter Book* (1895; see III[44]), 67, however, also takes the passage as a single sentence.

Swylce geac monað   geomran reorde,
singeð sumeres weard,   sorge beodeð
55   bitter in breosthord.

[The cuckoo too prompts, summer's watchman, sings with sad
voice, announces bitter sorrow to the feeling heart.]

The kenning *sumeres weard* for the cuckoo 'watchman of summer' uses succinctly the notion expressed in *Guthlac A* line 744 *geacas gear budon* [cuckoos
announced the spring].[139] As we shall see, personification is not uncommon in
Old English verse, and striking personifying kennings, of which *sumeres weard*
is a good example, are an occasional grace central, as has been thought, to
poetry. These lines provide also an example, relatively rare in Old English, of
'variation' on verbs: *monað* 'reminds, prompts, urges', *singeð* 'sings', and
beodeð 'proclaims, announces'.

So common are kennings in Old English verse that, whenever a passage is
considered of interest for some other literary reason, it is likely to include one or
more kennings. In the present brief section on ornament we have so far
gathered: *The Phoenix* line 250 *(mid) wintergewædum* 'with the raiments of
winter' that is hoar-frost and snow; *Christ and Satan* line 308 *in sceldbyrig* 'in
the defenced city',[140] that is varying *in heora fæder rice* (line 307) 'in the
kingdom of their father' (of Matthew 13:43); *The Metres of Boethius* 20 line 173
lagufloda gelac translated 'the play of the water floods', varying *streamas* 'the
seas, the currents'. Perhaps the poetic word *gelac* should have been translated
'tumult' or 'strife' or 'swift motion'; but 'play' seems best, for the word is used
as the second element of the battle kennings *sweorda gelac* 'play of swords'
Beowulf line 1040, and *æt ecga gelacum* 'at the play of blades' *Beowulf* line
1168. Cynewulf twice uses a battle kenning with 'shield' as first element and
gelac as the second; *lindgelac* is used in a straightforward way in the glorification of the Apostles as if for martial prowess, *The Fates of the Apostles* line 76.
But in his reference to the devil's venemous strike weapons which puts the
shield of faith to the test, Cynewulf's use of *biter bordgelac* 'bitter shield-play'
Christ II line 769. It forms part of a subtle and complex figure, and is an
essential ingredient of the long passage, *Christ II* lines 756-77, the basis of
which appears to be the great conflict of Ephesians 6:11-17, especially verse
16:[141] 'in al things taking the shield of faith, wherewith you may extinguish al

---

139 See H. Marquardt, *Kenningar* (1938; see II[60]), 190 [= 88]; for copious references, cf. J.
Roberts (ed.), *The Guthlac Poems of the Exeter Book* (Oxford, 1979), 156-7.
140 The underlying concept appears to be biblical, but none of the various relevant phrases in the
Bible is applied to heaven (without resorting to figural exegesis): *civitas munita, urbs
munita* 'defenced city'; *civitas munitissima, urbs munitissima* 'city most strongly defended';
urbs fortis, civitas firma 'strong city'; *civitas murata, urbs murata* 'walled city'; *confugii
civitas, confugii urbs* 'city of refuge'.
141 Though the notes on lines 756-77 by A. S. Cook (ed.), *The Christ of Cynewulf* (1st edn
Boston, Massachusetts, 1900; 2nd edn 1909; reprinted Hamden, Connecticut, 1964), 146-

the fiery dartes of the most wicked one.' Within the long passage of the fight against the devil's weapons,[142] the immediate context of the battle kenning is *Christ II* lines 766-70:

> Forþon we fæste sculon   wið þam færscyte
> symle wærlice   wearde healdan,
> þy læs se attres ord   in gebuge,
> biter bordgelac,   under banlocan,
> 770   feonda færsearo.

[Therefore we must staunchly, always warily, keep watch against that sudden missile, lest the poisonous point turn within under the enclosing bones – a grievous shield-play – the sudden device of the enemies.]

Perhaps it is indulging too enthusiastic an appetite for spiritual exegesis, an appetite of which I do not feel myself guilty: 'Legt ihr's nicht aus, so legt was unter' – but, as the enemies' weapons are both the afflictions of the body and also the temptations of the spirit, with the shield of faith a good defence against both, so the *biter bordgelac* is both physically 'a grievous shield-play' and also spiritually 'a bitter conflict of faith'.

As in Old Icelandic, with especially in skaldic verse a greater wealth of kennings, swords are the referents of some subtle kennings in Old English. Good examples in *Beowulf* are *fela laf* line 1032 and *homera laf* line 2829. Two of the senses of *laf* may be applicable: 'that which is left' or 'heritage, heirloom'. Therefore, *fela laf* can mean either 'that which is left when the files have done their work', that is, the sword's edge or edges sharpened by files, or 'that which the files bequeath', again referring to the edge or edges of the sword. The kenning *homera laf* refers to the blade, that is, 'that which the hammers leave when they have done their work', or 'that which the hammers bequeath'. In both kennings, by means of a different figurative conception, play is made with the idea that a sword was often an heirloom in Anglo-Saxon times.

Metonymy and synecdoche are common features of kennings,[143] but are not confined to kennings in Old English verse. For example, 'edge' often stands for 'sword', and so did 'blade' (as it still does in Modern English). The poetic word *grima* refers to the visor-like front part of the helmet; it can also mean 'spectre', and the sense 'visor' may be a metaphor, perhaps a dead metaphor. In a clearly martial context, it is possible that an Anglo-Saxon, hearing *grima*, would think

---

50, give a wealth of references, the Epistle to the Ephesians is not among them. Like G. P. Krapp and E. V. K. Dobbie in the ASPR edition, III, 253, Cook favours a simple equivalence of *bordgelac* (line 769) with 'strife'. The Pauline use seems to make that too simple a solution.

[142] On the devil's weapons, cf. E. G. Stanley, 'Poetic Diction', reprinted in *Collection of Papers* (1987; see I[45]), 238-42.

[143] So also in skaldic verse; cf. E. Marold, *Kenningkunst* (1983; see IV[134]), 30-2, 50-1, 208, 211.

only of the helmet and not of some spectral manifestation; thus in *Elene* lines 125-6:

125   Gylden grima,   garas lixtan
      on herefelda.

[The golden visor (and) spears shone on the battlefield.]

We cannot regard the metonymy 'visor' as a kenning, and could not do so even if we thought that it meant 'spectre', because it consists of a single element only, and the colour word *gylden* is not an element revealing the true nature of the 'spectre', but is merely descriptive. The two compounds for 'helmet' in *Beowulf* are, however, kennings because they consist of two parts, neither of which alone means 'helmet', though the two elements together make the meaning 'helmet' clear: *beadogrima* 'battle visor' and *heregrima* 'army visor'. We do not know if in these compounds the sense 'spectre' inheres in *grima*; if it does, 'battle spectre' and 'army spectre' might be quite good poetic circumlocutions for 'helmet'.

In Old English kennings, metonymy is less common than synecdoche with the second element in sense wider, usually more general, than the referent; but the defining first element narrows down the sense, so that the referent can be recognized. Thus there are many Old English words for clothes in general, *-hama* 'garment', *hrægl* 'dress', *syrce* 'shirt. Much as in Modern English *mail-shirt* is a particular kind of 'shirt', what kind is made clear by 'mail-', so Old English words for dress are narrowed down by first elements such as *beado* 'battle', *fyrd* or *here* 'army', *hilde* 'war', resulting in compounds meaning 'armour'.

In Old English, *bæð* presumably meant literally, as does Modern English *bath* which is derived from it, either 'an act of immersion (in water)' or 'the place where one immerses oneself (in water)'. It can be an aspect of the sea, but is not synonymous with it. When defined by another element, however, the sense of the two elements together may be 'the sea'; for examples, *fisces bæð* 'the place where the fish is immersed' or *ganotes bæð* 'the place where the gannet immerses itself'.

In connection with Old English kennings, it is profitable to consider the nature of some Old English poetic descriptions which are not kennings, and the way in which the Anglo-Saxons delighted in analysing what they saw and putting such analysis to use in descriptions, for example, often in their riddles, but not only in riddles, as the description of the hail of weaponry in *Beowulf* lines 3114-19 shows:

                    'Nu sceal gled fretan,
3115 weaxan wonna leg,   wigena strengel,
      þone ðe oft gebad   isernscure,
      þonne stræla storm   strengum gebæded

> scoc ofer scildweall: sceft nytte heold,
> fæðergearwum fus   flane fulleode.'

['Now fire, the dark flame full-grown, must consume the prince of warriors who often lived through the hail of steel, whenever impelled by strong strings the storm of arrows hastened over the shield wall: the shaft did duty, made eager for its journey by the feather-gear it helped the arrow-head on its way.']¹⁴⁴

In this description there is a figurative, half-personifying conception. If the interpretation is right, the arrow-head has the other parts' of the arrow serving it eagerly and dutifully on its flight.

As a rule, I am suspicious of most attempts to relate the written word of the Anglo-Saxons to their visual arts, and, therefore, I do not find much enlightenment in some assumed parallel between the organization of narrative poems and the interlace ornaments of some manuscript pages. But the *Beowulf* poet's analysis of the arrow in flight is reminiscent of the anatomizing manuscript initials of the Anglo-Saxons. The arrow's head, body and tail, that is, arrow-head, shaft and feather-gear, are not unlike those strange, stylistically refined, but unrealistic, zoomorphic creatures in, for example, the initials of the Junius Psalter (authoritatively discussed by Francis Wormald),¹⁴⁵ in which a head, with jaws that bite, is connected to a stylized body by a slender, excessively long neck, and the creature is in turn bitten by another with taloned hoofs. These creatures are fantastic: one cannot always guess what they might be, or how they hang together. Their *raison d'être* is purely ornamental; the analyis of the parts to the whole has, however, been carefully considered, and that gives an impression of reality to the construct, a reality which, moreover, makes the construct recognizably zoomorphic. My comparison of the arrow in flight with the psalter initial must not be pressed or extended: I do not believe that the poem shares either provenance (Winchester has been suggested) or date ('stylistically

---

¹⁴⁴ Several items in this translation are problematic. MS *weaxan* line 3115 is taken as a spelling for the past participle *weaxen* [see W. J. Sedgefield (ed.), *Beowulf* (3rd edn; Manchester, 1935), 146; and cf. for the confusion of vowels in unstressed syllables, including *-an* for *-en*, Kemp Malone, 'When Did Middle English Begin?', in J. T. Hatfield, W. Leopold and A. J. F. Zieglschmid (eds), *Curme Volume of Linguistic Studies*, Language Monographs (supplement to *Language*), VII (1930), 110-17, for *Beowulf* pp. 115-16. The sense of *strengum* line 3117 is uncertain; my translation 'strong strings' uses both of the possible meanings, because I believe that both are present here in wordplay: *strengum* is the dative plural of both *strengu* 'strength' and of *streng* '(bow)string'. The interpretation of *flan* line 3119 as 'arrow-head', instead of the normal sense 'arrow' in Old English, is perhaps not wholly contextual; cf. F. Holthausen (ed.), *Altenglisches etymologisches Wörterbuch* (Heidelberg, 1934), 106 s.v.; J. de Vries (ed.), *Altnordisches etymologisches Wörterbuch* (Leiden, 1961), 129-30 s.v. *fleinn*; A. Jóhannesson (ed.), *Isländisches etymologisches Wörterbuch* (Berne, 1956), 905-6 s.v. *(s)plei-*.

¹⁴⁵ F. Wormald, 'Decorated Initials' (1945; see IV¹⁸), especially 116-19, and Plate IV d. illustrating the psalter initial, Bodleian MS Junius 27, fo 20ʳ.

it would seem to belong to the second quarter of the tenth century') with the psalter. I think it shares only, and only to some extent, a mode of perception.

A similar mode of perception is found in several of the riddles of the Anglo-Saxons. I do not turn to the riddles and to Anglo-Saxon riddling in any generalizing spirit, like that of Socrates in the Platonic dialogue *Alcibiades*, if Plato means us to take Socrates straight – which I rather doubt:[146]

> He [*scil.* Homer], like almost every other poet, speaks in riddles. For poetry as a whole is by nature inclined to riddling, and it is not every man who can apprehend it. And furthermore, besides having this natural tendency, when it gets hold of a grudging person who [in his poetry] wishes not to show forth to us his own wisdom but to conceal it as much as possible, we find it an extraordinarily difficult matter whatever this or that one of them may mean.

Though in some Old English poetry, as often throughout the history of poetry, obscurity, and therefore a reader's puzzlement, may be an unintentional result of the use of figurative language, or, as Socrates seems to allege, the result of the essential indirection of almost all poetry, the Anglo-Saxon poets do not appear to have produced deliberate obscurity, except for riddles. Some of these are similar in analysis to some of the best kennings used in verse, and the imaginitive leap required to recognize the referent in the analytical description of the kenning is similar to the imaginitive leap required to solve the riddle. The context of the kenning usually makes clear, sometimes by variation, what the referent is, and there is no indirection or real obscurity in Old English kennings, unlike skaldic kennings. The riddle does not usually reveal the solution easily: we are meant to admire its cleverness in concealing the solution, not its obviousness.

Riddle 17 is a good example of riddling by parts, and that it has no generally accepted solution is not detrimental to using it as an example:

> Ic eom mundbora   minre heorde,
> eodorwirum fæst,   innan gefylled
> dryhtgestreona.   Dægtidum oft
> spæte sperebrogan.   Sped biþ þy mare
> 5   fylle minre.   Freo þæt bihealdeð
> hu me of hrife fleogað   hyldepilas.
> Hwilum ic sweartum   swelgan onginne
> brunum beadowæpnum,   bitrum ordum,
> eglum attorsperum.   Is min innað til,
> 10   wombhord wlitig,   wloncum deore.
> Men gemunan   þæt me þurh muþ fareð.

[146] I use the translation in W. R. M. Lamb (ed.), *Plato, Charmides, Alcibiades*, etc., Loeb Classical Library (1927), *Alcibiades*, II, 147 (Loeb edn, p. 261).

[I am the protector of my flock, secure by means of the wire-
enclosures, filled within with noble treasure. By day I often
spew forth spear-terror. My success is all the greater for my
being full. My lord beholds how the warlike darts fly from my
belly. At times I endeavour to swallow battle-weapons, black
and brown(?), bitter points, hideous poison-spears. My womb
is good, the treasure in my belly beautiful, precious to the
proud. People remember what passes through my mouth.]

A solution often accepted is *ballista*; the solution 'fortress' has sometimes been
preferred, though *eodorwirum fæst* seems to be against it. The anatomizing
perception underlying the description of the object, whatever that may be, in
terms of mouth spitting forth weapons and of belly holding rich treasure, is not
unlike the perception underlying the analysis in *Beowulf* lines 3117-19 of the
arrow in flight, head foremost and body helping it onwards.

Riddle 31 is similar in this respect. Its solution, widely accepted, is 'bagpipe',
for the playing of which by Anglo-Saxons this riddle appears to provide the only
evidence, though glosses attest to knowledge of the instrument among learned
Anglo-Saxons:[147]

> Is þes middangeard   missenlicum
> wisum gewlitegad,   wrættum gefrætwad.
> Ic seah sellic þing   singan on ræcede:
> wiht wæs *no*[wer][148]   werum on gemonge
> 5   sio hæfde wæstum   wundorlicran.
> Niþerweard wæs neb hyre,
> fet ond folme   fugele gelice;
> no hwæþre fleogan mæg   ne fela gongan.
> Hwæþre feþegeorn   fremman onginneð,
> 10   gecoren cræftum,   cymeð geneahhe,
> oft ond gelome   eorlum on gemonge,
> siteð æt symble,   sæles bideþ
> hwonne ær heo cræft hyre   cyþan mote
> werum on wonge.   Ne heo þær wiht þigeð
> 15   þæs þe him æt blisse   beornas habbað.
> Deor, domes georn,   hio dumb wunað;
> hwæþre hyre is on fote   fæger hleoþor,
> wynlicu woðgiefu.   Wrætlic me þinceð
> hu seo wiht mæge   wordum lacan

[147] See C. Williamson (ed.), *The Old English Riddles of the Exeter Book* (Chapel Hill, 1977),
233-4.
[148] Most editors follow this emendation, first suggested by G. Herzfeld, *Die Räthsel des Exeter-
buches und ihr Verfasser* (Berlin, 1890), 68. The manuscript reads *wiht wæs onwerum onge
monge*, with *ge-* attached to the word preceding it and space between the prefix and the word
to which it belongs, as is not uncommon in the manuscript [cf. E. G. Stanley, review of I. L.
Gordon (ed.) *The Seafarer*, in *MÆ*, 31 (1962), 59; cf. V²³, below].

20 þurh fot neoþan.   Frætwed hyrstum,
 hafað hyre on halse   þonne hio hord warað,
 bær, beagum deall,   broþor sine,
 mæg mid mægne.   Micel is to hycgenne
 wisum woðboran   hwæt [sio] wiht sie.

[This earth is made beautiful in a variety of ways, richly
adorned. I saw a wondrous thing singing in hall: nowhere
among men was a creature that had a more marvellous shape.
Its face was downwards, its feet and hands like a bird; yet it
cannot fly nor walk much. However, eager to march forth, it
begins to perform, select in its skills, again and again it turns
many times in the assembly of men, sits at banquet, awaits the
time till soon it can make known its skill to men on earth. It
partakes of nothing there of what men have in joy. Brave, eager
for glory, it stays dumb; yet sweet melody is in its foot, a
joyous gift of song. It seems miraculous to me how that creature can play with words through its foot from below. Adorned
in its trappings, whenever it holds treasure, naked, proud of its
rings, the sibling strongly carries on its neck its brothers. It is
much to be pondered by anyone who utters wisely what that
creature may be.]

The bagpipe is anatomized, part by part considered in anthropomorphic and
zoomorphic terms; and there is wonder, as not infrequent in the riddles, at the
contrariety of things. Litotes, common in Old English, is used to describe the
creatures ability to walk: *ne fela* 'not much'. Some of the details are like
kennings. For example, the drones are brothers carried by the bagpipe, their
kinswoman, on her neck. The creature carries verbal song or poetry in its foot,
and it gives forth without partaking of what is provided at the feast, where it sits
mutely till its time to perform has come: wise rhetoricians, prophets and singers,
whose utterance teaches the world, have reason to ponder that.

Old English metaphorical language at its most difficult may be exemplified
from an obscure passage in *Exodus*. Explication of obscurities is a self-pleasing
exegetical activity, often satisfying only the explicator. The following explication of the word *sæcir* at line 291 as a kenning for the turbulent waters of the sea
is far from obvious and perhaps wrong.[149] I give it to illustrate how elaborate
and elaborately figurative some Old English verse can be in its diction, especially *Exodus*. In the manuscript, Bodleian Junius 11 p. 158, lines 289-91a
read (here set out in verse lines, with modern word-division and punctuation,
and with initial capital for the first word):

---

[149] See E. G. Stanley, 'Notes on the Text of *Exodus*', in M. Collins, J. Price and A. Hamer (eds),
Sources and Relations: Studies in Honour of J. E. Cross, LSE, n.s. XVI (1985), 242.

Sælde sægrundas   suðwind fornam,
290   bæðweges blæst;   bring is areafod,
      sand sæcir span.

Manuscript *bring*, though it has been defended as meaning 'offering' (the abstract of *bringan* 'to bring'),[150] is usually emended to *brim* 'the sea'. The most common meaning of *blæst* is 'flame', but here it varies *suðwind* 'south wind' and presumably means 'gust of wind', a sense common in Middle English, with dependent genitive *bæðweges* 'of the ocean', with *bæðweg* a kenning for 'sea'. Manuscript *span* is the preterite of *spinnan* 'to spin'. The compound *sæcir* occurs only here. I interpret half-line 290a, *sand sæcir span*, as a spinning metaphor; *-cir* is the noun related to *cirran* 'to turn', and could refer to part of the turning mechanism of spinning machinery, perhaps the whorl (assuming the Anglo-Saxons had whorls), or the spindle, or the reel.[151] If so, *sæcir* is some technicality used metaphorically and perhaps to be translated by 'the whorl of the sea', referring to the south wind (which stirs up the waters). The passage of the Israelites through the sea is described as if their Exodus took them on the sandy path spun by that sea-whorl. Whether *sæcir* is strictly a kenning depends on whether the compound refers primarily to the waters or to the wind. If *sæcir* were the sea, it would not be a kenning since the first element is 'the sea' explicitly. But if line 290b is emended to *brim* 'sea', *bri*m *is areafod* 'the sea is carried off', *sæcir* cannot refer to the sea which has been removed from the path through the sea, and must, therefore, refer to the wind. The compound would then be a kenning, its sense to be inferred from the combination of its elements. We may, therefore, perhaps translate the lines (emending *bring* to *brim*): 'The south wind took away the fettered sea-depths, the gust of the ocean; the sea is carried off, the sea-whorl spun out sand.'

Many Old English kennings are not very imaginative. Terms for the deity are typical: *heofoncyning* 'King of heaven', *wuldorcyning* 'King of glory' and *cyninga wuldor* 'Glory of kings', *wuldres aldor* 'Prince of glory', *lifes aldor* 'Prince of life', *weoroda dryhten* 'Lord of hosts', *þeoden engla* 'Prince of angels', *sigora waldend* 'Lord of glories', *fæder mancynnes* 'Father of mankind'. *gasta scyppend* 'Creator of souls', *sawla nergend* 'Saviour of souls', and a great many more, using different combinations of elements some of which are exemplified here.[152]

---

[150] It is found in the plural *bringas* in four Old English Psalter glosses to Psalm 50:21 (see *DOE* s.v.), including the gloss with variant *bringas ł oflaten* glossing 'oblationes' in the very late Eadwine's Psalter, Psalm 50:21; see F. Harsley (ed.), *Eadwine's Canterbury Psalter*, EETS, o.s. 92 (1889), 89; in early Middle English the word is used by Laȝamon. Cf. Bosworth-Toller and *MED* s.v. *bring*.

[151] For the Old English vocabulary of spinning, cf. *Gerefa* 15, 1, in F. Liebermann (ed.), *Die Gesetze der Angelsachsen*, I (Halle, 1898-1903), 455. Which part of spinning machinery may be referred to cannot be deduced from the etymological sense of *-cir*, except that it turns.

[152] Cf. H. Marquardt, *Kenningar* (1938; see II⁶⁰), 267-91 [= 165-89].

Of course, many of these religious kennings derive from Latin biblical or liturgical use. In such contexts a warlike Germanic sense 'victory' is not to be looked for strenuously in phrases like *sigora dryhten* and *sigora waldend* or in compounds like *sigedryhten*: 'Lord of glories' and 'glorious Lord' are probably better translations.[153] Such religious kennings come so often in the extant, preponderantly religious verse of the Anglo-Saxons that it requires an effort to remember that they must once have been new in Old English poetry.

Personification and allegory

Anthropomorphization takes various forms in Old English poetry, as we have seen: the arrow-head is helped by the shaft and made eager for flight by the feather-gear, at *Beowulf* lines 3118-19; and − is it like an animal or are its human characteristics such as to make it human? − the bagpipe of *Riddle 31* is a wondrous performer, sits mute at the banquet without partaking of the delights provided, and then gives forth of the sweet melody stored in its foot with its brothers borne on its neck helping somehow. Such zoomorphizing and anthropomorphizing arises from a playful perception.

Full personification involves more than that. It has been thought to be an imaginative exploitation of grammatical gender in languages that have a system of gender. In a chapter on 'personifications' immediately preceding a chapter on 'the art of poetry' in Jacob Grimm's account of Germanic mythology, personification is seen as a central feature of the poetry in the Germanic languages, and his view of how gender arose in language is a piece of central doctrine of German Romanticism, a movement in which the Grimms had a not unimportant place.[154]

---

[153] Cf. E. G. Stanley, 'Some Problematic Sense-Divisions in Old English: 'glory and victory; noble, glorious, and learned', in H. Damico and J. Leyerle (eds), *Heroic Poetry in the Anglo-Saxon Period – Studies in Honor of J. B. Bessinger, Jr.* (Kalamazoo, 1993), 174-210.

[154] J. Grimm, *Deutsche Mythologie* (2nd edn, 1844; see I²⁵), ch. xxix, Personificationen (pp. 834-51), ch. xxx, Dichtkunst (pp. 852-64). These chapters were added in the second edition; that on personification is the more fundamental. Grimm's discussion in *Deutsche Mythologie* is based on his *Deutsche Grammatik*, III (Göttingen, 1831), ch. vi Genus (pp. 311-563, especially pp. 311, 317-18, 344-6, 348). Cf. E. G. Stanley, *Paganism* (1964-1965; reprinted 1975; see I²), reprint pp. 95-6, where a central passage from *Deutsche Mythologie* is translated and (p. 133) quoted; the opening of that quotation is also given at p. 200, below.

Readers more concerned than Grimm with English literature may see shortcomings in his linguistic approach to poetry as revealed in his sweeping statement about the formal unfitness of the English language for poetry (*Deutsche Grammatik*, III, p. 345):

> Beide, flexion und genus bedingen einander und mit dem untergang der flexions- und ableitungssilben mindert sich zugleich das gefühl für den geschlechtsunterschied; wie wir in der reihe deutscher sprachen zumal in der englischen sehen, welche gewissermaßen die geistigste, formell aber auch die am wenigsten poetische ist.

> [Infexional system and gender are interdependent, and with the decline of

Johann Winckelmann, the historian of Classical art, has an earlier, influential statement on the relationship of grammatical gender to personification and, more particularly, to allegory; a better statement perhaps though not in tune with current feminist understanding of gender, and in its way as Romantic as anything in Grimm, but earlier than German Romanticism and firmly attached to Classicality:[155]

> Die Natur selbst ist der Lehrer der Allegorie gewesen, und diese Sprache scheinet ihr eigener als die nachher erfundene Zeichen unserer Gedanken: denn sie ist wesentlich, und giebt ein wahres Bild der Sachen, welches in wenig Worten der ältesten Sprachen gefunden wird, und die Gedanken mahlen, ist unstreitig älter als dieselben schreiben, wie wir aus der Geschichte der Völker der alten und neuen Welt wissen. . . .
>
> Die in Bildern redende Natur und die Spuren von bildlichen Begriffen erkennet man so gar in dem Geschlechte der Worte, welches die ersten Benenner derselben mit den Worten verbunden haben. Das Geschlecht zeuget von einer Betrachtung der wirkenden und leidenden Beschaffenheit, und zugleich des Mittheilens und des Empfangens, welches man sich Verhältnißweise in den Dingen vorgestellet, so daß das Wirkende in männlicher Gestalt und das Leidende weiblich eingekleidet worden. Die Sonne hat in den alten und in den mehresten neuen Sprachen eine männliche Benennung, wie der Mond eine weibliche, weil dort Wirkung und Einfluß erkannt worden, hier aber Annehmen und Empfängniß, und daher haben Aegypter, Phoenicier, Perser, Hetrurier und Griechen die Sonne männlich und den Mond weiblich gebildet. In der deutschen Sprache ist in beyden Worten das Gegentheil, wovon ich den Grund anzugeben andern überlasse. So scheinet Gott, der Tod, die Zeit und andere Begriffe mit dieser Betrachtung des Wirkens und Einflußes in den alten Sprachen männlich benennet zu seyn. Die Erde hat eine Benennung weibliches Geschlechts und ist in weiblicher Gestalt gebildet, weil dieselbe den Einfluß des Himmels und die Witterung empfängt, und nur durch Mittheilung wirket. Es ist also hieraus zu schließen daß die ältesten Zeichen der Gedanken muthmaßlich bildliche Vorstellungen derselben gewesen.
>
> [Nature itself has been the teacher of allegory, and allegorical language seems to belong more properly to nature than the signifiers[156] of our thoughts devised at a later stage: for the language of allegory is essential, giving a true picture of the things such as is to be found in only a small number of words of the earliest languages and which depict thoughts, a language indisputably older than the written earliest languages, as we know from the history of nations ancient and modern. . . .

> inflexional and derivational syllables the feeling for the difference between genders is diminished also; as we see, in the Germanic group of languages, especially in the English language, which is, as it were, the most intellectual, but at the same time in its grammatical forms the least poetic of these languages.]

[155] J. J. Winckelmann, *Versuch einer Allegorie, besonders für die Kunst* (Dresden, 1766), 3-4.
[156] I use the English equivalent of the Saussurean *signifiant* because Winckelmann's use of *Zeichen* 'sign' is close to it, and anticipates it in its relationship to the 'signified' thoughts.

We recognize nature speaking in images and the traces of figurative concepts in the very gender of words which their first users have connected with these words. Gender bears witness to a perception of active or passive characteristics, and at the same time of imparting and conceiving which were imagined as proportionately significant in the things, with the result that the active was invested with masculine, the passive with feminine. The sun has in the ancient and most of the modern languages a masculine name, while the moon has a feminine name, because in the former effectiveness and influence were recognized, but in the latter acceptance and conception, and therefore the Egyptians, the Phoenicians, the Persians, the Etrurians, and the Greeks have figured the sun as masculine and the moon as feminine. In the German language both words have the opposite gender; I leave it to others to state the reason for that. Thus it seems that in the ancient languages god, death, time and other concepts perceived as effective and influential were designated masculine. The earth has a designation of feminine gender because it is passively subject to the influence of heaven and of climatic conditions, and is effective only by impartment. It is therefore to be deduced that the most ancient signifiers of thoughts were probably figurative representations of them.]

Like Winckelmann in his 'Essay of Allegory', so Grimm in *Deutsche Grammatik*, vol. III, expressed belief in the interpendence of the allegorical mode of personification and the linguistics of gender, mysteriously rooted in each other. He praises the operation of linguistic gender in Greek and Latin syntax, word-order presumably. Since in German (as, somewhat differently, in English Feminist language) *Geschlecht*, like Greek *genos* and Latin *genus*, has among its senses both 'sex' and 'gender' Grimm thought personification a fundamentally natural form of expression (p. 346):

Das grammatische genus ist . . . eine in der phantasie der menschlichen sprache entsprungene ausdehnung des natürlichen auf alle und jede gegenstände. Durch diese wunderbare operation haben eine menge von ausdrücken, die sonst todte und abgezogene begriffe enthalten, gleichsam leben und empfindung empfangen, und indem sie von dem wahren geschlecht formen, bildungen, flexionen entlehnen, wird über sie ein die ganze sprache durchziehender reiz von bewegung und zugleich bindender verknüpfung der redeglieder unvermerkt ausgegoßen. Man kann sich, wäre das genus in der sprache aufgehoben, verschlingungen der worte, wie wir sie in der griechischen oder lateinischen syntax bewundern, nicht wohl gedenken.

[Grammatical gender is an extension of natural gender to each and every object, an extension that arose in the fancy of human language. As a result of this marvellous operation a great number of expressions, which otherwise contain dead or abstract concepts, have, as it were, received life and feeling. Since they have borrowed their forms, morphology and inflexions from true gender, a charm has effused these expressions, imperceptibly filling the whole language, endowing them with emotion and at the same time with a syntactical means of connecting the parts of an utterance. If gender were lost in language, one could not imagine easily the complexities of word-order which we admire in Greek and Latin syntax.]

There is a hint in this statement, and more than a hint in the many pages from which a less Romantic grammarian might have deduced that the system of gender in the Germanic languages (and elsewhere in Indo-European) is the result of morphological groupings rather than of an animation of dead or abstract concepts through an imaginative extension born of the very nature of language. In *Deutsche Mythologie* (p. 835) the Romantic interpretation of the morphology of gender is raised to near-mystical heights not scaled in *Deutsche Grammatik*:

> Was in sprache und sage tief verwachsen ist kann der mythologie niemals fremd geblieben sein, es muss auf ihrem grund und boden eigenthümliche nahrung gesogen haben, und jene grammatische, dichterische allbelebung darf sogar in einer mythischen prosopopöie ihren ursprung suchen.

> [Whatever has deep roots in language and spoken tradition can never remain outside mythology; it must have imbibed fit nourishment on its soil, and this universal animation, at once grammatical and poetic, may even trace its origin to a mythical prosopopoeia.]

The ideas are grand: personification is at the heart of poetry and is so natural an imaginative extension of gender in its sexual aspects that it must have arisen inevitably in the preliterate world of the common Germanic tradition. The History of Ideas, viewed positively, traces the aggrandizement of thought, often its imaginative advancement, and so the notions of Winckelmann and Grimm about gender, personification and allegory, language-based within Indo-European, shine forth more brightly than the random groupings into masculine, feminine and neuter to which the detailed morphological evidence presented by Grimm might, or even should, have led him. Winckelmann was wise in his refusal to speculate on the origin of masculine for the moon and feminine for the sun in Germanic. It is only one example of the lack of reason in the gender of nouns. There is no good reason in nature (though it is explicable in morphology) why Old English *mase* 'titmouse' should be feminine, *wrenna* 'wren' masculine; or why Old English *mæw* 'seagull' (and probably the Old Saxon cognate *meu*) should be masculine, while Middle Low German *mewe* is feminine (whence Modern German *Möwe*, also feminine), as is Middle and Modern Dutch *meeuw(e)*; or more to the point, why Old English *wif* 'woman' should be neuter, and with masculine second element *wifman* should be masculine. In short, the equation of gender with sex, or of grammatical category with a division of humankind, is too simple to be true. Viewed negatively, the History of Ideas traces the development and rejection of error, and in retrospect it may seem that the grander the idea, the greater the error. In detailed application too, the rightness of gender is a nonsense. One is reminded of Christian Morgenstern's view on contemplating the physiognomy of seagulls:[157]

> Die Möwen sehen alle aus,
> als ob sie Emma hießen.

[The seagulls all look as if their name were Emma.]

An explanatory note by Morgenstern on these lines says, 'Eine Erfahrung, die sich jedem aufdrängt, sobald er eine Möwe daraufhin betrachtet' [An experience unavoidably arrived at by anyone as soon as he contemplates a seagull with this in mind]. I cannot help feeling that, if German *Möwe* had the gender of *Löwe*, the idea that they are all called Emil might have forced itself as inevitably on a beholder with the literary sensitivity of a Morgenstern, or with the linguistic sensitivity of a Grimm. But Morgenstern is at play, Grimm always in earnest: Morgenstern is aware that the feeling for the appropriateness of an appellation can be amusing and based on self-suggestion; Grimm was a frequent victim of self-suggestion when he let his linguistic erudition harden a vague, poetic feeling into what he thereafter accepted as a fact.

There is no evidence to tell us if allegory was known to the Anglo-Saxons before they were in touch with Latin Christianity, but it is unlikely. On the other hand, personification may well have existed before they met with it in Latin, though there is no evidence for that either.

In Latin, of course, abstractions, whether allegorized or not, are often feminine; for example, *philosophia* (as also its Greek etymon). The Old English equivalent is *wisdom*, which is masculine. Sometimes in Old English *wisdom* is personified. As it happens, whereas *wisdom* is masculine, *snyttro* 'sagacity' like *sapientia* and *gesceadwisnes* 'discrimination, reason' like *ratio* are feminine.

Alfred, translating (often very freely) Boethius or *The Soliloquies* of St Augustine, takes over many of the personifications of his source, and uses them regardless of gender. A very striking use of Wisdom personified, superficially regardless of the masculine gender of the word in Old English, comes in Alfred's exposition, erotic as it may seem, of St Augustine's *amator sapientiae* in the *Soliloquies* I.xiii:[158]

Ac ic wolde þæt wyt sohten nu hwilce ðæs wysdomes lufiendas beon scolen. Hu ne wost ðu nu þæt ælc þara manna þe oðerne swiðe lufað þæt hine lyst bet þaccian and cyssan ðone oðerne on bær lic, þonne þer þær claðas betweona beoð? Ic ongyte nu þæt lufast þone wisdom swa swiðe, and þe lyst hine swa

---

157 The opening lines of 'Möwenlied', M. Cureau (ed.), Christian Morgenstern, *Werke und Briefe*, III Humoristische Lyrik (Stuttgart, 1990), 86 and 310.
158 I quote, with some alteration, the text of W. Endter (ed.), *König Alfreds des Grossen Bearbeitung der Soliloquien des Augustinus*, [C. W. M. Grein's] Bibliothek der angelsächsischen Prosa, XI (1922; reprinted Darmstadt, 1964), 42-4. Cf. R. Waterhouse, 'Tone in Alfred's Version of Augustine's *Soliloquies*, in P. E. Szarmach (ed.), *Studies in Earlier Old English Prose* (Albany, New York, 1986), especially 68-71 'Lovers and Clothes'.

wel nacode ongitan and gefredan þæt þu noldest þæt*te* ænig clað betweuh
were. Ac he hine wyle swiðe seldon ænegum mæn swa openlice geawian; on
ðam timum þe he ænig lim swa bær eowian wile þonne eowað he hyt swiðe
feawum mannum. Ac ic nat hu þu hym onfon mage mid geglofedum handum;
ðu scealt æac don bær lic ongean gyf ðu hine gefredan wilt. Ac sege me nu gyf
ðu hwilc ænlic wif lofodest swiðe ungemetlice ofer æalle oððer þing, and heo
ðonne þe fluge and nolde þe lufian on nan oðer gera*d* butan þu woldest ælce
oðer lufe aletan for hyre anre lufe, woldest þu þonne swa don swa heo
wylnode? Ða cwæð ic: . . . Hu ne were þu ær geðafa þæt ic nanwiht ne lufode
ofer wisdom? . . . Ic ne lufige ðeah nan ðing æalles on ðam wisan þe ic ð*one*
wisdom lufige. Ælc þara þinga þe ic swiðost lufige, þa hwile þe ic hyt swiðost
lufige, ne an ic hy*s* nanum men butan me selfum, buton wisdome anum. Hine
ic lufige ofer eallum oðrum þing*um*; and þeah ic hys uðe ælcum men, minum
willan ælc man þe on þis myddangearde wære hine lufode and hym æfter
spirede and hyne æac funde, and hys syððan bruce; forðam ic wot þæt ure
lufede ælc oðerne swa micle swiðor swa ure willa and ure lufu swiðor on
anum were. Ða cwæð heo: Hu ne sæde ic ær, se se þe bær lic gefreddan wolde
þæt he hyt scolde myd barum gefredan? And ic segge eac, gyf þu ðone wisdom
selfne geseon wilt swa bærne, þæt þu ne scealt nannæ clað betweon lætan þinum
eagum and hym, ne furðum ne*nne* myst. To ðam ðu ne meaht þeah on þis
andweardan life becuman, þeah ic hyt þe lære and þea*h* ðu hys wilnige.

[But I should like that the two of us now find out of what kind the lovers of
Wisdom must be. Don't you know that every person who very much loves
another would rather pat and kiss the other on the naked body than where there
are clothes between them? I now apprehend that you so very much love
Wisdom, and so much long to get to know and perceive Wisdom nakedly that
you don't want that any clothes come between. But Wisdom will only rarely
appear so openly to anybody; at those times when Wisdom is willing to display
any part thus naked it is to very few persons. But I don't know how you can
receive Wisdom with gloved hands; you too must put your naked body against
Wisdom's if you wish to perceive Wisdom. But tell me now, supposing you
were to love a unique woman very boundlessly beyond everything else, and
she were then to shun you and would not love you on any other condition than
that you would renounce every other love for her love alone, would you then
do as she desired? Then I spoke: . . . Didn't you admit that I loved nothing
above Wisdom? . . . Yet I love nothing else the way I love Wisdom. Except only
Wisdom, everything that I love most for as long as I love it most, I will not
share any of it with anyone else. I love Wisdom beyond all else; and though I
were to share Wisdom with everyone I would willingly let everyone in this
world love, and search after, and find Wisdom too, and then enjoy Wisdom;
because I know that each of us would love the other by so much more as our
desire and love were more in unison. Then she [Philosophy] spoke: Didn't I
say before, whoever might wish to perceive the naked body must perceive it
with naked limbs? And I say moreover, if you want to see the very person of
Wisdom thus naked you must let no clothes come between your eyes and
Wisdom, not even any mist. To that, however, you cannot attain in this present
life, though I were to instruct you in it and though you were to wish for it.]

The Old English text uses masculine gender throughout for both Wisdom and the lover of Wisdom (as well as, of course, the pronouns referring to them); but in my translation I have avoided gender specificity for Wisdom. In the account of the boundless love for *sum ænlic wif*, however, we are dealing, by way of similitude, with a man's love for a woman, not with a relationship with an abstraction personified; and for the love of her the feminine gender seems appropriate in Modern English. By contrast, love of Wisdom is sexless in Alfred: the lover naked perceives Wisdom naked, and the sexlessness of it is proved by the unjealous pleasure felt when another shares in that love, unjealous when that other lover searches for Wisdom and finds Wisdom, unjealous even when the other lover too enjoys Wisdom. Wisdom, in Alfred's writing, remains an abstraction personified, and the eroticism is only a semblance in a love-relationship of mind and spirit.

Wisdom can stand for an aspect of the Second Person of the Trinity, as it does, together with Power, in I Corinthians 1:20-4:

Hath not God made the wisedom of this world folish? For because in the wisedom of God the world did not by wisedom know God: it pleased God by the folishnes of the preaching to saue them that beleeue. For both the Iewes aske signes, and the Greekes seeke wisedom: but we preach Christ crucified, to the Iewes certes a scandal, and to the Gentiles, folishnes: but to the called Iewes & Greekes, Christ the power of God and the wisedom of God.

There is no trace of Wisdom as the Second Person of the Trinity in Alfred's adaptation of *The Soliloquies*, though Wisdom is sought and, through the teaching of Philosophy, is to be found. A trace of it, however, occurs in Cynewulf's Epilogue to *Elene* lines 1239-42:[159]

Nysse ic gearwe

1240   be ðære [rode] riht   ær me rumran geþeaht
þurh ða mæran miht   on modes þeaht
wisdom onwreah.

[I did not know clearly the truth about the Cross, before Wisdom disclosed to me wider-ranging understanding in thought of mind through that glorious Power.]

Similarly, *Snyttro* 'Wisdom' is an allegorical aspect of God in *Christ I* lines 239-40:[160]

---

[159] Cf. A. S. Cook (ed.), *The Old English Elene, Phoenix, and Physiologus* (New Haven and London, 1919), 97, who makes the connection with I Corinthians 1:24, and, believing Cynewulf to be the poet of *Christ I* also, adduces also the use of *seo Snyttro* 'the Wisdom' at *Christ* line 239.

[160] See the preceding note, and A. S. Cook (ed.), *Christ* (2nd edn 1909; see IV[141]), 101; cf. J. J. Campbell (ed.), *The Advent Lyrics of the Exeter Book* (Princeton, 1959), 94 note on on Lyric VIII lines 26-7.

Þu eart seo snyttro   þe þas sidan gesceaft
240   mid þi waldende   worhtes ealle.

[Thou art the Wisdom that with God [the Father] didst shape
entirely this spacious creation.]

As has been pointed out in connection with *Christ I* lines 239-40 by its editor
A. S. Cook,[161] clear expression is given by Ælfric in a Catholic Homily that the
Wisdom is allegorically the Son of God and is as powerful as the Father:[162]

Crist is Godes Sunu swa þæt se Fæder hine gestrynde of him sylfum buton
ælc`e´re meder. Næfð se Fæder nænne lichaman, ne he in ða wisan his Bearn
ne gestrynde þe men doð. Ac his Wisdom, þe he mid ealle gesceafta geworhte,
se is his Sunu se is æfre of þam Fæder and mid þam Fæder, God of Gode, eall
swa mihtig swa se Fæder.

[Christ is the Son of God in that the Father begot him of himself without any
mother. The Father has no body, nor did he beget his Child in the manner
which humans do. But his Wisdom, with which he made all creatures, is his
Son who is ever of the Father and with the Father, God of God, even as
powerful as the Father.]

Less complex, less allegorical and less theological personifications are to be
found more frequently in the poetry. At *Guthlac A* line 275 hunger and thirst are
hearde gewinnan 'cruel adversaries'. It might be thought that that is a kenning,
yet, unlike true kennings, it is used, not in variation with its subject, but as a
predicate in the devils' speech of temptation, lines 271-7:

Ðu þæt gehatest   þæt ðu ham on *u*s
gegan wille.   Eart ðe Godes yrming:
bi hwon scealt þu lifgan,   þeah þu lond age?
Ne þec mon hider   mose fedeð;
275   beoð þe hungor ond þurst   hearde gewinnan
gif þu gewitest   swa wilde deor
ana from eþele.

[You vow that you wish to gain a home with us. God's indigent
you are: what are you to live on, though you possess land? No
one will feed you with victuals here; hunger and thirst will be
cruel adversaries to you if you go forth solitary from your
home as do wild beasts.]

Another personification is used at *Andreas* line 1088, a kenning for hunger, a
pale guest at table, perhaps, with wordplay on *gast* with long *ā*, a pale spectre at
the feast:

161 Cook's *Christ*, p. 101 note on line 239, with several further references.
162 My text is from N. Eliason and P. Clemoes (eds), *Ælfric's First Series of Catholic Homilies,
British Museum Royal 7 C. xii*, EEMF, XIII (1966), fo. 91ʳ; cf. B. Thorpe (ed.), *the Homilies
of Ælfric*, Ælfric Society, I, iii (1843), 258.

<pre>
1085   Þa wearð forht manig
          for þam færspelle folces ræswa,
          hean hygegeomor,   hungres on wenum,
          blates beodgastes.
</pre>

[Then many a prince of the people was afraid on account of
the terrible news, dejected, sad in mind, expecting hunger, that
pale guest at table.]

At *Christ III* line 972 fire is described in a personifying kenning as *se gifra
gæst* either 'that voracious guest' (or perhaps, with long *æ*, a kenning but not a
personification, 'that devouring spirit', or with wordplay on both senses),[163]
varied in the next line by *hiþende leg* 'ravaging flame'; followed at line 984a by
another personifying kenning *weallende wiga* 'a raging or seething warrior',
varying *fyrswearta leg* 'fiery-dark flame' of the preceding half-line, in the
account of the great conflagration on Judgement Day, lines 972-84:

<pre>
          Swa se gifra gæst   grundas geondseceð:
          hiþende leg   heahgetimbro
          fylleð on foldwong   fyres egsan,
975   widmære blæst   woruld mid ealle,
          hat heorogifre;   hreosað geneahhe
          tobrocene burgweallas;   beorgas gemeltað
          ond heahcleofu,   þa wið holme ær
          fæste wið flodum   foldan sceldun,
980   stið ond stæðfæst,   staþelas wið wæge,
          wætre windendum.   Þonne wihta gehwylce
          deora ond fugla   deaðleg nimeð,
          færeð æfter foldan   fyrswearta leg,
          weallende wiga.
</pre>

[Thus that voracious guest will overtake the regions, ravaging
flame will, with terror of fire, strike down the lofty buildings
on to the terrestrial plain, the flame famed far and wide, hot
(and) fiercely greedy, [will strike down] the world altogether;
utterly broken, the fortifications of cities will fall in plenty; the
mountains will melt and the towering cliffs that had protected
the land against the sea, stoutly against the floods, positions of
strength against the wave, against the eddying water. When the
deadly flame will seize every creature, beast and bird, fiery-
dark flame will run over the earth: a raging warrior.]

These are touches of personification, not more. For the poet there is a linguistic
link between the destructive action of the final conflagration on Judgement Day

---

163 Cf. *gæsthof*, in Cynewulf's *Christ II* line 820 (that is, in a poem on the Ascension, not now
   thought to be by the poet of *Christ III* on Judgement Day). Cf. the discussion of wordplay
   pp. 40-1, above.

and the ravages by fire and sword of a hostile army. The word *gifre* 'greedy' points that way, often in combination with *grædig*, its synonym; together used of hell fire in *Genesis B* line 793 where the Old Saxon source had only *gradag*,[164] and elsewhere; and the superlative *gifrost* is used of the flame of the great pyre for Hnæf in *Beowulf* lines 1122-4, again qualifying *gæst*, either (and here more probably) 'spirit' with long vowel, or with short vowel 'guest, visitant', or perhaps with wordplay on both senses:

> Lig ealle forswealg,
> gæsta gifrost, þara ðe þær guð fornam
> bega folces.

[Flame, greediest of spirits (? visitants), devoured all of those whom warfare had destroyed there of both nations.]

Fire and flame are readily anthropomorphized as the greediest of invaders, and it is impossible to tell if this is true personification, or, as I believe, only offering in descriptive epithets opportunity for anthropomorphic moments.

Wyrd 'issue, outcome', sometimes 'final outcome' — it is the feminine abstract noun related to the verb *weorðan* 'to become, to come to pass, to be' — may mean 'Fate' personified. The word is used in both verse and prose. This is not a matter of their poetic art, but of us seeking to understand how the Anglo-Saxons might have perceived an abstract to which mythologizing lends itself. The scholarship of this controversial subject is voluminous, with, forming one party in the dispute, those who see the word at every occurrence as a divinity originating in Germanic mythology and, where no longer pagan, as Providence in Christian theology, and, forming the other party (towards which I incline but am too eclectic to belong), those who doubt if the word, in the singular or plural, ever means more than 'issue, outcome', except when glossing or translating words for the Fates (or, less often, Fortune).[165] The Anglo-Saxons may not have distinguished sharply between anthropomorphic overtones and full-fledged personification.

In *Beowulf* it is easy to take *wyrd* as the abstract 'outcome' in such uses as lines 734-6:

---

[164] No Old Saxon cognate of *gifre* is recorded; for Old Saxon poetic usage of *gradag* with 'fire' and 'flame', cf. E. Sievers (ed.), *Heliand* (1878; 2nd edn with supplement by E. Schröder, 1935; see IV[16]), 409 'Formelverzeichnis' s.v. *feuer*. Cf. A. N. Doane (ed.), *The Saxon Genesis* (Madison, Wisconsin, 1991), 229 and 232.

[165] The following studies survey the subject and give many references: G. W. Weber, *'Wyrd' Studien zum Schicksalsbegriff der altenglischen und altnordischen Literatur*, Frankfurter Beiträge zur Germanistik, 8 (1969); B. J. Timmer, 'Wyrd in Anglo-Saxon Prose and Poetry', *Neophilologus*, xxvi (1941), 24-33, 213-28, and 'Heathen and Christian Elements in Old English Poetry', *Neophilologus*, xxix (1944), 180-5; and cf. E. G. Stanley, *Paganism* (1964-1965; reprinted 1975; see I[2]), reprint pp. 92-121.

Ne wæs þæt wyrd þa gen
735   þæt he ma moste   manna cynnes
ðicgean ofer þa niht.

[By no means was that the outcome that he might feed on
more of humankind after that night.]

Yet most of the translations into Modern English prose introduce an element of
fatalism, for example: D. Wright (1957) 'it was not his luck to devour any more
. . .', J. R. Clark Hall revised by Wrenn (1911, 1940 and 1950) 'That was no
longer his fortune, that he should devour more . . .', E. T. Donaldson (1966) 'It
was not his fate that . . .', C. B. Hieatt (1967) 'But it was not destined that he
would be able to partake . . .', G. N. Garmonsway (1968) 'But never again
would fate decree that he could take any more . . .'.[166] Of course, if the translators of the 1950s and '60s invest even this, to my mind, quite unfatalistic use
with the influence of a presumably supernatural agency, no wonder that they do
the same for line 455b: *Gæð a wyrd swa hio scel* 'The event always takes its
course as it must' if interpreted fatalistically is not far from 'Fate always goes as
it must', and this has been seen by an editor of Old English gnomic poetry as a
statement limiting the operation of Fate.[167]

In a superlative sequence, Fate, the manifestations of Nature, the Seasons,
Truth and Treasure, they all appear to be personifications in the Cotton *Maxims
II* lines 3-11:

Wind byð on lyfte swiftust,
þunar byð þragum hludast.   Þrymmas syndan Cristes myccle.
5   Wyrd byð swiðost.   Winter byð cealdost,
lencten hrimigost: he byð lengest ceald;
sumor sunwlitegost,   swegel byð hatost,
hærfest hreðeadegost   hæleðum bringeð
geres wæstmas   þa þe him God sendeð.
10   Soð bið swicolost.   Sinc byð deorost,
gold gumena gehwam.

[Wind is swiftest in the sky, thunder at times is loudest.
Christ's powers are great. Fate is strongest. Winter is coldest,
spring rimiest: it is cold the longest; summer (is) the most
beautiful and sunniest, the sun is the hottest, harvest-time is
glorious in its prosperity, brings to men the year's crops which
God sends them. Truth is the most deceptive.[168] Treasure, gold
is most precious for every man.]

166 D. Wright, *Beowulf* (Harmondsworth, 1957), 44; J. R. Clark Hall, *Beowulf*, revised by C. L.
Wrenn (1940; edn 1950, see II[64]), 58; E. T. Donaldson, *Beowulf* (New York, 1966; London
1967), 13; C. B. Hieatt, *Beowulf and Other Old English Poems* (Indianapolis, 1967), 38; G.
N. Garmonsway and J. Simpson, *Beowulf and Analogues* (1968; see I[66]), 21.
167 B. C. Williams (ed.), *Gnomic Poetry* (1914; see III[12]), 37.
168 Cf. C. W. M. Grein, *Sprachschatz der angelsächsischen Dichter* (Cassel and Göttingen,

The superlatives have the effect of inviting comparison. But with what? The wind with birds? Thunder with other noise-makers? The seasons with each other? Truth with all utterance and not as transparent as one might think? Treasure and gold with everything we desire? And fate, is Fate compared with God's powers and found stronger, as early commentators thought? Probably not, but the very act of comparison often suggests humanity as the yardstick.

If the emendation to *switolost* 'most open and transparent, clearest' is not accepted, then the manuscript of line 10a must be regarded as right, though paradoxical: *Soð bið swicolost* 'Truth is the most deceptive, deceitful'. Though someone has defined 'paradox' as 'Truth standing on its head to gain attention', the bald assertion, 'Truth is most untruthful', makes no obvious sense. As a personification, however, such a paradoxical reading might make sense. Truth becomes a speaking person, a truth-speaker. Set within an imagined juridical context, the words appear to mean, 'When witnesses are heard, the truth-speaker's testification will prove stronger than any liar's deception could.' That is perhaps too particular an imagined context for such a personification; the paradox *Soð bið swicolost* may mean, more generally, 'Truth will outargue Mendacity'.

The degree of personification depends also on how we translate pronouns: *he* in line 6, *lencten hrimigost: he byð lengest ceald*, might have been rendered by 'he' not by 'it'; and *hio* in *Beowulf* line 455b, *Gæð a wyrd swa hio scel*, might have been rendered by 'she'; and then we should have ensured a personifying perception of seasons and events. Languages in which gender has a firmer grammatical role than in Modern English slip more easily, imperceptibly as it seems at times, into personification than does Modern English. Old English was such a language; but it is far from certain that the Anglo-Saxons resorted to personification as easily and naturally as Romantic Critical Theory might lead one to expect.[169]

As regards *lencten*, there is little sign that in Old English literature it and the other seasons were habitually personified, as they are in many literatures, earlier and later. One thinks of Winter and Summer in debate,[170] in English not least at the end of *Love's Labour's Lost*. In Middle English that kind of personification

1861-1864), 511 s.v. *svicol* [retained in J. J. Köhler's revised edn (Heidelberg, 1912-1914), 658 s.v. *swicol*]: 'sich leicht entziehend, leicht entgehend?', perhaps 'readily evasive', an attractive rendering, but not supported by the semantic evidence for *swicol*, namely 'deceitful, deceptive'; and cf. T. A. Shippey (ed.), *Poems of Wisdom and Learning in Old English* (Cambridge and Totowa, New Jersey, 1976), 77 and 134, 'Truth is most deceptive'. Many editors emend to *switolost* 'the most evident', or attempt other emendations.

169 Other figurative ornaments in *Beowulf*, especially when weapons, the beasts of battle, buildings, ships, and natural phenomena appear to some extent sentient or volitional, are discussed as personifications by N. D. Isaacs, 'The Convention of Personification in *Beowulf*', in R. P. Creed (ed.), *Old English Poetry* (1967; see II¹²), 215-48.

170 Cf. H. Walther, *Das Streitgedicht in der lateinischen Literatur des Mittelalters*, Quellen und Untersuchungen zur lateinischen Philologie des Mittelalters, V/2 (Munich, 1920), *Altercatio Yemis et Estatis*, 37-45, 191-211.

leads to poetry such as is found in *The Owl and the Nightingale*, when the Owl says, lines 489-92:[171]

> Vor Sumeres tide is al to wlonc
> And doþ misreken monnes þonk,
> Vor he ne recþ noȝt of clennesse:
> Al his þoȝt is of golnesse.

[For the season of Summer is all too wanton and causes mankind's thought to go astray, for he [Summer – rather than *monn* 'man'] does not care for chastity: all his [Summer's] thinking is of lechery.]

In *Sir Gawain and the Green Knight*, after the wintry journey to the hospitable castle of Hautdesert, Gawain changes his armour for the fine clothes brought for him to wear, and the poet half-personifies Spring to describe how springlike Gawain looked after that change (lines 862-70):[172]

> Ryche robes ful rad renkkez hym broȝten
> For to charge and to chaunge and chose of þe best.
> Sone as he on hent and happed þerinne,
> 865 Þat sete on hyn semly wyth saylande skyrtez,
> Þe Ver by his uisage verayly hit semed
> Welneȝ to vche haþel, alle on hwes
> Lowande and lufly, alle his lymmez vnder
> Þat a comloker knyȝt neuer Kryst made
> 870   hem þoȝt.

[Men brought him very promptly splendid garments to put on and change into, making choice of the best. As soon as he had taken one and was clad in it, one that fitted him elegantly with flowing lower parts, truly by his looks he semed the very Spring almost to every one, all in colours brilliant and beautiful, and under his clothes his limbs such that, as it appeared to them, Christ had never made a handsomer knight.]

---

[171] See E. G. Stanley (ed.), *The Owl and the Nightingale* (London and Edinburgh, 1960; rev. edn, Manchester, 1972), 63 and the note on these lines (p. 117), with further references.

[172] See J. R. R. Tolkien and E. V. Gordon (eds), *Sir Gawain and the Green Knight* (2nd edn, revised by N. Davis; Oxford, 1967), 24 and (p. 100) the note on lines 864 ff. Cf. M. Andrew and R. Waldron (eds), *The Poems of the Pearl Manuscript* (London, 1978), 240; the suggestion, not rejected in this edition, that *ver* (line 866) is not 'spring' but a form of Old French *veir* 'fur' seems unlikely in the context and without *gris*; for the phrase *vaire and gryse* see *OED* s.v. *vair*, sb., *MED* s.v. *grīs*, n. (2), and cf. A. Tobler and E. Lommatzsch (eds), *Altfranzösisches Wörterbuch*, fascicule 88 ed. H. H. Christmann (Stuttgart, 1989), col. 87 s.v. *vair*.

Variation

Kennings often depend on the device of variation, appositional parallelism: by means of that device light may be shed on the sense of the kenning. When well used, variation singles out the centrally important, stressed word in a sentence and refers by another term or other terms to what the important word denotes. Words used in variation may be either synonymous or reveal different aspects of the central word. Fred C. Robinson gives a good definition:[173] 'Simply stated, I regard variation as apposition (Sweet's old term), if apposition be extended to include restatements of adjectives, verbs, and phrases as well as of nouns and pronouns.' Perhaps that definition is too wide if interpreted as including in the term variation unstressed finite verbs and pronouns.

A good example of variation of several kinds occurs in *Beowulf* lines 907-13:

> Swylce oft bemearn   ærran mælum
> swiðferhþes sið   snotor ceorl monig,
> se þe him bealwa to   bote gelyfde,
> 910   þæt þæt ðeodnes bearn   geþeon scolde,
> fæderæþelum onfon,   folc gehealdan,
> hord ond hleoburh,   hæleþa rice,
> eþel Scyldinga.

> [So too many a wise man, who looked to him for a remedy from afflictions, often regretted the exploit of the man strong in spirit in former times, that that prince's son was destined to prosper, was to accede to his paternal rank, was to rule the nation, the treasure and the citadel, a realm of warriors, the homeland of the Scyldings.]

The infinitive *gehealdan* has several objects in variation: *folc, hord ond hleo-burh, hæleþa rice,* and *eþel Scyldinga.* They are obviously not synonymous, but they refer to and magnify the central concept, namely, the polity over which Heremod, the subject of these lines, was to hold sway, listing one after the other aspects of that concept of governance. The finite verb *scolde* (line 910b) has three dependent infinitives: *geþeon, onfon* (with one dative object, *fæderæþelum*), and *gehealdan* (with the string of objects in variation). If we define variation as of *nomina* only (rather than of words bearing metrical stress, as I think we should), it could be argued that infinitives like participles and 'verbal nouns' are in verse in the same class of stress as *nomina.* Variation is not parallelism of units consisting of phrases with finite verbs as well as their nouns (object or subject) in variation. In this important respect, variation is very

---

[173] F. C. Robinson, 'Two Aspects of Variation in Old English Poetry', in D. G. Calder (ed.), *Old English Poetry* (1979; see I[71]), 127-45; his definition of the term is at p. 129. He gives valuable bibliographical references. Many examples from *Beowulf* are given by A. G. Brodeur in chapter ii 'Variation', in *Art of Beowulf* (1959; see II[59]), 39-70.

different from Hebrew parallelism familiar to us in translations of the Bible; for example, Psalm 5:2-6:

> Receive ô Lord my wordes with thine eares, vnderstand my crie.
> Attend to the voice of my prayer, my king and my God.
> Because I wil pray to thee: Lord in the morning thou wilt heare my voice.
> In the morning I wil stand by thee and wil see: because thou art not a God that wilt iniquitie.

Or with parallelism formally dependent on 'let', Psalm 34:4-6:

> Let them be counfounded & ashamed, that seeke my soule.
> Let them be turned backward, and be confounded that thinke euil against me
> Be they made as dust before the face of winde; and the angel of our Lord straictning them.
> Let their way be made darkenesse and slippernes: and the angel of our Lord pursewing them.

The quality of the Psalmist's parallelism in terms of poetic art is too bound up with the literary art of translation for an assessment to be possible without familiarity with Biblical Hebrew. In the psalms the poetic art of iteration of an idea, parallelism, is expressed by a whole clause; in Germanic poetry, the poetic art of iteration of an idea, variation, is expressed by single stressed words. Variation is found also in Old High German alliterative poetry, and especially in Old Saxon poetry which has had the advantage of S. Colliander's thorough systematizing of the patterns of variation.[174]

Skilfully used, variation is a neat resumptive device, helped by inflexional endings, for achieving clarity when within a sentence a parenthetical clause has to be bridged.[175] We must always have in mind that the Old English poetic manuscripts have no syntactic punctuation such as might clarify complicated sentence structures, certainly no dashes or parentheses. For example, in Hrothgar's 'sermon', *Beowulf* lines 1745-7 (where there is no punctuation in the manuscript):

> 1745 þonne bið on hreþre   under helm drepen
> biteran stræle   – him bebeorgan ne con –
> wom wundorbebodum   wergan gastes.

[Then he beneath his helmet is struck at heart by a sharp arrow – he does not know how to guard himself – by the crooked, mysterious instigations of the damned spirit.]

Variation is used occasionally to bring together opposites, contrary to its

---

[174] S. Colliander, *Der Parallelismus im Heliand* (1912; see II[63]).
[175] F. C. Robinson (1979; see IV[173]), 137, has introduced the term 'clarifying variation' when the device is used to achieve lucidity.

usual functions of clarifying the referent by synonyms for it or of aggrandizing it by further aspects. A good example of adversative variation[176] occurs near the beginning of *Elene* (lines 14-18):

> Hine God trymede
> 15 mærðum ond mihtum þæt he manegum wearð
> geond middangeard mannum to hroðer,
> werþeodum to wræce, syððan wæpen ahof
> wið hetendum.

[God strengthened him [Constantine] with glory and power, so that, to many throughout the world, he came to be a comfort to people, an affliction to nations, from the time that he first took arms against enemies.]

Manegum, mannum and *werþeodum* are in variation, the first two with *to hroðer*, the third with *to wræce* which has the opposite sense of *to hroðer*.

Hebrew parallelism, as far as may be discerned in translations of the Psalter, does not resort to chiasmus, but operates strictly in parallels; for example, Psalm 14:1: 'who shal dwel in thy tabernacle? or who shal rest in thy holie hil?' And similarly, Psalm 21:13: 'Manie calues have compassed me: fatte bulles haue besieged me.' In Old English variation chiastic order is common. For example, *The Dream of the Rood* lines 23-4:

> Hwilum hit wæs mid wætan bestemed,
> beswyled mid swates gange, hwilum mid since gegyrwed.

[At times it was with wetness bedewed, bedrenched with the flow of blood, at times with treasure adorned.]

The unstressed finite verb *wæs* governs three past participles in the three phrases: in the first, it ends the phrase; in the second it begins the phrase; and in the third it ends the phrase (which is introduced by *hwilum*).

In *Christ I* lines 408-10 three appellations are introduced for God, the last two of which are kennings: *weoroda God* 'God of hosts', *wigendra hleo* 'Protector of warriors' and *helm alwihta* 'Shield of all creatures'; in the first two appellations the genitive plural precedes, in the last it comes second, thus constituting a chiasmus of the elements of the kennings:

> þu eart weoroda God,
> forþon þu gefyldest foldan ond roderas,
> wigendra hleo, wuldres þines,
> 410 helm alwihta.

---

[176] Cf. C. Schaar, *Critical Studies in the Cynewulf Group*, Lund Studies in English, XVII (1949), 173 in his section on 'Adversative asyndeton', not, in fact, in his next section (pp. 184-234), his very good discussion of 'The Use of Variation'. I have used some of his examples of chiastic order as well as his example of a bad use of variation in *Andreas*.

[Thou art God of hosts, because thou, Protector of warriors, hast filled earth and the heavens with thy glory, Shield of all creatures.]

And similarly in the next Advent Lyric, *Christ I* lines 426-8, using *folca nergend* 'Saviour of nations' and *dryhten weoroda* 'Lord of hosts':

> Ond swa forðgongende   folca nergend
> his forgifnesse   gumum to helpe
> dæleð dogra gehwam,   dryhten weoroda.

[And so going forth the Saviour of nations, grants as a help to men forgiveness every day, the Lord of hosts.]

It is not easy for a modern reader faced with the device of variation to judge when it is used badly. It is so different from the poetic devices to which a reader of Middle English or Modern English verse is accustomed. We cannot be sure if the Anglo-Saxons were content when, within one set of variations, the same word was used twice, and the uncertainties of textual transmission have made editors and commentators indulge in variously happy and unhappy emendations to get rid of repetition within variation, imperfections as they seem to modern eyes.[177] I am not a great admirer of *Daniel*, and not unwilling to impute want of art to him; but, like the most recent editor of the poem,[178] I am not sure if the repetition of *ðeoden* 'lord' (referring to God) as well as of *dyrust* 'most precious, dearest' in 33-7 lines is to be regarded as a fault or as a rhetorical device which the Anglo-Saxons might have admired:

> Þa wearð reðemod   rices ðeoden,
> unhold þeoden   þam ðe æhte geaf.
> 35 Wisde him æt frymðe   ða ðe on fruman ær ðon
> wæron mancynnes   metode dyrust,
> dugoða dyrust,   drihtne leofost.

[Then the Lord of the realm grew angry, the Lord [grew] hostile to those to whom he had given dominion. He had guided them in the beginning, those who at first had previously been the dearest of humankind to the Lord, dearest among nations, most beloved to the Lord.]

This seems feeble; but I doubt if it is corrupt. The repetition seems to accord with the vapid variation of *æt frymðe* and *on fruman* in line 35. On the other

---

177 See the excellent discussion in F. C. Robinson, 'Two Aspects of Variation' (1979; see IV[173]), 138-45.

178 R. T. Farrell (ed.), *Daniel* (1974; see III[73]), 48-9 note on lines 33b-34a. Cf. Robinson, 'Two Aspects of Variation (1979; see IV[173]), 141. Manuscript *þeoden* causes difficulty at line 412 also, and is emended by almost all editors and commentators.

hand, the repetition in *Beowulf* lines 2283-4, 'Ða wæs hord rasod ‖ onboren beaga hord' [Then the hoard was opened up, the hoard of rings diminished] seems good. The order is chiastic. The verb *rasian* comes only here (*arasian* 'search out, open up' is more common), and there may be a gradation from *rasian* 'to open up, explore' to *onberan* 'to diminish, destroy'.

It is clear that the device of variation is not everywhere used with the skill shown by the poet of *Beowulf*. Sometimes the heaping up by variation increased by an 'and' phrase may seem excessive to modern taste. Thus in *Andreas* lines 195-8, the saint's speech labouring the praise of the skill in seamanship characteristic of God's angel:

> 195   Con him holma begang,
> sealte sæstearmas[179]   ond swanrade,
> waroðfaruða gewinn   ond wæterbrogan,
> wegas ofer widland.

> [He knows the expanse of the seas, the salt ocean streams and the swan's way, the perturbation of the eddying surf and marine terrors, the paths over distant lands.]

One may doubt if the *Andreas* poet's piety justifies his use of repetitive epithets at lines 325-6 and their repetition word for word at lines 702-3:

> w(e)aldend ond wyrhta   wuldorþrymmes,
> an ece God   eallra gesceafta.

> [Lord and Creator of glorious might, one eternal God of all creatures.]

At least, it can be said that God matters in the poem, and the nature of praise of God, as shown in the liturgy, is that repetition cannot easily be too much: it is to be presumed that there shall be joy in heaven, not a sinful, bored sense of having heard it all before, when souls in bliss hear the angelic choirs praise God reiteratively for as long as eternity lasts. The heaping of terms for the sea in order to give expression to the angel's skill as a seaman, however, is far less excusable on religious grounds, and not at all perhaps on literary grounds; the enthusiastic poet pulled out the stop Maritime Variation because it chanced to be ready to hand.

Similarly, in *The Battle of Maldon*, Offa's speech has (at lines 232-7) an inessential accumulation of weapons, in variation. No doubt, the versifier recalled happier uses of such variation when greater poets sang of arms and the

---

[179] MS *sæstearmas* is usually emended to *sæstreamas*; but see A. Campbell, *Grammar* (1959; see III[32]), § 459 (4), 'Low stress promotes metathesis of *r*'; and cf. F. C. Robinson, 'Metathesis in the Dictionaries: A Problem for Lexicographers', in A. Bammesberger (ed.), *Problems of Old English Lexicography: Studies in Memory of Angus Cameron*, Eichstätter Beiträge, 15 (Regensburg, 1985), 245-65.

man, and brought back the tumult of war in high-sounding words of gleaming weapons and armour, the clash of shields, and the shouting of men. In the extant Old English poetry, so much of it religious, little space is given to that. In the messenger's speech near the end of *Beowulf* (lines 3021-2) *gar . . . // monig morgenceald* [many a morning-cold spear], unvaried, serves only as a symbol for a last, brave stand. An echo of martial poetry is, however, a strong feature of the beginning of *Elene* when Huns and Goths, Franks and Hugas, gather under arms for that battle of nations, and Constantine conquered in the sign of the Cross. There, at lines 23b-24a, *garas lixtan, // wriðene wælhlencan* [spears gleamed, woven coats of mail], with the rare kenning *wælhlenca* the first part of which means 'corpse, slaughter' and the second 'linked ring' (for ring-armour). That is the background for the words which in *The Battle of Maldon* are put into the mouth of Offa, who, after varying effectively *þeoden* 'lord' with *eorl* 'earl', has said, with the formula[180] *habban and healdan* 'to have and to hold', all he has to say by way of encouraging Byrhtnoth's men to die on the field on which their lord was slain; but, before resuming his theme of encouraging all to die, he is made to lose his way in vapid variation of weapons without achieving emphasis on either valour or self-sacrifice (lines 232-7):

> Nu ure þeoden lið,
> eorl on eorðan, us is eallum þearf
> þæt ure æghwylc oþerne bylde,
> 235 wigan to wige, þa hwile þe he wæpen mæge
> habban and healdan, heardne mece,
> gar and god swurd.

[Now that our lord lies dead, the earl on the ground, it is needful for us all that each of us should encourage the other, (each) warrior to the fight, for as long as he can maintain and hold a weapon, a hard blade, a spear and a mighty sword.]

Though the device of variation may give emphasis to an unimportant element in the discourse when badly handled, that is rare. When handled well, the device enables a skilful poet to wield long sentences and still retain clarity. Good examples are to be found in *Beowulf*; thus lines 874-84:

> Welhwylc gecwæð
> 875 þæt he fram Sigemunde secgan hyrde,
> ellendædum, uncuþes fela,
> Wælsinges gewin, wide siðas,
> þara þe gumena bearn gearwe ne wiston,
> fæhðe ond fyrena, buton Fitela mid hine

---

[180] It is used also, for example, in poetry at *Christ III* line 1648, and in the Wulfstanian laws, II Cnut 66,1; see F. Liebermann, *Gesetze*, I (1898-1903; see IV[151]); and cf. D. Whitelock, 'Wulfstan and the Laws of Cnut', *EHR* 63 (1948), 433-52.

880   þonne he swulces hwæt   secgan wolde,
       eam his nefan,   swa hie a wæron
       æt niða gehwam   nydgesteallan,
       hæfdon ealfela   eotena cynnes
       sweordum gesæged.

[He said everything that he had heard tell of Sigemund, of
deeds of valour, much that was little known, the strife of the
son of Wæls, distant journeys of which the children of men
would not have known readily, the feuding and the crimes, had
not Fitela (been) with him whenever he wished to say something of such a matter, the uncle to his nephew, as they always
were in all hostilities comrades in peril, had humbled a great
multitude of the race of giants with their swords.]

The poet of *Beowulf* singles out, by means of variation, elements for emphasis (as, for example, in lines 875-7), each new item providing new information. He uses variation also to give clarity to the structure of the sentence,
especially when resuming what was first expressed by a pronoun (as, for
example, in lines 879b-82). In the hands of this poet the device of variation
probably does not become tedious to most modern readers who, if they wish,
can justify its use on the grounds that it helps the listener or reader to understand
a complex sentence. That, however, is not a good argument for justifying a
poetic ornament which often operates by expressing more than the minimum
needed for comprehension: economy of utterance cannot justify poetic
ornamentation, and figurative language may please without being a necessity.

It is in the nature of variation to increase the density of stressed words,
especially of nouns, with the effect of greater stasis in the narration than we are
used to in narrative verse. In Modern English lively movement is achieved by a
versatile use of finite verbs, and, as we have seen earlier in this chapter (pp.
152-3), the poet of *Judith* employs variation including variation of nouns to give
a sense of movement at one point of the narrative.

Older English-speaking readers may have received, at first or second hand,
some part of their sensibility of what is good style in Modern English usage
from H. W. Fowler (and Sir Ernest Gowers) who treated 'elegant variation' as an
object of derision to be avoided in Present English.[181] We learnt that we must
avoid calling Rome anything other than Rome. No elegancy will serve in
modern variation, 'the Eternal City, the City of the Seven Hills, the Papal City,
the Empress of the Ancient World, the Western Babylon', and more matter-of-
fact appellations, like 'the Italian capital', all alike are to be shunned: just repeat

---

[181] H. W. Fowler (ed.), *A Dictionary of Modern English Usage* (Oxford, 1926; 2nd edn, ed. Sir
Ernest Gowers, Oxford 1965), s.vv. *elegant variation* and *sobriquet*. A good account of the
work and its faults is given by R. W. Burchfield, 'The Fowler Brothers and the Tradition of
Usage Handbooks', in G. Leitner (ed.), *English Traditional Grammars* (Amsterdam and
Philadelphia, 1991), 93-111.

'Rome' or use 'there' for 'in Rome', in such sentences as, 'It was her first visit to Rome, and, in spite of the heat, she enjoyed her time in Rome.' We have to unlearn the Fowlerian prescription probably for much poetry in most languages of most ages, and certainly for Old English verse. Apparent novelty in Old English variation occurs, but whether it is truly new is not demonstrable since we can never know what figure was newly coined and admired as a novelty. Comparison with verse in other Germanic languages may help us to identify what figure reaches back to a venerated antiquity and was perhaps recognized as such by the Anglo-Saxons and perhaps admired by the Anglo-Saxons because they too loved ancient things and locutions, as Anglo-Saxonists, who, as a class, love ancient things and locutions, would wish and hope.

V

Prayers, Praise, and Thanksgiving in Old English Verse

Pagan or Christian?

'Pagan or Christian?': that old contrariety has long been laid to rest, one had hoped given decent burial,[1] though perhaps still manifesting an occasional galvanic spasm.[2] On the other hand, Heusler's less loaded 'secular and ecclesiastic', 'weltlich und kirchlich' (rather than 'pagan or Christian?', 'heidnisch oder christlich'?) has more life in it.[3] Those who like to construct diagrammatic presentations of evidence could produce a pie diagram with, for Old English verse, a large slice 'ecclesiastic and Christian', a goodly slice 'secular and Christian' with *Beowulf* a tasty morsel in it, and a tiny slice for 'pagan and secular' with some of the metrical charms perhaps, the pagan elements of which may well be, in the extant, mainly monastic manuscripts, superstitious survivals with only the rarest recollections of prayer to the gods of pre-Christian English antiquity.

Some lines from 'The Nine Herbs Charm' are often quoted, especially lines 30-3 in which Woden is mentioned:

30 Ðas *nigon magon*[4] wið nygon attrum.
  † Wyrm com snican, toslat he nan.
   Ða genam Woden *nigon* wuldortanas.
   Sloh ða þa næddran þæt heo on *nigon* tofleah.

---

1 For an attempt to contribute towards a record of the life and death of that debate, see E. G. Stanley, *Paganism* (1964-1965; see I[2]); cf. L. D. Benson, 'The Pagan Coloring of *Beowulf*', in R. P. Creed (ed.), *Old English Poetry* (1967; see II[12]), 193-213.

2 See, for example, J. D. Niles, 'Pagan survivals and popular belief', in M. Godden and M. Lapidge (eds), *The Cambridge Companion* (1991; see II[33]), 126-41, who treads in the footsteps of W. Bonser, 'Survivals of Paganism in Anglo-Saxon England', *Transactions of the Birmingham Archaeological Society*, Proceedings for 1932, 56 (1934), 37-70. See also E. A. Philippson, *Germanisches Heidentum bei den Angelsachsen*, Kölner anglistische Arbeiten, 4 (1929), who assembles much pagan material well.

3 A. Heusler, *Altgermanische Dichtung* (Wildpark-Postdam, 1923; 2nd edn, Potsdam, 1941), 146.

4 Manuscript *VIIII ongan*.

[These nine avail against nine poisons. [Sign of the Cross.] A
serpent came crawling, it bit none to death. Then Woden took
nine twigs of glory. He struck then the adder so that it flew
apart into nine pieces.]

The text is preserved in British Library MS Harley 585, which has been described as a 'medico-magical commonplace book';[5] but then English medicine
before such pioneering work as that of William Harvey, William Withering and
Edward Jenner would hardly be respected as scientific by modern practitioners,
and continental medicine was no better. Anglo-Saxonists have been so lost in
admiration that in this charm Woden is named, and is surrounded by many nines
– dare one hope, magic nines? – that they have made much of that, but they have
made less of the fact that the herbs are the addressees of the charmer's words
(lines 1-3):

> Gemyne ðu, mucgwyrt,   hwæt þu ameldodest,
> hwæt þu renadest   æt Regenmelde.
> Una þu hattest,   yldost wyrta.

[Remember thou, O Mugwort, what thou didst make known,
what thou didst arrange at the Great Parliament. Thou art
called Una, foremost of herbs.]

Is this address to the herb a relic of paganism? Is its form ancient? It matters
when assessing the nature of prayer-like apostrophes in Old English literature.
For there are many prayers in Old English, of course; it could not be otherwise
in such a dominantly Christian literature.

For two centuries or so, and still occasionally, Germanic scholars, many of
them in real life mild bookish people at their desks, have sought out as their
favourites, not the Christian verities in Anglo-Saxon poems, but rather the
Teutonic antiquities. As if driven to it by the subject-matter of the poems, they
strive to reconcile the martial and heroic manifestations in Bible-story and
hagiography with the wished-for Teutonism. These are the characteristic preoccupations and predilections of most earlier Germanic scholars, and of some
modern Germanic scholars to this day.

Perhaps in the lost world of pre-Christian, pre-Cædmonian Anglo-Saxon
poetry, the direction of the Anglo-Saxons' own interest was not in prayer either.

---

5 Thus by J. H. G. Grattan and C. Singer, *Anglo-Saxon Magic and Medicine Illustrated
Specially from the Semi-Pagan Text 'Lacnunga'*, Publications of the Wellcome Historical
Medical Museum, 3 (London, 1952), 95 and running title; the appellation is accepted and
extended to the whole manuscript by C. E. Wright (ed.), *Bald's Leechbook British Museum
Royal Manuscript 12 D. xvii*, EEMF, V (Copenhagen, 1955), 29. Grattan and Singer print
'The Nine Herbs Charm' (with translation) at pp. 150-7, and have for it a wonderful title and
subtitles. In the manuscript the charm has no title, as is usual. Cf. G. Storms (ed.), *Anglo-
Saxon Magic* (The Hague, 1948), p. 24; he prints the text (with translation) at pp. 186-91.

But that speculation provides scholars and critics with no excuse for seizing on the few vestiges of a supposed paganism as the firm basis of Teutonic glory, with the plentifully extant Christian poetry as a sad decline. One is reminded of Wordsworth critics held fast in the young Wordsworth's enthusiastic attitudes to the French Revolution and resenting the adult poet's distancing himself from the presentation of it 'as it appeared to Enthusiasts at its Commencement'.[6]

Cædmon

Because we know nothing of Old English writings till we have Christian writings it is essential that we look especially hard at the evidence we have for the beginning of Anglo-Saxon Christian verse in the vernacular. The Anglo-Saxons themselves took a deep interest in their origins, not merely where on the continent they had their roots, but also in how they received the new faith, and in how that new faith was given utterance in their vernacular, a language inherited of course from pagan times.

The earliest English poet of whom we have both the name and some lines of verse is Cædmon.[7] Bede celebrated the beginning of English Christian verse in his account of how the gift of song came to Cædmon, a neat-herd of the monastery of Whitby (Streoneshealh) during the time when St Hild was abbess (AD 657 to 680).[8] Bede's pious account is not to be read by us *de haut en bas* as a characteristic piece of medieval hagiography, a load of chaff from which some grains of fact may perhaps be won by a careful process of historical winnowing. Nor is the extant poem itself, *Cædmon's Hymn*, to be considered as a poor Christian thing which one would gladly trade in for any one of the secular songs sung by Cædmon's fellow-servants at the beer-drinking.

There was merry conviviality, Bede tells us, and everybody present took his turn and sang when the harp, as it went round, was in his hands. But Cædmon, the songless man, left the group of monastery servants, and tended cattle till he fell asleep. A man came to him in his dream, and spoke to him saying that he should sing *principium creaturarum* [the beginning of all creation]. Cædmon did so, and, because he derived his existence as a poet from God himself, *non ab hominibus neque per hominem* [not from human beings nor through a human being], he sang with greater skill and with a higher seriousness than any ordinary singer. Bede speaks of the source of Cædmon's poetic calling in words reminiscent of St Paul's on his apostolic calling (in the opening verse of

---

6   Cf. the title 'FRENCH REVOLUTION as it appeared to Enthusiasts at its Commencement', E. de Selincourt (ed.), *The Poetical Works of William Wordsworth*, II (Oxford, 1944), 264.

7   Cf. E. G. Stanley, 'The Oldest English Poetry Now Extant' (1974, pp. 1-24; reprinted 1987, pp. 127-31); see III[2]); and E. G. Stanley, 'New Formulas for Old' (1994; see IV[12]).

8   B. Colgrave and R. A. B. Mynors (eds), *Bede's Ecclesiastical History*, IV, xxiv (1969; see III[16]), 414-21.

Galatians), 'Paul an Apostle not of men, neither by man, but by Jesus Christ, and God the Father'.

Nine lines of song in praise of God the Creator are all we have: they form the beginning of Cædmon's divine gift. Some critics make these lines sound inferior: 'their short abrupt rhythm suggests a late rather than an early date';[9] 'incomplete control is suggested in some unemphatic repetitions, as if the poet seized on e.g. *Ece Drihten* (Eternal Lord) because the phrase was a metrical half-line and made a sensible statement';[10] 'it is easy to see how [Bede's] story could be turned into a miracle, and how "Caedmon's Hymn" could be tailored to fit the legend';[11] 'Parallelism and variation can be used with more propriety and skill than Caedmon shows here'.[12] 'Cædmon's simple nine-line hymn, unpretentious, trivial even, by later standards'.[13]

It is improbable that any modern reader, no matter how keen on Old English verse should come to *Cædmon's Hymn* in the venerative spirit in which it is likely to have been received by the monks of Hild's abbey when the poem was first communicated – should one presume, sung? – by Cædmon. Bede, when he lay dying and uttered his *Death Song*, seems not to have had need of a harp, and Cuthbert describing the scene does not advert to the lack of a harp. Bede nowhere mentions the harp in connection with Cædmon's divinely inspired song or poetry. The view sometimes expressed that for the nine lines of verse which we call *Cædmon's Hymn* his own delivery must have been to the harp is no more than a speculation, perhaps based on the comparative study of Christian hymnody, perhaps based on the mention of making music *bi hearpe* 'to the harp' in *Widsith* (line 105), by many still thought to be an early poem,[14] perhaps based on the not infrequent mention of the harp in *Beowulf* and the finding at Sutton Hoo of fragments which more than once have led to reconstructions of a harp or lyre.[15] It cannot be based on what is known of the music of Anglo-Saxon England, for none is known from before the Benedictine Reform in the late tenth century, liturgical music that has been shown to owe much to the Church

9 Stopford A. Brooke, *History of Early English Literature* (1892; see II[74]), II, 71-2 footnote quoting *Cædmon's Hymn*.
10 J. E. Cross, in W. F. Bolton (ed.), *The Middle Ages*, Sphere History of Literature in the English Language, I (London, 1970), 20.
11 D. Pearsall, *Old English and Middle English Poetry* (1977; see II[18]), 27.
12 M. Alexander, *Old English Literature*, in A. N. Jeffares (ed.), Macmillan History of English Literature (London and Basingstoke, 1983), 52.
13 M. J. Swanton, *English Literature before Chaucer* (1987; see I[81]), 71.
14 Thus Kemp Malone (ed.), *Widsith* (1936; see I[45]), 54, retained in 2nd edn (1962), 116: 'The evidence of the language . . . leads us to conclude that *Widsith* was composed and reduced to writing in the latter part of the seventh century'; and 56-7 (2nd edn, 117): 'We may conclude that the metrical confirms the linguistic evidence pointing to an early date of composition'. But see G. Langenfelt, 'Studies on *Widsith*', *Namn och Bygd*, 47 (1959), 70-111.
15 See pp. 42-4, above.

music better recorded on the continent, and is unlikely to owe anything to the music of pre-Christian English song.[16]

Bede writing of Cædmon's singing uses *canere* and *cantare* both of which can mean either 'to sing' or 'to recite verse', and also *dicere carmen* 'to recite a song'.[17] He gives details of the regulation of singing at the monastery servants' merry-making, *ut omnes per ordinem cantare deberent* [that they should all sing in turn], and speaks of Cædmon leaving *ubi adpropinquare sibi citharam cernebat* [when he saw the harp approaching him]. In the standard edition by B. Colgrave and R. A. B. Mynors, there is an explanatory footnote attached to *cithara* 'harp' in which the editors describe the first reconstruction; the second, with different dimensions, was made after the publication of their edition:

> The type of harp which was passed round would probably be like the one reconstructed from the fragments found in the hanging bowl at Sutton Hoo, which is now in the British Museum. It is about 6 in. high and could easily be passed from hand to hand. Unfortunately Bede tells us neither the nature nor the substance of the songs sung. The context implies that they may have been 'foolish or trivial', which might mean simple folk-songs or ballads and possibly some heroic fragments. Again Bede does not tell us whether they were made up for the occasion, either on the spot or beforehand, but again the context suggests that they were traditional songs which Cædmon for some reason had never learned.

In short, the monastery servants at their merry-making performed, in the unfounded opinion of these editors, much of the repertoire of genres of Germanic song in accordance with Romantic and post-Romantic theory, longed for in vain by their fond hearts within the extant literary corpus.

Let us return to the first audience, the monks of Whitby. When on the morrow of Cædmon's night of dream-vision, they heard him and reflected on the pre-Christian poetry of the English, known to them but lost to us, and as they ranged the new song in the same category of intellectual experience, it is not unlikely that they felt the wonder of it, that the latest song which they received was the best, in much the same way as did at the Marriage in Cana (John 2:1-11) the 'cheefe steward' (Rhemes), 'the gouernor of the feast' (Authorized Version), 'But thou hast kept the good wine vntil now'. *Carmen dulcissimum* [the sweetest song], Bede calls Cædmon's paraphrases of Holy Scripture which followed that first song. By divine gift song came to Cædmon, in a way reminiscent of the gift of tongues of many prophets in many civilizations; but there is nothing vatic in Cædmon's song, neither in the hymn of praise of God the Creator which we have, nor, probably, in the biblical paraphrase which he instituted in English,

---

[16] See S. Rankin, 'From memory to record: musical notations in manuscripts from Exeter', *ASE*, 13 (1984), 97-112.

[17] B. Colgrave and R. A. B. Mynors (eds), *Bede's Ecclesiastical History*, IV, xxiv (1969; see III[16]), 416-18.

and of which none of his making survives. That Bodleian MS Junius 11, containing *Genesis A* and *B*, *Exodus*, *Daniel*, and *Christ and Satan*, is often called 'The Cædmon Manuscript', is due to the belief by early scholars that these poems were by Cædmon;[18] and now perhaps the name is retained because it indicates that these poems belong to a class of biblical paraphrase in vernacular verse which, according to Bede, was Cædmon's gift to the English people.

The ubiquity of prayer in Old English writings in prose and verse

In the extant Old English prose and verse prayers come often, whether we like it or not. Presumably, the wording of Latin Christian liturgy, including, of course, the psalms, underlie the wording of formal prayers. Perhaps Irish Latin Christianity has contributed to wording not directly relatable to Roman Latin liturgy;[19] but most often Roman and Irish liturgy agree in wording.

There are poetic renderings of liturgy, such as paraphrases of the Lord's Prayer, the Gloria and the Creed, as exemplified in the verse of the Wulfstanian Benedictine Office.[20] In a literary judgement, the best Old English versified prayers are the paraphrases of the O's of Advent, the twelve lyrics with which the Exeter Book opens (incomplete at the beginning).[21] The Latin antiphons to which these lyrics go back take their name from their opening with the exclamation 'O' (*Eala* in the Old English translation). The Latin antiphons are subtle and varied expressions of piety, and the Old English versions, which often differ from their source, are similar in that quality. The seventh Advent lyric, for which no source is known, has within it speeches spoken alternately by the Virgin Mary and Joseph, and some have sought and found in it a piece of Anglo-Saxon dramatic endeavour, as they read with the characteristic hindsight of the literary historian 'this vivid anticipation of the later medieval mystery plays'.[22] It is seen as drama, partly, because most of the speeches have no indication of who is

18 See the earliest reference, Franciscus Junius, the Younger, *Observationes in Willerami Abbatis Francicam Paraphrasin Cantici canticorum* (Amsterdam, 1655), 248; reprinted in facsimile, N. Voorwinden (ed.), Early Studies in Germanic Philology, 1 (Amsterdam, and Atlanta, Georgia: 1992).

19 Cf. H. Gneuss, 'Anglo-Saxon Libraries from the Conversion to the Benedictine Reform', *Settimane di studio del Centro italiano di studi sull'alto medioevo*, XXXII (Spoleto, 1986), 660; and especially P. Sims-Williams, *Religion and Literature in Western England, 600–800* (Cambridge, 1990), ch. 10 'Prayer and magic'.

20 See J. Ure (ed.), *The Benedictine Office*, Edinburgh University Publications Language & Literature, 11 (1957), 83-9; also ASPR, VI, pp. 74-80.

21 See J. J. Campbell (ed.), *Advent Lyrics* (1959; see IV[160]).

22 Cf. R. Wülker, *Grundriss zur Geschichte der angelsächsischen Litteratur* (Leipzig, 1885), 385-6: 'Dramatische Bestrebungen der Angelsachsen' [Dramatic Endeavours of the Anglo-Saxons], inevitably a very brief section in the survey. The phrase quoted is from M. Alexander, *Old English Literature* (1983; see V[12]), 170.

speaking; but that is not so in the case of the Virgin's final speech to Joseph (VII, 32b-50 = *Christ* lines 195b-213):

<blockquote>
195   Þa seo fæmne onwrah
ryhtgeryno,   ond þus reordade:
"Soð ic secge   þurh Sunu Meotudes,
gæsta Geocend,   þæt ic gen ne conn
þurh gemæcscipe   monnes ower,
200 ænges on eorðan,   ac me eaden wearð,
geongre in geardum,   þæt me Gabrihel,
heofones heagengel,   hælo gebodade,
sægde soðlice   þæt me swegles Gæst
leoman onlyhte: sceolde ic Lifes Þrym
205 geberan, beorhtne Sunu,   Bearn eacen Godes,
torhtes Tirfruman.   Nu ic his tempel eam
gefremed butan facne,   in me Frofre Gæst
geeardode,   nu þu ealle forlæt
sare sorgceare.   Saga ecne þonc
210 mærum Meotodes Sunu   þæt ic his modor gewearð,
fæmne forð seþeah,   ond þu fæder cweden
woruldcund bi wene.   Sceolde witedom
in him sylfum beon   soðe gefylled."
</blockquote>

[Then the Virgin revealed the true mystery, speaking thus: 'Truth I utter through the Son of God, the Saviour of souls, that I have still not known at any time a man by sexual union, not any on earth, but to me, young in my dwellings, it was granted that Gabriel, heaven's archangel, offered me a salutation, saying truly that the heavenly Spirit would illumine me with radiance. I am destined to bear the Glory of Life, the luminous Son, the great Child of God, of the bright Prince of Glory. Now that I am his temple, made immaculate, the Paraclete in me indwelling, so now do you leave off all grievous and sorrowful anguish. Give eternal thanks to the glorious Son of God that I have become his mother, a virgin henceforth none the less, and you, in the supposition of the world, called (his) father. The prophecy was to be truly fulfilled in Himself.']

Echoes of prayers and psalms are to be heard in many Old English poems, and that is not to be wondered at: we may assume that the literate poets of the extant verse were steeped in the wording of church services, since medieval literacy north of the Alps has its roots and its first practice in Christianity.

Thus lines 97-102 of *The Seafarer* have been connected with verses of Psalm 48 as rendered and explained in the Paris Psalter, together with its argument:[23]

---

[23] For the argument and text of the psalm, see J. W. Bright and R. L. Ramsay (eds), *Liber Psalmorum The West-Saxon Psalms being the prose portion . . . of the . . . Paris Psalter* (Boston, Massachusetts, and London, 1907), 114, and cf. B. Colgrave (general ed.) *The Paris*

    Þeah þe græf wille   golde stregan
    broþor his geborenum, byrgan be deadum,
    maþmum mislicum   þæt hine mid wille,
100 ne mæg þære sawle þe biþ synna ful
    gold to geoce   for Godes egsan,
    þonne he hit ær hydeð þenden he her leofað.

[Though a brother desires to strew with gold his brother's grave, to bury him among the dead with divers treasures which he [the survivor] wishes to go with him [the dead], before the terror of God gold cannot be of avail to the soul that is full of sins, when he had been keeping it in a hiding-place during his life-time here.]

The argument of Psalm 48 is:

Dauid sang þysne eahta and feowertigoðan sealm, on þam he lærde ealle men, ge on his dagum ge æfter his dagum, þæt hy hy upp ne ahofen for heora welum, and þæt hy ongeaton þæt hi ne mihton þa welan mid him lædan heonon of weorulde; and eac he lærde þæt þa ðearfan hy ne forðohton ne ne wenden þæt God heora ne rohte. And eac he witgode þæt ealle rihtwise menn sceoldon þæt ylce læran; and eac þæt Crist wolde þæt ylce læran þonne he come.

[David sang this forty-eighth psalm, in which he taught all people, both in his time and after his time, that they would not elevate themselves on account of their riches, and that they might learn that they could not take those riches away with them out of this world; and also he taught that they should not despise the needy nor suppose that God did not care about them. And also he uttered as a prophet that all the righteous must teach that same doctrine; and that Christ likewise would teach that whenever he comes.]

In the Paris Psalter Psalm 48:7-10 is rendered and explained:

Psalter, EEMF, VIII (1958), fos 59ʳ-59ᵛ. For the Vulgate, I quote the Doway rendering (as usual in this book), though that is not of the Roman Psalter; cf. K. Sisam, '*Seafarer* lines 97-102', *RES*, 21 (1945), 316-17, 'Now compare Psalm 48 in the Roman version (the Gallican or Hebrew would serve)'; and note K. and C. Sisam, EEMF, VIII (1958), 16/1:

    The method of rendering varies from pure translation to translation with
    explanatory comment . . . The text translated is generally that of the
    Roman psalter, though occasionally the rendering agrees with Jerome's
    Gallican or Hebrew versions.

That the prose psalms and prefaces are by King Alfred has been advanced especially by J. I'a. Bromwich, 'Who was the translator of the prose portion of the Paris Psalter?', in C. Fox and B. Dickins (eds), *The Early Cultures of North-West Europe (H. M. Chadwick Memorial Studies)* (Cambridge, 1950), 289-303, confirmed by several of the studies listed in E. G. Stanley, 'The Scholarly Recovery' (1981; see I⁵⁶), 240 note 57, reprinted in *A Collection of Papers* (1987; see I⁴⁵), 23 note 57. For *The Seafarer* lines 97-102, see, in addition to Sisam's article, I. L. Gordon (ed.), *The Seafarer* (London, 1960), 45-6. For the text and the translation of the end of the poem, see also E. G. Stanley, *A Collection of Papers*, 270-1, note 50.

Ongitan nu, þa þe truwiað heora agenum mægene, and þære mycelness hiora speda gylpað and wuldrað:

Þæt nan broðor oþres sawle nele alysan of helle, ne ne mæg, þeah he wylle, gif he sylf nanwuht nyle ne ne deð to góóde þa hwile ðe he her byð. Gylde for þy him sylf and alyse his sawle þa hwyle þe he her sy; for þam se broðor oþþe nyle oððe ne mæg, gif he sylf na ne onginð to tilianne þæt he þæt weorð agife to alysnesse his sawle; ac þæt ys wyrse þæt full neah ælc mann þæs tiolað, fram þæm anginne his lifes oþ þæne ende, hu he on ecnesse swincan mæge.

[Let them now understand, those who put trust in their own strength, and boast of and glory in the greatness of their riches: that no brother can redeem another's soul from hell, though he wishes to, if he himself will not at all (do so) nor act for his benefit while he is here (on earth). May he himself therefore achieve his reward and redeem his soul while he is here; because his brother is either unwilling or unable (to do so), if he himself in no way begins to strive that he may pay the price for the redemption of his soul; but that is worse that almost everyone, from the beginning of his life till the end, strives how he may travail for ever.]

In the Vulgate (Doway translation) Psalm 48:7-10 reads:

They that trust in their strength: and glorie in the multitude of their riches. A brother doth not redeme, man shal *not*[24] redeme: he shal not geue vnto God his reconciliation. And the price of the redemption of his owne soule: and he shal labour for euer, and shal liue yet vnto the end.[25]

---

[24] In 'man shal not redeme', *not* is omitted in Doway following the Latin, with an explanation of the textual problem.

[25] Verses 11-12 and 18 may be relevant too:

> And they shal leaue their riches to strangers: and their sepulchers their houses for euer. . . . Because when he shal dye, he shal not take al thinges: neither shal his glorie goe downe with him.

In the Paris Psalter these verses are rendered:

> and læfað fremdum heora æhte þeah hy gesibbe hæbben: hy beð him swyðe fremde þonne hi nan góód æfter him ne doð; ac heora byrgen byð heora hus on ecnesse. . . . For þam þe he ðyder ne læt þæt eall mid him þonne he heonan færþ, ne hit him æfter þyder ne færeð.

> [and they leave their wealth to strangers though they have kindred: they are very much estranged from them when they did not act for their post-humous benefit; but their sepulchres will be their houses for ever. . . . Because he [God] does not allow it to go there, that all (is) with him [the dying] when he departs, it does not go there along with him.]

In the last clause of verse 18 the free Paris Psalter rendering is closer to the Gallican Psalter in not including *domus* of the Roman Psalter (*domus* is in the Roman Psalter Latin written parallel with the Old English in the manuscript), *neque simul descendit cum eo gloria domus eius* [neither does the glory of his house go down with him]. Nothing like that Roman reading is in the relevant passage of *The Seafarer* where the glory of one's house on earth might have provided another mutability symbol.

The second half of *The Seafarer* gives commonplaces in illustration of the theme of mutability, ending in a prayer of thanksgiving (lines 117-24):

> Uton we hycgan   hwær we ham agen,
> ond þonne geþencan   hu we þider cumen;
> ond we þonne eac tilien   þæt we to moten
> 120 in þa ecan   eadignesse.
> Þær is lif gelong   in lufan Dryhtnes,
> hyht in heofonum.   Þæs sy þam Halgan þonc
> þæt he usic geweorþade,   wuldres Ealdor,
> ece Dryhten,   in ealle tid.
>   Amen.

[Let us think where we have our home, and then consider how we may reach it; and may we then also strive that we may be allowed to go there into that everlasting bliss. There life consists in the love of the Lord, joy in heaven. Thanks be to the Holy One, that he, the Prince of Glory, the eternal Lord, has distinguished us for ever and ever. Amen.]

It is no difficult matter to find elsewhere in Old English literature many of the phrases in these lines and many of the ideas that underlying them: notions of our true home, eternal bliss, love of the Lord, joy in heaven, thanks be, the Holy One, *Dominus gloriae*, the eternal Lord, and expressions to render *in saecula saeculorum*. The identifying either of *Parallelstellen* in Old English literature, made easy now by the availability of the *Microfiche Concordance*, or of *loci classici* in the *fontes Anglo-Saxonum latini*, or of both, therefore represents no surprising gain in scholarship or literary awareness. The recognition that in *The Seafarer* the experiences recounted in the first half of the poem lead – inevitably lead, I think – to the final prayer is central to an understanding of the poem, and involves the now general rejection of earlier critical views. K. Reichl expresses that central understanding succinctly in a section devoted to *The Wanderer* and *The Seafarer* of an encyclopaedia article on elegy:[26]

Das nahtlose Ineinandergreifen von weltlichen und geistlichen Elementen läßt die Gedichte als Einheit erscheinen, in der die christl[ich]-meditative Komponente keineswegs, wie dies die ält[ere] Forsch[ung] annahm, als späterer Zusatz zu einem urspr[ünglich] heidn[ischen] Klagelied anzusehen ist.

[The seamless meshing together of secular and spiritual elements allows the poems to appear as unities in which the Christian meditative components are by no means to be regarded, as did earlier scholarship, as later additions to an originally pagan lament.]

Prayer was a deeply ingrained Anglo-Saxon habit of mind, and its expression

---

[26] In the article *Elegie*, in J. Hoops (ed.), *Reallexikon* (2nd edn; see II[22]), VII/1-2 (1986), 131.

therefore a recurrent manifestation of their poetic art. The language of prayer is
to be seen in such passages as the prayer of Judas in *Elene* lines 725-801,
including, lines 750-3a, clearly a paraphrase of the Sanctus in a context naming
cherubim at line 749 and seraphim at line 754b:[27]

> 750   Halig is se Halga,   heah engla God,[28]
>   weoroda Wealdend. Is ðæs wuldres ful
>   heofun ond eorðe, ond eall heahmægen
>   tire getacnod.

[Holy is the Holy One, the high God of angels, the Lord of
Hosts. Heaven and earth are full of that glory, and all (his) high
might is set forth in glory.]

The prayer culminates in lines 795b-801:

> 795   Ic gelyfe þe sel
>   ond þy fæstlicor   ferhð staðelige,
>   hyht untweondne,   on þone ahangnan Crist
>   þæt he sie soðlice   sawla Nergend,
>   ece ælmihtig,   Israhela Cining:
> 800   walde widan ferhð   wuldres on heofenum,
>   a butan ende,   ecra gestealda.

[I believe the better and set (my) spirit, (my) unwavering hope,
the more firmly on the crucified Christ, that he is truly the
Saviour of souls, Eternal Almighty, King of Israel: that he
holds sway for ever over the glory of heaven, over the eternal
mansions, always without end.]

In such passages, often guided by the source, a devout habit of thought finds
expression in recurrent liturgical phrases. When in Old English poetry we have

---

[27] Following the source, an edited text of which is conveniently available in the editions of
Cynewulf's Elene by J. Zupitza (3rd edn, Berlin, 1888), 32, C. W. Kent (Boston, New York,
etc., 1889), 46 (with a confusing note on the orders of angels, p. 77), and F. Holthausen (2nd
edn; Heidelberg and New York, 1910), 28. Cf. J. J. Campbell (ed.), *Advent Lyrics* (1959; see
IV[160]), 99; cf. further the beginning of the Te Deum and similar prayers, such as that in
British Library MS Harley 7653; see W. de Gray Birch (ed.), *An Ancient Manuscript*,
Hampshire Record Society (London and Winchester, 1889), 117.

[28] The editors, both here and in the paraphrase of the Sanctus at *Christ I* line 403b *heah engla
brego* follow B. Thorpe's editions in compounding *heah-engla*; see *Report on the New
Edition of Rymer's Foedera by C. P. Cooper – Appendix B* (printed 1836; cf. IV[18]), 123 line
1504, and *Codex Exoniensis* (1842; see II[85]), 25 line 20 (= *Christ* line 403b); and similarly
heah-engla cyning, Thorpe, *Codex Exoniensis*, 33 line 19 (= *Christ II* line 528a), which is not
a version of the Sanctus. The compound *heahengel* means 'archangel', and in the Sanctus
there is no reason for calling God 'Lord of archangels'; nor probably at *Christ II* 528a, where
J. J. Conybeare (ed. W. D. Conybeare), *Illustrations* (1826; see I[7]), 216 and footnote, had
understood the half-line (correctly, I think), namely, *heah engla cyning* rendered '*Rex
angelorum altissimus*'.

no source and when the subject matter is secular, or less immediately religious, that habit of thought nevertheless makes itself felt from time to time.

The involvement of Germanic fatalism in putative pre-Christian prayer

Germanic fatalism used to be discerned most clearly in the use of *metod* in *Waldere* I.19: '*metod*, here, as originally, "fate," "destiny" (cf. O.N. *mjǫtuðr*); usually an epithet applied to the Creator.'[29] That interpretation is still accepted in editions of 1979 and 1983.[30] The word comes in a pious passage in the speech by Waldere's beloved, whose name (*Hild(e)gyþ) happens not to occur in the Old English fragments, I.19-23:

> Ðy ic ðe metod ondred,
> 20   þæt ðu to fyrenlice   feohtan sohtest
>   æt ðam ætstealle   oðres monnes
>   wigrædenne.   Weorða ðe selfne
>   godum dædum   ðenden ðin God recce.

[On your behalf I therefore feared the Lord,[31] that you strove to fight too fiercely at that hostile place of battle in warfare against the other man. Achieve honour for yourself in deeds of valour as long as God has you in his care.]

Whether the story of Waldere goes back to some heroic original is far from certain. 'Most likely, both the Latin epic [*Waltharius*] and the Old English fragment have a heroic lay as the original source,' it has been suggested;[32] but the evidence for the existence of 'the Germanic heroic lay' remains slight, however ardently and constantly believed in by Germanic scholars.[33] I presume, with no better evidence than the universality of Christian thought in the extant

---

29 B. Dickins (ed.), *Runic and Heroic Poems of the Old Teutonic Peoples* (Cambridge, 1915), 58. Cf. R. Jente, *Die mythologischen Ausdrücke im altenglischen Wortschatz*, AF, 56 (Heidelberg, 1921), 72, who gives this use first place in a list of occurrences which, he believes, appear to preserve the ancient pagan meaning 'fate'.

30 A. Zettersten, *Waldere* (Manchester, 1979), 38 s.v.; and J. Hill (ed.), *Minor Heroic Poems* (1983; see III[80]), 67 s.v.; nothing in the notes in either edition indicates the possibility of any other interpretation. On *Metod* in *Beowulf*, cf. A. G. Brodeur, *Art of Beowulf* (1959; see II[59]), p. 193. See also pp. 237-8 n. 43, below.

31 The interpretation goes back to S. Bugge, 'Spredte iagttagelser vedkommende de oldengelske digte om Beowulf og Waldere', *Tidskrift for Philologi og Pædagogik*, 8 (1868), 74. It is accepted by Dobbie, ASPR, VI, 138; and G. Nickel (general ed.), *Beowulf und die kleineren Denkmäler der altenglischen Heldensage Waldere und Finnsburg*, I (Heidelberg, 1976), 207; cf. E. G. Stanley, *Paganism* (1964-1965; reprinted 1975; see I[2]), reprint p. 111.

32 A. Zettersten (ed.), *Waldere* (1979; see V[30]), 5; cf. K. Langosch, *"Waltharius" Die Dichtung und die Forschung*, Erträge der Forschung, 21 (Darmstadt, 1973), 1-3, especially 8-14, and 85; and K. Langosch, 'Die Vorlage des "Waltharius" ', in J. Autenrieth and F. Brunhölzl, *Festschrift Bernhard Bischoff zu seinem 65. Geburtstag* (Stuttgart, 1971), 229-30, 241-54.

33 Cf. E. G. Stanley 'Heroic Lay', in *A Collection of Papers* (1987; see II[39]) 282-97.

literature of literate Germania (including England), that the story of Walter was created in Christian times, and that the habit of prayer resided in the Christian originator.

For pre-Christian Germania, the propitiation through prayer of a personified Fate (or of a triad of Weird Sisters)[34] is an article of faith among some Germanic scholars, with Hildegyth's *Ðy ic ðe metod ondred* interpreted (as by Bruce Dickins) 'wherefore I trembled for thy fate' an important confirmatory text 'proving' that both *wyrd* and *metod* must have been Fate, so that the Anglo-Saxons slipped easily from, originally, prayer to pagan *metod* to, later, prayer to the Lord God for whom the word was therefore used in verse.

Prayer and thanksgiving to God in Beowulf

The figures of *Beowulf* too not infrequently resort to prayer and pious thought (or are reported by the poet as resorting to prayer and pious thought). Outside prayer too, the poet employs language which implies prayer and pious thought.[35] The following are most of the relevant passages.

The poet attributes to God the birth of Beow(ulf) the Dane and the help he gave to his nation in their need, lines 12-17:

> Ðæm eafera wæs   æfter cenned,
> geong on geardum,   þone God sende
> folce to frofre.   Fyrenðearfe ongeat,
> 15 þæt hie ær drugon   aldorlease
> lange hwile.   Him þæs Liffrea
> wuldres Wealdend   woroldare forgeaf.

[Afterwards a son was born to him, a boy in the courts, whom God sent as a help to his people. He [God] had seen the dire need, that being lordless they had endured for a long time.[36] The Lord of life, the Ruler of glory, gave him honour in the world for that reason.]

As at the end of the poem the poet makes Wiglaf say that the dead Beowulf will live forever in the Ruler's keeping (line 3109, see p. 240, below), so at the beginning of the poem the poet says of the dead Scyld, lines 26-7:

---

[34] Cf. A. Brandl, 'Zur Vorgeschichte der *Weird Sisters* im 'Macbeth', in M. Förster and K. Wildhagen (eds), *Festgabe für Felix Liebermann* (1921; see IV[31]), 252-70.

[35] Cf. A. G. Brodeur, *Art of Beowulf* (1959; see II[59]), 190-5.

[36] For this interpretation of the unemended reading (the normal abbreviation for *þæt*), see C. L. Wrenn (ed.) *Beowulf* (1953; see IV[82]), 185, retained in W. F. Bolton's revised edn (1973, see IV[75]), 97. For a different defence of the unemended reading, cf. R. W. Chambers (ed.), A. J. Wyatt's edition, *Beowulf with the Finnsburg Fragment* (revised edn; Cambridge, 1920), 2 note on line 15.

> Him ða Scyld gewat   to gescæphwile
> felahror feran   on Frean wære.

[Then Scyld, very aged, journeyed at the destined hour into the
keeping of the Lord.]

Hrothgar's *scop* sings a song of creation, lines 90-8, of which Klaeber in the
notes to his edition of *Beowulf* says well, '**90-98 The Song of Creation** bears no
special resemblance to Cædmon's famous Hymn, but follows pretty closely
upon the lines suggested by the biblical account.' Klaeber is, of course, object-
ing to earlier scholars who found a Cædmonian echo in the words of these lines.
For the present purpose, however, what matters is that these lines constitute a
song of praise of God the Creator, which is in that general respect similar to
Cædmon's Hymn. In the Bible story of Creation there is no song of praise, no
prayer till much later Seth calls upon the name of the Lord (Genesis 4:26).

Beowulf and his men thank God after crossing from Geatland to Denmark,
lines 227b-8: 'Gode þancedon ‖ þæs þe him yþlade eaþe wurdon' [They thanked
God because the sea-voyagings had been pleasant for them].

The coastguard utters a prayer for Beowulf and his men, lines 316b-18a:

> Fæder alwalda
> mid arstafum   eowic gehealde
> siða gesunde!

[May the omnipotent Father in his mercy preserve you safe
and sound in (your) exploits!]

Hrothgar attributes to God the coming of Beowulf to help the Danes in their
need, lines 381b-4a:

> Hine halig God
> for arstafum   us onsende,
> to West-Denum,   þæs ic wen hæbbe
> wiþ Grendles gryre.

[Holy God of his grace sent him to us, to the West-Danes, as I
hope in hostility to the terror of Grendel.]

Hrothgar believes that God has the power to put an end to the ravages
wrought by Grendel, lines 478b-9: 'God eaþe mæg ‖ þone dolsceaðan dæda
getwæfan' [God can easily put an end to the actions of that desperate ravager].

Wealhtheow thanks God for a hero like Beowulf in whom she could trust for
timely relief from the national disaster of Grendel, lines 625-8a:

> 625 Grette Geata leod;   Gode þancode
>   wisfæst wordum   þæs ðe hire se willa gelamp
>   þæt heo on ænigne   eorl gelyfde
>   fyrena frofre.

[She saluted the prince of the Geats, thanking God in wise
words because her wish had come to pass that she might trust
in some warrior for relief from evil deeds.]

Beowulf, whom God had set against Grendel as men heard say (lines 665b-
7a), puts his trust in his strength and God, lines 669-70 (cf. lines 1270-4a, pp.
233-4, below):

> Huru Geata leod   georne truwode
> 670   modgan mægnes,   Metodes hyldo.

[Truly, the prince of the Geats readily trusted in (his own)
brave strength (and) in the grace of the Lord.]

Beowulf in the weaponless fight with Grendel looks to God to assign victory
to whom he will, lines 683b-7:

>   Ac wit on niht sculon
> secge ofersittan   gif he gesecean dear
> 685   wig ofer wæpen;   ond siþðan witig God
> on swa hwæþere hond,   halig Dryhten,
> mærðo deme   swa him gemet þince.

[But the two of us must in the night forgo (the use of) the
sword if he dare seek weaponless battle; and thereafter may
the wise God, the holy Lord, adjudge glory on whichever of
our two sides it may seem fitting to him.]

That resigned trust that God will deal justly with Beowulf and Grendel in their
fight is answered in lines 696b-702a:

>   Ac him Dryhten forgeaf
> wigspeda gewiofu,   Wedera leodum,
> frofor ond fultum,   þæt hie feond heora
> ðurh anes cræft   ealle ofercomon,
> 700   selfes mihtum.   Soð is gecyþed,
> þæt mihtig God   manna cynnes
> weold wideferhð.

[But the Lord granted to them, to the people of the Geats, the
fortunes of successes in battle, help and support, that they all
overcame their enemy through the strength of one, through the
powers of his own person. The truth is made manifest that
mighty God ruled humankind for ever and ever.]

Hrothgar gives thanks to God for Beowulf's victory over Grendel, and the
whole speech (lines 928-56) is relevant. I select from it three passages; thanks
for the victory symbolized by the trophy of Grendel's hand, lines 928-31; the
deed was performed through the Lord's power and Beowulf is to be praised in

terms applicable to Mary's joy at her Son's birth,[37] lines 939b-46a; and the final
prayer that God will requite Beowulf liberally, 955b-6. Lines 928-31:

> Ðisse ansyne Alwealdan þanc
> lungre gelimpe! Fela ic laþes gebad,
> 930 grynna æt Grendle: a mæg God wyrcan
> wunder æfter wundre, wuldres Hyrde.

[To the Ruler of all let thanks be given at once for this sight! I
have experienced many a grief, afflictions at the hands of
Grendel: God can always work wonder upon wonder, the
Shepherd of glory.]

Lines 939b-46a:

> Nu scealc hafað
> 940 þurh Drihtnes miht dæd gefremede
> ðe we ealle ær ne meahton
> snyttrum besyrwan. Hwæt, þæt secgan mæg
> efne swa hwylc mægþa swa ðone magan cende
> æfter gumcynnum, gyf heo gyt lyfað,
> 945 þæt hyre Ealdmetod este wære
> bearngebyrdo.

[Now, through the Lord's might, a retainer has performed a
deed which all of us before could not contrive with (our) skill.
Behold, whoever of women bore that son among mankind can
say, if she still lives, that the Lord God of old[38] was gracious to
her in child-bearing.]

Lines 955b-6: 'Alwalda þec ‖ gode forgylde, swa he nu gyt dyde' [May the
Ruler of All reward you with good, as he even now has done].

In the fight against Grendel, Beowulf puts his trust in his God-given strength
and in divine favour, lines 1270-4a (cf. lines 669-70, p. 232, above):

> 1270 hwæþre he gemunde mægenes strenge,
> gimfæste gife ðe him God sealde,
> ond him to Anwaldan are gelyfde,
> frofre ond fultum: ðy he þone feond ofercwom,
> gehnægde helle gast.

---

[37] Cf. Klaeber's note on lines 942 ff. refers to Luke 11:27 ,'Blessed is the wombe that bare thee,
and the pappes that thou didst sucke'; and to his comments, 'Notizen zur Texterklärung des
Beowulf', *Anglia*, 28 (1905), 441-2, 'Die christlichen Elemente', *Anglia*, 35 (1912; cf. II[44]),
468. In the introduction to his edition (3rd edn, 1936), p. xvii note 3, he dismisses a detail in
a Faroese ballad, 'viz. the exclamation in praise (blessing) of the hero's mother after the
slaying of the giant', as a 'coincidence' that 'need not be considered of importance'.
[38] Cf. F. Klaeber, 'Die christlichen Elemente', *Anglia*, 35 (1912; cf. II[44]), 124.

[however, he was mindful of the strength of might, the liberal gift which God had given him, and he put his trust in the Ruler for grace, help and support: by that means he overcame the enemy, laid low the spirit from hell.]

After Æschere's death Beowulf was summoned to where Hrothgar sat, anxious if God would ever bring to pass change for the better, lines 1311b-15:

> Samod ærdæge
> eode eorla sum   æþele cempa,
> self mid gesiðum,   þær se snotera bad
> hwæþer him Alwalda   æfre wille
> 1315   æfter weaspelle   wyrpe gefremman.

[At break of day the noble warrior went together with his men, he himself with his companions, to where the wise one awaited whether the Ruler of all would ever bring about change after that woeful tale.]

After Beowulf's speech stating his readiness to fight Grendel's mother, Hrothgar gives thanks to God for Beowulf's words, lines 1397-8:

> Ahleop ða se gomela,   Gode þancode,
> mihtigan Drihtne,   þæs se man gespræc.

[The aged one leapt up, thanked God, the mighty Lord, for what the man had said.]

God decides to give Beowulf victory over Grendel's mother, lines 1550-6 (echoed in lines 1657b-64, see p. 235, below):

> 1550   Hæfde ða forsiðod   sunu Ecgþeowes
> under gynne grund,   Geata cempa,
> nemne him heaðobyrne   helpe gefremede,
> herenet hearde,   ond halig God
> geweold wigsigor: witig Drihten,
> 1555   rodera Rædend,   hit on ryht gesced
> yðelice   syþðan he eft astod.

[The son of Ecgtheow, warrior of the Geats, would have met with disaster under the wide earth if his battle-corslet had not afforded him help, the hard war-net, and if holy God had not brought about victory in battle: the wise Lord, Ruler of the heavens, easily decided it aright as soon as he [Beowulf] stood up again.]

Beowulf's men give thanks to God for his safe return, lines 1626-8:

> Eodon him þa togeanes,   Gode þancodon,
> ðryðlic þegna heap,   þeodnes gefegon,
> þæs þe hi hyne gesundne   geseon moston.

[Then they, a splendid company of retainers, went to meet him, gave thanks to God, rejoiced in their prince, that they might see him sound.]

In his speech to the Danes Beowulf echoes the words quoted above (lines 1552-4a) in which the poet had stated that the hero would have met with disaster if God had not assigned him victory by providing him with a gigantic sword, lines 1657b-64:

> Ætrihte wæs
> guð getwæfed, nymðe mec God scylde.
> Ne meahte ic æt hilde   mid Hruntinge
> 1660 wiht gewyrcan, þeah þæt wæpen duge,
> ac me geuðe   ylda Waldend
> þæt ic on wage geseah   wlitig hangian
> ealdweord eacen   – oftost wisode
> winigea leasum –   þæt ic ðy wæpne gebræd.

[The battle would have been put an end to straightaway if God had not protected me. In that conflict I could not achieve anything with Hrunting, good though that weapon be, but the Lord of mankind granted me that I should see hanging on the wall a gigantic ancient sword in all its beauty – most often he has guided the friendless – (granted me) that I should draw that sword.]

Most of Hrothgar's speech, his 'sermon' (lines 1700-84), is relevant, central, in fact, to any discussion of prayer and pious thought in *Beowulf*, and will be dealt with at some length in the next section of this chapter.

Hrothgar, lines 1841-45a, attributes to God Beowulf's wisdom which had found expression in the young hero's speech:

> Þe þa wordcwydas   wigtig Drihten
> on sefan sende.   Ne hyrde ic snotorlicor
> on swa geongum feore   guman þingian.
> Þu eart mægenes strang   ond on mode frod,
> 1845 wis wordcwida.

[The wise Lord sent that utterance of words into your mind. I have not heard a man at so young an age speak more wisely. You are strong of might and sage of mind, wise in utterance of words.]

Hygelac gives thanks to God for Beowulf's safe return from the land of the Geats after his perilous exploit there, lines 1997b-98: 'Gode ic þanc secge, ‖ þæs ðe ic ðe gesundne geseon moste [I give thanks to God because I may see you safe and sound].

The poet, contrasting Beowulf's virtues with the wicked behaviour of which a

Heremod may be accused (though Heremod is not mentioned by name), attributes the virtuous hero's great strength to God, lines 2177-83a (before going on to tell of Beowulf's inglorious youth):

> Swa bealdode   bearn Ecgðeowes,
> guma guðum cuð,   godum dædum,
> dreah æfter dome.   Nealles druncne slog
> 2180   heorðgeneatas,   næs him hreoh sefa;
> ac he mancynnes   mæste cræfte,
> ginfæstan gife   þe him God sealde,
> heold hildedeor.

[Thus Ecgtheow's son, a man renowned in battles for great deeds, gave proof of valour, bore himself gloriously. Not at all did he drunkenly slay his hearth-companions, his spirit was not savage; but he, a man brave in war, possessed the greatest human ability, the ample gift which God had given him.]

The poet explains how the man who pillaged the dragon-hoard survived the dragon's wrath by the grace of God, lines 2291-3a:

> Swa mæg unfæge   eaðe gedigan
> wean ond wræcsið   se ðe Waldendes
> hyldo gehealdeþ.

[Thus one not yet doomed to die, who keeps the Almighty's grace, can easily come through misery and hardship.]

Beowulf, his people in danger from the dragon and his own palace and throne destroyed, meditates with dark contrition how he may have offended against the Lord, *ofer ealde riht* 'contrary to ancient law', perhaps 'in contravention of time-honoured law',[39] lines 2329-32:

---

[39] It is unclear if what is referred to is 'natural law', that is, outside the Judaeo-Christian tradition, perhaps deliberately pre-Christian for our pagan hero, or such 'natural law' equated with the Mosaic Dispensation, or Divine Law less precisely, or even the Law as interpreted by the Fathers of the Church. The half-line is well discussed by M. W. Bloomfield, 'Patristics and Old English Literature: Notes on Some Poems, B. *Beowulf*, line 2330', in S. B. Greenfield (ed.), *Studies in Old English Literature in Honor of Arthur G. Brodeur* (Eugene, Oregon, 1963), 39-41 [reprinted in L. E. Nicholson (ed.), *Anthology* (1963; see I[78]), 369-72]. In the Anglo-Saxon Laws, the phrase *an eald riht* (Hlothære and Eadric 12), *an ald reht* (Wihtræd 5), is confined to the very early Kentish Laws [extant only in the twelfth-century Textus Roffensis; see P. H. Sawyer (ed.), *Textus Roffensis Rochester Cathedral Library Manuscript A. 3. 5.*, part 1, EEMF, VII (1957), fos. 4ᵛ line 14, 5ᵛ lines 14-15], in both cases marked off by points, perhaps to indicate the formulaic nature of the phrase. F. Liebermann, by an argument of doubtful logic [*Die Gesetze der Angelsachsen*, III (Halle, 1916), 22/1 and 27/1, as well as II/2 Rechts- und Sachglossar (Halle, 1912), 276/3 *altes Recht*, 1], resists the obvious sense, and believes *eald* in these laws means 'vollkommen, gut, ehrwürdig, echt; erprobt' [perfect, good and true, honourable, valid and genuine; tried and not found wanting]. D. Whitelock, *English Historical Documents*, I *c.* 500-1042 (2nd edn; London and New York,

<pre>
         Wende se wisa   þæt he Wealdende
2330 ofer ealde riht,   ecean Dryhtne,
         bitre gebulge.   Breost innan weoll
         þeostrum geþoncum, swa him geþywe ne wæs.
</pre>

[The wise one thought that he had bitterly angered the Ruler,
the eternal Lord, contrary to ancient law. Within him his breast
surged with dark thoughts as was not usual with him.]

In a much discussed place in Beowulf's last speech before battle – perhaps an
echo of *Pater, in manus tuas commendo spiritum meum* [Father, into thy handes
I commend my spirit][40] – the aged king, going into the fight with the dragon,
resigns himself to whatever may be his destiny, with *Metod* only two words after
wyrd.[41] By making Beowulf thus resign himself to whatever outcome Divine
Providence holds for him, the poet seems to allow the dying king as nearly a
holy end verbally as a pagan can hope to achieve, and, in fact, more nearly so
than he appears to be achieving in what is his actual dying speech (at lines
2729-51, see p. 238, below); lines 2524b-7a:

<pre>
                           Nelle ic beorges weard
2525 oferfleon fotes trem;   ac unc[42] sceal
         weorðan æt wealle   swa unc wyrd geteoð
         Metod manna gehwæs.
</pre>

[Not a footstep will I flee from the guardian of the barrow; but
it must be with the two of us at the wall as the Lord of each of
humankind determines the outcome.]

Translations of these lines usually make more of Germanic Fatalism here.
That depends on taking *wyrd* in the nominative as varied by *metod* (nominative)
with a comma after *geteoð*. An early, poetic rendering, not generally familiar,
may be quoted as exemplifying this interpretation:[43]

1979), 395 and 397, translates the phrase 'according to ancient law', and that seems better
both for the Kentish Laws and for the antonymous use with *ofer* 'contrary to' in *Beowulf*. The
legal uses make a religious application of the phrase in *Beowulf* certainly unnecessary,
perhaps unlikely. In both the poem and the Laws *eald* may carry overtones of 'time-
honoured', but that is as far as I should wish to go in Liebermann's direction.

40 With these last words on the Cross (Luke 23:46, cf. Psalm 30:6), Jesus provides the supreme
example of holy dying.

41 See pp. 206-8 and 229-30, above, on 'Germanic fatalism'.

42 The half-line lacks alliteration and is short; editors supply a word after *unc*, for example,
furður 'further on' for which support has been found in the quite different use of *furðor* at
The Battle of Maldon line 246-7 (where only *nelle* ‖ *fleon fotes trym* is close); but also a noun
(in the dative or instrumental) for 'in the battle', *fæhðo* or *feohte*, has been suggested. R. P.
Tripp, *More about the Fight* (1983; see II²), 382, supplies *faehð* without explaining how he
scans the half-line.

43 A. D. Wackerbardt, *Beowulf An Epic Poem Translated from the Anglo-Saxon into English
Verse* (London, 1849), 97-8. *Maxims I* line 173, 'wineleas wunian hafaþ him wyrd geteod'
[fate has ordained for him to dwell without friends], may lend some support to translations of

> Nor to the Barrow's Guardian dread
> A single Footstep will I yield;
> But it shall be unto us twain
> As Fate, Man's Maker, shall ordain.

Wiglaf's reference to the deity may amount to little more than a 'God knows' protestation, rather than a full calling on God as witness, in lines 2650b-2:

2650   God wat on mec
      þæt me is micle leofre   þæt minne lichaman
      mid minne goldgyfan   gled fæðmiæ.

[God knows of me that I would far rather that the flame engulf
my body together with my generous lord.]

In Beowulf's speech near the end of his life there are expressions of satisfaction that he has led a virtuous life and has governed well. I have expressed elsewhere my doubts if his last speeches, with elements of avarice and vainglory, are such as a devout Christian might hope to make when death is near.[44] There may even be a touch of smugness in his dealings with the Almighty, lines 2732b-43a:

                           Ic ðas leode heold
      fiftig wintra.   Næs se folccyning
      ymbesittendra   ænig ðara
2735 þe mec guðwinum   gretan dorste,
      egesan ðeon.   Ic on earde bad
      mælgesceafta,   heold min tela,
      ne sohte searoniðas,   ne me swor fela
      aða on unriht.   Ic ðæs ealles mæg
2740 feorhbennum seoc   gefean habban:
      forðam me witan ne ðearf   Waldend fira
      morðorbealo maga   þonne me sceaceð
      lif of lice.

[I ruled this nation for fifty years. There was not one king of
any of those peoples dwelling round about that dared attack
me with war-allies, (dared) threaten with terror. I awaited in
the land whatever time might bring, I conducted myself well, I
sought no contrived hostilities, nor did I swear many wrongful
oaths. Sick with mortal wounds I can rejoice in all that:
because when life departs from my body the Ruler of humankind has no cause to blame me for the murderous slaying of
kinsmen.]

the *Beowulf* passage taking *wyrd* (line 2526) in the nominative, and varied by *metod* in the
following half-line.

44 Cf. 'Hæþenra Hyht in *Beowulf*', in S. B. Greenfield (ed.), *Studies in Honor of A. G. Brodeur* (1963; see V[39]), 147; reprinted in E. G. Stanley, *A Collection of Papers* (1987; see I[45]), 203.

At the beginning of his last speech, Beowulf is nearer to a good Christian's dying speech, in an utterance close to a prayer of thanksgiving for divine favours received for the benefit of his people, than towards the end when he reverts to a vainglorious wish to be commemorated by a monument, and at the very end when he remembers the dynasty of the Wægmundings and Wiglaf, prince of that dynasty. This is the prayer, lines 2794-8:

> Ic ðara frætwa   Frean ealles ðanc,
> 2795 Wuldurcyninge,   wordum secge,
> ecum Dryhtne,   þe ic her on starie,
> þæs ðe ic moste   minum leodum
> ær swyltdæge   swylc gestrynan.

[I speak words of thanks to the Lord of all, to the King of glory, the eternal Lord, for the treasures which I gaze on here, that I was able to acquire such for my people before the day of (my) death.]

Wiglaf's inability to halt Beowulf's fleeting life by applying water in the hope of rousing him becomes a poetic expression of human incapability in contrast with divine power, unchanging and inexorable, lines 2852b-59:

> He gewergad sæt,
> feðecempa   frean eaxlum neah,
> wehte hyne wætre: him wiht ne speow.
> 2855 Ne meahte he on eorðan,   ðeah he uðe wel,
> on ðam frumgare   feorh gehealdan,
> ne ðæs Wealdendes   wiht oncirran:
> wolde dom Godes   dædum rædan
> gumena gehwylcum,   swa he nu gen deð.

[He sat wearied, the foot-soldier close to his lord's shoulder, attempted to awaken him[45] with water: it availed him nothing. He could not, however much he might wish it, retain life on earth in that war-chief nor change anything of the Ruler's (ordainment): God's decree would rule the actions of every man, as it still does now.]

Wiglaf attributes Beowulf's slaying of the dragon to God, lines 2873-6:

> Nealles folccying   fyrdgesteallum
> gylpan þorfte.   Hwæðre him God uðe,
> 2875 sigora Waldend,   þæt he hyne sylfne gewræc
> ana mid ecge,   þa him wæs elnes þearf.

---

[45] Cf. B. Mitchell, *On Old English* (1988; see III[39]), 159 footnote 21a, and the references there given; see also J. R. R. Tolkien (ed. A. J. Bliss), *Finn and Hengest* (London, 1982; see I[69]), 87 note on *The Battle of Finnsburh* line 18.

[By no means did the nation's king have reason to boast of his
comrades in arms. However, God, Ruler of glories, granted
him that he might avenge himself with his sword single-
handed when he stood in need of valour.]

Wiglaf, commanding Beowulf's funeral rites, ends his speech with the hope
that Beowulf shall dwell in the Lord's keeping,[46] lines 3105b-9:

3105   Sie sio bær gearo,
        ædre geæfned,   þonne we ut cymen,
        ond þonne geferian   frean userne,
        leofne mannan,   þær he longe sceal
        on ðæs Waldendes   wære geþolian.

[Let the bier be prepared, quickly made ready, for such a time
as we come out and when we carry our lord, the beloved man,
where he must forever dwell in the Ruler's keeping.]

Hrothgar's 'sermon'

The densest concentration in *Beowulf* of pious thoughts, 'Christian elements', is
to be found in Hrothgar's so-called 'sermon', lines 1700-84 at approximately
the centre of the poem. Divine worship as well as homiletic matter are suitably
expressed by Hrothgar. These themes, reinforced by wording that recalls Christian prayer and homily, have led to the speech being given the appellation
'sermon'. At first, and perhaps still, that appellation was, no doubt, designed to
emphasize the distance between Hrothgar's moralizing and the true world of
Germanic heroes, as by Ettmüller's explanatory note to his translation published
of 1840:[47]

1731-1796. Eingeschobenes Stück. Bis v. 1739 enthält es nur Wiederholung
von v. 1726-1728, und das Folgende ist eine allegorisirende Predigt, die sich
im Munde eines alten heidnischen Königs etwas sonderbar ausnimmt, selbst
wenn man seine Priesterwürde in Anschlag bringt. An sich hat das Stück
manche Schönheiten.

[1716-81. Interpolated passage. Up to line. 1724a it contains only a repetition
of lines 1711-[?]1714a, and what follows is an allegorizing sermon which
sounds a little peculiar in the mouth of an aged pagan king, even if one takes
his priestly office into account. Considered on its own terms, the passage
includes some beautiful features.]

---

[46] Cf. line 27b, quoted pp. 230-1, above.

[47] This was, I think, the first application to lines 1700-84 of the term 'sermon', German
Predigt; L. Ettmüller, *Beowulf. Heldengedicht, stabreimend übersetzt* (1840; see I⁸), 136 note
on lines 1716-81 (= Ettmüller's lines 1731-96).

When nearly thirty years later Müllenhoff takes up the appellation *Predigt* the assurance of the Higher Criticism makes itself felt in the easy recognition of two differing elements in the speech (one element being characteristic of his hypothesized interpolater B):[48]

1700-1768. sieht man etwas genauer zu, so hält Hroðgar zwei reden, die nicht wohl demselben hirn entsprungen sein können. die eine, kürzere 1769-1784 ist der situation ganz wohl angemessen. . . . die andre längere rede 1700-1768 ist eine in mehr als einer hinsicht unpassende predigt, wie sie von dem theologisch gelehrten und zugleich sagenkundigen B erwartet werden darf.

[1700-68. If one observes the matter a little more closely, then Hrothgar makes two speeches which can hardly have originated in the same brain. One of them, the shorter (lines 1769-84), is quite well suited to the situation. . . . The other speech, the longer of the two (lines 1700-68), is a sermon, unsuitable in more than one respect, such as is to be expected from Interpolator B, who is theologically learned and, at the same time, knows Germanic legends.]

Müllenhoff (p. 214 [= 131]) exemplifies Interpolator B's theological learning by relating *biteran stræle . . . wom wundorbebodum wergan gastes* (lines 1745-6) [with the bitter arrow, the crooked mysterious commands of the accursed spirit] to Ephesians 6:16, 'the firie dartes of the most wicked one', part of the allegorical passage introduced by verse 11, 'Put you on the armour of God, that you may stand against the deceites of the Deuil.' Other, feebler biblical echoes have been pointed out: Luke 10:42, 'Marie hath chosen the best part which shal not be taken away from her', has been related to lines 1759-60, *ond þe þæt selre geceos, ece rædas* [and choose the better for yourself, eternal counsel].[49]

There is no need to quote all 85 lines of Hrothgar's speech, or to say more of it than that increasingly it has been felt by critics to be 'the centrepiece of the poem', as John Earle suggested a century ago:[50]

This long address of the old king to the young hero has been too hastily slighted as mere sermonizing, whereas it is appropriate and affecting; and moreover it affords valuable light for the interpretation of the poem. . . .

There is one great thought which animates the whole poem, and it is a thought proper to the time. It is the germinant thought of social organism, and it provides a theme adequate for an Epic, because it is coextensive with moral and political life so far as it had then been developed, and accordingly it embraces human interests of the highest order.

The thought is this:– *Mutual dependence is the law of human society.* No one is independent; not the strongest or noblest or most exalted; for he depends upon the support of those who are under him. Consideration and gener-

---

[48] K. Müllenhoff, 'Innere Geschichte' (1869; see I[33]), 213-14 [= *Untersuchungen* (1889), 130-1].

[49] See Klaeber, 'Die christlichen Elemente', *Anglia*, 35 (1912; cf. II[44]), 457-8.

[50] *The Deeds of Beowulf* (1892; see I[45]). I quote from pp. lxiv-lxv and lxxxvii-lxxxviii.

osity from him to them; honour and fidelity and devotion from them to him; these are the rudimentary foundations upon which alone it is possible to erect and edify a stable fabric of government, to build up a State.

This thought pervades the allegorical narrative as a whole, and this thought is the text of that well-abused discourse which is the centrepiece of the poem. The unity of the poem is manifested by the readiness of every part, whether action or discourse, to be interpreted by reference to this thought. . . .

Hrothgar's discourse is a warning of the dangers which attend high success. Nothing is worse for men, nothing more hurtful to their understanding, than the consciousness of possessing a power which none can control.

This is a high Victorian ideal of good government. Whether it truly chimes with an Anglo-Saxon ideal seems doubtful, though perhaps no more doubtful than the critics' application, as if Germanic polity had undergone no change, of the comitatus spirit expressed in Tacitean terms. King Alfred would not have formulated the ideal of good government as did Earle, but he might well have understood that formulation and sympathized with it, since to him as to Hrothgar good government is the royal exercise of virtue. One recalls Alfred's words about Nero, 'the unrighteous emperor' (*Boethius*, ch. xvi § 4):[51]

Eala eaw! hu hefig geoc he beslypte on eallæ þa þæ on his tidum libbende wæron on eorðan, ond hu oft his sweord wæron besyled on unscyldegum blode! Hu ne wæs þær genog sweotol þæt se anweald his agenes ðonces god næs þa se god næs þe he to com?

[Alas and alas! how heavy a yoke he slipped on all those who in his time were alive on earth, and how often his swords were polluted in innocent blood! Was it not clear enough there that power of itself was not good when he was not good to whom it came?]

Earle's notion of interdependence of governor and governed has no place in Alfred's judgement of Nero. Earle discerned in Hrothgar's ideal of kingship that the grace and bounty of kings rests on and answers to the loyalty of retainers, best when least like that of Heremod and his subjects, lines 1709b-22a. Addressing Beowulf, to whom sway will come through merit (lines 1845b-53a), Hrothgar gave that as a lesson (lines 1722b-3a): *Đu þe lær be þon: gumcyste ongit!* [Take instruction from that: perceive sovereign bounty!]. Another central theme in the 'sermon', as in many of the passages of thanks and prayer throughout the poem, is praise of the munificent power of God, lines 1724b-7:

Wundor is to secganne,
1725   hu mihtig God   manna cynne

[51] W. J. Sedgefield (ed.), *King Alfred's Boethius* (1899; see IV[63]), 39-40; *þam unrihtwisan kasere*, p. 39. The source, Boethius, *De Consolatione Philosophiae*, II met. vi, has only a short reference to the wicked violence of Nero's sword.

þurh sidne sefan   snyttru bryttað,
eard ond eorlscipe: he ah ealra geweald.

[It is a wonder to say how mighty God in his largeness of spirit distributes to mankind wisdom, land and dominion:[52] he has power over all.]

Nothing is known of the prayers, if they had them, of pre-Christian Anglo-Saxons to the gods of Germanic antiquity; nothing is known of their moralizing eloquence, if they practised it in pre-Christian times as we know they did in historical times. And so it is difficult to take as anything other than a grudging concession to the non-disintegrators of the poem K. Sisam's remarks on Hrothgar's speeches (in his 'Note B: Christianity in *Beowulf*'):[53]

And it is worth noting that, if all Hrothgar's speeches are accepted as belonging to the original composition, they put forward no characteristically Christian doctrine. Most intelligent men would agree that overweening is a vice, especially in the crude forms that Hrothgar thinks of – miserliness, rapacity, and the wanton killing of companions (1709 ff.). Reversals of fortune (1769 ff.) are a commonplace subject of reflection and story among pagans. So are the shortness and uncertainty of human life (1753 ff.)

Doctrine does not appear in Hrothgar's moral eloquence, less so than in Sisam's reference to Overweening as a Vice, Lucifer's Vice as it may seem to the Christian reader (if not to the intelligent pre-Christian or post-Christian on the Clapham omnibus): Christian thought and phrasing are in evidence in many lines of the poem, not confined to Hrothgar, but more frequent and consistent in his 'sermon' than elsewhere in the poem.

Christian thought and phrasing, reminiscent of prayer and homily, do not individualize any one speaker in the poem, here the old king. They characterize Wisdom in the recognition of God's greater power than any man's, and in the recognition of God's grace through the divinely just exercise of that power. They constitute Christian eloquence expressing – in wonder (line 1724b) – the gratitude and praise humanity owes individually and collectively to God in acknowledgement of divine favours received. That wisdom and eloquence pervade the poem.

---

[52] For the notion that humankind has dominion over the creatures of the earth, perhaps cf. Genesis 1:26.
[53] *The Structure of* Beowulf (1965; see II[27]), 78-9.

VI

Postscript

Many books on Old English literature and on many other subjects have a last chapter with the title 'Conclusion(s)', in German even *Fazit* or *Ergebnisse* 'Result(s)', as if there were something solid at the end of it all. Doctoral candidates, after labouring away at a dissertation for more years than was thought possible at the outset, more than in retrospect is thought justifiable, must give the impression to parents, teachers and funding agencies that the so-called research was all worth while. Scientists, after long labour, at last come to the stage when they can write it up, to announce, if they were lucky, something new and real, one or more results. A fairly wide reading of doctoral dissertations in English studies, including Anglo-Saxon studies, makes me think that results, though often claimed, are a rare outcome of much honest labour. Sometimes, especially in old-fashioned theses with long tabulations and listings, each item patiently analysed, the permanent value may lie, not in the conclusions drawn or the results claimed, but in the chapters leading up to them. This book, which is far from being a doctoral dissertation, has this final brief chapter called 'Postscript': everything dissolved, nothing resolved, nothing solved, no conclusion.

Accuracy and doubt should attend academic literary study. Accuracy is hard to achieve, and if a postscript were to include a general confession of sins of omission and commission it would be appropriate here; for every time I have published I have had cause to regret misprints as well as errors not attributable to the printing. I recall Thomas Adams' apology at the foot of the final page of a great work of exegesis, below a list of *Errata*:[1]

> There be diverse other misplacings, mispointings, and mistakings of words, with which no ingenious and ingenous Reader will charge the Author. . . . These which I transiently found . . . I have set downe. By which you may ghesse at the rest, and in your fair charity pardon all.

---

[1] T. Adams, *A Commentary Or, Exposition upon the Divine Second Epistle Generall Written by the Blessed Apostle St. Peter*, II (London, 1633). In the opening sentence 'ingenous' may be a mere misprint for 'ingenuous'.

Forgiveness in fair charity does not come easily to academics. Accuracy is a great goal in academic work: the study of Anglo-Saxon literature arose out of the study of the language, and an age that saw the rise of criticism saw the fall of accurate philological knowledge. Accurate philological knowledge was only rarely attended by literary good sense. Literary good sense seems to me more often a result of salutary doubt than of assurance based on a security rooted in accurate factual knowledge, for any assurance is likely to be unjustified, and may amount to no more than smugness.

Doubt comes more easily than assurance. This book began with Goethe's contemptuous *Xenion* on exegesis, and that remains central to it:

> Im Auslegen seyd frisch und munter!
> Legt ihr's nicht aus, so legt was unter.
>
> [As exegetes, you in each text display,
> Not what it says, but what you'd have it say.]

Too rarely, the exegetes of Old English verse have said, 'I cannot understand this, and what I understand I do not like as I understand it.' Academic work is usually performed by scholars teaching the subject, and when the teacher confesses frequent inability to understand, the pupil is unlikely to be impressed. It may be doubted if the sceptical pupil is more readily impressed by a teacher's utterances delivered with a false and often pompous display of certainty. After all, it is usually easy to recognize as nonsense what is offered in expert teaching even when better sense is not yet achieved fully by the newcomer to the subject. The newcomer may lack the courage to reject as improbable or impossible the consensus of scholars, for an opinion or theory advanced with force by an established scholar soon becomes a consensus.

Because this literature is so distant in time, many scholars have imposed on it Romantic theories of origination, and in support of their theories they look to traces supposedly earlier than anything the vernacular offers in hard evidence of extant texts. The theories are in tune with the preoccupations and predilections of the scholars promoting them in their exegesis, but often do not chime with the overt sense of the texts in which they seek covert meanings apparent to them because they think themselves experts. The exegetes could, therefore, say, but usually are not ingenuous enough to say so, 'I do not like what I understand the text to say, but I like my understanding of what the text should say.'

The greatest difficulty for the critic of medieval literature may be that it is imbued with Christianity. If the exegete is a devout Christian, perhaps a Roman Catholic steeped in Patristics, theological learning will be a help towards understanding, though it may lead to some minor difficulties because of the many changes in doctrine over the centuries; at least, such a reader will understand some of the underlying doctrinal features of early Christian literature. If the reader is not a Christian there is the danger of missing the centrality of holiness in most of the Anglo-Saxons' extant writings, or, worse still, the danger of thinking them all hypocrisy, and the writers no better than Chaucer's Pardoner, in the Host's view, forcefully expressed and accompanied by a pious oath, 'by the croys which þat seint Eleyne foond'.

Some of the great moments in Old English poetry lie in the glory of the Faith, and are not, in the first place, glories of literature, a concept not easily accommodable to Anglo-Saxon writings in the vernacular. In this book I may well have emphasized more heavily than readers will like those moments in vernacular verse when the Faith is glorified, partly perhaps because my own preoccupations and predilections do not tend in that direction. Of little faith myself, I have tried to respond to utterances of greater faith in medieval literature: the sense of wonder manifested in the writings of Anglo-Saxon England, which I cannot share in personal experience, I strive to understand by a deliberate act of imagining. To Horace, in the opening words of Epistle VI, *Nil admirari*, 'to marvel at nothing', was the key, if not to Philosophy that is Wisdom, at least to happiness. If we are to read the literature of the Anglo-Saxons with sympathy we must invert that dictum, and strive to reenact their sense of wonder at every divine mystery, their sense of wonder at many secularities perceived as manifestations of the divine.

Beowulf is in the foreground of this book. *Beowulf* is a secular poem, suffused with piety including a sense of wonder at the shaping of events such as humans cannot predict or justify. The book deals at some length with the art of expression shown in this and other Old English poems. In selecting passages for discussion, both from *Beowulf* and from other writings, I have often preferred what I believe the Anglo-Saxons might have valued more highly than do modern readers. That led to emphasis on pious lines in *Beowulf* rather than on heroic formulations.

I have deliberately gone against views which I believe to have been widely held at one time, many of which are still held today, though often less strongly or naïvely than formerly. It may be that I have quoted too many opinions about Old English poetry which I believe to be untenable. *Untenable* may be merely a polite word for 'silly': *silly* 'illogical', *silly* 'unsupported by evidence', and very occasionally *silly* 'simple-minded'. But let us never forget that, as we find our predecessors silly, that is, their views untenable, so shall those who succeed us find us silly, our views untenable.

The history of our subject, Old English literature as understood by scholars over a long time, is of interest to me, and I am inclined to read new articles and books on Old English literature in the light of old articles and books on it. The texts themselves are at the centre: *monumenta litterarum*. They have been a centre of intellectual interest for over four hundred years and a university subject for only a little over a hundred years. The texts will remain whether read or unread by academics and their pupils. Our views will perish. It is good that the Anglo-Saxons themselves, as revealed in their extant vernacular writings including *Beowulf*, are strong on mutability.

INDEX I

Bibliographical Index of Scholars and Critics named in the footnotes

This bibliographical index of names, mainly of scholars including editors, and also other writers including poets, Church Fathers, and critics (followed by date of publication) lists the references in the notes. For Classical and medieval authors no date of publication is given (other than under the editor's name); similarly for post-medieval writings of uncertain date. Joint authors are listed under the name of the first (in the order as given). The chapter numbers are in roman numerals, followed by the note number in arabic numerals. References to bibliographical information in the Preface have 'Preface' followed by either (small) roman page numerals or arabic numerals for footnotes.

Index II, the literary index, should be consulted for authors and writings, ancient, medieval and modern, and Index IV, the general index, includes some references to more extended mention of scholars, critics, and other authors. Index I alone is virtually confined to the footnotes.

(1900, 2nd edn 1909) IV 141, 160, 161
(1919) IV 159
(1922) II 87
(1925) I 68
Cooper, C. P. (printed 1836) IV 18; V 28
Crawford, S. J. (1928) II 72
Creed, R. P. (1967) II 12, 15; IV 169; V 1
Cross, J. E. (1970) V 10
(1972) I 85
Cureau, M. (1990) IV 157

Dale, E. (1907) II 74
Damico, H., and Leyerle, J. (1993) IV 153
Damico, H., and Olsen, A. H. (1990) II 82
Davis, N. (1959, 2nd edn of Zupitza, J.)
    Preface xiii
    and Wrenn, C. L. (1962) IV 24
de Boor, H. (1930) IV 91
de Marco, M. (1968) IV 112
de Selincourt, E. (1944) V 6
de Vries, J. (1961: *Altnordisches
    etymologisches Wörterbuch*) IV 144
    (1961: *Heldenlied und Heldensage*) II 26,
    38
    (1964) IV 15
Dickens, C. (1841) IV 7
Dickins, B. (1915) V 29
    (1939) I 6
    and Ross, A. S. C. (1934) III 64
Dietrich, F. E. C. (1859) I 46
Doane, A. N. (1991) IV 164
Dobbie, E. V. K. (1936-1953: ASPR)
    Preface xiii
    (1937) III 16, 37; IV 90
Dodsley, R. (1740) III 48
    and J. (1755, 1761, 1768) III 48
Dodwell, C. R., and Clemoes, P. A. M.
    (1974) IV 100
Donaldson, E. T. (1966) IV 166
Donoghue, D. (1986) III 35
    (1987: *Style in OE Poetry*) III 35, 39, 62,
    72
    (1987: 'Classification of b-Verses') IV 51
Drögereit, R. (1951) IV 18
Düwel, K. (1968) IV 15
Duggan, H. N., and Turville-Petre, T. (1989)
    IV 80, 115

Earle, J. (1884) I 81
    (1884 and 1885) I 45, 62
    (1892) I 45, 59; V 50
    and Plummer, C. (1892-1899) III 62
Ebert, A. (1880-1887, 2nd edn 1889) IV 2,
    20
Ehrismann, G. (1909) II 71

Eliason, N., and Clemoes, P. A. M. (1966)
    IV 162
Emerson, O. F. (1906) II 72
Endter, W. (1922) IV 158
Erhardt-Siebold, E. von (1925) IV 112
Ersch, S., and Gruber, S. G. (1819) III 21
Ettmüller, L. (1840) I 8, 18; V 47

Farmer, D. H. (1978) IV 9
Farrell, R. T. (1974) III 73; IV 178
Faulkes, A. (1987) III 31; IV 1, 133
Fell, C. (1984) II 86
Finkenstaedt, T. (1974) II 22
Förster, M., (1913) Preface xiii
    festschrift (1929) I 58; IV 31
    (1941) IV 86
    and Wildhagen, K. (1921) IV 31; V 34
Fowler, H. W. (1926; 1965 rev. Gowers, Sir
    E.) IV 181
Fox, Sir C., and Dickins, B. (1950) V 23
Frank, R. (1972) II 5
    (1991) II 33
Fry, D. K. (1968) I 82
    (1969) II 71
    (1974) I 69
Fuhrmann, J. (1886) IV 79

Ganz, P. (1978) IV 31
Garmonsway, G. N., Simpson, J., and
    Davidson, H. E. (1968) I 66; IV 166
Gering, H. (1906; 2nd edn 1913) I 54
Gerould, G. H. (1924-1925) IV 11
Gladstone, W. E. (1858) IV 113
Gneuss, H. (1972) IV 13
    (1986) V 19
Godden, M. (1978) IV 11
    (1979) III 62
    (1980) IV 12
    (1991) III 61
    and Lapidge, M. (1991) II 33; III 61; V 2
Göller, H. (1971) II 78
Goethe, J. W. von (1828) I 1
    (1833) IV 111
Goldsmith, M. E. (1970) II 48
Gollancz, (Sir) I. (1895) III 44, 71; IV 138
    (1927) Preface xiii; IV 100
Gordon, E. V. (1937) IV 39, 42, 43
Gordon, I. L. (1960) IV 148; V 23
Grattan, J. H. G., and Singer, C. (1952) V 5
Gray, T. (1751) III 48
Green, D. H. (1965) IV 12
Green, J. R. (1874) III 53
Greene, R. L. (1935, 2nd edn 1977) III 46;
    IV 64
Greenfield, S. B. (1963) V 39, 44

Karg-Gasterstädt, E., Frings, T., and Grosse, R. (1952-) IV 127
Kaske, R. E. (1958) I 79
Kastovsky, D., and Bauer, G. (1988) IV 81, 86
Kato, T. (1974) III 46
Kauffmann, F. (1887) IV 34, 53, 54
Kemble, J. M. (1833; 2nd edn 1835-1837) I 6, 23, 31
(1836) I 25, 32, 38
(1856) III 63
Kendall, C. B. (1991) IV 25
Kendrick, Sir T. D., Brown, T. J., et al. (1960) IV 109
Kennedy, B. H. (1871) IV 52
Kennedy, E. D., Waldron, R., and Wittig, J. S. (1988) IV 60
Kent, C. W. (1889) V 27
Ker, N. R. (1956) III 34
(1957; new edn 1990) III 3, 22, 29; IV 18
Ker, W. P. (1897) II 75
(1904) I 84; II 35
Kiernan, K. S. (1981) II 88; III 9
King, K. C., and McLintock, D. R. (1976, revision of Bostock, J. K.) III 21; IV 18, 21, 38
Kirby, T. A., and Woolf, H. B. (1949) IV 120
Klaeber, F. (1905) V 37
(1910) II 37
(1911) II 42
(1912) II 44, 45; V 37, 38, 49
(1918) II 37
(1922; 2nd edn 1928; 3rd edn 1936, with supplements 1941, 1950) Preface xii; I 26, 48, 54, 77; II 44; III 51; IV 45, 58, 93, 95; V 37
Kock, E. A. (1922) I 77
Köhler, J. J. (1906) IV 92
König, G. (1957) IV 107
Korhammer, M. (1992) III 38, 78; IV 14, 56
Kotzor, G. (1981) II 5
Krackow, O. (1903) II 62; IV 122
Krämer, E. (1902) IV 95
Krapp, G. P. (1931-1936: ASPR) Preface xiii
Krause, W., and Jahnkuhn, H. (1966) IV 15
Kuhn, H. (1933; reprinted 1969) III 35, 72; IV 25
Kuhn, S. M. (1972; reprinted 1984) IV 11
Kurath, H., Kuhn, S. M., Reidy, J., Lewis, R. E., and Williams, M. J. (1952-) Preface xii
Kuryłowicz, J. (1948-1949) IV 29
(1970) IV 11, 29
(1974) IV 29

Lachmann, K. (1819; reprinted 1876) III 21
(1832; reprinted 1876) III 21

(1835; reprinted 1876) IV 21
Lamb, W. R. M. (1927) IV 146
Langenfelt, G. (1959) V 14
Langosch, K. (1971) V 32
(1973) V 32
Lardet, P. (1983) III 4
Lawrence, W. W. (1909) I 64
(1928; reprinted 1961) I 24, 65
Leake, J. A. (1967) II 29, 30
Lee, A. A. (1969) II 51
(1972) II 49, 51
Lehmann, E. (1901; German translation 1906) I 36
Lehnert, G. (1905) III 4
Leitner, G. (1991) IV 181
Leo, H. (1838) I 23
(1839) I 23, 24, 31
Levison, W. (1946) IV 18
Leyser, K. (1983) IV 18
Liebermann, F. (1898-1903: *Gesetze* I) IV 151, 180
(1912-1916: *Gesetze* II and III) V 39
Lindheim, B. von (1951) III 45
Liuzza, R. M. (1991) I 11
Locherbie-Cameron, M. A. L. (1978) IV 71
Lockhart, J. G. (1837) IV 94
Löhe, H. (1907) III 15
Lonsdale, R. (1969) III 48
Lord, A. B. (1949) II 9
(1960) II 9
Loyn, H. R. (1953) IV 70
Lucas, P. J. (1977) III 52, 58; IV 49
(1985) III 35
(1988) IV 34
Lübke, H. (1889) I 33
Luick, K, Wild, F., and Koziol, H. (1929-1940) IV 121
Lutz, A. (1984) IV 89
Lye, E., and Manning, O. (1772) IV 99

Macrae-Gibson, O. D. (1983) IV 59
McIntosh, A. (1949; reprinted 1990) IV 4
McKinnell, J. (1975) IV 70
McNamee, M. B. (1960; reprinted 1963) II 46
Magoun, F. P., Jr (1953) II 9
(1955) II 11
Malone, K. (1930) IV 144
(1936, 2nd edn 1962) I 45; IV 15; V 14
(1951) II 28
(1963) Preface xiii; II 28
Manitius, M. (1911) IV 2
Marold, E. (1983) IV 134, 143
Marquardt, H. (1938) II 60; III 59; IV 134, 137, 139, 152
(1940) II 37; III 1

INDEX II

Literary Index of Authors and Writings

CLASSICAL AND MEDIEVAL

GREEK

Aristotle,
  on colour, 174
Homer,
  colour words, 173-5
  epithets, formulas, and scenes, in Homer
    and *Beowulf*, 41, 45, 50
  'speaks in riddles', 193
Plato,
  Alcibiades,
    Socrates, 193

LATIN

Alcuin, 58-9, 74
Aldhelm,
  Riddles,
    V *Iris,* 173
    XXXIII *Lorica,* 79 n. 22
Altercatio Yemis et Estatis, 208 n. 170
Augustine of Hippo, St,
  Enarratio in Psalmus XLI,
    on Psalm 41, 58
  Soliloquia, 201
Bede, 58, 74, 76; see also *Bede's Death Song*
  De die iudicii, 77 and n. 15
  De metrica arte, 115, 125-6
  Hexaemeron, 54
  Historia ecclesiastica gentis Anglorum,
    on Cædmon, 50, 125, 220-3; see also
      Cædmon
Bible,
  Vulgate,
    text and translation used, Preface xiii-xiv
  Genesis,
    1:1-10 and *Cædmon's Hymn,* 86
    1:26: 243 n. 52
    4:26: 231
    6:4: 54
  Iob, 28:21: 183
  Psalmi,
    5:2-6: 211
    13:2: 161

14:1: 212
21:13: 212
30:6: 237 and n. 40
34:4-6: 211
41 and 'hart' symbolism in *Beowulf,* 57
43:3: 183-4
48:7-12, 18: 224-6 and notes 23-5
102:5: 185
Isaias, 53:2: 183-4
Danihel, 3:36: 184
Evangelia,
  Mattheus,
    13:31-2: 183 n. 128
    13:43: 185, 189
    26:51: 153 n. 77
  Marcus,
    14:47: 153 n. 77
  Lucas,
    10:42: 241
    11:27: 233 n. 37
    13:18-19: 183 and n. 128
    22:50: 153 n. 77
    23:46: 237 and n. 40
  Johannes,
    2:1-11: 222
    18:10: 153
Epistolae Pauli,
  I ad Corinthios I:20-4: 203
  II ad Corinthios 3:6 and *Exodus* 523-6: 98
  ad Galatas 1:1: 220-1
  ad Ephesios 6:11-17: 189-90, 241
Boethius,
  De Consolatione Philosophiae, 201
    II met. vi: 242 n. 51
    III met. ix: 181
    scholia, 181 n. 126
Cuthbert,
  'Epistola de obitu Bedae', 77 and n. 16,
    221
Gregory the Great,
  Moralia in Iob, XIX, 3: 183-4
Gregory of Tours, 12 n. 23
Henry of Huntingdon, 15 n. 29

POST-MEDIEVAL

INDEX III

Lexical Index of Words and Phrases

In the alphabetization of Old English words the prefix *ge-* is ignored, and similarly *gi-* prefixed to Old Saxon words.

General Index

For the names of **scholars and critics** see Index I, with references to the footnotes in which they are named; here only more extended treatments are listed, as well as names (including those of scholars) referred to but not in the footnotes (and therefore not in Index I). For the names of **authors** and for the titles of individual **texts** see Index II, the literary index.